Afrofuturism in *Black Panther*

Afrofuturism in *Black Panther*

Gender, Identity, and the Re-Making of Blackness

Edited by
Renée T. White
Karen A. Ritzenhoff

LEXINGTON BOOKS
Lanham • Boulder • New York • London

Published by Lexington Books
An imprint of The Rowman & Littlefield Publishing Group, Inc.
4501 Forbes Boulevard, Suite 200, Lanham, Maryland 20706
www.rowman.com

6 Tinworth Street, London SE11 5AL, United Kingdom

Copyright © 2021 by The Rowman & Littlefield Publishing Group, Inc.

All rights reserved. No part of this book may be reproduced in any form or by any electronic or mechanical means, including information storage and retrieval systems, without written permission from the publisher, except by a reviewer who may quote passages in a review.

British Library Cataloguing in Publication Information Available

Library of Congress Cataloging-in-Publication Data

Names: White, Renée T., editor. | Ritzenhoff, Karen A., editor.
Title: Afrofuturism in Black Panther: gender, identity, and the re-making of blackness edited by Renée T. White, Karen A. Ritzenhoff.
Description: Lanham : Lexington Books, 2021. | Includes bibliographical references and index. | Summary: "This book examines Black Panther not only as a film grounded in Afro-futurism, but also as an invitation for viewers to think about relevant real-world social questions about identity, liberation, and racial justice, ultimately posing the question of how Black Panther invites a reimagining of Blackness"—Provided by publisher.
Identifiers: LCCN 2021022735 (print) | LCCN 2021022736 (ebook) |
ISBN 9781793623577 (cloth) | ISBN 9781793623584 (epub) |
ISBN 9781793623591 (paper)
Subjects: LCSH: Black Panther (Motion picture: 2018) | Motion pictures—Social aspects—United States. | Afrofuturism. | Blacks in popular culture—History—21st century. | Blacks—Race identity—21st century. | Future, The, in popular culture.
Classification: LCC PN1997.2.B5815 A37 2021 (print) | LCC PN1997.2.B5815 (ebook) | DDC 741.43/72—dc23
LC record available at https://lccn.loc.gov/2021022735
LC ebook record available at https://lccn.loc.gov/2021022736

∞™ The paper used in this publication meets the minimum requirements of American National Standard for Information Sciences—Permanence of Paper for Printed Library Materials, ANSI/NISO Z39.48-1992.

*For Jeff Harman
And my grandnieces and nephew*
Renée T. White

*For Cindy and Medici,
My fellow warriors and allies*
Karen A. Ritzenhoff

Contents

Preface   ix
Zeinabu irene Davis

Acknowledgments   xiii

Introduction   1

1. I Dream a World: *Black Panther* and the Re-Making of Blackness   21
   Renée T. White

2. The Power in Numbers: Ensemble Stunt Performance in *Black Panther* and Histories of Practice   33
   Lauren Steimer

3. From Expressivity to Equanimity: Locating New Black Action Aesthetics in *Black Panther*   53
   Wayne Wong

4. Paid the Cost to be the Boss: Chadwick Boseman, *Black Panther*, and the Future of the Black Biopic   73
   Mikal J. Gaines

5. Let Ayo Have a Girlfriend: Resisting Black Lesbian Erasure on Twitter   87
   Sarah E. S. Sinwell

6. "Tell Me a Story Baba": *Black Panther* and Wakanda's Foreign Policy in the Age of Neoliberalism   103
   Clarence Lusane

7 The Underground Railroad as Afrofuturism: Enslaved Blacks That Imagined Freedom, Future, and Space   127
dann j. Broyld

8 The Evolution of the Dora Milaje: Wakanda's Greatest Warriors in Comics and Film   153
Joshua Truelove

9 "The Prince Will Now Have the Strength of the Black Panther Stripped Away": Reading Disability and Queerness in Killmonger   171
Dominique Young

10 Only When She Wants To: Code-Switching in *Black Panther*   187
Paul Moffett

11 The Dora Milaje in Real Life: A Continuing Legacy of African Warriors   203
Myron T. Strong, K. Sean Chaplin, and Giselle Greenidge

12 Echoes of the History of Black Utopian Visions, "Black Manhood," and Black Feminism in the Making of *Black Panther*   215
Dolita Cathcart

13 Tradition, Purpose, and Technology: An Archaeological Take on the Role of Technological Progress in *Black Panther*   245
Shayla Monroe

14 Reflections on *Black Panther* and the Traditions of Third Cinema   267
Cynthia Baron

15 The Depiction of Homeschooling, Black Identity, and Political Thought in the Film *Black Panther*   287
Khadijah Z. Ali-Coleman

16 Two Paths to the Future: Radical Cosmopolitanism and Counter-Colonial Dignity in *Black Panther*   299
Neal Curtis

17 My Bloodright: A Critical Analysis of *Black Panther*'s Erik Killmonger, Colonialism, and Hybrid Identity   315
Gabriel A. Cruz

18 The Other Worlds of *Black Panther*'s Purple Heart-Shaped Herb   333
Paul Karolczyk

Index   351

About the Contributors   359

Preface

Zeinabu irene Davis

American cinema and Black culture cannot underestimate the lasting influences of Ryan Coogler's *Black Panther*. Its impacts on American cinema and more importantly Black culture worldwide are phenomenal. The film has jump-started and fortified our introductions, definitions, awareness, and discussions of Afrofuturism as a conceptual matrix for both celebrating and interrogating world-African popular culture. Culturally, the film moves us to a beautiful complex simmering gumbo of ideas and ideals around Black identity and representation, manifestations of Pan Africanism, Third World and national cinemas, debates about gender and class, and African diaspora culture. The textures and understanding of the film seem to only improve with time.

I am a proud, card-carrying member of a group of Black filmmakers now known as the *LA Rebellion Film Movement*. Our mission, borne out of the ashes of the Watts uprisings in Los Angeles in 1965, was to create cinematic stories that genuinely reflected our families and our communities. Our stories were raw and unpolished, imperfect creative representations of our lives and our struggles, and our victories and sometimes quiet successes. Guided by outstanding professors and mentors, such as Elyseo Taylor and Teshome Gabriel, we were exposed to cinemas from all over the world, especially the cinema of social change reflected by Third World filmmakers and the national cinemas from the African continent and its diasporas. Many of my friends, collaborators, and mentors of the movement—Charles Burnett, Julie Dash, Carroll Parrott Blue, Billy Woodberry, Barbara McCullough, Ben Caldwell, and Haile Gerima—experimented and made cinematic innovations with both form and content that still provokes audiences today. Our creative output should have been more significant; it does not match the wealth of our collective talent. Yet, it laid a basis for what we see happening now in contemporary

Black cinema. One of the LA Rebellion's hallmarks and lasting contributions is that we all dedicated our lives to passing on what we learned while making cinema. Some of us started and sustained film collectives and cultural institutions; several of us became teachers and college professors.

As a professor and independent filmmaker for over thirty years, I am grateful that I still make films and pass on what I know by teaching. I constantly revise and reinvent my courses to reach as many students as I can. So, I teach a class on *Black Panther*. The film provides a rich space to discuss so many topics, many of which you will see covered by the extraordinary range of authors in this book. From an analysis of stunt work, martial arts, the impact of colonialism, and the many meanings of the heart-shaped herb, this book has something for everyone.

I am lucky enough to live in San Diego, the home of the original Comic-Con. Every July, San Diego is filled with people who walk around as superheroes and villains, monsters and geeks for nearly a week. In the last few years, the convention has become much more ethnically diverse than it had been five years ago. It has indeed been a pleasure to see so many people dressed as Black Panther and Killmonger. Families come dressed as an entire clan of Black Panthers, and there are Black Panthers who are both male and female, straight and queer. It is incredibly awesome to see Black women dressed as Okoye, Shuri, and Nakia's characters. *Black Panther* led many people to read comic books and graphic novels by authors such as Ta-Nehisi Coates, Nnedi Okorafor, and Roxane Gay. It opened people up to old questions and debates about superheroes to conversations and celebrations of culture.

For me, specifically, *Black Panther: Afrofuturism, Gender, Identity, and the Re-making of Blackness* will provide an excellent resource for my students to read, think, and interrogate the film and its context for the lives of Black people. *Black Panther* provides an exciting space to get students hooked on discussing cinema, the role of superheroes, and to engage a film beyond the pleasurable enjoyment it provides. More importantly, it lays the groundwork to explore the more complex topics of race, class, and gender roles. The film provides an entry point for students to discover and begin to read or continue to read comics and graphic novels, and it begs for the inclusion of a deep discussion of the Black Panther Party. The film and this book will open a dialogue of representation, culture, colonialism, and neoliberalism, and also the ideals of Pan-Africanism. In these troubled times where the killing of Black people by the police is still an ongoing tragedy, *Black Panther* has provided a safe space for my Black students to have pride and for my other students to listen, learn, and become better citizens and hopefully eventual allies.

It is impossible to write this and not acknowledge Chadwick Boseman who played the titular role of T'Challa as the Black Panther and his passage in August 2020. Mr. Boseman's real-life courage to privately deal with cancer while portraying a fictional superhero is not lost on most of us. Chadwick's incredible resilience and grit in honoring this beacon of representation are what made him a real-life superhero who will not be forgotten. I was fortunate enough to be in the Cinemark Theaters (formerly Magic Johnson Theaters) in south-central Los Angeles the week of the film premiere in February 2018. Although we could not get a seat in the theater, we experienced the roar of the crowd as Chadwick made a brief, unannounced appearance right before the screening started, much to the delight of fans of all ages. It was a magical moment and time that I will not forget.

Let this book take you back to the magical moments you spent when you first watched this film. Or let this book inspire you to watch it for the first time. However, you experience it, these rich and illuminating chapters will unpack layers of rich details and perspectives that are both exciting and evergreen.

By no means is *Black Panther* a perfect movie, but I deeply admire and love what the director Ryan Coogler has done within the Hollywood studio system. He has helped expand women's roles in front of and behind the camera, facilitated a more equitable and diverse collaborative process, and offered many talented people a space to learn, create, grow, and see themselves. This was the LA Rebellion filmmakers' objective, and I am happy to see it passed on to a new generation of filmmakers.

Figure P.1 Oil painting of the Dora Milaje by Karen A. Ritzenhoff, 2021.

Acknowledgments

We would like to thank our contributors for their steadfast commitment during the most unusual year any of us will have experienced: we became a community, a support group of sorts, working through the difficulties and coming up with the goods. We would also like to thank Zeinabu irene Davis, a trailblazer in her own right, for believing in the book before it was ready and agreeing to write our preface. Many thanks go to our fabulous editor at Lexington Books/Rowman and Littlefield, Jessica Tepper, who has been a constant source of optimism and support. Furthermore, the cover art has special significance because it is a picture of Makena Randolph, taken by her mother Naomi Randolph. Naomi is Renée T. White's niece.

Renée T. White—First I must thank Jocelyn Boryczka, former coeditor of *New Political Science*. A passing conversation we had about Black Panther turned into an invitation for me to write a critical essay for the journal. That invitation has evolved into this book, which has been a joy to do with my colleague and friend Karen A. Ritzenhoff. I am most appreciative to her for the patience and care she has brought to this project. Few people could make videoconferencing as energizing as she can. She has boundless energy and optimism, loves film, has faith in collaboration and is an inspiration, always. My niece Naomi Randolph is behind the lens that captured our cover photo of my grandniece Makena.

There is a beauty to this—that my young grandniece sees herself in the film that undergirds our book. She is the essence of our point: people identify with *Black Panther* beyond its entertainment value. They feel a kinship and an invitation. For Makena, as a young Black girl, Black Panther is her possibility. Her idea of superheroes is tied to and grounded in her still-forming Black identity and transcends it too. It makes sense to her that she

Figure A.1 Makena Randolph Makes the Universally Recognized Wakanda Forever Gesture. Photograph by Naomi Randolph.

can be the hero of her own story in ways not circumscribed by rules of race and gender.

Thank you as well to the readers of "I Dream a World: *Black Panther* and the Re-Making of Blackness" who have contacted me over the past two years; this was evidence of the ongoing interest in further academic examination of the film. My thanks to faculty at Wheaton who have assigned it in their classes. To the students I met in Wheaton College Professor Nick Dorzweiler's 2019 class POLS 269: Popular Culture and World Politics—you were prepared with really challenging and insightful comments regarding the article. You didn't let me off the hook just because I was Wheaton's Provost. You pushed my analysis, shared some new and interesting interpretations of the film that informed this project. To Sharmeen Inaam '20 in particular, our ongoing conversations were wide ranging in scope and led me to rethink elements of the film. Other Wheaton colleagues have checked on my progress,

Acknowledgments

Figure A.2 The Ferocity of Superheroes as Interpreted by Makena Randolph. Photograph by Naomi Randolph.

always with a positive word to encourage me. There are too many to list but please know that the thanks is genuine. I do have to acknowledge the supergroup I get to work with daily: Touba Ghadessi, Jim Mancall, and Alison Ricco. I would be remiss if I didn't mention two former Provost Office colleagues Meg Kirkpatrick, who has the uncanny ability to text exactly when I need it and Shawn Cristian, with whom I have had the most wonderful discussions of music, art, and literature. Also, too, friends from President's Council (past and present) were supports along the way.

This project is a love letter of sorts to my friends and family who nourish my passion. Even as a social scientist focused on widely divergent issues, they always understood how and why visual and performing arts ground me. My dear sister-friends Dina Strachan and Lisa Jones Gordon have claim to some of the formative years for me when my interest in visual arts also took hold in my academic inquiry. I have many movie-themed memories defined by hours of conversation and laughter. Many years ago, I completed a National Endowment for the Humanities Black Film Studies Institute at the University of Central Florida, which further instilled in me the desire to engage in critical analysis of films. Luckily since then, friends continued to indulge my curiosity in ways great and small and inspire me with their own creative, multidisciplinary work—Beth Boquet, Breanna McDaniel, Tricia Elam-Walker, Lindsay Johnson, Roxana Walker-Canton, Robbin Crabtree. Evelyn Newman-Phillips, I am grateful to you for inviting me to one of my academic homes where I worked out some of my ideas and to Warren Perry for bringing the CCSU Africana Studies love. Lauren Slingluff, Crystal Williams, and Patty Poulter—even if we didn't talk about this project, your steadfast friendship and expansive range as artistic people serve as ballast for me. I come from a family defined by art, for whom the experience of works that reflect the complexities of Blackness and Afro-Latinidad was always a driving force. My father Richard was my movie-going "ride-or-die" who never hesitated to take me to see films that were way too mature for my age but were ones he knew I'd love. My mother Clara was my theatre and museum-going partner. We would discuss the choices directors made, the position of figures in paintings. And we spent many hours deconstructing where and how we saw ourselves depicted in works. I regret that they aren't here to enjoy this moment, but I know that they would be very excited and proud.

I hope my family—my stepchildren and their own families, my cousins, and my chosen kin—see themselves in this book. My husband Jeff Harman gamely accompanied me for repeat viewings of *Black Panther* because he knew I would need someone to work through my ideas in real time. We had many wonderful and animated discussions as a result. He's my bedrock and co-conspirator in all things. And finally, there are the funny, curious, bright, and endlessly entertaining ones—my grandnieces Soraya, Makena, and Sasha and my grandnephew Javi. In addition to having the best parents and grandmas, there is this basic fact. They are wondrous beings to me. They fill me with immeasurable joy. I hope the world will be kind, safe, and ready for their brilliance.

Karen A. Ritzenhoff would like to thank Sabrina Cofer who has been our trusted indexer. A recent graduate from Central Connecticut State University, she is already a terrific editor and writer. I am thankful to Judith Grant, editor of the Taylor and Francis journal *New Political Science* who helped us get the reprinting rights of Renée T. White's ground-breaking chapter. I am grateful for the incredible team of scholars we have assembled for this collection. They produced revised versions of their chapters in record time despite the challenges we all faced in the midst of a global pandemic. We are proud of what we have accomplished together in a short time span to add such a strong collection of research to the discussions about *Black Panther*. Our volume will contribute to scholarship of colleagues, and most importantly our students.

I would like to thank my immediate family: my husband Michael, my three kids Jan-Philipp, Dominik, and Lea-Karoline, my mother Birgit in Germany, and my brother Burkhart in Copenhagen. My trusted girlfriend Chez Liley keeps me on track, always. During the COVID pandemic, these extended members of my American family helped me stay sane: Amy Dumschott, Bonnie Baldwin, Susan Caplan, Elizabeth Eden, Raquel Pega, Elizabeth Seewald Hill, Doreen Hampton, Melora Mennesson, Grail Kearney, Tracy Thrall, Lisa Judd, Jennifer Osborne, Susan Yancy with our "Cup of Conversation" tribe: Deborah Thomas, Pat Brett, Diane Turner, Pam Feinberg, Elena Vishnevetsky, Patti Giannini, Sherry Shanbrom, and Angela Rugambwa. My international friends/sisters/colleagues who are always by my side: Karen Randell, Elena Caoduro, Janis L. Goldie, Dijana Metlić, and Clémentine Tholas. Thanks to the troika who envisioned the Action Cinema Conference at the University of Reading in spring 2019 that helped set the wheels for this volume on *Black Panther* in motion: Lisa Purse, Yvonne Tasker, and Chris Holmlund. My allies at Central Connecticut State University, especially Kathy Hermes, Aimée Pozorski, Jacqueline Cobbina-Boivin, Melissa Mentzer, Candace Barrington, Fumi Showers, Charisse Levchak, Diana Cohen, Fiona Pearson, and Jessica Greenebaum deserve my heartfelt thanks as does our relentlessly supportive group of CCSU Communication "women warriors" Cindy L. White, MJ Moriarty, Rati Kumar, Joan Walden, Carolyn Lumsden, Julie Kim, Betsy Louys, Lois Koteen, and Kathy Bantley. Many thanks also to the "Badass Female Filmmakers" (BFFs) in Connecticut: Jennifer Boyd, Karyl Evans, Ágnes Mócsy, Heather Elliott-Famularo, Suzanne Colton, Ilvi Dulack, Tracy Heather Strain, Annaliesa Russell-Smith, and Roxana Walker-Canton. Last but not least my trusted male university warriors over the years at CCSU and the University of Hartford have my heartfelt thanks: Bob Kagan, Christopher Pudlinski, Yonty Friesem, Keith Hughes, Michael North, Robert Wolff, Leroy Temple, Chad Valk, Ryan Wark, Robert Lang, Jack Banks, Michael Walsh, Burlin Barr, Frederick Wasser, and Gil Gigliotti. I am incredibly thankful for my students at CCSU as well as the University of Hartford who watch full-length movies with me via zoom during the pandemic and have helped me understand their perspectives on *Black Panther* and *BlacKkKlansman* and many other films via extensive chat conversations. The book is dedicated to Cindy L. White, a fellow warrior who has been my trusted ally since the journey as a teacher at university started.

My friend and colleague Renée T. White and I have enjoyed our editing journey together. I felt so privileged to have access to her schedule, basking in her attention during our hour-long zoom meetings where we explored our next steps as coeditors, laughed, tried to make sense of and talked politics. I am so hopeful that we will continue to collaborate and help our joint collection to gain a broad audience in academia and beyond.

Introduction

Renée T. White and Karen A. Ritzenhoff

Black Panther's global box office success in the Marvel Cinematic Universe has exceeded even the wildest expectations for a superhero movie, directed by the thirty-four-year-old Black director Ryan Coogler, featuring a predominantly African American star cast and creative team. As director Ava DuVernay, one of the few female directors of color who is working on blockbuster films in Hollywood, has said loud and clear: filmmaking is about connections and Hollywood's "old white boys' club" mentality filters down to the below-the-line workers as well.[1] Many Black designers, musicians, stunt workers, and behind-the-scene staff are excluded from profitable projects. Ryan Coogler made a point by giving key creative positions to African American talent. Ruth E. Carter won the Oscar for best costume design in 2019. The film was nominated for seven academy awards and won altogether three: best original score as well as best production design also went to *Black Panther*. The superhero film was a trailblazer not only due to his enormous financial success at the box office but also due to its underlying philosophy to base a superhero story on a narrative that is reliant on Afrofuturism, describing a fantasy country, Wakanda, hidden in the African continent. The strategy to appeal to a broad audience with a contemporary fairytale that featured strong Black female protagonists and an intriguing storyline about good winning over international antagonists paid off. On the IMDb website it lists the box office success of the movie at almost $1.35 billion. In the United States alone, *Black Panther* made over $700 million, compared to a $200-million production budget. As we are completing this manuscript, *Black Panther 2* is scheduled for release by the Marvel Studio in the summer 2022. After the lead character Chadwick Boseman passed away in 2020 of colon cancer, no new King T'Challa, loved by so many, will take his place. Boseman was mourned by a global fan community. The tweet announcing his death in August 2020 is the most retweeted to that point.² All of this—the huge financial success and the global appeal of *Black Panther*—warrants an entire collection of essays to help explain its role in American Cinema in the twenty-first century.

The journey of the character Black Panther begins in July 1966, when Jack Kirby and Stan Lee introduced the world to "The Sensational Black Panther!" in *Fantastic Four* no. 52. As Stan Lee later explained, "I wanted to create the first black super-hero, but I wanted to avoid stereotyping.... But, to avoid stereotyping, he [T'Challa] doesn't live in a regular tribe and so forth; he is the prince of a nation, and the nation is hidden under the ground. It's a country called Wakanda, and he is one of the greatest scientists in the world and his area; his country is more scientifically advanced than any," Lee continued.

> "When you get to the hidden entrance and go down to Wakanda, it looks like you're in a scene from a science-fiction movie of the thirtieth century! But, in order not to be discovered by the rest of the world, 'cause he doesn't want his nation contaminated by today's civilization, it's hidden underground, and up above it looks like just thatched villages where nobody would ever suspect what's really below.... he's one of the characters I'm most proud of because he was the first important black super-hero."³

Previous images of people of African ancestry in comics reified long-held racialized stereotypes that centered whiteness by trading in the *lingua franca* of minstrelsy. Stan Lee and Jack Kirby are linked with one of the more infamous characters, Whitewash Jones, as part of the Captain America storyline published by Timely Comics (which later became Marvel Comics). Jack Kirby and Joe Simon conceived of Washington Carter (Whitewash) Jones as a sidekick to Bucky Barnes (himself a sidekick of Captain America), who was introduced to readers in *Young Allies* in 1941. His first line of dialogue has him confirming that he can play the harmonica: "Yeah Man! I is also good on de watermelon."⁴ These kinds of images of Black America echo what psychiatrist, philosopher, and political theorist Frantz Fanon observed in his seminal text *Black Skin, White Masks*, published in 1967: "look at the children's picture magazines: Out of every Negro mouth comes the ritual 'Yassuh, boss' ... to make [a black man] talk pidgin is to fasten him to the effigy of him, to snare him, to imprison him, the eternal victim of an essence, of an appearance for which he is not responsible."⁵ Visual culture and popular entertainment have been used as vehicles for the reproduction of circumscribed and reductionist notions of Blackness. This sort of racial propaganda is intended to deny readers the agency to imagine beyond the possible.

Obviously, there is a rich storytelling tradition in literature and other arts where the humanity of Black people has been expressed and where Black stories are at the center. For example, in 1919 Oscar Micheaux directed *Homesteader*, which is the first feature length film with an all-Black cast. His 1920 movie *Within Our Gates* is the earliest known surviving film directed by an African American, and it deals directly with anti-Black terrorism and sexual violence by Whites and the effects of living under White supremacy and oppression. Critics often see the film as a response to D. W. Griffith's 1915 racist blockbuster *Birth of a Nation*.[6]

But within the world of comics, the introduction of Black Panther by Marvel Comics is arguably the first Black superhero (some claim that Lion Man, introduced by Orrin Evans in 1947 in *All Negro Comics* is really the first one).[7] T'Challa/Black Panther would only appear sporadically in stories featuring The Avengers or The Fantastic Four. He did not have a significant solo storyline until the early 1970s when Don McGregor, a White proofreader at Marvel, argued that up until then the Africa-focused storylines of the series *Jungle Action* were not only unrealistic but were racist. They lacked any viable African characters and were centered on White protagonists traversing an imagined, non-specific, Africa. Not only did McGregor (along with artists Rich Buckler, Gil Kane, and Billy Graham, the first Black art director in the comics), end up reintroducing Black Panther to the public in 1973 and centering him in *Jungle Action*, in a two-year story called "Panther's Rage." He created the character Erik Killmonger and is credited with shifting the storyline to Wakanda so that all the characters were African or Black.[8]

Some fifty-two years later, the release of the film in 2018 caused reverberations. As journalist Micah Peters observes in "The Evolution of Marvel's *Black Panther*,"

> We have a blockbuster movie with a black lead, and a black director, premiering during Black History Month. The Black Panther exists (if you ask Stan Lee) because Stan Lee noticed that there weren't enough black superheroes and thought hey, let's make some. But now the story has been carried to the silver screen in the hands of the people who are best equipped to tell the truest and most interesting version of it. It's still a movie, and it won't save us, so to speak. But it is, like I said before, a gigantically big deal. Started as a refugee from a Tarzan movie, now we're here.[9]

Why do superheroes matter, and why are they especially important for Black fans? A hero faces challenges and taps into all their abilities to overcome them. Heroes highlight what is possible. In contrast, author and blogger Balogun Ojetade writes in "Ain't no Such Thing as Superman!" "superheroes possess fantastic powers, fight their battles with advanced technology, or possess uncanny beauty, bravery, skill, or luck. Superheroes are heroes who cannot possibly exist in our own world today."[10]

If we follow this line of argument a bit further, while Black heroes are welcome and important, what they achieve is tethered to our current realities and involves them surviving within a racialized reality. In contrast, Black superheroes can exist in any realm including ones in which what it means to be Black can be redefined altogether, because the only rules that apply are the ones shaped by the imagination of the creator. They challenge the narrative conceit that superheroes are supposed to be White, or rather, non-Black. Given that, the Black superheroes that are "ensconced in a SF motif function not only as counter-hegemonic symbols of black racial pride and racial progress but possibly even as Afrofuturistic metaphors for imagining race and black racial identity in new and provocative ways," argues African American Studies scholar Adilifu Nama in "Brave Black Worlds: black superheroes as science fiction ciphers."[11] The notion of Afrofuturism, which grounds this book, according to cultural critic Taylor Crumpton in "Afrofuturism Has Always Looked Forward."

> [I]s a fluid ideology shaped by generations of artists, musicians, scholars, and activists whose aim is to reconstruct "Blackness" in the culture. Reflected in the life and works of such figures as Octavia Butler, Sojourner Truth, Sun Ra, and Janelle Monáe, Afrofuturism is a cultural blueprint to guide society. The term was coined by Mark Dery in 1993 but birthed in the minds of enslaved Africans who prayed for their lives and the lives of their descendants along the horrific Middle Passage. The first Afrofuturists envisioned a society free from the bondages of oppression—both physical and social. Afrofuturism imagines a future void of white supremacist thought and the structures that violently oppressed Black communities. Afrofuturism evaluates the past and future to create better conditions for the present generation of Black people through the use of technology, often presented through art, music, and literature.[12]

Afrofuturism encourages freethinking that focuses on what is possible without constraints, to see beyond the known world.

The importance of that comic book character remains clear, even in the years since the release of the film version of *Black Panther*. February 16, 2021, marks the third anniversary of the U.S. release of the movie. As fans mark the occasion on social media, debates, and discussions regarding the film—its narrative arc, special effects, costuming, and cultural meaning—have also made a resurgence. That the film was released in the month of February, Black History Month in the United States, adds to its social and cultural meaning. In perusing some of the discussions on Twitter marking this anniversary, it was evident why *Black Panther* still resonates, has meaning and continues to stir debates. Fans of color, particularly Black ones, see the film as offering a needed counter-narrative:

> 3 years ago today, i watched black panther for the first time in theatres this movie gave us a mainly darkskin cast, no trauma centred around blackness, a lil love story, the celebration of african culture— man that was a great day #WakandaForever. (@mensahnicolee, Feb 20, 2021)
>
> I don't like Black Panther for obvious reasons like the third act. But overall, it's a decent movie. I support my black brothers and sisters especially during February, and I'm Native American. I wished we had our Black Panther but I guess we unite under Wakanda. (@sectionxp12, Feb 16, 2021)
>
> What anti-SJW don't get about entertainment like #WakandaForever is that the industry is simply meeting the demands of a new generation of consumers. WE want entertainment that reflects us & we're willing to spend for it. In other words, "woke" is capitalism. (@padresj, Feb 16, 2021)

The film's story line also continues to push viewers to think about relevant real-world social questions:

> This movie succeeds in MCU's weakest area. It gave us one of the best villains ever with Killmonger because everything he believes in is actually true. Wakanda was a terror to withhold its resources from its own people around the world. Killmonger became a villain from his trauma. (@InthecutZine Feb 16, 2021)
>
> not everything is celebrated the way black panther is. it is much more than just another mcu movie to a whole community, and i'm talking about the habitual negativity targeted at invalidating that. and that's unique to black panther. (@dannyonfilm on Feb 16, 2021)

Ongoing interest in *Black Panther* is not only about the film as a form of entertainment. It encourages underrepresented groups to celebrate storytelling from their own vantage points. Furthermore, it is a showcase of artistry by and about the African diaspora. It has become a space in which imagined futures are possible. This volume recognizes all of these vantage points, particularly how film as text can tell us a great deal about how art interrogates daily life.

RYAN COOGLER AND SPIKE LEE: TWO BLACK DIRECTORS WITH A MISSION

The same year as Ryan Coogler's *Black Panther* was released in 2018, Spike Lee's *BlacKkKlansman* hit the screens. It is important to see *BlacKkKlansman* and *Black Panther* in their similarities and differences in the context of what was roiling the United States in 2018: Spike Lee addresses police violence and racism in the United States, connecting the realities of the 1970s, described by Ron Stallworth, with the violent rise of White supremacy in the past decade. Ryan Coogler directs a film that offers an alternate universe, independent of the current realities of the racial divisions that marked the summer of 2020 with global protests to raise awareness that *Black Lives Matter*. *Black Panther* is a film that affirms Black creativity, self-rule, global independence of an African nation, and non-violent protest to create awareness of racial inequality in the world. Both films use the strategy of telling stories within the framework of cinema. However, differently from the notoriously racist *Birth of a Nation*, American film history is re-written by these two Black directors. Lee shows the continuity of White supremacy as an arch that reaches from the early twentieth century to the 1970s, the summer of 2017, and Donald Trump's Presidency.

Lee juxtaposes two groups in parallel editing that could not be more different: one chants "Black Power" while the other chants "White Power" and "America First." The first is congregating around Jerome Turner (played by Harry Belafonte) who tells activists of the Black Student Union in Colorado Springs in the 1970s about lynchings he had witnessed. Turner also explains the power of images and tells his audience of D.W. Griffith's silent racist film about the Confederate States, *Birth of a Nation* (1915), a "blockbuster" which ushered in a renewed rise of the Ku Klux Klan in America. It was screened by U.S. president Woodrow Wilson in the White House: "he said, it was history written with lightning," says Turner to the students who are listening to him. The Black students raise their fists and chant "Black Power" together. The other group listens to the Grand Wizard of the KKK, David Duke (played by Topher Grace) who has come to Colorado to induct new members to the "organization." The new Klan members and their wives all watch *Birth of Nation* together. The audience is seen clapping while watching the racists scenes, performed by White actors in blackface; they are frantically chanting "string him up, bring him up" when a Black man is declared "guilty" by a KKK mock trial. The music suddenly changes and Lee cuts to Ron Stallworth (John David Washington), the protagonist of the film, the first African American policeman in Colorado Springs who wrote the memoirs on which *BlacKkKlansman* is based. Stallworth successfully infiltrated the Klan as an undercover agent and has another colleague, Philipp Zimmerman, "Flip" (Adam Driver) stand in for him at the Klan meetings. "Flip" is Jewish and has to swear in the induction ceremony that he is a "white, non-Jewish American citizen."

Ron and Flip help prevent violent attacks and cross burnings by the KKK members during their undercover investigation; they not only reveal racists within their own police force but also KKK members in the Colorado military base, who steal ammunition for bomb attacks, clandestinely investigated by the FBI. In his speeches, Duke promotes "America First"; at the end of the *Birth of a Nation* screening, all viewers rise, lift their right hand in a fascist salute, and scream "White Power." Spike Lee ends his dark satire with documentary footage of the Tiki Torch bearing White supremacists in Charlottesville in August 2017.

Lee also includes an authentic clip of President Trump during a press conference, calling the extremist protesters with their torches and swastikas "very fine people." He claimed that "you had a group on one side that was bad; and you had a group on the other side that was also very violent. Not all of those people were neo-Nazis, believe me." While Trump says these words, footage of the White supremacists with confederate flags and neo-Nazi attire are shown, marching down the streets in Charlottesville. *Black Lives Matter* activists are calling out off-camera "Nazis go home." Spike Lee uses the power of images to undermine the statements of the American President. Ultimately, the real David Duke who attended the rally in Virginia is pictured, creating the link between the movie and contemporary America. Lee also makes painfully clear that movie images like those of *Birth of a Nation* continue to promote cultural stereotypes, model violence, and create an atmosphere of hate. D.W. Griffith's "master piece" is still screened in American and international film history classes as a classic. Its racist legacy may or may not be emphasized, depending on the respective instructors. The fact that Spike Lee filters the racist footage of *Birth of a Nation* with cross-cutting back and forth to the Black Student meeting in Colorado Springs is a deliberate strategy to depict the toxic legacy of film history and break the spell of the images. In contrast, *Black Panther* has built an alternate universe, a fantasy world, and is thereby actively reversing the course of history. The film is providing a lasting imprint, a legacy of a story that is empowering and inspirational, and requires critical engagement in its own right.

Rather than invoking the racist past of American film history (and repeating some of the pitfalls of contemporary Hollywood directors who showcase racism and segregation by creating stories around White saviors), Coogler has created a world that is self-contained and almost devoid of White actors. It is not a mirror of racist modern America but a world in Africa, entirely driven by its own rules: while honoring ancestors, the country of Wakanda combines tradition with science fiction and modernity. It is technologically more advanced than the contemporary United States. Contrary to Spike Lee, Ryan Coogler uses a distinctly different strategy of storytelling to build a narrative about the racial divide within the United States. He displaces the story of Black Americans and the legacy of slavery, Jim Crow and segregation, while creating an alternate universe, a fantasy country, Wakanda, hidden from the world underneath a dome on the African continent. Rather than being vulnerable and out in the open, as the *Black*

Lives Matter protesters were in Charlottesville to protest racial injustice and police violence, Wakanda thrives in hiding, kept apart from the rest of political movements while observing those from afar. However, the movie ends with the King T'Challa (Chadwick Boseman) addressing the General Assembly of the United Nations, supposedly in Geneva, and opening up his country and its wealthy natural resources to a global community.

Whether or not to protest for racial inequality in the open as well as supporting or rejecting violent/armed struggle is at the heart of *Black Panther*. As many of our authors in the collection argue, Ryan Coogler's superhero film reinvents history for African-Americans and Africans outside of slavery, White supremacy and the legacy of the transatlantic passage. Africans in *Black Panther* have access to the United States as visitors and observers, but their identity is not defined by the rules of a racist government. Wakandans, despite being governed by an elected king who must prove himself in hand-to-hand combat, are represented by powerful tribes. Leadership roles are held by both male and female alike; the army that protects the king consists of women warriors only, the Dora Milaje ("the adored ones")—a fierce collective reminiscent of Amazonians—who fight with traditional Wakandan spears and vibranium weapons. Their heralded role, as strong, respected women who will fight and die for the nation, deviates from popular depictions of Black women in film, and more specifically of African women. These re-inscriptions of who and what constitutes traditional African womanhood are arguably more acceptable within an Afrofuturist, comic book-defined realm. The same is true of Wakanda, which is steeped in tradition but at the same time profits from a technology that is far advanced to the United States. Wakanda is a nation that could win any war but has not shared its weapons, manufactured from the precious metal *vibranium*, with anybody *Black Panther* does not advocate for violence, even though Ryan Coogler does show racial injustice in the United States and alludes to the U.S. history of slavery when antagonist Killmonger (Michael B. Jordan) dies toward the conclusion of the film. He prefers to perish than live in "bondage" as did his ancestors who came on slave ships to America. The conflict whether to bear arms or not is battled out in Wakanda itself between two Black protagonists. They stand for opposing ideologies on how to overcome injustice in a modern world: King T'Challa chooses diplomacy and education; Killmonger advocated for an armed struggle.

HISTORICAL CONTEXT IN CONTEMPORARY SOCIETY

Tiki torch carrying White supremacists and right-wing, neo-Nazi and KKK sympathizers marched in Charlottesville in the summer 2017. They had clashed with BLM protesters who had assembled on the street, and a young woman, Heather Hever, was killed instantly in an act of violence when a male driver smashed into the group. The Charlottesville resident who was thirty-two years old died on the spot. Spike Lee's *BlacKkKlansman* shows the portrait of Heather Heyer at the end of his dark satire about police violence and racial discrimination in Colorado Springs in the 1970s. Ryan Coogler's *Black Panther* does not end on a dark note but promotes hope for change: T'Challa returns to Los Angeles into a predominantly African American neighborhood and asks his sister Shuri to run an educational foundation for Black youth. Coogler added the epilogue with T'Challa at the United Nations to provide closure for a global platform, thereby merging the local with the international. Both films by Lee and Coogler and their creative teams were nominated for Academy Awards: *Black Panther* was in competition for seven nominations and won three of them in 2019, among them the Oscar for best costume design for Ruth E. Carter, the first African American woman to win this award. *BlacKkKlansman* had six nominations and won one for "Best Adapted Screenplay."

This snub of both films for the "Best Film" Award in 2019 was seen as yet another example of the "Oscars-So-White." The winner of that year was *Green Book* (2018), a nostalgic story about historical racism in the South of the United States, proving that the American Academy was more comfortable with a somewhat light-hearted story about segregation with a White hero Tony "The Lip" Vallelonga (played by Viggo Mortensen) who dominates the screen performances as a "white savior" for a Black classical musician, Dr. Donald Shirley (Mahershala Ali) during the Jim Crow era. While Ali won the Oscar for Best Supporting Actor that year, Mortenson was heralded as the real hero of the movie. It is a so-called buddy film, a comedy, directed by Peter Farrelly, a White director. Criticisms from Don Shirley's family, as well as viewers, focused on the centering of the White hero, the invocation of Dr. Shirley as the vehicle for his discovery of racism in the segregated United States of the 1960s. Furthermore, given family members' claims that Don Shirley never wanted his story made into a film, the question of narrative agency and control over one's life story must also be considered.[13] Are these trends in storytelling because few people of color have seats at the tables where stories are green-lit and script are written, where actors are cast, and where films are underwritten? Continued tensions regarding race and film require that we continue to ask: Why is Hollywood still dominated by White male directors and why are most crew members White? In response to this continued trend, and the debates regarding inclusion and representation in film, African American contemporary director Ava DuVernay is an advocate for a new database where below-the-line-talent is promoted so that it is easier to get hired in film production.[14]

What is distinctly different in *Black Panther* from films, such as *Green Book,* is that the cast features only few and not plot carrying White actors. In *Black Panther*, there is no "knight in shining armor" who needs to come to King T'Challa's rescue. Although there are also antagonists and opposing interests of power, the central conflict takes place between cousins: T'Challa and Killmonger, who grew up in Los Angeles. Killmonger's father was dissatisfied as a young man, sent to Los Angeles as an observer, with the decision of his brother, the King T'Chaka (John Kani) to hide Wakanda from the world and not provide access to its riches to liberate Black Americans from discrimination. Not only does T'Chaka criticize his brother who is involved in arms deals and sells vibranium to weapons dealers but he actually has him killed, leaving Killmonger as an orphaned child behind. In the story, based on the comic series *Black Panther*, Killmonger arrives in Wakanda as an adult man, a charismatic American army trained sniper and warrior who not only challenges the new young king but tries to kill him to avenge his father's death, and then assumes the throne. Killmonger wants to change Wakanda's role in the world. He advocates for armed struggle and violence, similar to the North African post-colonial wars to free countries from European colonial rule. He does not believe in peace. He rejects the tribal past and honoring the heritage of elders contrary to the way, T'Challa does. Killmonger orders the magic herb that allows the king to connect with the forefathers in a ritual to be burned to the ground and destroyed. He announces that Wakanda's army and the female Amazonian tribe, the Dora Milaje, will launch an international revolution and take power over other countries and governments by force.

Black Panther has been a huge box office success. It is the first superhero film with an almost exclusively African American and African cast to have crossed the 1 billion profit margin. Children across the world emulate and idealize the characters of the Dora Milaje and the female protagonists in Wakanda, Princess Shuri (Letitia Wright) and T'Challa's mother Ramonda (Angela Bassett) and girlfriend Nakia (Lupita Nyong'o). The film has also been incorporated into discussions surrounding Afrofuturism in music and culture.

Our collection of essays, by a broad array of international scholars, reflects the intersecting topics, as indicated by our book's title *Black Panther: Afrofuturism, Gender, Identity and the Re-Making of Blackness*; it alludes to the multifaceted and multidisciplinary points of interest and scholarship of our diverse group of international authors. The title is a direct reference to Renée T. White's first chapter "I Dream a World: *Black Panther* and the Re-Making of Blackness." Originally published in 2018 by the journal *New Political Science* (Vo 40, No.2), White's research was the spark for this project. Lauren Steimer and Wayne Wong, authors of chapters 2 and 3 in this volume, attended an international conference on Action Cinema at the University of Reading in the United Kingdom in spring 2019, organized by the scholars Lisa Purse, Yvonne Tasker, and Chris Holmlund. Karen A. Ritzenhoff attended the conference to present a paper on Ruth Carters' Afrofuturist philosophy when she refined the costume design for *Black Panther*. Steimer and Wong quickly agreed to contribute their work to our co-edited collection and were joined by researchers from a broad spectrum of fields. We publish eighteen chapters in this book, despite all the trials and tribulations that the global COVID pandemic unleashed on our contributing scholars. We are drawing from research outside the realm of Western-centric film studies. We are also addressing different analytical approaches from many different disciplines. Our preface by filmmaker and scholar Zeinabu irene Davis anchors our volume in the legacy of the L.A. Rebellion and the roots of contemporary New Black Cinema.

In chapter 1, "I Dream a World: *Black Panther* and the Re-Making of Blackness," Renée T. White describes how the film's importance as an Afrofuturistic tale can be best understood through the lens of Third Cinema and the Black Arts Movement. Its popularity rests in part, because it is a film that rejects tropes of Blackness often imposed by Hollywood productions and keeps a diasporic imagining of Blackness at its center.

Lauren Steimer's chapter "The Power in Numbers: Ensemble Stunt Performance in *Black Panther* and Histories of Practice" positions the film at the epicenter of a seismic shift in the history of Hollywood stuntwork. That so many talented stuntwomen and Black stunt performers found work on *Black Panther* is not due to, but rather, despite the actions of the Screen Actors Guild. Steimer's chapter is divided into three sections on histories of practice within stunting communities: practices of exclusion; practices of inclusion; and expert performance in practice.

In chapter 3, "From Expressivity to Equanimity: New Black Action Aesthetics in *Black Panther*," Wayne Wong argues that *Black Panther* (2018) is a landmark moment in the history of Black action cinema in the sense that it represents the consolidation of a new action aesthetics in the genre, which he calls "martial ideation," emphasizing not on the cathartic release of emotions but more on the cultivation of tranquility amidst violent bodily conflicts. The turn from ruthless outburst of rage to tranquil recollection of powerful emotion in quietness presents an alternative vision to the view by Frantz Fanon of violence as a form of resistance to colonialism and opens up new aesthetics possibilities for Black action cinema in the future.

Mikal J. Gaines explores in chapter 4, "Paid the Cost to be the Boss: Chadwick Boseman, *Black Panther*, and the Future of the Black Bioptic," how Ryan Coogler's *Black Panther* and more specifically, the casting of the late Chadwick Boseman, exemplifies the peculiar intersection between the Black biopic and the superhero movie. The idea that the success or failure of a (Black) superhero movie should come with higher stakes than the biopics in which Boseman previously starred, signals an important shift in how Black audiences are conceptualizing Black representation. Despite the biopic's persistence as one of the chief genres through which Hollywood approaches blackness, other genres, namely horror and the superhero film, have undeniably become the more important metric of progress.

If the biopic has often served as mechanism of legitimacy, a reward and proof of the actor's special capabilities, it now functions as a stepping-stone to what has become the more culturally prestigious and significant work of rendering truth from myth.

In chapter 5, "Let Ayo Have a Girlfriend: Resisting Black Lesbian Erasure on Twitter," Sarah E. S. Sinwell goes back to 2017. When it was announced that Marvel would be releasing Ryan Coogler's *Black Panther* in February 2018, fans were excited that two of the titular character's bodyguards, Ayo and fellow female warrior Okoye, would get together as Ayo and Aneka do in the comics. However, when it was clear that the relationship between Danai Gurira's Okoye and Florence Kasumba's Ayo in *Black Panther* would not be romantic, this lesbian erasure from *Black Panther* sparked outrage among fans of the comic books. Thus, these fans of *Black Panther* turned to Twitter to encourage Marvel to #LetAyoHaveAGirlfriend.

This chapter maps out the ways in which social movements on Twitter function as a contradictory space for political and social advocacy: both facilitating online activism and cultivating online harassment and bullying. Pushing up against the whiteness and heteronormativity of corporate-sponsored media culture, the campaign to #LetAyoHaveAGirlfriend draws attention not only to the absence of people of color and LGBTQ characters within contemporary media more generally but also to alternative possibilities for diverse media representation.

In chapter 6, "'Tell Me a Story Baba': *Black Panther* and Wakanda's Foreign Policy in the Age of Neoliberalism," Clarence Lusane addresses how the groundbreaking symbolism of the Black Panther masks critical political issues that confront contemporary Black global resistance. From an international relations perspective, the film raises a question that is at the very center of the film's narrative arc: What should be the foreign policy doctrine of an all-powerful Black nation? *Black Panther* sets up a false dichotomy that ignores an alternative model for achieving power that challenges neoliberalist assumptions without extremist violence as a strategy. Lusane argues that the film settles on a resolution that fails to address the global devastation of neoliberalism that cannot be resolved by one nation no matter how (secretly) wealthy in resources and advanced technology. Ultimately, the question of the unequal distribution of political and economic power must be named and changed through a collective resistance to the current configuration of neoliberal tenets, policies, and institutions.

In chapter 7, "The Underground Railroad as Afrofuturism: Enslaved Blacks that Imagined Freedom, Future, and Space," dann j. Broyld employs the lens of Afrofuturism to address *Black Panther* and the Underground Railroad, detailing what imagination, tact, and technology, it took for fugitive Blacks to flee to the "outer spaces of slavery." Black enslavement was as terrifying as any exotic fictional tale, but it happened to real humans alienated in the "peculiar institution." Escaping slavery brought dreams to life, and at times must have felt like "magical realism" or an out-of-body experience, and the American North, Canada, Mexico, Africa, Europe, and free Caribbean islands were otherworldly and science fiction-like, in contrast to where Black fugitives ascended. This chapter will address Black Panther and the intersections of race, technology, and liberation, by retroactively applying a modern concept to historical moments.

In chapter 8, "The Evolution of the Dora Milaje: Wakanda's Greatest Warriors in Comics and Film," Joshua Truelove discusses how the characters of the Amazonian tribe have changed. The Dora Milaje in the comic were very representative of the "sex sells" culture and era of cynicism of the 1990s. The women were sexualized, looked like supermodels, and were described as promised future wives to the king of Wakanda. As the comics moved forward, and the Marvel films were released, the characters became more adaptable to their current era. By exploring the origins, background, characters, technology, and image of the Dora Milaje, this chapter argues that the Dora Milaje have a deeper history and lore than just the one expressed in the Marvel Cinematic Universe and that the women warriors of Wakanda have reflected and adapted to the eras in which they existed.

Dominique Young argues in chapter 9, "'The Prince Will Now Have The Strength of The Black Panther Stripped Away': Reading Disability and Queerness in Killmonger," that the intersection of a disability studies and Black feminist framework in Sami Schalk's book *Bodyminds Reimagined: (Disability), Race and Gender in Black Women's Speculative Fiction* and Cathy Cohen's essays, "Deviance as Resistance" and "Punks, Bulldaggers, and Welfare Queens" allow us to read the character, Killmonger, as both a psychologically disabled and queer character. When analyzed through Schalks' definition of bodymind and metaphor of disability, in the end, Young encourages readers to consider how disability studies and Black feminism offer new ways of thinking about Black masculinity and disability in the film.

In chapter 10, "Only When She Wants To: Code-Switching in *Black Panther*," Paul Moffett focuses on a memorable moment in the Ryan Coogler-directed *Black Panther* (2018), when N'Jobu, played by Sterling K. Brown, abruptly changes from speaking in an American accent to speaking in the movie's Wakandan accent. This moment of code-switching not only reveals N'Jobu's double identity to the audience, it also signals the complexity and fluidity of that identity. In this chapter, Moffett explores the role of code-switching, both successful and unsuccessful, and both literally linguistic and metaphorical, as it is employed throughout the film. Each of these instances functions differently, but each informs the others as the film explores the performance of identities, both public and secret.

Myron T. Strong, K. Sean Chaplin, and Giselle Greenidge address in chapter 11, "The *Dora Milaje* in Real Life: A Continuing Legacy of African Warriors," Afrofuturism's embrace of divine feminism—this idea that women themselves have complete agency over both their lives and choices that they make—was on full display in the movie *Black Panther*. It is the elevation of *Dora Milage* along with Shuri and Nakia in the movie that's the driving force of the movie and real African history to the big screen. While many modern views of African women are framed with Eurocentric ideas about their roles and abilities, the *Dora Milage* challenge these notions and bridge the fictional warrior force with the real traditions of African women. The *Dora Milage* pulls from many aspects of precolonial African women, including the Kingdom of Dahomey (modern day Benin), which had fearsome female warriors and powerful kings. *Black Panther's* celebration of this history was both culturally and socially significant. It speaks the necessity of Afrofuturism as vehicle to challenge, change, and highlight those important aspects of being Black.

Chapter 12 by Dolita Cathcart discusses "Echoes of the History of Black Utopian Visions, 'Black Manhood,' and Black Feminism in the Making of *Black Panther*." Cathcart illustrates how *Black Panther*—a film of two utopias, one of an African nation not infected by the disorganization and destructive forces of a colonial past with that of Black Americans who lived a life defined by racism and discrimination—incorporates the ongoing battle of Black feminists' struggle for justice and equality for all Americans and Black male activists' fight for Black manhood rights alone, with their utopian visions of a future America. In Cathcart's analysis, the fictional nation of Wakanda resembles an African version of Booker T. Washington's Tuskegee Institute, while Killmonger's history, similar to that of Malcolm X, contributes to his desire for a revolution. Cathcart compares and contrasts the characters of the film with Booker T. Washington, WEB DuBois, William Monroe Trotter, Josephine St. Pierre Ruffin, Harriet Tubman, and Ida B. Wells. These activists are examples of the countless Black women and men in the early twentieth century, known to history and forgotten, who committed their lives to a near-impossible vision of building a just nation for all. *Black Panther* is an Afrofuturist re-imagining of the fabled Prester John, the king of a mythical and powerful nation in Africa for which the Portuguese and other Europeans searched as they sought allies to defeat the Moors in the

1400s, with the dystopian aspects of over 400 years of Black struggle in North America. Black Americans and activists have exhibited an optimistic and resilient persistence in both re-imagining a better world and striving to make it so. What they imagined for themselves and for their country was ultimately utopian, because whether they were reformers or revolutionaries, they had to convince the majority of White Americans that Blacks and all women deserved first class citizenship. Cathcart concludes that their struggles and utopian visions of America's past history are echoed throughout the film, *Black Panther*.

Shayla Monroe explores in chapter 13, "Tradition, Purpose, and Technology: An Archaeological Take on the Role of Technological Progress in *Black Panther*." Monroe's chapter takes an archaeological approach to understanding the intricate relationship between technology, ideology, and culture, in the movie *Black Panther* (2018). The film illustrates a central tenet of the anthropology of technology: technological innovation is culturally situated, culturally contingent, and adopted selectively. By comparing the perspectives of T'Challa and his sister, Shuri, with those of M'Baku and Nakia, this chapter seeks to: (1) examine the shared Wakandan cultural foundations of that allowed for such dramatic tech development while the Jabari opted out, (2) contrast those foundations with the capitalistic motivations of an influential, real-world center of tech invention, Silicon Valley, (3) unpack the hegemonic exaltation of technological innovation and its motivating principles, and (4) imagine a real-world future with technology origination in service to distinctly African ethics and ideals.

In chapter 14, "Reflections on *Black Panther* and the Traditions of Third Cinema," Cynthia Baron looks at *Black Panther*'s wide international audience and reflects on the film's material conditions, with its financial success grounded in the transnational dominance of Hollywood studios. At the same time, the film is an international cultural-aesthetic artifact that can be studied in relation to international cinema movements. Specifically, one can consider it in light of Third Cinema, which has represented an alternative to corporate filmmaking and apolitical art cinema since the mid-twentieth century and international action cinema, which sometimes offers representations of individuals and communities rarely featured in highbrow productions. Looking at *Black Panther* through these two cultural-aesthetic lenses allows Cynthia Baron to clarify its ideological perspectives; it also makes the film's aesthetic innovations visible. Arguably, *Black Panther*'s rich depiction of Black subjectivity emerges from its use of both Third Cinema principles and action cinema strategies.

Khadijah Z. Ali-Coleman introduces in chapter 15, "The Depiction of Homeschooling, Black Identity and Political Thought in the film *Black Panther*" the disparate viewpoints and personalities of two fictional Black male characters, Killmonger and T'Challa. Both characters, largely homeschooled by their fathers during their primary years, hold worldviews shaped by parents who emphasized cultural practice and history as integral to identity. Homeschool is PK-12 instruction that is implemented and/or curated by the student's parent(s) within a structured or unstructured learning environment. Homeschooling rates have continued to grow in the United States, moving from 1.7 percent of school-aged children being homeschooled in 1999 to 3.4 percent being homeschooled in 2012. Overall, although more than 5 percent of homeschooled students are African American and steadily rising, the literature focusing on African American homeschoolers is not proportionate to their presence.

Khadijah Z. Ali-Coleman argues that the main characters of *Black Panther* provide a lens in which to discuss the impact of homeschooling. While the character Killmonger has been characterized by most as villainous, serving as the antagonist to T'Challa's role as the protagonist, his articulated viewpoints have polarized audiences, garnering many fans. Some viewers of the film agree with Killmonger's articulated anger and viewpoints in the film, while others find his perspective divisive and violent. Using critical race theory to present the literature on homeschooled students in relation to analysis of the film *Black Panther*, this chapter asserts that homeschooling is a form of liberatory practice for Black children. Consequently, as American society operates from a White, patriarchal positioning, this chapter discusses how homeschool education for African American children provides an armor of cultural awareness that empowers and emboldens.

Neal Curtis explores in chapter 16, "Two Paths to the Future: Radical Cosmopolitanism and Counter-Colonial Dignity in *Black Panther*," how the film managed to mix mainstream success with an unflinching meditation on the legacy of colonialism and slavery. He argues the film espouses two forms of politics in response to this legacy. The first is represented by Killmonger's global project for liberation based on the need for unflinching counter-colonial violence. Here, the film is rooted in the work of Frantz Fanon, as presented in *Black Skin, White Masks*, and *The Wrteched of the Earth*. Against this, T'Challa's politics might be said to represent a more pacific but equally radical cosmopolitanism representative of the work of W. E. B. DuBois. The chapter argues that while Killmonger might move from radical activist to villain within the film, his final refusal to submit to T'Challa's wishes maintains the dissent that is at the heart of his politics. This dissent also works to remind us that the universal claims of cosmopolitanism cannot be secured in the face of universal injustice. This helps explain why the film remains true to radical protest in a post-colonial context. On the way, the chapter also addresses the important cultural politics of the original comic.

Chapter 17, "My Blood Right: A Critical Analysis of *Black Panther's* Killmonger, Colonialism, and Hybrid Identity," allows Gabriel A. Cruz to analyze how throughout American history, our society has grappled with the concept of racial hybridity, and the third space, that is created relative to the constructions of race in the United States. Culturally positioned as belonging to both-and-neither cultures of their respective heritages, individuals of mixed racial backgrounds have long occupied a space fraught with tensions surrounding acceptance and legitimacy. Cruz's chapter critically engages with the conceptualization of hybrid identity within the film *Black Panther* by examining the character Erik Killmonger and his hybrid identity of being both-and-neither Wakandan and African American.

In chapter 18, "The Other Worlds of *Black Panther's* Purple Heart-Shaped Herb," Paul Karolczyk uses ethnobotany to show how *Black Panther's* heart-shaped herb spotlights the deep enduring influence of psychotropic plants on traditional and contemporary culture, human consciousness and identity, religious cosmology and ritual, and medicine and psycho-spiritual healing. The herb's cinematic portrayal as a powerful consciousness-altering plant overturns racist stereotypes of African traditional religion and elevates a Black perspective from the excluded margins of White-dominated prevailing discourses that express the West's taboo cultural fascination with hallucinogenic plants. Consequently, *Black Panther* stands alone in American popular cinema as a film that sheds serious light on sacred and medicinal psychotropic plant use and gives it a cultural visibility that rarely appears in comparison to the widespread imagery of secular recreational drug and alcohol use. Karolczyk's ethnobotanical chapter considers *Black Panther's* heart-shaped herb as an invitation to the humanist study of African and other indigenous traditional psychotropic plant uses to capture their symbolic and practical importance in relation to past, present, and future social and environmental problems in the real world.

NOTES

1. Ava DuVernay has announced that she will help create a database to help diversify creative talent in Hollywood. She argues that many Black crew members do not get picked for major Hollywood productions. See Yvonne Villarreal, "Ava DuVernay and Peter Roth have a plan to diversify crews. And Hollywood is on board." *The Los Angeles Times*, December 29, 2020. https://www.latimes.com/entertainment-arts/tv/story/2020-12-29/ava-duvernay-peter-roth-hollywood-diversity-array-crew-database (access on February 18, 2021).

2. The tweet that announced Chadwick Boseman's death has been labeled as the most widely distributed "of all time" according to CNN coverage on August 20, 2020.

"Twitter's most liked tweet of all time now belongs to Chadwick Boseman." https://www.cnn.com/2020/08/29/us/most-liked-tweet-of-all-time-chadwick-boseman-trnd/index.html (accessed on February 18, 2021).

3. Roy Thomas, "Stan Lee's Amazing Marvel Interview: Two Extraordinary 2005 Sessions with the Man Who Spearheaded Marvel Comics," *Alter Ego* 3, no. 164 (2011): 38.

4. Blair Davis, "*All-Negro Comics* and the Birth of Lion Man, the First African American Superhero," *Inks: The Journal of the Comics Studies Society* 3, no. 3 (2019): 275, KHAL, "The 7 Most Racist Moments in Comic Book History," *Complex* (April 2018) https://www.complex.com/pop-culture/2018/04/racist-moments-in-comic-book-history/.

5. Frantz Fanon, *Black Skin, White Masks* (New York: Grove Press, 1967), 34–35.

6. Kristin Hunt, "How Oscar Micheaux Challenged the Racism of Early Hollywood," *JSTOR Daily* (October 3, 2019) https://daily.jstor.org/how-oscar-micheaux-challenged-the-racism-of-early-hollywood/.

7. Davis, "All-Negro Comics," 274, 291.

8. Abraham Riesman, "How an Untested Young Comics Writer Revolutionized Black Panther." *Vulture* (February 16, 2018) https://www.vulture.com/2018/02/don-mcgregor-panthers-rage-black-panther.html; Tucker Stone and David Brothers, "Fear of a Black Panther," *The Comics Journal* (February 16, 2018) http://www.tcj.com/fear-of-a-black-panther/; Ben Morse, "Don McGregor on Breaking Boundaries with Black Panther." *Marvel*. November 12, 2020, https://www.marvel.com/articles/comics/don-mcgregor-on-breaking-boundaries-with-black-panther.

9. Micah Peters, "The Evolution of Marvel's 'Black Panther': Tracing the Comic Book Origins of a Complex, Exciting Character—and the Series that (Sometimes) Bears His Name," *The Ringer* Feb 14, 2018 https://www.theringer.com/pop-culture/2018/2/14/17012374/marvel-black-panther-comics-history.

10. Balogun Ojetade, "Ain't no Such Thing as Superman! Do Black People Need Black Superheroes…or Just Black Heroes?" *Chronicles of Harriet* (February 2015) https://chroniclesofharriet.com/2015/02/17/heroes/.

11. Adilifu Nama, "Brave Black Worlds: black superheroes as science fiction ciphers," *African Identities* (May 2009).

12. Taylor Crumpton, "Afrofuturism Has Always Looked Forward: How can the ideology serve as a blueprint for cultural growth?" *Architectural Digest*, August 24, 2020, https://www.architecturaldigest.com/story/what-is-afrofuturism.

13. Kate Erbland, "'Green Book': Real-Life Friends of Dr. Don Shirley Defend 'Simply Wonderful' Film," IndieWire. https://www.indiewire.com/2019/01/green-book-friends-don-shirley-defend-film-1202033954/ (January 19, 2019); Brooke Obie, "How 'Green Book' and The Hollywood Machine Swallowed Donald Shirley Whole," Shadow and Act, December 13, 2018, https://shadowandact.com/the-real-donald-shirley-green-book-hollywood-swallowed-whole.

14. Ava DuVernay, "Ava DuVernay on Array Crew, A Database to Diversify Hollywood Production Personnel," interview by Ailsa Chang, *All Things Considered*, National Public Radio, February 18, 2021, audio, 8:00. https://www.npr.org/2021/02

/18/969151083/ava-duvernay-on-array-crew-a-database-to-diversify-hollywood-production-personnel.

WORKS CITED

CNN. "Twitter's most liked tweet of all time now belongs to Chadwick Boseman." August 20, 2020. https://www.cnn.com/2020/08/29/us/most-liked-tweet-of-all-time-chadwick-boseman-trnd/index.html.

Crumpton, Taylor. "Afrofuturism Has Always Looked Forward: How can the ideology serve as a blueprint for cultural growth?" *Architectural Digest*, August 24, 2020, https://www.architecturaldigest.com/story/what-is-afrofuturism.

Davis, Blair. "All-Negro Comics and the Birth of Lion Man, the First African American Superhero." *Inks: The Journal of the Comics Studies Society* 3, no. 3 (2019): 273–297.

Erbland, Kate. "'Green Book': Real-Life Friends of Dr. Don Shirley Defend 'Simply Wonderful' Film." IndieWire, January 19, 2019, https://www.indiewire.com/2019/01/green-book-friends-don-shirley-defend-film-1202033954/.

Fanon, Frantz. *Black Skin, White Masks*. New York: Grove Press, 1967.

Hunt, Kristin, and Kristin Hunt. "How Oscar Micheaux Challenged the Racism of Early Hollywood." *JSTOR Daily*, October 3, 2019, https://daily.jstor.org/how-oscar-micheaux-challenged-the-racism-of-early-hollywood/.

KHAL. "The 7 Most Racist Moments in Comic Book History." *Complex*, April 2018, https://www.complex.com/pop-culture/2018/04/racist-moments-in-comic-book-history/.

Lee, Stan and Jack Kirby. The Black Panther. *Fantastic Four*. July/August 1966, New York: Canam Publishers Sales Corp.

Morse, Ben. "Don McGregor on Breaking Boundaries with Black Panther." *Marvel*. November 12, 2020, https://www.marvel.com/articles/comics/don-mcgregor-on-breaking-boundaries-with-black-panther.

Nama, Adifu. "Brave Black Worlds: Black Superheroes as Science Fiction Ciphers." *African Identities* (May 2009).

Obie, Brooke. "How 'Green Book' and The Hollywood Machine Swallowed Donald Shirley Whole." *Shadow and Act*, December 13, 2018, https://shadowandact.com/the-real-donald-shirley-green-book-hollywood-swallowed-whole.

Ojetade, Balogun. "Ain't no Such Thing as Superman! Do Black People Need Black Superheroes…or Just Black Heroes?" *Chronicles of Harriet*, February 2015, https://chroniclesofharriet.com/2015/02/17/heroes/.

Riesman, Abraham. "How an Untested Young Comics Writer Revolutionized *Black Panther*." *Vulture* (February 16, 2018) https://www.vulture.com/2018/02/don-mcgregor-panthers-rage-black-panther.html.

Stone, Tucker and David Brothers. "Fear of a *Black Panther*." *The Comics Journal*, February 16, 2018, http://www.tcj.com/fear-of-a-black-panther/.

Thomas, Roy. "Stan Lee's Amazing Marvel Interview: Two Extraordinary 2005 Sessions with the Man Who Spearheaded Marvel Comics." *Alter Ego* 3, no. 164 (2011): 37–38.

Villarreal, Yvonne. "Ava DuVernay and Peter Roth have a plan to diversify crews. And Hollywood is on board." *The Los Angeles Times*, December 29, 2020, https://www.latimes.com/entertainment-arts/tv/story/2020-12-29/ava-duvernay-peter-roth-hollywood-diversity-array-crew-database.

Womack, Ytasha L. *Afrofuturism: The World of Black Sci-Fi and Fantasy Culture*. Chicago Review Press, 2013. ProQuest Ebook Central, http://ebookcentral.proquest.com/lib/wheatonma-ebooks/detail.action?docID=1381831.

FILMS

BlaKkKlansman. Directed by Spike Lee. USA, 2018.
Homesteader, The. Directed by Oscar Micheaux. USA, 1919.
Within Our Gates. Directed by Oscar Micheaux. USA, 1920.

Chapter 1

I Dream a World

Black Panther *and the Re-Making of Blackness*[1]

Renée T. White

Black Panther has been a critical and financial success and a defining moment for Black storytelling in Hollywood. This is the first superhero movie with a predominantly Black creative team and cast.[2] Like Langston Hughes describes in "I Dream a World,"[3] in *Black Panther* writer/director Ryan Coogler dreams a world of freedom for Black people. The story of Black Panther and the Kingdom of Wakanda has been so evocative that to have been an existential moment, particularly for some Black viewers.

STORYTELLING AND NARRATIVE AGENCY

In mainstream Hollywood, Black-themed films are considered too financially risky. It comes as a surprise when they are critical and financial successes.[4] As director and producer Reginald Hudlin observed,

> The confusion starts with the definition of 'black film,' as if it was a genre. There are musicals, action movies, comedies, horror films, but 'black' is not a storytelling genre. And the fact that these movies [with black casts] that can be wildly different are all put in the same category as if they're all the same, ignoring actual genres, which can have a huge effect on its ability to travel, already leads to people misunderstanding its worldwide box office potential.[5]

Superhero films, in particular, are expected to utilize a narrative-absent racial consciousness in order to be financially lucrative in the global market. Therefore, they must signify "different things to different segments, who have fundamentally different understandings of history, justice, and policy."[6]

Black Panther challenges these old tropes about superheroes and actively rejects the hegemony of whiteness.

There is no magical Negro (or as Spike Lee described it, the "super-duper Magical Negro")[7] who serves as a vehicle for White self-discovery but whose own interiority is irrelevant.[8] *Black Panther* also functions in contrast to films that introduce the White savior, who single-handedly improves the fate of the Black characters.[9] Part of what makes *Black Panther* so notable is that the film imagines a wholly self-contained, autonomous African ecosystem.

Since being introduced in 1966 by co-creators Stan Lee and Jack Kirby, *Black Panther* has evolved, both as a character and as a narrative vehicle. Authors shrugged off stereotypic ideas of African people and culture that were present in earlier iterations of the comic book. More recently, writers like Ta-Nahesi Coates and Roxane Gay expanded and complicated the stories and created storylines for queer and female characters. Writer/director Ryan Coogler and his co-writer John Robert Cole have drawn:

> from many different versions of *Black Panther* . . . . This slow decolonization of the Black Panther is the effort to decenter the white perspective from the construction of the character. If we recognize that representation matters, and that Black representation has been a tool in white supremacy, tracing the character over decades illustrates an epic struggle to make a "real" Black character out of something that was a white fantasy of blackness.[10]

The film is a commentary on African lives with minimal interest in, or need for, the approval of the White gaze. Cultural critic Mark Dery posits, "Can a community whose past has been deliberately rubbed out and whose energies have subsequently been consumed by the search for legible traces of its history, imagine a possible future?"[11]

AFROFUTURISM: BLACK TO THE FUTURE

Black Panther is Afrofuturist, unlike other superheroes and anti-heroes depicted in movies, such as *Blade* (1998), *The Meteor Man* (1993), *Blankman* (1994), *Spawn* (1997), and *Hancock* (2008). Afrofuturists create science fiction that disrupts our understanding of blackness by rethinking the past, present, and futures of the African Diaspora; they merge culture, tradition, time, space, and technology to present alternative interpretations of blackness. Afrofuturism "does not seek to deny the tradition of countermemory [defined as 'an ethical commitment to history, the dead, and the forgotten']. Rather, it aims to extend that tradition by reorienting the intercultural vectors of Black Atlantic temporality towards the proleptic as much as the retrospective."[12]

Black Panther looks to the past and pulls those threads into an alternate present and future, conjuring a fully liberated African nation into being for the audience. It starts with the origin story of Wakanda. Five African tribes war over vibranium, an otherworldly metallic substance. A shaman from the Black Panther tribe consumes a "heart-shaped flower" that gives him superhuman and mystical powers, leading him to unify the tribes into one nation. After this preamble, *Black Panther* tells multiple stories: the ascent of young Wakandan King T'Challa following his father's assassination, an arms dealer's pursuit of vibranium, and the evolution of the dealer's partner who turns out not to be who we think. The film embraces Sankofa, a Twi word from the Akan tribe in Ghana which means "it is not taboo to fetch what is at risk of being left behind."[13] By wedding pan-African languages, symbols, design, iconography, and tradition, *Black Panther* offers an Afrofuturist take on Sankofa. It inverts simplistic representations of Africanity, exploring the tensions between a never-colonized African nation and its diasporan kin whose history is inextricably linked to captivity. It serves as a reclamation project as described by Lisa Yazsek, Professor of Science Fiction Studies:

> [the writers] do more than simply combat the erasure of black subjects from Western history . . . [their] Afrodiasporic histories insist both on the authenticity of the black subject's experience in Western history and the way this experience embodies the dislocation felt by many modern peoples.[14]

As an Afrofuturist reclamation project, *Black Panther* is also indebted to both the Black Arts Movement and Third Cinema.

The Black Arts Movement emerged from the activism of writers and focused on developing a Black esthetic which places the experience and voice of Black people at the center of the narrative. Larry Neal, renowned scholar of African American Theater, explains that as the esthetic and spiritual sister of Black Power,

> the Black Arts Movement proposes a radical reordering of the western cultural esthetic. It proposes a separate symbolism, mythology, critique, and iconology. The Black Arts and the Black Power concept both relate broadly to the Afro-American's desire for self-determination and nationhood.[15]

Also a product of the late 1960s, Third Cinema emerged from Latin American filmmakers' critiques of traditional film fare and was embraced by African and Black American artists as well. "What makes Third Cinema third (i.e., a viable alternative to Western cinema) is . . . a film's political orientation within the hegemonic structures of post-colonialism. [And it] contributes ideologically to the advancement of Black people, within a context of systematic denial."[16]

Proponents of Third Cinema deployed a close reading of Frantz Fanon's body of work to critique and revolutionize filmmaking. Fanon documented the structural and psychosocial destructiveness of colonialism, the violence it metes out to the colonized, and unpacks how violence becomes a characteristic trait of anti-colonial resistance. He demonstrated how culture is used to rationalize colonialism. The culture produced by colonial powers reifies them while also denying the colonized their humanity. Colonized people, much like the mirror in a house of horrors, are disfigured and distorted beyond recognition. Culture produced by colonizing powers erases the particulars of the lives of the colonized, because this is irrelevant to the colonizing project. Cultural production by marginalized people, then, is intended to reject the violent erasure of their selfhood at the hands of Western colonial powers. What Third Cinema and the Black Arts Movement did was to claim "stories, epics and songs of the people," using the tools of cultural production to mold "national consciousness, giving it form and contours and flinging open before it new and boundless horizons .... The formula of 'This all happened long ago' is substituted with that of 'What are we going to speak of happened somewhere else, but it might well have happened here today, and it might happen tomorrow.'"[17] These arts movements reimagine the culture of a people, insisting that they too have a past, present, and future.

Wakanda is a reimagining of a pan-African past, present, and future. Characters speak both English and Xhosa, a South African dialect. Wakanda is a country of vibrant colors; each clan wears clothes specific and distinctive in style; beading, cowrie shells, prints, resins, and clay—meld the traditional and modern. Head costume designer Ruth Carter carefully studied and was inspired by the clothes, headdress, and jewelry from Kenya, Nigeria, Ghana, Lesotho, Namibia, and South Africa.[18] *Black Panther* unambiguously rejects colorism and embraces dark-skinned actors. Female characters wear natural hairstyles—braids, twists, clay covered coils, shaved heads, and locs—in clear relief to narrow and Westernized notions of beauty and womanhood. Even in its styling *Black Panther* suggests what could happen to the culture and practice of a nation that has been untouched by the colonizing sweep of the West.

THE UNCOLONIZED IMAGINATION

As King T'Challa (Chadwick Boseman) returns home following his father's assassination, the aircraft glides over herders and disappears into the tree line, when suddenly a metropolis appears below. "This never gets old," he says. All this time, the real Wakanda remained hidden under an undetectable dome. Wakanda had sustained the myth that it was a "backward" nation with little of consequence to offer, especially in the technologically driven twenty-first century. The residents took full advantage of this supremacist and paternalistic conceit and used it against the West. Wakanda was able to develop without interference; its residents understood the West without being defined by it. They consider Western science and technology substandard: bullets are barbaric, fabric and jewelry have limited applications, and communication devices are clumsy. The world outside of Wakanda appears more chaotic, violent, and less vibrant. In contrast, Wakanda is a stable, centuries-old nation where the ancient and sacred coexist with modern, sleek, ultra-high-tech gadgetry. For example, in the name of peacemaking and national security, T'Challa consumes the heart-shaped flower for superhuman strength and dons the vibranium-laced Black Panther costume. His teenage sister Princess Shuri (Letitia Wright) is a genius inventor and head of the Wakanda Design Group. There are virtual reality cars and aircraft, costumes in necklaces, and bracelets made of communications beads called Kimoyo ("of the spirit").

This movie does not need a White savior. Instead, it interrogates the centrality of whiteness for the main White characters, CIA agent Everett K. Ross (Martin Freeman) and the arms dealer Ulysses Klaue (Andy Serkins). Everett K. Ross had interacted with the Wakandan monarchy for some time. He is aware of the existence of the Black Panther, knows it is T'Challa's secret identity, and yet dismisses this as the rather quaint behavior of the monarch of what he calls a "Third World country." It never occurs to him to think much of this behavior, perhaps because it fits with the presumption of "simple" performative African traditions. In the film he reunites with T'Challa purely by accident at a casino where he intends to buy a stolen weapon from Klaue. T'Challa is also pursuing Klaue, accompanied by his ex-girlfriend Nakia (Lupita Nyong'o), a War Dog, and General Okoye (Danai Gurira), leader of the Dora Milaje (all-female royal guard) (see figure 1.1.). They are hoping to extradite Klaue to Wakanda because many years earlier he had invaded Wakanda and stolen vibranium, leaving many dead in his wake.

Though many nations had been looking for the source of vibranium, only Klaue knows where it is located. This knowledge does not only drive his greed but also his rage. It is unconscionable to him that any African "savage" has sole access to something so valuable. Therefore, his drive to extract it from them—because they have no right to something the West should possess—is a modern version of the colonizing mentality. Though he is demonstrably different from Klaue, Ross is temporarily unable to see beyond his Eurocentric lens. Even after seeing the technology used by the T'Challa, Nakia, and Okoye during their confrontation with Klaue and his

Figure 1.1 The Dora Milaje, Led by Okoye (Danai Gurira), Are Presented as an Amalgam of African Traditions in Their Dress and Appearance. *Source*: Screenshot taken by author.

men, it still does not occur to Ross that there might be something unusual about these Wakandans. It is not until later, when he is transported to Wakanda for life-saving surgery that he realizes what Wakanda really is—the most advanced technological power in the world. Ross is in a country where his CIA credentials have little currency. He is frequently reminded of his proper place—by Shuri who calls him "colonizer" and by a tribal leader who silences Ross first by grunting, then by tapping into an old trope about African cannibals and gleefully threatening to feed Ross "to his children." Outside of offering comic relief, Ross is important and along with Klaue serves a symbolic purpose. Both are reminders that it is virtually impossible to have contact with the outside world without consequence.

AM I MY BROTHER'S KEEPER?

Those who lived outside of Wakanda come to realize the cost of their nation's isolationist politics. It resulted in the country becoming a bystander to centuries of anti-Black racism, violence, and White supremacy. Nakia confronted the unintended consequences of her country's inaction while serving as a spy who infiltrated human trafficking operations. She witnessed the suffering of others and has seen their dehumanization for profit. She pleads with T'Challa to reconsider their country's isolationist stance. For her, Wakandan technology should be made available to provide healing for the dispossessed and disadvantaged. Another character struggled to reconcile the Wakandan monarchy's decision to remain separate from the suffering of the African diaspora. Erik Killmonger (Michael B. Jordan), a violent mercenary aligned with Klaue, is actually Wakandan royalty (see figure 1.2.). His father N'Jobu

I Dream a World

Figure 1.2 Killmonger (Michael B. Jordan) Embodies the Confluence of Wakandan and U.S. Black Traditions as he Engages in Conflict between These Parts of His Own Identity and History. *Source*: Screenshot taken by author.

(Sterling K. Brown) was King T'Chaka's (Atandwa and John Kani) brother (and thus T'Challa's uncle) and was a spy assigned to a post in Oakland, California. When we meet N'Jobu and Erik (as a child) it is 1992, the year of the Los Angeles (LA) uprisings. N'Jobu has witnessed police violence in Black communities, the impact of the influx of drugs plus the ongoing disinvestment in and abandonment of these communities. He is disillusioned by his brother's unwillingness to end mass Black suffering. N'Jobu's anger led him into a dangerous and unstable alliance with Klaue, presumably to fund some revolutionary plan. King T'Chaka uncovered this plot, confronts N'Jobu and kills him, leaving Erik behind.

Killmonger grows up seeking to avenge his father's death and destroy Wakanda for abandoning him and leaving the African diaspora vulnerable to White supremacy. He becomes a CIA operative and mercenary and like his father aligns with Klaue as a ploy to get close to Wakanda. Killmonger's very existence, like his nickname, has been defined by violence—and is memorialized by the scarification ritual he engages in following each "kill." But his is not the "purifying" violence often associated (sometimes inaccurately) with Fanon. He has witnessed and perpetrated violence against non-White countries and peoples (Iraq, Afghanistan, and throughout Africa). Through it all, he remains a Black man descended from African royalty, who is using the tools of oppression against his own people. He sees the Kingdom of Wakanda as complicit in the loss of his father, his exile, and his rootlessness. Killmonger becomes vigilante and avenger. He eventually kills Klaue, buying him entry into Wakanda where he successfully challenges T'Challa for the crown. When facing the Wakandan elders he tells them, "Where I'm from, when Black folks started revolutions, they never had the firepower or the resources to fight their oppressors . . . . Y'all sitting up here comfortable. Must feel good. Meanwhile, there are about 2 billion people all over the world that looks like us. But their lives are a lot harder. Wakanda has the tools to liberate them all." During his temporary reign over Wakanda, he attempts to use their technology to lay waste to White supremacist regimes, unconcerned about the damage to his homeland. Killmonger's use of violence fails because it is decoupled from a fully developed narrative of liberation; he is willing to kill his own people in the service of his own personal needs.[19] His violence is unfocused, driven by vengeance rather than the need to liberate. Faced with his failure, he chooses suicide, proclaiming to his cousin T'Challa, "Bury me in the ocean with my ancestors who jumped from ships, 'cause they knew death was better than bondage.'"

There is an important ideological debate throughout the film. Can Black people ever be untouched by the reach of White supremacy? Did Wakanda's leaders have an obligation to aid other people of African ancestry, even at some cost to themselves? Can technology simultaneously be used as tools of destruction and liberation? What does it mean to be truly free? Can one justify using violence if it is in the service of another's freedom? All of these questions, apart from serving as compelling plot devices, are mechanisms for introducing the audience to some of the political themes raised by Black revolutionary thinkers and artists.

#WAKANDAFOREVER

Since its opening, *Black Panther* has become a destination event. Its impact on people of African ancestry has been especially notable. The seismic reaction from Black audiences around the globe is not only a response to the esthetic beauty and storytelling of the movie. It is as if audiences are experiencing mass psychic relief. The film-going experience is often a complicated one for Black viewers because "Knowing yourself as a Black person—historically, spiritually, and culturally—is not something that's given to you institutionally; it's an arduous journey that must be taken by the individual."[20] But as a variant of Third Cinema, *Black Panther* offers the audience

> representations of black people [that] are presented from a wholly black cultural perspective instead of through the racist frame imposed by studios on many mainstream films . . . [and] relief from studio films that rely primarily on an inversion of racial codes—a structural feature that positions black spectators to view themselves from a mainstream perspective.[21]

In the end, the film may offer hope; while Killmonger has died, the inter-tribal conflict he causes is resolved and Wakanda reveals itself to the world. In a moment fully evocative of Sankofa, T'Challa buys the Oakland apartment complex where his father killed his uncle—where Killmonger's radicalism and rage are cultivated—with plans to turn it into a community center under Nakia's and Shuri's leadership. As children playing on the nearby basketball court clamor about the Wakandan aircraft before them, one young man looks at it in wonder then asks T'Challa who he is, and if the craft belongs to him; before T'Challa can answer, the screen fades to Black. This scene hints at a new origin story—that of T'Challa as a rightful global leader. It is a new origin story for the children as well, and by extension the Black viewers. For T'Challa is gateway to the past and a bridge to a different future. Here is a film that might just hold up a mirror, not one distorted by racism and White supremacy but one that allows the viewer to say, "I am." As The Weeknd and Kendrick Lamar remind viewers in the closing song, "You need a hero, look in the mirror, there go your hero"[22]

NOTES

1. This chapter has been first published in *New Political Science* 40, no. 2 (2018): 421–427. I wanted to thank NPS for allowing me to reprint it here.

2. American actors Chadwick Boseman (T'Challa/Black Panther), Michael B. Jordan (Erik Killmonger), Angela Bassett (Ramonda), and Forest Whitaker (Zuri); Afro-Caribbean actors Letitia Wright (Shuri) and Winston Duke (M'Baku) plus several actors with African parents including Lupita Nyong'o (Nakia), Danai Gurira, (Okoye), Daniel Kaluuya (W'Kabi).

3. Langston Hughes, "I Dream a World," in *The Collected Poems of Langston Hughes*, ed. Arnold Rampersad (New York, NY: Alfred A. Knopf, 1994), 311.

4. See *The Butler* (2013), *Selma* (2014), *Moonlight* (2016), *Get Out* (2017), *Hidden Figures* (2017), and *Girls Trip* (2017).

5. Tre'vell Anderson, "Disproving the 'Black Films Don't Travel' Hollywood Myth," *Los Angeles Times*, March 24, 2017, http://www.latimes.com/entertainment/movies/la-et-mn-black-movies-global-audience-myth-20170324-story.html.

6. Ezra Claverie, "Ambiguous Mr. Fox: Black Actors and the Interest Convergence in Superhero Film," *The Journal of American Culture* 40, no. 2 (2017): 156.

7. Susan Gonzalez, "Director Spike Lee Slams 'Same old Stereotypes in Today's Films," *Yale Bulletin and Calendar*, March 2, 2001, http://archives.news.yale.edu/v29.n21/story3.html.

8. *The Green Mile* (1999), *Shawshank Redemption* (1994), *The Legend of Bagger Vance* (2000), and *Mr. Church* (2016).

9. *The Blindside* (2009), *Mississippi Burning* (1988), and *The Help* (2011).

10. Rebecca Wanzo, "And All Our Past Decades Have Seen Revolutions: The Long Decolonization of Black Panther," *The Black Scholar*, February 19, 2018, https://www.theblackscholar.org/past-decades-seen-revolutions-long-decolonization-black-panther-rebecca-wanzo/.

11. Mark Dery, "Black to the Future: Interviews with Samuel A. Delaney, Greg Tate, and Tricia Rose," in *Flame Wars: The Discourse of Cyberculture*, ed. Mark Dery (Durham, NC: Duke University Press, 1994), 180.

12. Eshun Kodwo, "Further Considerations of Afrofuturism," *CR: The New Centennial Review* 3, no. 2 (2003): 289.

13. "The Power of Sankofa: Know History," Carter G. Woodson Center, Berea College, accessed February 2018, https://www.berea.edu/cgwc/the-power-of-sankofa/.

14. Lisa Yaszek, "Afrofuturism, Science Fiction, and the History of the Future," *Socialism and Democracy* 20, no. 3 (2006): 47.

15. Larry Neal, "The Black Arts Movement," *The Drama Review: TDR* 12, no. 4 (1968): 39.

16. Tommy Lott, "A No-Theory Theory of Contemporary Black Cinema," *Black American Literature Forum* 25, no. 2 (1991): 231.

17. Frantz Fanon, *The Wretched of the Earth* (New York, NY: Grove Press, 1963), 240.

18. Melena Ryzik, "The Afrofuturistic Designs of 'Black Panther'," *The New York Times*, February 23, 2018, https://www.nytimes.com/2018/02/23/movies/black-panther-afrofuturism-costumes-ruth-carter.html.

19. Kalpana Seshadri-Crooks, "I am a Master: Terrorism, Masculinity, and Political Violence in Frantz Fanon," *Parallax* 8, no. 2 (2002): 84–98.

20. Mark Dery, *Flame Wars: The Discourse of Cyberculture*, 210.

21. Tommy Lott, "Esthetics and Politics in Contemporary Black Film Theory," in *Film Theory and Philosophy*, eds. Richard Allen and Murray Smith (UK: Oxford Press, 1997), 291.

22. The Weeknd and Kendrick Lamar, "Pray for me," *Black Panther: The Album*.

WORKS CITED

Anderson, Tre'vell. "Disproving the 'Black Films Don't Travel' Hollywood Myth." *Los Angeles Times*, March 24, 2017, http://www.latimes.com/entertainment/movies/la-et-mn-black-movies-global-audience-myth-20170324-story.html.

Claverie, Ezra. "Ambiguous Mr. Fox: Black Actors and the Interest Convergence in Superhero Film." *The Journal of American Culture* 40, no. 2 (2017): 158–168.

Dery, Mark. "Black to the Future: Interviews with Samuel A. Delaney, Greg Tate, and Tricia Rose." In *Flame Wars: The Discourse of Cyberculture*, edited by Mark Dery, 179–222. Durham, NC: Duke University Press, 1994.

Fanon, Frantz. *The Wretched of the Earth*. New York, NY: Grove Press, 1963.

Gonzalez, Susan. "Director Spike Lee Slams 'Same Old Stereotypes in Today's Films." *Yale Bulletin and Calendar* 29, no. 21, March 2, 2001. http://archives.news.yale.edu/v29.n21/story3.html.

Hughes, Langston. "I Dream a World." In *The Collected Poems of Langston Hughes*, edited by Arnold Rampersad, 311. New York, NY: Alfred A. Knopf, 1994.

Kodwo, Eshun. "Further Considerations of Afrofuturism." *CR: The New Centennial Review* 3 no. 2 (2003): 287–302.

Lott, Tommy. "A No-Theory Theory of Contemporary Black Cinema." *Black American Literature Forum* 25, no. 2 (1991): 221–237.
———. "Aesthetics and Politics in Contemporary Black Film Theory." In *Film Theory and Philosophy*, edited by Richard Allen and Murray Smith, 291. UK: Oxford Press, 1997.
Neal, Larry. "The Black Arts Movement." *The Drama Review: TDR* 12, no. 4 (1968): 28–39.
Ryzik, Melena. "The Afrofuturistic Designs of 'Black Panther'." *The New York Times*, February 23, 2018. https://www.nytimes.com/2018/02/23/movies/black-panther-afrofuturism-costumes-ruth-carter.html.
Seshadri-Crooks, Kalpana. "I am a Master: Terrorism, Masculinity, and Political Violence in Frantz Fanon." *Parallax* 8, no. 2 (2002): 84–98.
Wanzo, Rebecca. "And All Our Past Decades Have Seen Revolutions: The Long Decolonization of Black Panther." *The Black Scholar*, February 19, 2018, https://www.theblackscholar.org/past-decades-seen-revolutions-long-decolonization-black-panther-rebecca-wanzo/.
Yaszek, Lisa. "Afrofuturism, Science Fiction, and the History of the Future." *Socialism and Democracy* 20, no. 3 (2006): 41–60.

FILMS

Black Panther. Directed by Ryan Coogler. United States: Marvel Studios, 2018.
Blade. Directed by Stephen Norrington. United States: Amen Ra Films, 1998.
Blankman. Directed by Mike Binder. United States: Columbia Pictures, 1994.
Blind Side, The. Directed by John Lee Hancock. United States: Alcon Entertainment, 2009.
Green Mile, The. Directed by Frank Darabont. United States: Warner Bros., 1999.
Hancock. Directed by Peter Berg. United States: Sony Pictures, 2008.
Help, The. Directed by Tate Taylor. United States: Walt Disney Studios, 2011.
Legend of Bagger Vance, The. Directed by Robert Redford. United States: DreamWorks Pictures, 2000.
Meteor Man, The. Directed by Robert Townsend. United States: Metro-Goldwyn-Mayer, 1993.
Mississippi Burning. Directed by Alan Parker. United States: Orion Pictures, 1988.
Mr. Church. Directed by Bruce Beresford. United States: Cinelou Releasing, 2016.
Shawshank Redemption. Directed by Frank Darabont. United States: Warner Bros., 1994.
Spawn. Directed by Mark A.Z. Dippé. United States: New Line Entertainment, 1997.

MUSIC

Black Panther: The Album. "Pray for Me." The Weeknd and Kendrick Lamar. Interscope Records, 2018.

Chapter 2

The Power in Numbers

Ensemble Stunt Performance in Black Panther *and Histories of Practice*

Lauren Steimer

This chapter positions the film *Black Panther* (Ryan Coogler 2018) at the epicenter of a seismic shift in the history of Hollywood stuntwork. In the U.S. film industry, stuntworkers and actors have been represented by the same union since 1933, the Screen Actors Guild. *Black Panther* is the first film to win the coveted Screen Actors Guild-American Federation of Television and Radio Artists awards for both "Outstanding Performance by a Cast in a Motion Picture" and "Outstanding Performance by a Stunt Ensemble in a Motion Picture." For a film that has broken so many records and one with the largest numbers of Black SAG-AFTRA members ever represented in cast and crew, this confluence of craft honors is still a surprise—not because it is unwarranted, but because the Screen Actors Guild is precisely the organization that fostered exclusionary practices limiting career growth for women and Black stuntworkers for most of the twentieth century. That so many talented stuntwomen and Black stunt performers found work on *Black Panther* is not due to, but rather, in spite of the historical actions of the Screen Actors Guild.

The chapter is divided into three sections on histories of practice within stunting communities: practices of exclusion; practices of inclusion; and expert performance in practice. The first section outlines the history of discriminatory practices used within Hollywood stunt communities to keep women and minorities from finding gainful employment as stunt performers. Such tactics include the formation of craft organizations that barred stuntwomen and minority stuntworkers from joining their ranks. Empowered by high-ranking positions in SAG, members of the Stuntmen's Association of Motion Pictures consistently blocked women and Black stunt performers from work, often arguing that their presence was a safety issue on set. White male stuntworkers were hired instead to double for actresses and Black actors. A process enabled by two distinct craft practices of concealment: "wig downs" and "paint downs." These techniques helped to "ensure safety" on set by making sure that the most experienced (White man) was tasked with the job of doubling actresses and Black actors and kept stuntwomen and Black stunt performers from gaining much-needed work experience as a form of on-the-job training, which is a requirement for future work in locally and transnationally networked stunt communities of practice.

The second section of this chapter addresses the means by which stuntwomen and Black stuntworkers fought back in the late 1960s through the early 1980s. They did so via the formation of their own craft organizations and through pressure on SAG to change the union policy on stunt hiring practices. These practices of inclusion contributed to larger numbers of stuntwomen and Black stunt performers finding work in American film and television productions between the 1970s and the present. Even so, the intentionally weak language of SAG's stuntwork diversity policy has not led to as many avenues for career growth for Black stuntworkers as was simultaneously made possible by the large ensemble action design work for the film *Black Panther*.

The final section of this chapter examines the action design work of the film in detail, including an analysis of the performance of Chadwick Boseman's main stunt double, Danny Graham. The chapter also considers the contributions and work history of the film's main fight coordinator, Jonathan Eusebio, and speaks with precision as to the influence of a Western South African combat style (Capoeira Angola), Nigerian martial art (*dambe*), and a hybrid of martial arts and breakdancing (tricking) on the action design. The chapter concludes with an investigation of the effects of working on *Black Panther* on the careers of Black stuntwomen Maria Hippolyte and Sadiqua Bynum.

PRACTICES OF EXCLUSION: PAINTING DOWN, WIGGING UP, AND SHUTTING OUT

On October 6, 2014, on the New York set of the Warner Brothers television show *Gotham*, at the request of the stunt coordinator, a White stuntwoman was covered in dark Black paint, outfitted with a wig, and set to double for guest actress Lesley-Ann Brandt. This practice, called a "paint down," is discouraged by Screen Actors Guild-American Federation of Television and Radio Artists (SAG/AFTRA) union policy, but it is not an outright violation of that policy. While the actress was reportedly dismayed at the sight, the White stuntwoman was so disgusted by her own participation, and after her consultation with other stuntwomen, the incident was quickly reported to the press. Warner Brothers made a public statement calling the incident a "mistake" and recast the position with a Black stuntwoman.[1] SAG/AFTRA National Director of EEO & Diversity, Adam Moore called the incident "presumptively improper . . . particularly so in a production center like New York City with so many qualified stunt women of color trained for this type of work."[2] Where exactly the practice of blackface might be "presumptively proper" to the union representing the stunt community is hopefully the questions you are asking yourself. Following the union, the answer to that question is predicated on arguments about safety and training. Those arguments have a history and a point of origin that is often obscured in the face of what seems like the common sense—that the most trained stunt person must be selected to ensure safety on set.

Rhetorics of "safety" and "training" in Hollywood stunt communities have historically functioned as both legitimate concerns given the higher rate of injury in the profession and as repressive operations toward gatekeeping in Hollywood stunt communities. Such rhetoric was deployed in response to stuntworkers' precarious position within the Screen Actors Guild (SAG), which primarily represented their major competitors in the workforce—actors. As actors were not trained in stuntwork, and their safety was of paramount importance to the studios who held their contracts, the safety and training rhetorics helped to delineate the domain of the stuntworker. However, these same rhetorics have continually resurfaced as arguments designed to discredit women and minority stuntworkers. We must interrogate these discursive strategies of safety and training, which continue to be employed, limiting job opportunities for women and minorities working in the U.S. stunt industry.

While stunt performers worked in Hollywood in the 1920s and 1930s, the stunt industry had not yet professionalized, work was rarely consistent, and stunt labor lacked any regulation for financial compensation or safety procedures. The decision to join the ranks of film actors and lobby for a standard pay scale seemed to be a rational step toward the twin goals of legitimating stunting as a profession and gaining more security of employment for stuntworkers. When the Screen Actors Guild was founded in 1933, the union represented both actors and stunt performers. Through collective bargaining, SAG secured a daily rate for stuntworkers which was 10 dollars more than the rate for actors. In the mid to late 1930s, this difference seemed so substantial that many actors sought work as stunt performers, a process which was facilitated by their representation by the same union. In order to distinguish their work from that of less physically adept actors and compete for the limited number of stunting jobs in a precarious labor environment, stunt performers marketed their work via two interrelated criteria: safety and training. Directors and producers want to minimize risk of injury and costly delays in production and they commonly relied upon stunt performers with a solid reputation of performance without injury to cast and crew.

As stuntworkers were regularly in charge of coordinating the action and also more knowledgeable than the director about the process, a group of them formed a fraternal organization to establish standards, provide training, and create a pipeline to employment. Over time, stunt work in Hollywood professionalized and the Stuntmen's Association of Motion Pictures, formed in 1961, was integral to that process. The Stuntmen's Association, which also included coordinators and second unit directors, was an invitation-only organization, did not accept women as members, and required members to maintain consistent work in the profession earning no less than $10,000 a year. The selective nature of the invitation process and the employment restrictions effectively eliminated non-White stuntmen from joining the group, as there was not enough work doubling non-White leads in the 1960s to attain the minimum required salary. The all-White, all-male Stuntmen's Association encouraged members to hire from within the group and, because SAG commonly referred producers, directors, and studios to hire from the Stuntmen's Association (up until the SAG was called out for this practice in 1984), work in the stunting profession was severely limited for women and minorities.

The two common craft practices to accompany these discriminatory rhetorics are "paint downs" and "wig downs," both of which remain under-addressed in film and media studies. In a "paint down," a White stunt double is covered in dark makeup to better approximate the complexion of non-White actors. Similarly, a "wig down" is a process in which a stuntman is costumed in long hair and makeup so as to double an actress. Female and minority stunt organizations have actively fought these tactics since the late 1960s, succeeding in 1970s with a new SAG policy meant to deter these activities. However, prominent members of the segregated Stuntmen's Association of Motion Pictures, who had ascended to advisory positions within SAG, inserted conditional policy language regarding safety that excused stunt coordinators from hiring women and minorities if they were deemed to be insufficiently trained.

Most stunt performers working in Hollywood from the 1920s to the late 1960s had previous training in disciplines as varied as wild west shows, the rodeo, and the circus, some were college gymnasts and competitive divers. These bodily disciplines are useful as precursors to a career in stunting, but training for stunt work generally came in three forms up until fairly recently: on the job training, knowledge passed down within a family, and training provided through the apprenticeship systems of craft organizations. The exclusionary tactics of the Stuntmen's Association limited the flow of stunting knowledge and job prospects for non-members in equal measure. Comparatively, very few stuntwomen and Black stunt performers found work until the 1970s, when "wig downs" and "paint downs" were still common practice in the industry. The formation the Black Stuntmen's Association as well as the Stuntwoman's Association of Motion Pictures in 1967 marked a turning point in the industry. These two groups organized women and Black stuntworkers to provide training, networking, and accreditation in order to counteract the rhetorical strategies used to keep stunting White and male.

The exclusionary tactics of the Stuntmen's Association and their union-endorsed advisory function effectively eliminated access to stunting jobs in Hollywood for most women and racial minorities. The few women and Black stuntmen who were employed often suffered various tactics designed to cause injury and demonstrate their lack of proper training including being repeatedly punched or kicked to provoke a reaction, having safety equipment removed, or not being accurately instructed on the nature of the stunts they were hired to perform. It was not uncommon for stunt coordinators to intentionally hire women or Black stuntmen with limited training in order to demonstrate that they could not be trusted to perform stunts and that properly trained White male performers should be hired to maintain safety on set.[3] The gatekeeping practices of the Stuntmen's Association eliminated most on-the-job training opportunities for women and minorities and efforts to discredit the few who were working reached a tipping point in the late 1960s.

PRACTICES OF INCLUSION: GETTING ORGANIZED, GETTING TRAINED, AND MAKING TROUBLE FOR HOLLYWOOD

The Black Stuntmen's Association (BSA) was formed in 1963 by Calvin Brown in Los Angeles as a coed craft organization. Calvin Brown was chosen as Bill Cosby's stunt double on *I-Spy* (created by David Friedkin and Morton Fine) in 1965 at Cosby's insistence because the star was disgusted by the practice of painting down. According to my discussion with Nonie L. Robinson, granddaughter of original BSA founding president Ernie Robinson, and producer of a documentary on the BSA called *Breaking Bones, Breaking Barriers* (Marques Miles 2021), Brown created the BSA in collaboration with a small group of working stuntmen in order to facilitate the training of Black stuntmen and women; pioneer members included Henry Kingi, Ernie Robinson, Greg Elam, Alex Brown, Eddie Smith, and Jadie David. Lacking the financial capital for a facility, their training occurred in a local L.A. park, under the watchful eye of the police, who assumed they were a militant civil rights organization.[4] Members, who included athletes from Historically Black Colleges and 10th Regiment Buffalo Soldiers, practiced the art of almost hitting each other, selling reactions, and falling onto mattresses, which they had brought with them to the park—because they did not have stunt equipment.[5]

The increase in lead roles for Black stars in major studio productions generated work prospects, but it was the star power of Cosby, Harry Belafonte, and Sidney Poitier and their active resistance to "paint downs" that ensured Black stuntworkers were employed as doubles. While their networking opportunities were limited because they were effectively blacklisted by Stuntmen's Association stunt coordinators, individual members like Calvin Brown, Willie Harris, and Eddie Smith used sympathetic high-profile Hollywood connections to help themselves and other BSA member to find work in the industry. Calvin Brown relied on his connection to Bill Cosby to lobby for more work for Black stunt performers. Willie Harris parlayed a casual encounter with Elliot Gould on the set of *Bob & Carol & Ted & Alice* (Paul Mazursky 1969) into the SAG card that he needed to pursue a career in stunts, as Gould paid Harris's $236 in membership dues and asked Robert Altman to write Harris the required letter of recommendation from a director.[6] Eddie Smith contributed most to the early networking efforts of the BSA, organizing practice sessions, and using his connections in Central Casting to get other member work as extras and stunt performers.[7] However, the efforts of the BSA made sure the available workforce was well trained, had access to an employment network, and could ensure the safety of others on set.

Founded the same year and with similar intentions to the Black Stuntmen's Association, the Stuntwoman's Association of Motion Pictures (SWAMP) was created by Jeannie Epper, May Boss, Stevie Myers, and other working female stunt professionals for the purpose of training stuntwomen, establishing standards, and effectively quashing the relentless paternalism of the White male stunt coordinators protecting them from gainful employment. The early members of SWAMP had trained with their male family members in the stunt industry or were accomplished horsewomen, drivers, fall down girls, and gymnasts. Most of these women learned the art of stunting on the job, if they were fortunate to find one. In Mollie Gregory's interview with SWAMP, founder Jeannie Epper for the book *Stuntwomen*, Epper explains that,

> [t]oday we have stuntwomen's organizations. We bring the younger girls in to show them the ropes. No group did that for us. We were fighting for basic recognition as stuntwomen. We warned the girls that if they took jobs they couldn't do as well as a guy or *better*, they were going to put a guy back in the clothes. That was the issue we were fighting—too many men were doubling women.[8]

In the 1960s–1980s, it was not uncommon for stuntwomen to have to consistently prove their merit on set. Often, they were asked to do excessively difficult stunts, just so that they would fail, and their job could be handed to a stuntman in a wig. One of the major problems faced by women in the stunt industry is that female actors hungry for work in Hollywood sometimes tried to pass as stuntwomen—a process facilitated by the fact that actors and stunt people carry the same union card (as mentioned above). In my discussion with original SWAMP member Julie Ann Johnson, she indicated that the SWAMP had become lax in fighting the problem of "wig downs" even though SWAMP's ranks were swelling.[9] Too few members were getting work and SWAMP failed to generate a pipeline to the industry because the Stuntmen's Association retained their monopoly. When a rogue group of young White stuntmen broke ties with the Stuntmen's Association in 1970 and formed their own organization, *Stunts Unlimited*, that monopoly slowly began to crumble. A collective of twelve stuntwomen followed suit in 1975 and created the *Society of Professional Stuntwomen* (SPS), which emphasized *safety* and *training* so as to distinguish their membership from other newly minted stuntwomen or actresses trying to pass as stunties and also to market their talents in a manner that would register with White male coordinators.[10] SPS ingeniously marketed their members by mobilizing the rhetorics of training and safety that had been previously been used against them.

The training efforts of the BSA and the stuntwomen's organizations prepared the workforce, but protests, litigation, and concomitant shifts in union policy forced more jobs to materialize. Certain brave stuntworkers like BSA member Marvin Walters and SPS member Julie Ann Johnson took it upon themselves to make trouble for Hollywood, and in doing so suffered blacklisting and threats of violence. Marvin Walters alerted the U.S. Justice Department to the discriminatory practices of the Hollywood stunt industry and filed complaints with the Equal Employment Opportunity Commission.[11] The BSA, with the help of the NAACP initiated public protests against the Warner Brothers film *Skin Game* (Paul Bogart and Gordon Douglas) in 1971, because Lou Gossett Jr. was doubled by a painted down stuntman. This is when the BSA, now *The Coalition of Black Stuntmen and Women* took legal action and won. One year later, the *Stuntmen's Association* hired their first Black member, Bob Minor, who joined the group instead of the BSA because of the networking prospects and chance to train with more experienced stuntmen.[12] Marvin Walters joined BSA member (and Pam Grier stunt double) Jadie David at Metro–Goldwyn–Mayer in 1976 as Affirmative Action Consultants to ensure that the studio acted responsibly to all of its employees. Stuntwoman Julie Ann Johnson worked with the SAG Stunt and Safety Committee Chair (and SAG's first female president), Kathleen Nolan on drafting language about discriminatory hiring practices in the stunt community during the early 1970s.[13] The result, though an example of progress at the time, is a policy Johnson herself resents. The policy reads,

> When the stunt performer doubles for a role which is identifiable as female and/or black, Hispanic, Asian Pacific or Native American, and the race and/or sex of the double is also identifiable, stunt coordinator shall *endeavor* to cast qualified persons of the same sex and/or race involved [emphasis added].[14]

Johnson told me that the word "endeavor" operates in practice as a loophole for discriminatory actions on set.[15] This single word allows stunt coordinators to argue that they tried but could not find a stunt performer of color or stuntwoman who had enough training. Some stunt coordinators will even intentionally hire an undertrained stunt performer of color or stuntwoman so as to immediately replace them when they cannot do the stunt. This dangerous practice is how some coordinators endeavor to fulfill union policy and still hire White people in their network. The primary difference on the set of *Black Panther* was the mass scale employment of expert and novice Black stunt workers as stunt doubles. This decision could have been because of the higher profile of Marvel Cinematic Universe productions and a desire to avoid controversy. At the same time, the decision to shoot some of the film in Atlanta, which has a well-networked community of Black stunt workers, would have had a major effect on the casting process.

Unsatisfied with the limited result of the policy change, in 1982, while Johnson was the Chair of SAG's Stuntwomen's Sub-Committee, she released a survey to assess the level of discrimination and harassment which stuntwomen faced on set. Many stuntwomen were afraid that answering the survey would result in being blacklisted. Johnson was herself blacklisted for her various efforts to reform Hollywood industry practices.[16] The results of Johnson's survey demonstrated a consistent culture of harassment, and Johnson pushed for further changes in SAG policy on discriminatory hiring practices in the stunt community. Henry Wills, the SAG Stunt Coordinator Sub-Committee Chair and Stuntmen's Association member, sent a letter to the union as a response to Johnson's efforts and the lawsuits brought by *The Coalition of Black Stuntmen and Women* and his statement is worth quoting at length,

> We seem to have become enmeshed with discrimination and legalities. Why? It seems to be because of personal desires and *not realities*. (. . .) Our basis of rating people as stunt persons is according to the individual's degree of experience and to his [sic] proper application of safety measures to everyone on set. Unfortunately, the theory that discrimination against youth, women, and ethnic groups seems to take precedent over the very most important factor that we need to achieve, and that is *safety* through knowledge and experience (. . .)

> Honesty must prevail in the use of women in certain fields of stunt work. There are several excellent women coordinators but they, along with men, need to realize their capacities. Most women do not have a knowledge of the mechanics involved in rigging. Most women are not mechanically inclined, and they should not rely wholly upon special-effects departments. They must rely on experience. It is not the intent of the stunt committee to deter or be discriminatory to anyone who can qualify. With the rating system as it is, everyone has an opportunity to improve his/her classification according to ability. Again, the most important thing to not lose sight of is *SAFETY*. [emphasis original][17]

While it is very obvious that safety and training are mobilized here to justify exclusionary practices, what is even more revealing is the emphasis on "reality" and the fairness of the rating system as based on ability and therefore an equal opportunity metric devoid of bias. That Black stuntworkers and stuntwomen exist in the same reality as White stuntmen, with the same rules, and access to money, work, training, and powerful networks is not called into question but is rather the premise for this "fair" system. While safety on set is always a primary concern for stuntworkers, the idea that stuntwomen or stunt people of color make the set unsafe, because they lack the requisite training, begs so many questions. Foremost among such inquiries, what can be done to ensure equal access to training, and networks, and job opportunities? In the last two years, SAG/AFTRA has finally been working toward answers to such questions. These efforts have been spearheaded by stuntwoman Julie Ann Johnson.

As of 2018, Julie Ann Johnson was still fighting to repair the damage done by the SAG/AFTRA policy language and told me that she submitted a petition and her most recent survey results in May of 2017, which demonstrated a consistent culture of sexual harassment. In addition, over 47 percent of respondents to her survey indicated that they had witnessed a "paint down" on set. Johnson requested the following of the union,

> I asked the negotiating team for our May [2017] contract to change the wording that says "stunt coordinator shall endeavor to hire." They don't "endeavor," this is the bad wording that came in in the 70's. I am asking SAG/AFTRA/AMPTP [Alliance of Motion Picture and Television Producers] to change that wording to "must hire same ethnicity and gender" and issue a $10,000 fine to the production company, the coordinator, and the stunt person who allows themselves to be painted or wigged if they are caught. Have to wait for the answer.[18]

The answer to Johnson's request was "no." While SAG/AFTRA has been working toward a more enforceable policy, they wanted to forego punishment in favor of a policy that would support training opportunities for stuntworkers of color and stunt women. The new policy asks stunt coordinators to self-report violations, and after an investigation takes places, may re-educate the coordinator on policy enforcement on "gender equity and diversity in casting."[19] While this approach is disappointing, the union has also added a mentorship program so that stuntworkers with 250 working days can work under a stunt coordinator to train on set while accumulating the 500 days required to advance from stunt performer to stunt coordinator.[20] This policy was instituted in April of 2020 and offers a step forward to stuntworkers who are underemployed due to the limited job opportunities for women and minorities.

The content boom of the last five years has been both beneficial and harmful to the Hollywood stunt community, because there is more work but a larger percentage than average of stunt performers have suffered career-ending or fatal accidents on set.[21] One such tragedy befell Black stuntwoman Joi "SJ" Harris, who died when she lost control of her motorcycle and crashed into a window while helmetless on the set of *Deadpool 2* (David Leitch 2018) in Vancouver. The death of SJ Harris, a motorcycle expert with no previous stunt work, was attributed by some in the stunt community to the dangers of union diversity initiatives. Stuntman Conrad Palmisano argued that, "the producers put pressure to have somebody of the same sex and ethnicity in a position she wasn't qualified to be in."[22] Additionally, another anonymous stuntman explained that "it absolutely could have been prevented" because "Joi was totally unqualified and never should have been there or put in that position (. . .) She was just a girl from Brooklyn who liked to road race—which was not remotely similar to what was required for the shots. She didn't have the experience or skills for the job they brought her in for." [23]

Preceding the accident, the stunt coordinator hired her knowing she had never done stunts before, had her do a few trial runs, and with that evidence approached the producer and director asking to replace her with a White stunt performer who could be painted down—a both tragic and very familiar story. To quote Miranda Banks, "precarity is not a new problem."[24] This history of exclusionary practices, which I have sketched, provided limited training opportunities to stuntwomen and minority stuntworkers. The industry rhetoric that bolsters union policy is that stuntwomen and Black stunt performers should not be hired, because they lack the proper on set training and create a perilous workspace. This begs the question, with White men taking their jobs, where might that training come from?

EXPERT PERFORMANCE IN PRACTICE: WORKING THE JOB, LEARNING THE ROPES, FIGHTING FOR A FUTURE

Black Panther facilitated three necessary elements of career growth for the Black stunt community: large-scale job opportunities, on-set training opportunities, and polylocal networking opportunities. The job market for stuntworkers is precarious not simply because of the inherent dangers of the job (e.g., falling from heights, being lit on fire, or crashing cars), but also because there are a limited number of positions available to double lead actors. Stunt doubling for a lead may increase the time span of an employment contract and can therefore lead to higher earnings for the stunt performer. Action-heavy films and television programs tend toward mostly White and mostly male lead actors. This choice not only limits the career growth and salary equity for women and actors of color (as big budget superhero films command bigger paychecks for actors), it simultaneously restricts the opportunities for women and stuntworkers of color to find work and more consistent incomes.

Many stunt performers more commonly rely on piecemeal work performing stunts for "nondescript" (ND) roles—unnamed characters or generic "good guy" or "bad guy" types. Women and stuntworkers of color are often overlooked for nondescript positions, as ND positions are not commonly identified in the script by any specified racial or gendered characteristics. Such positions create a loophole in union policy restrictions on racial and gender equity and are therefore often filled by White male stunt performers.

Black Panther was certainly not the first film with a large Black cast or the first Black superhero film, but it defied most of the industry conventions for stunt doubling and ND stunt performance work in two ways. The film required Black stuntmen and women to double a much larger than average number of Black leads in an action-heavy production context and, by the Afrocentric nature of its narrative and character design, necessitated extensive ND work for large numbers of women and Black stunt performers. Many of the stuntwomen and Black stuntworkers who worked on the film gained exposure to new stunting and fighting techniques, which they could then add to their repertoires. Additionally, these stuntworkers showcased their skills on set in a way that was memorable to other stunt team members and to stunt and fight coordinators—a process that allows them to make use of those networks to find future work in the industry. Lastly, many of the stunt team members utilized the Atlanta-based production context of the film to build polylocal networks, creating stunt teams and training groups in Atlanta and using the connects that they made on set to also find work and build new networks in Hollywood. The following two sections focus on the unique training and networking opportunities fostered by *Black Panther* for Black stunt doubles and stunt performers.

There are nine action set pieces in the film *Black Panther*. Each of these set pieces was organized, plotted, and realized by the film's second unit directors, stunt coordinators, fight choreographers, and stunt performers, each of whom may be named in the credits of the film, but their individual contributions to the end product are harder to identify. Stunt industry professionals perform a type of labor that is simultaneously hypervisible as a form of spectacle and invisible in its depersonalization. People mistake their work for that of the actor they double, and those actors sometimes falsely and regrettably take credit for "doing their own stunts." In order to best identify the contributions of these laborers, we must first look to their training histories. This process is easier for fight coordinators, stunt coordinators, and stunt doubles because their previous work yields clues to their histories of bodily performance. It is a much more difficult process to assess the skillset of ND stunt performers and stunt doubles for actors whose characters have minimal action scenes. For these reasons, the breakdown of training and choreography in *Black Panther* that follows will address the work of stunt double Danny Graham in more elaborate detail and will conclude with an analysis of the current career trajectories of Black stuntwomen Maria Hippolyte, as Lupita Nyong'o's double, and Sadiqua Bynum, who performed stunts as an unnamed member of the Dora Milaje.

The fight choreography for *Black Panther* is a mix of dambe, Capoeira Angola, and martial arts tricking and was choreographed by world-renowned fight director and member of the 87eleven Action Design team Jonathan "Jojo" Eusebio, who is well known for his work on the *John Wick* series (Chad Stahelski 2014–2019). Eusebio assigned individual characters and teams defined martial arts styles, as is evident in the manner in which individual stunt performers move as well as in their modes of attack and defense. While it is a common 87eleven tactic to establish symmetry between the narrative elements and the fight design so that the fight advances the narrative and fits the character arc, Eusebio also attempted to maintain cultural affinity between the pre-fight narrative elements and the ethos of combat expressed in individual fight sequences. As such, he "consult[ed] on movement and chants with South African playwright/actor John Kani (T'Challa's father T'Chaka)."[25] Eusebio explains that they "made sure the fights connected in an authentic way with the ceremonial pageantry."[26] This connection is most clear in T'Challa's fights for the throne.

While the combatants use weapons and shields instead of their fists, the basic structure of these two challenges to the throne mimics the format and defensive positioning of dambe. Dambe is a Nigerian combat ritual that serves dual purposes as a contest of masculine prowess and local entertainment. Historically in dambe, a challenger from outside the local village would compete against a local fighter in a three-round fight. The first man to submit or touch the ground loses and is considered "killed." Both combatants use their hands to fight, one as a spear and the other as a shield as the crowd plays drums. It is clear, given the structure of the fights for the throne, that dambe contributed to the use of three major take down moves in each fight, the use of spears and shields, and the choice to include drums in the ceremony, as well as the rules governing failure and success.

While both T'Challa/Black Panther (Chadwick Boseman) and Erik Killmonger (Michael B. Jordan) are, by Eusebio's design, more likely than any other characters to take flight during combat, T'Challa's early fights with Killmonger and M'Baku (Winston Duke) tend toward attacks positioned low to the ground and to acrobatic gestures because T'Challa's forms of defense and attack also inherit from the Western South African tradition of Capoeira Angola. Capoeira Angola is the origin of Afro-Brazilian capoeira and is an adapted form of *NGolo*, a South African martial art form in which the hands are commonly positioned toward the ground and the combatant thrust themselves into the air feet first in an attempt to kick or sweep an opponent.

African slaves brought this tradition to Brazil and disguised the defensive function of this combat sport from their captors through the choice to incorporate elements of African dance, in essence portraying it as a form of ceremonial performance.

We can see the explicit use of Capoeira Angola in this image from T'Challa's fight with M'Baku. T'Challa, here played by stunt double Danny Graham, positions both of his hands on the ground and thrust his legs upward into a cartwheel, with his leading knee hitting M'Baku in the head. This capoeira move is called *aú batendo* or "broken cartwheel." The prominence of techniques styled after Capoeira Angola in the film explains the selection of Danny Graham as Chadwick Boseman's stunt double, as Graham is master of tricking—an acrobatic form of martial arts drawn from capoeira, parkour, and breakdancing.

Danny Graham won the 2012 World Tricking Championships and has been working as stunt performer since 2010. While he has some ND stunt performances to his credit, his career as a stunt performer has grown exponentially in the last five years with the increased interest many Los Angeles-based fight coordinators have in tricking. Tricking originated as a form of "Xtreme Martial Arts" that incorporates jumps and spinning kicks. The style is similar to the more acrobatic tendencies of individual *wushu* routines, the terpsichorean flow of capoeira, and the presentational dynamism of breakdancing.

Tricking has become popular among LA-based fight coordinators primarily because of the belief that action audiences have grown tired of wirework and additionally due the presence of the Joining All Movement (JAM) tricking training gym in Southern California. Masters in the sport of tricking can achieve heights and perform flips that would normally require a wired harness rig and this skill puts them in high demand for superhero comic book film adaptations.

In this scene in which *Black Panther* is attacking members of W'Kabi's forces, Graham showcases his ability to fly without the aid of wires by taking a running jump off a stuntman's chest and spinning to complete a back-sided vertical kick with an in-air 540° rotation and finishing with a kick to the head of another opponent, a maneuver otherwise known as a "cheat 900" in the tricking community (see figure 2.1). If *Black Panther* can fly, kick, flip, and flow through the air, it is because of Graham's unique abilities, which have helped to secure his future in the stunt industry at a time when many Black stuntmen are struggling to find work (see figure 2.2.).

Black Panther provided jobs to hundreds of Black performers and craftspeople, but one film alone cannot resolve the decades-old equity problems in the U.S. stunt industry. The film bolstered the careers of many young Black

Figure 2.1 Stunt Double Danny Graham Executes a *aú batendo* or "Broken Cartwheel." Screenshot taken by author.

Figure 2.2 Danny Graham Thrusts Himself through the Air by Jumping off the Chest of Another Stuntman. Screenshot taken by author.

stunt performers, but even before the COVID-19 pandemic, there were not enough roles to keep them working. The film's team made some questionable decisions, like hiring mostly White and Asian American coordinators and using non-Black stunt performers for motion capture work. While the production team can make the arguments that they could not find available Black stunt coordinators or that they could not find a Black stunt performer with motion capture experience, the problem comes down to a failure of their personal networks or lack of proper training and support for minority stuntworkers by their union.

While SAG/AFTRA is making strides to correct such problems, Black stuntworkers are, yet again, organizing on their own behalf.

Maria Hippolyte, who doubled Lupita Nyong'o as Nakia, was originally trained as a circus performer and acquired the necessary skills to join the British Stunt Register by passing qualifying examinations in trampolining, taekwondo, gymnastics, high diving, scuba diving, and climbing. Her circus and gymnastic skills are in full view in this shot from the film in which she has been catapulted via air ram over a hillside, only to tuck and roll and land on her feet (see figure 2.3). She trained for years in these disciplines in order to become the one of only two Black stuntwomen on the British Stunt Register, working first on *Wonder Woman* (Patty Jenkins 2017) before joining the Marvel Cinematic Universe. Being one of only two registered Black stuntwomen in the United Kingdom has not led to endless doubling opportunities because many stunt coordinators are still painting down White stunt performers to double Black actresses.[27] Additionally, as there are fewer roles for Black actresses in action films than for their White and male contemporaries, Hippolyte was fortunate to start her career when she did. Securing a doubling role for *Black Panther* has led to more doubling rolls in other Marvel films.

Figure 2.3 Circus-trained Stuntwoman Maria Hippolyte Flies through the Air and Braces Herself for a Fall. Screenshot taken by author.

Working on *Black Panther* was the stunt role of a lifetime for a number of Black stuntwomen, as stunt coordinator Shahaub Roudbari explains, "because of [Black Panther], right now I could name 30 or 40 performers just in Atlanta more qualified and talented than people who've been doing this for over 20 years. They got that one opportunity."[28] One of those stuntwomen was former UCLA gymnast Sadiqua Bynum, who has parlayed her work in *Black Panther* into networking prospects in Los Angeles and Atlanta. Her work for the film increased her visibility to coordinators in both markets and she joined the Stunt POC group, which was formed to help coordinators find trained stunt performers of color.[29] Bynum has ridden the content boom and the small increase in action-heavy roles for Black actresses has helped her to find work doubling Regina King on *Watchmen* (Damon Lindelof 2019) and *The Harder They Fall* (Jeymes Samuel 2021), as well as doubling work on *Lovecraft Country* (Misha Green and Jordan Peele 2020). As Anne Cohen has argued, Bynum is "part of the new generation of Black stuntwomen taking on the industry . . . determined to create a sisterhood that not only stands on the foundation built by the trailblazing women who came before them, but also ensures that their sacrifices won't have been in vain."[30]

Black Panther, while by no means faultless in its production practices in regard to certain equity regulations in stunt work, remains a historic catalyst for change in the U.S. stunt industry. That being said, as demonstrated, *Black Panther* represents neither the beginning nor the end of this half-century-long fight for equality in the U.S. stunt industry. However, it stands on a precipice in this historical struggle that was formed by the revolutionary efforts of the pioneering women and Black stunt labor organizers of the past.

NOTES

1. Warner Brothers Television Press Release, quoted in David Robb, "Plan to Film 'Gotham' Stunt Woman in Blackface Scrapped by Warner Bros. TV," *Deadline*, October 9, 2014, accessed October 15, 2014, https://deadline.com/2014/10/gotham-stunt-woman-blackface-warner-bros-848969/.

2. Adam Moore, quoted in Carolyn Cox, "*Gotham* Cancels Plans to Film White Stuntwoman in Blackface: Head, Meet Desk," *The Mary Sue*, October 10, 2014, accessed October 15, 2014, https://www.themarysue.com/gotham-blackface-stuntwoman/.

3. Mollie Gregory, *Stuntwomen: The Untold Hollywood Story* (Lexington, Kentucky: University Press of Kentucky, 2015), 259–260; and Nonie L. Robinson, interview with Author, 30 June 2017.

4. Nonie L. Robinson, interview with Author.

5. Jocelyn Y. Stewart, "The Stuntmen Who Blacklisted Blackface," *Narratively*, October 16, 2014, accessed January 10, 2018, https://narratively.com/the-stuntmen-who-blacklisted-blackface/.

6. Ibid.
7. Ibid.
8. Jeannie Epper, quoted in Mollie Gregory, *Stuntwomen*, 67.
9. Julie Ann Johnson, email correspondence with author, April 25, 2017.
10. Gregory, *Stuntwomen*, 85–87.
11. Anne Cohen, "Black Stuntwomen Are Ready to Fight—Will Hollywood Let Them?," *Refinery29*, August 3, 2020, accessed August 3, 2020, https://www.refinery29.com/en-gb/2020/08/9946933/black-stuntwomen-hollywood-experience.
12. Gregory, *Stuntwomen*, 88.
13. Julie Ann Johnson and David L. Robb, *The Stuntwoman: The True Story of a Hollywood Heroine* (Scotts Valley, CA: CreateSpace Independent Publishing Platform, 2013), 53–55.
14. SAG/AFTRA, *Stunt and Safety Digest* (Los Angeles, CA: SAG-AFTRA, 2014), 18.
15. Julie Ann Johnson, email correspondence with author.
16. Johnson and Robb, *The Stuntwoman*, 60–62.
17. Henry Wills, "Letter to Screen Actors Guild," *Harvey Parry Papers* (Los Angeles: Margaret Herrick Library, File 55).
18. Julie Ann Johnson, Email Correspondence with Author.
19. "Stunt Coordinator Standards & Practices," SAG/AFTRA, accessed July 25, 2020, https://www.sagaftra.org/contracts-industry-resources/stunt-safety/stunt-coordinator-standards-practices.
20. "Stunt Coordinator Eligibility Process," SAG/AFTRA, accessed July 25, 2020, https://www.sagaftra.org/contracts-industry-resources/stunt-safety/stunt-coordinator-eligibility-process.
21. Scott Johnson, "Stunted: How Hollywood's Content Boom is Leading to More Stuntperson Injuries and Deaths," *Hollywood Reporter*, October 31, 2018, accessed October 31, 2018, https://www.hollywoodreporter.com/features/dark-side-hollywoods-content-boom-1156094.
22. Conrad Palmisano, quoted in Oren Peleg, "Crew had Raised Concerns about 'Deadpool 2' Stunt Person's Ability Before Death," *LAist*, August 23 2017, accessed October 31, 2018, https://laist.com/2017/08/23/crew_had_raised_concerns_about_deadpool_2_stunt_persons_ability_before_death.php.
23. Anonymous, quoted in Ben Arnold, "'Deadpool 2' Investigation over Stuntwoman's Death Finds 'Multiple Safety Violations'," *Yahoo Movies UK*, October 3, 2019, accessed October 10, 2019, https://sports.yahoo.com/investigation-over-stuntwomans-death-on-deadpool-2-finds-multiple-safety-violations-085845985.html.
24. Miranda Banks, "Diversity and Equity in Film Schools and Industry Fellowships: A Study of Gatekeepers and Mandates for Change," presented at The Society for Cinema and Media Studies Conference, March 15, 2018.
25. Hugh Hart, "How Jackie Chan, Ancient Sparta and Zulu Spear-Fighting Inspired *Black Panther*'s Stunt Coordinator," *The Credits: Profiles Below the Line*, March 1, 2018, accessed October 31, 2018, https://www.motionpictures.org/2018/03/jackie-chan-ancient-sparta-zulu-spear-fighting-inspired-black-panthers-stunt-coordinator/.

26. Jonathan Eusebio, quoted in Hugh Hart, "How Jackie Chan, Ancient Sparta and Zulu Spear-Fighting Inspired *Black Panther*'s Stunt Coordinator," *The Credits: Profiles Below the Line*, March 1, 2018, accessed October 31, 2018, https://www.motionpictures.org/2018/03/jackie-chan-ancient-sparta-zulu-spear-fighting-inspired-black-panthers-stunt-coordinator/.

27. In the UK this process is known as a "black up," instead of a paint down.

28. Shahaub Roudbari, quoted in Anne Cohen, "Black Stuntwomen Are Ready to Fight—Will Hollywood Let Them?," *Refinery29*, August 3, 2020, accessed August 3, 2020, https://www.refinery29.com/en-gb/2020/08/9946933/black-stuntwomen-hollywood-experience.

29. Anne Cohen, "Black Stuntwomen Are Ready to Fight."

30. Ibid.

WORKS CITED

Arnold, Ben. "'Deadpool 2' Investigation over Stuntwoman's Death Finds 'Multiple Safety Violations'." *Yahoo Movies UK*, October 3, 2019. Accessed October 10, 2019. https://sports.yahoo.com/investigation-over-stuntwomans-death-on-deadpool-2-finds-multiple-safety-violations-085845985.html.

Banks, Miranda. "Diversity and Equity in Film Schools and Industry Fellowships: A Study of Gatekeepers and Mandates for Change." Presented at The Society for Cinema and Media Studies Conference, March 15, 2018.

Cohen, Anne. "Black Stuntwomen Are Ready to Fight—Will Hollywood Let Them?" *Refinery29*, August 3, 2020. Accessed August 3, 2020. https://www.refinery29.com/en-gb/2020/08/9946933/black-stuntwomen-hollywood-experience.

Cox, Carolyn. "*Gotham* Cancels Plans to Film White Stuntwoman in Blackface: Head, Meet Desk." *The Mary Sue*, October 10, 2014. Accessed October 15, 2014. https://www.themarysue.com/gotham-blackface-stuntwoman/.

Gregory, Mollie. *Stuntwomen: The Untold Hollywood Story*. Lexington, Kentucky: University Press of Kentucky, 2015.

Hart, Hugh. "How Jackie Chan, Ancient Sparta and Zulu Spear-Fighting Inspired *Black Panther*'s Stunt Coordinator." *The Credits: Profiles Below the Line*, March 1, 2018. Accessed October 31, 2018. https://www.motionpictures.org/2018/03/jackie-chan-ancient-sparta-zulu-spear-fighting-inspired-black-panthers-stunt-coordinator/.

Johnson, Julie Ann, and David L. Robb. *The Stuntwoman: The True Story of a Hollywood Heroine*. Scotts Valley, CA: CreateSpace Independent Publishing Platform, 2013.

Johnson, Scott. "Stunted: How Hollywood's Content Boom is Leading to More Stuntperson Injuries and Deaths." *Hollywood Reporter*, October 31, 2018. Accessed October 31, 2018. https://www.hollywoodreporter.com/features/dark-side-hollywoods-content-boom-1156094.

Peleg, Oren. "Crew had Raised Concerns about 'Deadpool 2' Stunt Person's Ability Before Death." *LAist*, August 23 2017. Accessed October 31, 2018. https://laist.c

om/2017/08/23/crew_had_raised_concerns_about_deadpool_2_stunt_persons_ability_before_death.php.

Robb, David. "Plan to Film 'Gotham' Stunt Woman in Blackface Scrapped by Warner Bros. TV." *Deadline*, October 9, 2014. Accessed October 15, 2014. https://deadline.com/2014/10/gotham-stunt-woman-blackface-warner-bros-848969/.

SAG/AFTRA. "Stunt Coordinator Eligibility Process." Accessed July 25, 2020. https://www.sagaftra.org/contracts-industry-resources/stunt-safety/stunt-coordinator-eligibility-process.

SAG/AFTRA. "Stunt Coordinator Standards & Practices." Accessed July 25, 2020. https://www.sagaftra.org/contracts-industry-resources/stunt-safety/stunt-coordinator-standards-practices.

SAG/AFTRA. *Stunt and Safety Digest*. Los Angeles, CA: SAG-AFTRA, 2014.

Stewart, Jocelyn Y. "The Stuntmen Who Blacklisted Blackface." *Narratively*, October 16, 2014. Accessed January 10, 2018. https://narratively.com/the-stuntmen-who-blacklisted-blackface/.

Wills, Henry. "Letter to Screen Actors Guild." *Harvey Parry Papers*. Los Angeles: Margaret Herrick Library, File 55.

FILM AND TELEVISION

Black Panther. Directed by Ryan Coogler. United States: Marvel Studios, 2018.

Bob & Carol & Ted & Alice. Directed by Paul Mazursky. United States: Columbia Pictures, 1969.

Breaking Bones, Breaking Barriers. Directed by Marques Miles. Written and Produced by Nonie L. Robinson. United States, 2021.

Deadpool 2. Directed by David Leitch. United States: 20th Century Fox, 2018.

Gotham. Created by Bruno Heller. Produced by Danny Cannon and Bruno Heller. Aired September 22, 2014 – April 25, 2019, on Fox.

The Harder They Fall. Directed by Jeymes Samuel. United States: Netflix, 2021.

I-Spy. Created by David Friedkin and Morton Fine. Produced by Sheldon Leonard. Aired September 15, 1965–April 15, 1968, on National Broadcasting Company.

Lovecraft Country. Created by Misha Green. Produced by Misha Green, J.J. Abrams, and Jordan Peele. Aired August 16, 2020–present, on Home Box Office.

Watchmen. Created and Produced by Damon Lindelof. Aired October 20, 2019–December 15, 2019, on Home Box Office.

Wonder Woman. Directed by Patty Jenkins. United Kingdom and United States: Warner Bros., 2017.

Chapter 3

From Expressivity to Equanimity
Locating New Black Action Aesthetics in **Black Panther**

Wayne Wong

INTRODUCTION

"My Pop said Wakanda was the most beautiful thing he ever seen. He promised he was gonna show it to me one day," Eric Killmonger (Michael B. Jordan) painfully utters with a spearhead thrust into his chest as he is dying. Rather than ruthlessly finishing off his nemesis, T'Challa (Chadwick Boseman), without saying a word, carries Killmonger to a precipice and watches the Wakandan sunset with him in silence. Black Panther is exceptionally calm and composed. By the standard of Hollywood action, such a scene is implausible. The climax of the film is highly anti-climactic in the sense that all the intense emotions of fighting are somehow sublimated into tranquility.[1]

Such a transition from expressivity to tranquility is the signature aesthetics of Hong Kong action cinema.[2] The enlightenment occurs not at the expressive amplification of rage, but at the intricate moment of equanimity. Just as Bruce Lee respectfully covers Chuck Norris' corpse with the latter's Black belt as a sign of respect in *The Way of the Dragon* (1973), T'Challa also carefully moves Killmonger's hands to form the Wakandan gesture and recognizes him as part of the family.

The aesthetic connection between *Black Panther* (2018) and Hong Kong action cinema can be traced back to the kung fu craze in the early 1970s when there was a crossover between kung fu and blaxploitation genres. Especially after the tremendous success of *Enter the Dragon* (1973), martial arts sequences were incorporated into blaxploitation films, such as *Cleopatra Jones and the Casino of Gold* (1975), in which Cleopatra Jones (Tamara Dobson) fights her way to Hong Kong.

However, while *Black Panther* continues the tradition of Black action cinema by incorporating a Black-focused theme and narrative and hiring a predominantly Black creative team, it presents a subtle shift in its action aesthetics. This chapter argues that *Black Panther* reinvents Black action cinema by incorporating the concept of "martial ideation." It refers to the synthesis of action and stasis in tranquility. In the current theorization of cinematic action, there are two dominant paradigms: one is authenticity, seeking the faithful reproduction of forms; another is expressivity, pursuing the expressive amplification of emotions. Tranquility, as the aesthetic and philosophical core of Hong Kong action cinema, is the third paradigm that incorporates yet transcends the first two.

Such an aesthetic turn, however, should not be considered merely as a result of the technological advancement of the cinematic apparatus. The availability of digital effects does not necessarily evoke martial ideation. The technology could be used to render more realistic and graphic reproduction of violence and further enhances the emotional impacts of cinematic action. Neither is such a turn, merely an attempt to tone down the violence of the film and fit *Black Panther* into the marvel universe that primarily targets young audiences worldwide for their increasing consumer power.[3] The paradigmatic shift needs to be approached from two distinctive yet interconnected genres—Black action cinema and Hong Kong action cinema. As the synthesis of the two, not only does *Black Panther* open up new aesthetic possibilities for Black action films but it also reveals Hollywood's subtle yet effective strategy to reach the audience at the other side of the Pacific.

For the structure of the chapter, I will first contextualize *Black Panther* in the long lineage of Black action cinema and identify the Blaxploitation era as one of the most influential sources of the genre's distinctive aesthetics. The discussion focuses on the expressivity of key Blaxploitation films such as *Sweet Sweetback's Baadasssss Song* (1971) and *Superfly* (1972) so as to accentuate the tranquility of *Black Panther*. Before delving into a close reading of the film, I will ground the theorization of ideation on Chinese aesthetics and explain how the concept can be applied to cinema studies, especially Hong Kong action cinema. Finally, the center of the discussion is *Black Panther*'s formulation of martial ideation, focusing on the authenticity of ritual combat, the expressivity of the Ancestral Plane, and the tranquility of the Wakandan sunset.

BLAXPLOITATION AND BLACK ACTION AESTHETICS

To fully comprehend the significant role that tranquility plays in *Black Panther* and the film's ideational connection with Hong Kong action cinema, it is essential to take a retrospective look at the expressivity of Black action films. One crucial period for the development of Black action cinema is the Blaxploitation era, which has a profound impact on the genre's themes, styles, narratives, and characterizations. The Blaxploitation formula "consist[s] of a pimp, gangster, or their baleful female counterparts, violently acting out a revenge or retribution motif against corrupt Whites in the romanticized confines of the ghetto or inner city."[4] In this light, the action aesthetics of the Blaxploitation films is the binary opposite of martial ideation and features the expressive amplification of emotions, desires, and violence.

On the one hand, the explicit violence featured in the Blaxploitation era was a commercial decision due to the popularity and prevalence of what Guerrero calls "popcorn violence" in mainstream cinema, which highlights "shootouts, car chases, pyrotechnics, quadraphonic noise, and ever increasing body counts."[5] With the collapse of Hollywood's Production Code and the Supreme Court's liberalization of obscenity laws in the mid-1960s,[6] graphic violence was well-received among the young audience, whose increasing purchasing power was an important source of revenue for filmmakers.

On the other hand, the increased violence in Black action also represents a strong post-colonial sentiment that strives to oppose Hollywood's ceaseless attempts to misrepresent Blackness on screen. Melvin Van Peebles once said, "Black films should deal with images of our position in the superstructure. They should all work toward the decolonization of black minds and the reclaiming of black spirit."[7] According to the French political philosopher Frantz Fanon, one of the most influential critical theorists in postcolonial studies, violence is an essential means of decolonization. The colonizer's violent oppression to the colonized compels the latter to respond with an equal, if not higher, level of violence. As Fanon writes, "As soon as [the colonized] are born it is obvious to them that their cramped world, riddled with taboos, can only be challenged by out and out violence."[8] In this light, Black action cinema's emphasis on violence is not a coincidence, as it is a symbolic act to fight against Hollywood's colonizing ideological maneuver.[9]

The violence of Blaxploitation films, to some extent, results from the need and desire of unreserved expression. Such yearning for expressivity can be traced back to the late 1960s when the Black audience's political and social consciousness was rising and wanted to "see their full humanity depicted on the commercial cinema screen."[10] Previous representation of Blackness became increasingly questionable. For example, Sidney Poitier's "ebony saint" or "noble Negro" screen personas in *Guess Who's Coming to Dinner?* (1967) and *In the Heat of the Night* (1967) were considered shallow, as they "did not speak to the aspirations or anger of the new black consciousness that was emerging."[11] These films propagate the perspective of the Black bourgeoisie, who strives to "leave behind the expressiveness of a much broader based lower-class African American culture for the assimilation and seeming progress of life in the suburbs and the illusory embrace of the dominant culture."[12] The increasing need for expressivity was reflected in the screen personas of Jim Brown, who "was able to do what Poitier was denied in his career to that point, to act in a violent assertive manner and express his sexuality openly and beyond dominant cinema's sexual taboos."[13]

The fusion of sex, violence, and expressivity can be found in many Blaxploitation films. For example, in *Sweet Sweetback's Baadasssss Song*, Sweetback (Melvin Van Peebles) grows up at a whorehouse and works as a stud performing sex shows. His over-the-top sexual prowess is highlighted in the film. It begins with Sweetback's first sexual experience at the age of ten with a much older female prostitute (potentially a rape). Ed Guerrero, one of the pioneers studying the representation of Blackness in cinema, sums up the film's exaggerating plot as follows:

> Sweetback uses his cocksmanship to outfornicate the white female leader of a motorcycle gang. He also evades the police by raping a black woman at knifepoint at a rock concert, spears a cop with a pool cue, kills a number of dogs tracking him, heals himself with his own urine, and bites off the head of a lizard before escaping across the Mexican border into the desert.[14]

Sweet Sweetback's Baadasssss Song evokes a sense of "overcompensation," meaning that Van Peebles strives to revert the "the black bourgeois ideal of the ever-striving, upright Negro" and represent Black at the other extreme end of the spectrum.[15] Such overcompensation can also be found in other Blaxploitation classics. For instance, the endings of *Shaft* (1971) and *Superfly* feature spectacular massacre of gangsters and junkies. *Foxy Brown* (1974) pushes the limit further by featuring a scene where the Black female superheroine (Pam Grier), after being drugged and gang raped, castrates the White villain (Peter Brown) and delivers his genital in a pickle jar to the villain's girlfriend (Kathryn Loder).

In brief, the expressivity of the Blaxploitation films, instantiated by extended sex scenes and shootouts, was influential to the aesthetics of the Black action cinema. Granted, not all Black action films follow the Blaxploitation formula. Considering the increasingly ambiguous definition of the genre, intense actions can be found in "plot and character driven" historical agonies such as *Malcom X* (1992), *Amistad* (1997), and *Rosewood* (1997).[16] However, in the case of *Black Panther*, one should see it as a "sensation driven" action-adventure film along the lines of *Menace II Society* (1993), *Bad Boys I* and *II* (1995, 2003), *Blade* trilogy (1998–2004), and *The Equalizer I* and *II* (2014, 2018).[17] Yet what makes *Black Panther* different from its predecessors is that it exudes an intricate sense of tranquility amidst expressive actions—an aesthetic trait not commonly found in mainstream Hollywood action but has been crucial in Hong Kong action. To expound on *Black Panther*'s paradigmatic shift, it is necessary to examine the concept of martial ideation, which places tranquility as the ultimate aesthetic goal.

MARTIAL IDEATION: THE AESTHETICS OF TRANQUILITY

The theorization of tranquility as an aesthetic experience can be traced back to the discussion of *yi* (意), or ideation, in Chinese literary-aesthetic criticism.[18] In the pre-Qin (ca. 2100–221 BCE) period, ideation was regarded by Confucian literati as an essential quality of a good ruler. In other words, the concept in its early interpretation has more affiliation with politics or pedagogy rather than aesthetics.[19]

However, the meaning of ideation had a significant change during the Wei (220–265) and Jin (265–420) dynasties. With the increasing influence of Daoism and Buddhism, the concept became subjectivized and used by literati to express personal feelings and philosophical thoughts.[20] In the Tang (618–907) dynasty, the theorization of ideation benefited from the translation of many Buddhist classics from Sanskrit into Chinese. Borrowing the Buddhist term, *jing* (境), or realm, Wang Changling (王昌齡), a Tang poet, divided the formulation of ideation into three steps, namely, *wujing* (物境), or the realm of objects; *qingjing* (情境), or the realm of affect; and *yijing* (意境), or the realm of ideation:

一曰物境，欲為山水詩，則張泉石雲峰之境，極麗絕秀者，神之於心，處身於境，視境於心，瑩然掌中，然後用思，瞭然境象，故得形似。
二曰情境，娛樂愁怨，皆張於意而處於身，然後馳思，深得其情。
三曰意境，亦張之於意而思之於心，則得其真矣。

The first kind is *wujing*. Concerning the poetry about mountains and rivers, the poet needs to amplify the images of precious stones and prominent hills. He needs to concentrate and emerge himself into the environment. After capturing the essence of the images, he needs to focus and carefully manifest them through his hands. In so doing, he can achieve faithfulness in shape. The second kind is *qingjing*. It requires the author to have a personal, in-depth experience of different emotions in life. By unleashing these emotions in all possible directions, they can express the object dynamically and genuinely. *Yijing*, the third kind, is also an authentic expression of emotion, but it goes further to incorporate reflexivity in the heart. In so doing, the author can obtain the essence of the object portrayed (my translation).[21]

What makes Wang Changling's theorization a milestone is that he offered a systematic schema for understanding the concept of ideation and expanded its applicability from canonized art forms, such as literature and painting to other forms of artistry. Following Wang's pioneering effort, influential poets and scholars from the late Tang dynasty (755–907) to the Song dynasty (960–1279) such as Jiao Ran (皎然), Sikong Tu (司空 圖), and Yan Yu (嚴羽) further consolidated the theoretical complexity of ideation.[22]

Until the Republican Era (1912–1949), Zong Baihua (宗白華), a renowned Chinese aesthetician, encapsulated the concept as the synthesis of *shi* (實), or presence, and *xu* (虛), or absence(虛), or absence.[23] Against conventional understanding of ideation as an abstract idea, Zong argued that the epitome of ideation requires both the presence and the absence. He used classical Chinese mountain-river paintings as an illustration and proposed that the ideational experience of artists and spectators arises from the dialogic relationship between visibility and invisibility.

Despite the long development of ideation in Chinese aesthetics, its potential contribution to cinema studies has not been discussed until the rising scholarship on Chinese cinema in the last decade. Currently, there are two different views regarding the formulation of ideation on screen. One view is that "the power of the concept [of ideation] lies in an acknowledgment that neither the cinematic nor painterly image is real."[24] In other words, ideation is best encapsulated by the notions of absence, such as the abstract, the invisible, and the exaggerating. *Hero*'s (2002) digitalized landscapes, as she asserts, are the embodiment of ideation due to their surreal qualities. Such a view can be traced back to the operatic root of Chinese martial arts cinema. As in Peking opera, martial arts performance is highly stylized and rhythmicized not for the sake of mimicking reality, but expanding it to incorporate "motion emotion."[25] Another view is that ideation "is best achieved not by abstracting forms out of such concrete reality; rather, it is attained when landscape and the human figures within it are captured as is."[26] Fan expounds ideation through the lens of Chinese realist cinema in the 1930s and 1940s Shanghai, such as Fey Mou's (費穆) *Spring in a Small Town* (1948). Using the renowned works of the poet-director, he argues that the ideational experience locates not at the images of fantasy, but reality.[27]

The above two views, however, fail to adequately account for the bifurcated nature of the cinematographic image and ideation. The sense of tranquility cannot be evoked merely by presence or absence alone but the interplay of both. If ideation in a presence and absence in a Chinese mountain-river painting refers to Black ink stokes and White empty space, what do they refer to in the context of martial arts action cinema?

The Chinese word *wu* (武), or martial arts, demonstrates the synthesis of presence and absence. The word has two components—*ge* (戈), or action, and *zhi* (止), or stasis, according to the earliest Chinese dictionary, *Shuowen jiezi*

(說文解字), or Explaining Graphs and Analyzing Characters, written in the Han (206 BCE–220CE) dynasty. The bifurcated meaning of *wu* endows the concept of ideation with a martial dimension and makes it applicable to the study of action cinema.

Connecting this new insight back to Wang Changling's three-step process, the first step is the realm of object (*wujing*), in which action and stasis are combined for the faithful reproduction of forms. The second step is the realm of affect (*qingjing*), highlighting the expressive amplification of emotions through the interplay of bursts and pauses. The last step is the realm of ideation (*yijing*). It emerges as a subtle moment of tranquility after the thresholds of authenticity and expressivity.

Undoubtedly, action and stasis play a key role in martial arts cinema that film historian David Bordwell coins the term "pause-burst-pause" pattern to describe the insertion of short breaks between action sequences.[28] Cinematographically, the pattern can be instantiated by rapid zooming to highlight the emotional intensity of the action. Narratively, the dialogic relationship of taking action and maintaining stasis can be demonstrated in situations where an action hero or heroine is placed at the blink of conflict outburst.

However, current discussions of action and stasis tend to treat the pair as a means to achieve expressivity. This imperative is derived from the domination of the operatic discourse, which stresses the amplification of emotions through rhythmic and stylized movements. Yet the performative and entertaining traditions of martial arts action should not overshadow other equally important traditions, such as the philosophical and the practical. From the perspective of classical Confucianism, martial arts practice can be seen as a ritual that helps a practitioner regulate their emotions and prepares them to be a good ruler. As to the practical dimension, southern Chinese martial arts schools emphasize the stability of the lower body, which is a martial manifestation of stability and control. During combat, emotions need to be contained and restrained so that a fighter can make a discreet decision.

In this light, the theorization of cinematic action needs to take into consideration various facets of martial arts as performance, philosophy, and practice. The focus should not merely fall on the alternation of action and stasis, or bursts and pauses, but more importantly, how the creative interplay of the two generates different aesthetic experiences highlighting authenticity, expressivity, and ultimately tranquility.

MARTIAL AUTHENTICITY: RITUAL COMBAT

"Guns, so primitive," Okoye (Danai Gurira), the general of the Wakandan armed forces, says with a contemptuous tone, when she is sitting in a sports car made in "vibranium," to which firearms have zero impacts. This is one of the most important lines that highlights the significance of hand-to-hand combat in *Black Panther*. What differentiates Black Panther from other Marvel superheroes relying on technology or mythic powers, such as Iron Man and Thor, is that he is portrayed to be a genuine fighter with excellent martial skills.

Such skills are demonstrated in the ritual combat, an inaugural ceremony of the new Wakandan king, or Black Panther. The rule is simple: all Wakandan tribes are allowed to send a representative to challenge the new king. If the king cannot defeat the challenger, he will lose his kingship immediately, and the challenger will take his place as the king. The implication is that the ruler of Wakanda should be the best fighter in his country.[29]

Generically, the incorporation of a tournament structure into the narrative of the film is common in martial arts cinema, as it provides a convenient platform for extensive martial arts performance. There are in total two ritual combat in *Black Panther*. The first takes place when T'Challa is challenged by M'Baku (Winston Duke), the leader of the Jabari Tribe, and the second combat is requested by Killmonger, the son of N'Jobu (Sterling K. Brown), the brother of T'Chaka.

The main feature of ritual combat is authenticity. Black Panther is required to have his superhuman power temporally taken away to ensure the fairness of the combat. Without those powers, Black Panther becomes another human being, and his real martial skills will be tested. There are three types of authenticity in Hong Kong action cinema—archival, cinematic, and corporeal—referring to real martial arts techniques, unmediated performance, and genuine martial capabilities and the presence of physical risks during the performance.[30] All three types are present in the two ritual combats in *Black Panther*.

In the first combat, T'Challa fights M'Baku with a single hand sword and a shield initially, and eventually only with bare hands. The transition demonstrates that T'Challa's martial skills are independent of his weapons (see figure 3.1.). The weapons only enhance his martial capabilities, and he is equally good, if not better, without them. In contrast, M'Baku, after losing his weapon, loses his advantage in the fight. As M'Baku loses his foothold and falls to the ground, T'Challa takes the opportunity and uses a submission hold to suffocate his opponent.

In terms of archival authenticity, T'Challa uses a Judo technique called "Ura Sankaku," which is a rear triangle choke that blocks the carotid arteries on both sides of the neck. As to corporeal authenticity, the technique involves a high degree of physical risk. To ensure that Winston Duke would not be suffocated, Chadwick Boseman alters the angle of the triangle choke so that there is a small gap between his leg and Duke's right carotid artery. Boseman also lowers the angle of Duke's left arm so that it wouldn't block the

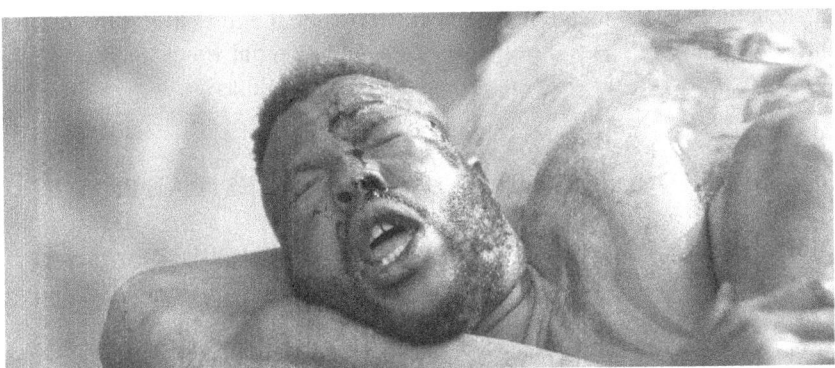

Figure 3.1 T'Challa Uses a Rear Triangle Choke to Suffocate M'Baku in the First Ritual Combat. To minimize the physical risks, Chadwick Boseman alters the angle of the choke so that Winston Duke's carotid arteries would not be blocked. Screenshot taken by author.

left carotid artery or break the arm by hyper-extension or hyper-rotation. For cinematic authenticity, it is done through well-executed constructive editing. Before the submission, M'Baku attempts to thrust T'Challa's torso with his sharp spear. The latter first evades it by rotating his body leftward, then uses his right knee to add his whole body weight to the spear and snatch it from M'Baku, and finally performs a left back kick to M'Baku's head through the rotating motion. Although the audience sees T'Challa's movement in constructive editing rather than a single long take, it is executed well through the medium-long shot, fulfilling cinematic authenticity.[31]

Compared to the first ritual combat, the second one is shorter and more violent. Killmonger kills Zuri (Forest Whitaker), the Wakandan priest associated with the death of his father, and throws T'Challa down the waterfall after piercing him with a spear. It is also worth noting that masks are taken off in the second combat. In the first one, T'Challa and M'Baku wear masks representing their tribes, and those masks eventually drop as the fight gets messy. The dropping of the masks signifies increased authenticity and violence. However, the second combat is without any masks, and it can be seen as a genuine face-off that would end with the death of one side. Furthermore, the scarred body of Killmonger corporeally authenticates him as a ruthless killing machine as he furiously tells T'Challa, one scar represents one kill.[32] Such extremity helps amplifying the emotions of the character and audience, which is crucial to the sketching of martial ideation.

In brief, although there are moments in the film where computer-generated imagery (CGI) is excessively used, such as the final fight scene between T'Challa and Killmonger in their Black panther suits, authenticity is undoubtedly highlighted as the essential quality of Black Panther. It is the first step of sketching martial ideation. The next step is about expressivity. In the film, the Ancestral Plane is the milieu that put the potential Black Panther to the test by evoking the deepest emotional pains and traumas.

EMOTIONAL EXPRESSIVITY: THE ANCESTRAL PLANE

At first glance, the Ancestral Plane is the place where the Black Panther meets his predecessors and receives the right to inherit their power and authority. However, at a deeper level, it is an ideational milieu where one relives his or her trauma. A worthy Black Panther is not merely one who demonstrates martial excellence in ritual combat, but more importantly, he needs to overcome his emotional weaknesses. After T'Challa beats M'Baku in ritual combat, he is allowed to take the "heart-shaped" herb and enter the Ancestral Plane. The unique shape of the herb points to the significance of the heart that the Black Panther's heart will be tested. The ritual that prepares T'Challa's entrance to the Ancestral Plane signifies a symbolic death and plays with the double meaning of burial. First, T'Challa needs to be buried by his traumatic past, where he witnesses his father's death in front of him. Second, he must courageously bury that past and have a rebirth. The restoration of his power depends on whether he could cultivate equanimity in face of his greatest fear.

The ability to control emotions is so vital that T'Chaka reiterates it in his last words, right before T'Challa's departure of the Ancestral Plane and rebirth from his burial (see figure 3.2.). T'Chaka says to his T'Challa, "You're a good man with a good heart. And it's hard for a good man to be

Figure 3.2 Entering the Ancestral Plane Requires a Burial Ritual, Which Has a Double Meaning. T'Challa, on the one hand, is buried by his traumatic past of witnessing his father's death; on the other hand, he needs to take courage and bury that past so that he can experience a rebirth. Screenshot taken by author.

king." The implication is that a king with a "good heart" would easily be swayed by his emotions, such as love and compassion. Because of that, it is difficult for him to strike a balance between personal feelings and national interests. However, as the story unfolds, T'Chaka gives up being "good" as a king in order to keep his throne and kingdom intact. His decision to leave N'Jobu's (his brother) son behind in Oakland demonstrates his failure to keep his "good heart" while being a king.

In contrast, T'Challa strives to reconcile the two by honestly facing his emotions and courageously taking up responsibilities. In his second entrance to the Ancestral Plane, T'Challa is again led to his deepest emotional pain—his disappointment with his beloved father due to his killing of his brother and decision to leave Killmonger behind as a child. Unlike the first entrance, he no longer kneels before T'Chaka but defiantly stands up to him (and the ancestors) and to the traditions. The background color of the Ancestral Plane has changed from purple red to golden yellow. Although these two can both be distinctive colors of sunset, the golden yellow signifies the possibility of change. T'Challa has turned from a loyal follower of tradition to a king bringing a whole new future to Wakanda. He has decided not to let the fear of exposing Wakanda to the world dominate him, as his father did. In this light, T'Challa has overcome his greatest fear and disappointment in his second entrance to the Ancestral Plane. His equanimity is neither the superficial placidness held by a series of lies nor the avoidance of conflicts. Rather, it is the result of fearless negotiation with fears and traumas, hence fulfilling the true meaning of ideation.

Achieving equanimity is not about cultivating a stone heart, which Killmonger does. Killmonger is the only other person who has the privilege of entering the Ancestral Plane. After defeating T'Challa in ritual combat, he is given the heart-shaped herb and enters his deepest consciousness where his trauma awaits him. Returning to his home in Oakland, he meets his father, N'Jobu. However, he shows no joy or sadness, but cynicism. When N'Jobu asks Killmonger if he wants to shed tear for him, he monotonously says, "everybody dies." N'Jobu feels very sad because his hopelessness is transferred to his son. He feels that he has failed as a father. Rather than giving Killmonger hope, he turns him into a monster of rage. Rather than helping the Black communities as Nakia (Lupita Nyong'o) does, Killmonger blames Wakanda for the world's problems, for his father's death, and for his own monstrosity. He is so bitter that he fails to take responsibility for his own choices and actions. When Killmonger wakes up from the red sand, he is overwhelmed with a sense of fear and rage, which is radically different from T'Challa's experience of joy and peacefulness after his first entrance. Killmonger's decision to burn all the heart-shaped herbs symbolically represents his reluctance to face his traumatic past. Without the herbs and the possibility of entering the Ancestral Plane, he lets his heart be consumed by fiery rage and bitterness, leading him to his destruction.

IDEATIONAL TRANQUILITY: THE WAKANDAN SUNSET

The sunset has been a key trope through *Black Panther*. It is first mentioned in Killmonger's entrance to the Ancestral Plane, where he meets his father. "The sunsets there [in Wakanda] are the most beautiful in the world. But I fear you still may not be welcome," said N'Jobu. Then later in the film, in the last sentence of his inaugural speech as Wakanda's new king, Killmonger quotes a hyperbolic phrase often used to describe the military might of the Habsburg, Spanish, and British Empires from the sixteenth to the nineteenth century: "the empire on which the sun never sets."[33] Killmonger attempts to expand Wakanda's territory to the world through military conquer so that there is at least one part of the empire that is always in daylight. At the end of the film, Killmonger is critically injured after his battle with T'Challa. In his last moments, he recalls his father's praise of the Wakandan sunset. Rather than killing his enemy, T'Challa carries Killmonger to a precipice facing the Wakandan sunset and let him fulfill his last wish of connecting with his father. In the above three examples, the second and the third represent a transition from the realm of affect to that of ideation, from expressivity to tranquility (see figure 3.3.).

When Killmonger expresses that "the sun will never set on the Wakandan empire," he is simultaneously denying Wakanda's "dark sides." To

Figure 3.3 T'Challa Brings Killmonger to a Precipice So That He Could See for the First (and Last) Time the Wakandan Sunset and Connect to His Deceased Father. Rather than ending the film with expressive violence, the beautiful sunset presents an intricate sense of tranquillity that helps the characters settle their emotions. Screenshot taken by author.

Killmonger, the sunset represents regression, flaws, and weaknesses. As Wakanda's new king, he hopes to rule the kingdom with absolute power and allows no room for failure. However, he has yet to see the beauty of imperfection. When N'Jobu, Killmonger's father, exclaims in the Ancestral Plane that the Wakandan sunset is the most beautiful sunset, he comes to the realization that Wakanda, despite its technological feats, has its inevitable defects and limitations. The kingdom's prosperity and stability, to a great extent, rely on its isolation from the world. Rather than being cynical, N'Jobu learns to accept and embrace them. In so doing, he eventually finds tranquility in the Ancestral Plane after death.

In contrast, Killmonger is unwilling to forgive and forget those who harm him, including N'Jobu. Rather than honestly facing his hurt and letting it go, Killmonger resorts to rage and makes his life bitter, which in turn amplifies his anger. Since Killmonger only chooses to see the good side and refuses to see or accept the darker side of things, he could neither show appreciation to the beauty of sunset nor cultivate equanimity. In a sense, equanimity is the moment when one sees all things as they are, no matter they are good or bad, and learns to face the imperfections of life. In the Ancestral Plane, N'Jobu hopes to enlighten Killmonger by encouraging him to shed a tear and accept weaknesses, but he failed. In fact, Killmonger would rather commit suicide rather than facing his own flaws and failure.

At the end of the film, when T'Challa offers him a chance to live, he rejects it. Refusing to be a prisoner, Killmonger pulls the spearhead out from his body and kills himself. Symbolically, his final act demonstrates the way he deals with his rage—he is not willing to take up the responsibilities for his actions (by facing the trial). Instead, he justifies his cowardice by aligning himself with his "ancestors" who committed suicide by "jump[ing] from the ships" and died in the ocean. By using this analogy, he sees T'Challa as the colonizer and himself as the colonized. Yet his plan to dominate the world using advanced weapons reveals that he is the true colonizer. From the beginning to the end of the film, Killmonger either looks for someone to blame or to justify his wrongdoings. He evades taking up responsibilities for his mistakes and let his strong emotions such as rage and bitterness overcome him. He would rather destroy himself (and those around him) than facing the consequences.

In contrast, T'Challa faces not only his mistakes but also those committed by his father and ancestors. As a character, he may not be as appealing as Killmonger due to his composure; however, as a king and warrior, his equanimity allows him to make the right decision and stay discreet under intense conflicts. It is such quality that makes Black Panther different from its predecessors and refines the Black action aesthetics. By embracing Killmonger in his last moment, T'Challa embodies the essence of martial ideation that tranquility incorporates expressivity in its constitution. T'Challa never wants to reject Killmonger but welcome him home. His embrace symbolically represents his willingness to negotiate with intense emotions and face his (and his father's) traumatic past. At the end of the film, T'Challa brings his sister, Shuri (Letitia Wright), to the building where his father killed his uncle (see figure 3.4.). Outside the building, there is a demolition sign written in capital letters, "WARNING: THIS BUILDING IS CONDEMNED PER CITY OF OAKLAND OFFICE OF THE BLDG. INSPECTOR. KEEP OUT." Noticing the sign, Shuri says to T'Challa, "They're tearing it down, Good." Shuri thinks that physically destroying the place associated could heal the traumas of his brother and father. Yet T'Challa replies, "They are not tearing it down. I bought this building. And that building. And that one over there. This will be the first Wakandan International Outreach Center." T'Challa looks deeper than the buildings themselves into the emotional root and turns his trauma into a powerful force that connects Wakanda to the world. N'Jobu's apartment, once signifying separation, is now endowed with a sense of connection. By facing his traumatic past proactively, T'Challa has cultivated equanimity and achieved martial ideation.

In short, martial ideation as an aesthetic paradigm is more than manifesting a sense of calmness in fight scenes. Rather, it is an attitude of life when facing challenges and confrontations. A true warrior needs to take control of not only their martial skills but also emotions, so that they can maintain stability amidst violent conflicts. This is what makes T'Challa different from Killmonger. The former has learned to genuinely face and carefully deal with their

Figure 3.4 At the End of the Film, T'Challa Brings Shuri to the Building Where His Father Kills His Uncle. Rather than attempting to erase his trauma, he overwrites it by turning the building into Wakanda's first International Outreach Center. In this light, T'Challa's tranquility is not the denial of expressivity. The tragedy cannot be undone, but he has learned to live, or even thrive, with it. Screenshot taken by author.

emotions, while the latter lets his feelings dominate him. In this light, *Black Panther* can be seen as a story of overcoming the fear of being exposed or discovered, of altering the established way of life, of making radical changes for a better future.

CONCLUSION

Black Panther's appropriation of marital ideation is more innovative than it seems. It is not literal transplantation of a Hong Kong action aesthetics; instead, it offers new approaches to the concept and makes it more flexible in global action filmmaking. If Hollywood two decades ago evoked tranquility through choreography, such as *The Matrix*'s (1999) direct reference to kung fu cinema, *Black Panther* focuses on narrative, characterization, and *mise-en-scène*. In so doing, martial ideation is increasingly detached from its narrow Chinese martial arts contexts and reconfigured as a universal aesthetics for global action blockbusters.

There are two ways to understand such a trend. First, martial ideation can be seen as a critical intervention to the excessive use of the digital effect in martial arts action, generating emotional and sensory overload among spectators. The over-reliance on CGI, on the one hand, results from the advancement of digital technology in cinema, including the deployment of higher-resolution cameras, more realistic graphic engines, and more powerful post-production digital editing. On the other hand, digital technology plays an essential role in compensating the lack of martial arts training and capabilities among contemporary action stars. With the transnational migration of Hong Kong action talents in films, such as *Rush Hour* (1998) and *Lethal Weapon 4* (1998), the global audience has developed a higher expectation of authenticity in Hollywood action. To keep up with the increased expectation, digital technology steps in to recreate the illusion of real martial and corporeal capabilities.

By shifting the focus from the expressivity of action to its tranquility, it is possible to open up a new path for the development of transnational martial arts action cinema. When human body performance can be replaced by CGI and even martial capabilities can be simulated by motion capture, action cinema's previous emphasis on authenticity and expressivity would easily become exhaustive. The incorporation of martial ideation, to some extent, shifts the global action paradigm from the corporeal to that of the aesthetic and philosophical.[34]

Another way to understand *Black Panther*'s uptake of martial ideation is Hollywood's desire to widen the audience base of its action genre. If the

Blaxploitation films in the late 1960s and early 1970s were part of Hollywood's strategy of capitalizing on Black audience's consumer power and rescuing the industry from its fiscal crisis,[35] *Black Panther* could also be serving that purpose now due to the continuing decline of the U.S. local box office in recent years. However, the difference is that Hollywood needs the support of not only the Black audience within the local U.S. market but also the overseas audience, especially in the massive Chinese market.

Considering China's heavy censorship and her careful attitude to Western ideologies, *Black Panther*, with its non-White casts and African cultures, is more appealing to the Chinese government than other Marvel superhero films propagating American values. In addition, the film's African settings also demonstrate a close tie with China's "Belt and Road" initiative, a campaign that aims at increasing the country's influence in the middle-east and African regions. Furthermore, by highlight tranquility, the film connects to the long history of Hong Kong action cinema, and hence more culturally, aesthetically, and philosophically familiar to the Chinese audience. Rather than making a film with a pro-Chinese theme and narrative, such as *The Great Wall* (2016), *Black Panther* is a more successful example balancing the diverse spectatorship across the Pacific.

However, what Hollywood would not expect is that the fusion of Black action cinema and martial ideation poses a stronger resistance to Hollywood's (mis)representation of Blackness. The new emphasis on tranquility challenges the Blaxploitation formula and redefines Black action aesthetics. On the one hand, resisting Hollywood's appropriation and absorption through the action genre is a meta-criticism revealing the contestation, struggle, and constantly changing the representation of Blackness on screen. On the other hand, the shared history of colonization and oppression featured in Black action cinema and Hong Kong action cinema makes the aesthetic uptake more sustainable and less prone to exhaustion as the Blaxploitation period did.

To sum up, the beauty of martial ideation is embodied in Black Panther's vibranium suit. In Shuri's words, it "absorbs the kinetic energy and hold it in place for redistribution." Rather than resorting to immediate retaliation or ignoring the physical (and emotional) pain, it promotes the idea of control and stability. The implication is that Black Panther has absolute mastery over when, how, and to whom he should unleash his power, or not unleash it at all. Such tranquility is the beginning of a new era of Black action cinema.

NOTES

1. The audience sees T'Challa and Killmongers's ascension from a dark vibranium pit filled with magnetically-levitated trains traveling in extreme speed to a precipice showing a panoramic view of the golden yellow Wakandan sunset.

2. In this article, I use Hong Kong action cinema as an umbrella genre for films featuring martial arts action, including kung fu (hand-to-hand combat), *wuxia* (swordplay), and gunfight.

3. Indeed, there are alternative ways to appeal to the young audience other than highlighting tranquility. Other Marvel superheroes, such as the Hulk and Thor, are known for their expressivity and impulsiveness. Black Panther, in contrast, has a more composed presence.

4. Ed Guerrero, *Framing Blackness: The African American Image in Film*, Culture and the Moving Image (Philadelphia: Temple University Press, 1993), 94.

5. Ed Guerrero, "Black Violence as Cinema: From Cheap Thrills to Historical Agonies," in *Violence and American Cinema*, ed. J. David Slocum (New York: Routledge, 2001), 212.

6. Guerrero, *Framing Blackness*, 94.

7. James P. Murray, *To Find an Image: Black Films from Uncle Tom to Superfly* (Indianapolis: BobbsMerrill, 1973), 165.

8. Frantz Fanon, *The Wretched of the Earth*, trans. Richard Philcox (1961; repr., New York: Grove Press, 2004), 3.

9. The Black Lives Matter (BLM) protests last year against police violence and social injustice points to the continued relevance of Fanon's ideas in contemporary racial and class struggles. Political civil disobedience conducted through the form of violence is deemed as a necessary means for liberation against institutional and systematic oppression. In this light, the protests can be seen as an invigorating expression of collective solidarity.

10. Guerrero, *Framing Blackness*, 69–70.

11. Guerrero, *Framing Blackness*, 72.

12. Guerrero, *Framing Blackness*, 88.

13. Guerrero, *Framing Blackness*, 79.

14. Guerrero, *Framing Blackness*, 87.

15. Lerone Bennett Jr., "The Emancipation Orgasm: Sweetback in Wonderland," *Ebony* 26 (1971): 106–116.

16. Neal Galber, "The Two Hollywoods; The End of the Middle," *New York Times*, November 16, 1997, 76; and Ed Guerrero, "The Spectacle of Black Violence as Cinema," in *Cinematic Sociology: Social Life in Film*, ed. Jean-Ann Sutherland and Kathryn Feltey, 2nd ed. (London: Sage Publications, 2010), 70.

17. Galber, "The Two Hollywoods," 76.

18. Wayne Wong, "Action in Tranquillity: Sketching Martial Ideation in The Grandmaster," *Asian Cinema* 29, no. 2 (2018): 202–207.

19. Michael J. Puett, *To Become a God: Cosmology, Sacrifice, and Self-Divinization in Early China* (Cambridge, MA: Harvard University Press, 2002), 289–315.

20. Shaokang Zhang, *Zhongguo wenxue lilun piping jianshi* [A concise history of Chinese literary criticism] (Hong Kong: The Chinese University of Hong Kong, 2004), 92.

21. Bowei Zhang, *Quantang wudai shige jiaokao* [A study of the poetic styles in Tang's Five Dynasties] (Xi'an: Shanxi renmin chubanshe, 1996), 172–173.

22. Ran Jiao, *Shishi* [On poetic forms] (Shanghai: Shangwuyinshuju, 1937); Tu Sikong, *Ershisi shipin* [Appreciating the twenty four forms of poetry] (Taipei: Jinfeng

chubanshe, 1987); and Yu Yan, *Canglang shihua* [Canglang poetry talks] (Taipei: Jinfeng chubanshe, 1986).

23. Baihua Zong, *Zong Baihua quanji* [Complete works of Zong Baihua], vol. 2 (Anhui: Anhui Jiaoyu Chubanshe, 1994), 361.

24. Mary Ann Farquhar, "The Idea-Image: Conceptualizing Landscape in Recent Martial Arts Movies," in *Chinese Ecocinema: In the Age of Environmental Challenge*, ed. Sheldon Hsiao-peng Lu and Jiayan Mi (Hong Kong: Hong Kong University Press, 2009), 100.

25. David Bordwell, *Planet Hong Kong: Popular Cinema and the Art of Entertainment*, 2nd ed. (2000; repr., Madison, WI: Irvington Way Institute Press, 2011), 127.

26. Victor Fan, "The Something of Nothing: Buddhism and The Assassin," in *The Assassin: Hou Hsiao-Hsien's World of Tang China*, ed. Hsiao-yen Peng (Hong Kong: Hong Kong University Press, 2019), 182.

27. Victor Fan, *Cinema Approaching Reality: Locating Chinese Film Theory* (Minneapolis: University of Minnesota Press, 2015), 122–136.

28. Bordwell, *Planet Hong Kong*, 138.

29. Such an idealistic representation of a king possessing both leadership and martial skills is the masculine ideal in kung fu cinema. The first kung fu hero Wong Fei-hung, for example, is an ideal ruler who excels at *wen* (the literary) and *wu* (the martial). Kam Louie and Louise Edwards, "Chinese Masculinity: Theorising Wen and Wu," *East Asian History*, December, no. 8 (December 1, 1994): 140.

30. Leon Hunt, *Kung Fu Cult Masters* (London: Wallflower Press, 2003), 29–41.

31. The gist of cinematic authenticity lies within "the *unity* of an action within a shot — the number of moves or techniques, the precision of a continuous combo, a single-take stunt." Hunt, *Kung Fu Cult Masters*, 36 (original italics).

32. The scarred body can also be seen as a subtle critique of the American government's active military operations in the Middle East. The prolonged warfare in Afghanistan, Iraq and Africa transforms Erik Stevens, a graduate of MIT, to Killmonger, a ruthless Black ops who rewards his kills through Crocodile Scarring.

33. David Armitage, *The Ideological Origins of the British Empire* (Cambridge; New York: Cambridge University Press, 2000), 32.

34. There are other Black action films featuring a strong sense of equanimity in action sequences. Despite its explicit violence, the protagonist of *The Equalizer* series (2014–18) is exceptionally calm during fight scenes.

35. Guerrero, *Framing Blackness*, 71–82.

WORKS CITED

Armitage, David. *The Ideological Origins of the British Empire*. Cambridge; New York: Cambridge University Press, 2000.

Bennett, Lerone, Jr. "The Emancipation Orgasm: Sweetback in Wonderland." *Ebony* 26(1971): 106–116.

Bordwell, David. *Planet Hong Kong: Popular Cinema and the Art of Entertainment*. 2nd ed. 2000. Reprint, Madison, WI: Irvington Way Institute Press, 2011.

Fan, Victor. *Cinema Approaching Reality: Locating Chinese Film Theory*. Minneapolis: University of Minnesota Press, 2015.

———. "The Something of Nothing: Buddhism and The Assassin." In *The Assassin: Hou Hsiao-Hsien's World of Tang China*, edited by Hsiao-yen Peng, 178–194. Hong Kong: Hong Kong University Press, 2019.

Fanon, Frantz. *The Wretched of the Earth*. Translated by Richard Philcox. 1961. Reprint, New York: Grove Press, 2004.

Farquhar, Mary Ann. "The Idea-Image: Conceptualizing Landscape in Recent Martial Arts Movies." In *Chinese Ecocinema: In the Age of Environmental Challenge*, edited by Sheldon Hsiao-peng Lu and Jiayan Mi, 95–112. Hong Kong: Hong Kong University Press, 2009.

Galber, Neal. "The Two Hollywoods; The End of the Middle." *New York Times*, November 16, 1997.

Guerrero, Ed. "Black Violence as Cinema: From Cheap Thrills to Historical Agonies." In *Violence and American Cinema*, edited by J. David Slocum, 211–225. New York: Routledge, 2001.

———. *Framing Blackness: The African American Image in Film*. Culture and the Moving Image. Philadelphia: Temple University Press, 1993.

———. "The Spectacle of Black Violence as Cinema." In *Cinematic Sociology: Social Life in Film*, edited by Jean-Ann Sutherland and Kathryn Feltey, 2nd ed., 69–85. London: Sage Publications, 2010.

Hunt, Leon. *Kung Fu Cult Masters*. London: Wallflower Press, 2003.

Jiao, Ran. *Shishi* [On poetic forms]. Shanghai: Shangwuyinshuju, 1937.

Louie, Kam, and Louise Edwards. "Chinese Masculinity: Theorising Wen and Wu." *East Asian History*, December, no. 8 (December 1, 1994): 135–148.

Murray, James P. *To Find an Image: Black Films from Uncle Tom to Superfly*. Indianapolis: Bobbs Merrill, 1973.

Puett, Michael J. *To Become a God: Cosmology, Sacrifice, and Self-Divinization in Early China*. Cambridge, MA: Harvard University Press, 2002.

Sikong, Tu. *Ershisi shipin* [Appreciating the twenty four forms of poetry]. Taipei: Jinfeng chubanshe, 1987.

Wong, Wayne. "Action in Tranquillity: Sketching Martial Ideation in The Grandmaster." *Asian Cinema* 29, no. 2 (2018): 201–223. https://doi.org/10.1386/ac.29.2.201_1.

Yan, Yu. *Canglang shihua* [Canglang poetry talks]. Taipei: Jinfeng chubanshe, 1986.

Zhang, Bowei. *Quantang wudai shige jiaokao* [A study of the poetic styles in Tang's Five Dynasties]. Xi'an: Shanxi renmin chubanshe, 1996.

Zhang, Shaokang. *Zhongguo wenxue lilun piping jianshi* [A concise history of Chinese literary criticism]. Hong Kong: The Chinese University of Hong Kong, 2004.

Zong, Baihua. *Zong Baihua quanji* [Complete works of Zong Baihua]. Vol. 2. Anhui: Anhui Jiaoyu Chubanshe, 1994.

FILMS

Amistad. Directed by Steven Spielberg. United States: DreamWorks Pictures, 1997.

Bad Boys II. Directed by Michael Bay. United States: Columbia Pictures, 2003.

Bad Boys. Directed by Michael Bay. United States: Don Simpson/Jerry Bruckheimer Films, 1995.
Black Panther. Directed by Ryan Coogler. United States: Marvel Studios, 2018.
Blade. Directed by Stephen Norrington. United States: Amen Ra Films, 1998.
Blade II. Directed by Guillermo del Toro. United States: New Line Cinema, 2002.
Blade: Trinity. Directed by David S. Goyer. United States: New Line Cinema, 2004.
Cleopatra Jones and the Casino of Gold. Directed by Charles Bail. United States: Harbor Productions, 1975.
Enter the Dragon. Directed by Robert Clouse. Hong Kong: Warner Bros., 1973.
Foxy Brown. Directed by Jack Hill. United States: American International Pictures [AIP], 1974.
Guess Who's Coming to Dinner? Directed by Stanley Kramer. United States: Columbia Pictures, 1967.
In the Heat of the Night (1967). Directed by Norman Jewison. United States: The Mirisch Corporation, 1967.
Malcom X. Directed by Spike Lee. United States: Largo International N.V., 1992.
Menace II Society. Directed by Albert Hughes and Allen Hughes. United States: New Line Cinema, 1993.
Rosewood. Directed by John Singleton. United States: Warner Bros., 1997.
Shaft. Directed by Gordon Parks. United States: Metro-Goldwyn-Mayer [MGM], 1971.
Spring in a Small Town. Directed by Fei Mu. China: Wenhua Film Company, 1948.
Superfly. Directed by Gordon Parks Jr. United States: Sig Shore Productions, 1972.
Sweet Sweetback's Baadasssss Song. Directed by Melvin Van Peebles. United States: Yeah Inc., 1973.
The Equalizer. Directed by Antoine Fuqua. United States: Columbia Pictures, 2014.
The Equalizer 2. Directed by Antoine Fuqua. United States: Columbia Pictures, 2018.
The Way of the Dragon. Directed by Bruce Lee. Hong Kong: Golden Harvest Films, 1972.

Chapter 4

Paid the Cost to be the Boss

Chadwick Boseman, Black Panther, *and the Future of the Black Biopic*

Mikal J. Gaines

In an October 2017 interview for *Metro*, a Boston free newspaper, lead Chadwick Boseman and co-star Josh Gad discussed the cultural significance of their new biopic, *Marshall* (Reginald Hudlin, 2017), which focuses on the first African American Supreme Court Justice and Civil Rights Activist. Boseman was decidedly reticent about labeling the film as "important," suggesting that the term made the film seem like obligatory viewing rather than a more fun, entertaining story about the "coolness" of Thurgood Marshall's early career. Boseman clarified that:

> Yes, he's important. But I also think he's a cool dude. He was cool for what he did. He was cool because he fought for justice. He was cool because he was courageous, arrogant, and selfless. When you start talking about how important movies are, it's like, "You have to see the movie!" But you don't want to see it. And I knew this was a movie people would want to see.[1]

We can sense in Boseman's statement a resistance not only to the often heavy-handed, didactic tone of the Black biopic but perhaps also an underlying concern about audiences growing weary of stories that they *have to see* in order to prove their commitment to social justice vis-à-vis supporting Black representation. Gad's comments were even more telling: "I think it is important without being self-righteous. And that's what I really respect about it. This really is a movie for everybody. At the same time, it is covering this incredible period of history and this incredible journey before he is the man in the robes. It's the origin movie of a superhero basically."[2]

Critics similarly picked up on *Marshall's* conflation of the superhero origin story and the biopic. Devan Coggan of *Entertainment Weekly* claimed in the title of her review that *"Marshall* is a Superhero Origin Story for the Legendary Civil Rights Lawyer"[3] while John Anderson of *America* magazine, a leading source on Jesuit perspectives, affirmed, "Thurgood Marshall Gets the Superhero Treatment in New Biopic."[4] Jessica Zack of the *San Francisco Chronicle* asserted: "Boseman knows a thing or two about playing heroes, and that they come in many guises—from the incognito versions in our comic book pages, to history's real life champions of justice and civil rights."[5] John Sullivan, writing for the *SMU Daily Campus*, noted that "Much like many of the superhero origin stories hitting the screen recently, *Marshall* depicts a young Thurgood Marshall, the first black supreme court justice, building up the mystique and prestige that defined his life" whereas a reviewer for *MTR Network* argued: "[Boseman] has taken mild mannered Supreme Court Justice, Thurgood Marshall and turned him into something more . . . a superhero."[6] Several of the reviews also discussed Boseman's previous roles as Jackie Robinson in *42* (Brian Helgeland, 2013) and as James Brown in *Get On Up* (Tate Taylor, 2014). Playing prominent Black historical figures with such gravitas seems to have given Boseman a brand of representational credibility that only the biographical film can offer. Moreover, his age, physicality, chameleon-like ability to slide into different personas, his apparent commitment to representations of Black heroism, and his proven track record as a box office draw made him if not the only logical choice to play the lead in Marvel's *Black Panther* (Ryan Coogler, 2018), certainly the most obvious one.[7] He has, as the Godfather of Soul himself would say, "paid the cost to be the boss." And with the film having broken the billion-dollar mark at the box office, it would be hard to argue that his casting was not a fortuitous choice.[8]

While Boseman offers convincing performances in *Black Panther* as well as the aforementioned biopics, I am less interested in the nuances of his acting than in what his playing all of these parts signifies about larger shifts in systems of meaning and knowledge production in American culture. I want to better understand how it is that we seem to have arrived at a point in the history of the biopic, of the superhero film, of Black cinema, and of film history more generally in which *Black Panther* feels, strangely, like the most important biopic of all time despite its being about a wholly fictional persona? Moreover, why and how does *Black Panther* seem to carry more historical weight, both in its desire to present a nuanced, multifaceted view of blackness and as a history-making Black cinematic event, than films about real Black historical figures? To clarify, I am not arguing that the Boseman-led biopics or other recent Black biopics have somehow been shortchanged by shallow audiences who prefer more escapist narratives. This argument is not intended as a moralist judgment about how the kind of popular myth, which the Marvel Cinematic Universe (MCU) has done such an effective job canonizing, garners a much bigger audience than films about real Black folks. After all, even if it were terrible (and it isn't) *Black Panther* would likely always have brought in more money than any of the more traditional Boseman-led historical films. What does seem worthy of further attention though is how Boseman's transition from starring in those biopics to then embodying King T'Challa, "The Black Panther," reveals continuities between the kinds of ideological work that both genres do, and how the superhero film potentially does so in ways that audiences find more satisfying.

Ostensibly based on real people and true historical events, biopics nevertheless often seek as film scholar Dennis Bingham asserts, "to enter the subject into the pantheon of cultural mythology," to create a fixed image that registers along with other easily associable signs in the popular imagination.[9] Alternatively, many Marvel films and particularly their superhero origin stories work to create a sense of history that foregrounds, solidifies, and ultimately lends seriousness to their mythological heroes. I contend that this blurring of biography and superhero mythos signals a deeper postmodern desire to challenge and replace established versions of history that fail to serve our present understandings. We seem to want and perhaps even *need* the superhero film to do things for us culturally, politically, and representationally that the biopic no longer can. Boseman's career trajectory also suggests that if the biopic has often served as mechanism of legitimacy, a reward and proof of the actor's special capabilities, it has now become a stepping-stone to the more prestigious and culturally significant work of rendering truth from myth.

This merging of the biopic and the superhero story begins to make much more sense if we consider that Marvel has arguably been in the biopic business for some time. *Iron Man* (Jon Favreau, 2008), *The Incredible Hulk* (Louis Leterrier, 2008), *Thor* (Kenneth Branagh, 2011), *Captain America: The First Avenger* (Joe Johnston, 2011), *The Guardians of the Galaxy* (James Gunn, 2014), *Ant-Man* (Peyton Reed, 2015), *Doctor Strange* (Scott Derrickson, 2016), and now *Black Panther* all seek to provide an account of how their respective heroes come into their power or in some cases, how they transition from boisterous and even reckless displays of that power to a more mature reckoning with the responsibility which attends it. As with the biopic, the heroes are put through their paces, they stumble, form allegiances, sever past bonds, and struggle with deep internal and external conflicts, all so that they can finally accept their new roles and prove why their special powers are precisely what are needed to save the day.[10] The underlying assumption—just as with Jackie Robinson, James Brown, Thurgood Marshall, or the focus of any other prototypical biopic—is that heroes are people born with gifts and a unique sense of character who find themselves elevated by destiny or circumstance, and who choose, to quote *The Avengers* (Joss Whedon, 2012) tagline, "to fight the battles that we never could." But what really allows these characters to become ones to whom audiences feel connected (and I would argue more so than to those in any biopic) and what also enables the MCU to cohere is that each of the heroes' stories are bound by a layered and decidedly complex brand of historicity. Even in the aforementioned origin stories, the heroes' emergence derives in large part from their ability to successfully grapple with the past: Iron Man Tony Stark (Robert Downey Jr.) hopes to counter the damage wrought by his father's violent legacy as an arms dealer. Thor (Chris Hemsworth) likewise seeks to reconcile his father's old rivalries and prove himself worthy of the powers he holds within. The whole Guardians team is a group self-professed "losers" wrestling to overcome past personal traumas. But this historicity extends to more than just the heroes' individual pasts.

In more recent Marvel films, the heroes discover that their whole worlds have been based on falsehoods and the revelation of the truth does nothing less than rewrite history itself, at least as it exists with the MCU. In *Captain America: The Winter Soldier* (Anthony Russo and Joe Russo, 2014), Steve Rodgers (Chris Evans) learns that S.H.I.E.L.D., the government agency whose missions he has been carrying out, has in fact been infiltrated by the evil secret society Hydra and is corrupt to its very core. *Thor: Ragnarok* (Taika Waititi, 2017) reveals that the entire mythical kingdom of Asgard's foundation rests not on the benevolent rule of King Odin (Anthony Hopkins) but rather on a colonialist reign of terror carried out by both Odin and Thor's outcast sister Hela, the Goddess of Death (Kate Blanchett). Most importantly for my purposes here, T'Challa in *Black Panther* finds out that his father T'Chaka (Atandwa Kani/John Kani) murdered his own brother N'Jobo (Sterling K. Brown) for betraying Wakanda and that he subsequently abandoned N'Jobo's son Erik (later Killmonger, Seth Carr/Michael B. Jordan) in America. This original sin, coupled with the decision to keep Wakanda and the ultimate natural resource, vibranium, a secret from the rest of the world becomes the animating conflict of the film.

As the MCU has grown then, each subsequent film adds more and more layers of backstory, constantly deepening the characters' journeys, instigating new conflicts, and creating a sense of interdependence with the past that ironically is not and perhaps cannot be duplicated by the standalone format of the biopic. Serialization affords Marvel films what the traditional biopic wants but can never deliver: a continually re-imaginable, fluid past and futurity without limit.

Jackie Robinson and James Brown can of course only integrate Major League Baseball and change the rhythm of American popular music once with what will always be the same results. And while Thurgood Marshall may have helped alter the course of American jurisprudence many times, the impact of that for audiences who still find themselves disenfranchised at the hands of an insidious criminal justice system feels both emphatically past and fundamentally limited. As Amen Oyiboke plainly states in a piece about the still circumscribed nature of Black screen representation: "Yes, biopics can sometimes be helpful in showcasing issues Black people have faced historically, but that can't be the only kind of Black stories we get. Our lives aren't one dimensional, and to understand the community means that Hollywood needs to explore our everyday lives in addition to those of historical figures."[11] In this sense, superhero films can both interrogate the past and give audiences futures that even they have not yet imagined.

BLACK HERO STATUS IN THE BIOPIC AND SUPERHERO FILM

To better understand this interconnected relationship between the Black biopic and the superhero film, we need only look at two moments, one from a Boseman-led biopic and another that features fans reacting to a surprise meeting with Boseman following a screening of *Black Panther*. An early scene in *42* (Brian Helgeland, 2013) shows Jackie Robinson (Boseman), the first African American baseball player in the U.S. Major League, arriving at the home of Mr. Brock (James Pickens Jr.), a local Black businessman who will host Jackie during training camp in Sandford, Florida. Brock, in classic integrationist posture proclaims that "The day belongs to decent-minded people." Brock then goes on to say that his wife earlier asked, "What do you serve when a hero's coming to dinner?" Jackie then modestly qualifies that "[he's] just a ball player." Immediately rejecting Jackie's attempt to downplay the significance of his representative role, Brock claims: "Naw, naw, naw. You tell that to all the little colored boys playing baseball in Florida today. To them, you a hero." The phrase triggers a triumphant swell of score music and a predictable medium close-up of Robinson's growing awareness of the great weight he carries. Although scenes like this that reinforce Robinson's heroic status permeate the film, this is easily the most explicit in its attempt to situate him within a recognizable framework of historic Black heroism. Yet these sign posting moments feel peculiar and overdetermined given the audience's almost guaranteed prior familiarity with Robinson's story and the frequency with which he already functions as common shorthand for racial barrier breaking. Even when dealing with a well-known figure like Robinson, the Black biopic still exhibits insecurity, requiring such deliberate claims about the gravity and magnitude of its subject.

An episode of *The Tonight Show with Jimmy Fallon* shortly after the release of *Black Panther* takes a different approach, positioning Boseman's role and the film itself as a landmark moment in Black history.[12] Black spectators stand in front of a large poster of Boseman in full costume and are asked to speak about the film's impact as he waits along with Fallon behind a curtain to surprise them. Their comments range from praise to gratitude to inspiration with the most telling doing nothing less than establishing Boseman as a true hero. In fact, the very first spectator interviewed, a man adorned in a blue suit, remarks: "I can't express how much it means to me and the community and my family. Thank you from the very bottom of my heart for all that you've done, for really being the hero that we need in a film like this."[13] When Boseman reveals himself from behind the curtain, the man literally screams and then begins bowing to Boseman while performing the Wakandan cross-armed salute and humbly repeating, "My king, my king, my king." Others talked about how much it meant to have him "step into the role as our king" and "to see a movie that's not like a black movie, but . . . just a great American superhero movie with you know, people that look like me."[14] A mother with her young son in tow even said that her son's childhood had "been defined by Barack Obama and now *Black Panther*." Although Boseman jokes that her statement seems like "too much praise," her implied equivocation between the President of the United States and a make-believe Marvel character coupled with the absence of any reference to Boseman's other work in historical films speaks to a profound shift in how Black audiences have come to conceptualize representation.

These real spectators' responses to an entirely fictional film, especially when read in contrast to the fictionalized but at least plausible moment from *42*, make apparent the stark contrast between a "historical" film that needs to announce its protagonist's importance in an explicit, even ham-fisted way, versus one where fans have implicitly interpreted the character's presence as having worth in their real lives. However respectful audiences might feel toward Boseman's work in biopics, that respect did not and *could not* warrant him the position as "our king" that we hear in fan responses to *Black Panther*. Moreover, the spectators' responses rely upon a powerful albeit not unproblematic conflation of Boseman with his Marvel persona based on the tacit recognition that a superhero film like *Black Panther* carries far higher representational stakes than any of his more "historical" roles. Rather than read these spectators as failing to understand the difference between myth and reality, their sentiments evince that the superhero film has clearly superseded the biopic both in regard to how Black history gets done both through and by popular culture and in terms of what constitutes a historic moment in Black screen representation.

I have been largely skeptical here about the biopic's power to leave audiences feeling moved or for it to do the kind of revisionist, corrective work that it once did. It seems difficult to imagine a collective rally around a biopic about any Black historical figure equivalent to what we have seen for *Black Panther* or for that matter, what we witnessed for Spike Lee's *Malcolm X* (1992) over a quarter century ago. Yet, we should not be too dismissive of how the biopic still performs a legitimizing function within the greater scheme of Black screen representation. Perhaps no single moment in *Black Panther* testifies more to its place as a kind of biopic and to the legitimacy that the biopic has granted to Black talent than the scene in which Erik Killmonger, played by Michael B. Jordan, challenges Boseman's T'Challa for the throne. Jordan himself became a household name after his breakout role in the Oscar Grant biopic, *Fruitvale Station* (2013), which was of course also Ryan Coogler's full-length directorial debut. Coogler and Jordan's next collaboration, *Creed* (2016), I would argue is itself really nothing less than a fictionalized biopic and Jordan would likely not have been given such a prominent role in *Black Panther* if not for his standout performance there. Jordan's more recent role as celebrated real-life civil rights attorney Bryan Stevenson in *Just Mercy* (Destin Daniel Cretton, 2019) could also be thought of as hybridizing superhero and biopic narratives, and potentially points toward the ways that Jordan might carry on Boseman's legacy.

Boseman and Jordan's biopic credentials firmly established, the scene also features Forest Whitaker as the shaman Zuri, who has no shortage of biopic bona fides: he played legendary jazz saxophonist Charlie Parker in Clint Eastwood's *Bird* (1988) and a character loosely based on civil rights activist Bob Hicks in *Deacons for Defense* (Bill Duke, 2003); he won the Best Actor award for his portrayal of Ugandan dictator Idi Amin in *The Last King of Scotland* (Kevin McDonald, 2006); played famous scholar and minister Dr. James Farmer, Sr. in *The Great Debaters* (Denzel Washington, 2007); played real-life Louisiana basketball coach Al Collins in *Hurricane Season* (Tim Story, 2009); and starred in *The Butler* (Lee Daniels, 2013), which is loosely based on the life of Eugene Allen.

Whitaker is flanked by Angela Bassett as T'Challa's queen mother Ramonda, who has twice played Dr. Betty Shabazz in *Malcolm X* (1992) and *Panther* (Mario Van Peebles, 1995), Katherine Jackson in *The Jacksons: An American Dream* (1992), Tina Turner in her Oscar-nominated performance for *What's Love Got to Do with It* (Brian Gibson, 1993), Rosa Parks in the TV-movie *The Rosa Parks Story* (Julie Dash, 2002), Voletta Wallace in *Notorious* (George Tillman Jr., 2009), Coretta Scott King in *Betty and Coretta* (Yves Simoneau, 2013), and Marie Laveau in *American Horror Story* (2013–2014), which, in a strange way, counts too. Also present are Danai Gurira as General Okoye, fresh off her turn as Afeni Shakur in the Tupac biopic *All Eyez on Me* (Benny Brown, 2017) and Lupita Nyong'o as T'Challa's love interest Nakia who of course won the Best Supporting Actress Oscar for her role as Patsy in the Solomon Northup biopic *12 Years a Slave* (Steve McQueen, 2013); she also starred in Disney's "based on a true story" uplift film, *Queen of Katwe* (Mira Nair, 2016). Thus, this otherwise standard Marvel showdown in which a superhero is deliberately set up to fail only so that he can later rise to his full potential is elevated in part because it populates the frame with Black actors whose pedigrees have been bolstered by their appearances in biopics and other Black historical films. These are actors who we trust not just to play real Black historical figures but who we trust with Black symbolic representation itself.

The only way the aforementioned scene of superhero self-making could have been further stacked with Black actors who have similarly found acclaim and clout playing real-life characters is if Don Cheadle, Jamie Foxx, Chiwetel Ejiofor, Will Smith, and Halle Berry showed up.[15] But then Cheadle aka James Rhodes aka "War Machine" was probably still recovering from his terrible fall in *Captain America: Civil War* (Anthony Russo and Joe Russo, 2016). As for Foxx, we can assume that since the MCU has been willing to accommodate Michael B. Jordan, Chris Evans, and Ryan Reynolds even after previously unsuccessful superhero roles, fans would probably also accept Foxx and put aside his turn as Max Dillon aka Electro in *The Amazing Spider-Man 2* (Marc Webb, 2014)—especially now that *Spiderman* has been rebooted and incorporated into the MCU as well.[16] Although one wonders how Foxx's *Django Unchained* (Quentin Tarantino, 2012) role—a lone Black anti-hero more interested in revenge than justice—might factor into the equation? But then again, fans do not seem to have any trouble distinguishing Samuel L. Jackson's highly offensive *Django* character Steven from his more assertive and wiser Nick Fury persona. And while Ejiofor's *Doctor Strange* (Scott Derrickson, 2016) character "Mordo" was absent for "Phase 3" of the MCU, he is set to return in *Doctor Strange: In the Multiverse of Madness* (Sam Raimi, 2022).

Halle Berry was arguably the first to transition between the biopic and the superhero film in her role as Storm in the *X-Men* movies (Bryan Singer, 2000; Singer 2003; Brett Ratner, 2006; Singer 2014) and less successfully in *Catwoman* (Pitof, 2004). Like Boseman, Berry's work as "Storm" might very well end up being the most significant of her career in terms of what it means for Black representation on screen and certainly more so than her performance in a biopic like *Introducing Dorothy Dandridge* (Martha Coolidge, 1999). Will Smith's star presence seems like it would have been too great a disruption to the carefully cultivated team dynamic that holds the MCU together, but the bigger issue is of course that Smith now plays the anti-hero "Deadshot" in the competing DC Comics universe. This part comes after multiple roles in biopics and as anti-hero turned superhero *Hancock* (Peter Berg) in 2008, which is ironically the same year that the MCU's inaugural film, *Iron Man*, was released.

I have been playing this postmodern game of degrees of separation between the Black biopic and the superhero film, because I suspect it has something to tell us about how American audiences in general and Black audiences specifically are making sense of their experience through the movies. American popular culture has in recent years become even more deeply invested in different articulations of heroism, individual and collective, Black, White, and otherwise. These narratives by their very nature offer more straightforward, simplistic solutions to what are largely intractable, systemic problems with deep historical roots. The appeal of biopics—"real life" examples of heroic individuals triumphing over enormous odds and against virulent resistance, and superhero films, stories about gifted individuals who use their power for a greater good—makes a certain obvious sense as a response.

What makes all of this especially interesting, however, is how blackness has come to be a pivotal part of this larger conversation about what makes someone a hero in the twenty-first century. Also worthy of closer consideration is how the mythmaking ethos of the biopic and the increasingly strong impulse of superhero films to historicize themselves have blurred the lines between fantasy and reality. No, Wakanda isn't real. Neither is *Black Panther*. But we need to take seriously the power this mythology holds for audiences and begin asking more critical questions about why conventional ways of doing Black history on screen, as with the biopic, no longer seem like the most meaningful or even true ways of framing a Black past so as to imagine a freer, more just, and more dynamic Black future.

NOTES

1. Gregory Wakeman, "Why the 'Superhero Origin' Story of Thurgood Marshall is 'Important,' but Still Entertaining," *Metro*, October 12, 2017, https://www.metro.us/entertainment/movies/marshall-superhero-josh-gad-chadwick-boseman.

2. Ibid.

3. Devan Coggan, "*Marshall* is a Superhero Origin Story for the Legendary Civil Rights Lawyer," *Entertainment Weekly*, October 13, 2017, http://ew.com/movies/2017/10/13/marshall-review/.

4. John Anderson, "Thurgood Marshall Gets the Superhero Treatment in New Biopic," *America*, October 12, 2017, https://www.americamagazine.org/arts-culture/2017/10/12/thurgood-marshall-gets-superhero-treatment-new-biopic.

5. Jessica Zack, "Marvel Superhero Boseman Plays Real-Life Hero Thurgood Marshall," *San Francisco Chronicle*, October 7, 2017, https://www.sfchronicle.com/movies/article/Marvel-superhero-Boseman-plays-real-life-hero-12252735.php.

6. John Sullivan, "'Marshall' is a New Kind of Superhero Story," *SMU Daily Campus*, October 11, 2017, http://www.smudailycampus.com/ae/marshall-is-a-new

-kind-of-superhero-story; Shanna, "'Marshall' Feels Like a Historical Superhero Origin Story," *MTR Network*, June 22, 2017, https://www.mtrnetwork.net/news/marshall-feels-like-historical-superhero-origin-story/.

7. Chadwick Boseman was considerably older than the characters were at the time when the films were set. For example, he was 36-37 when *42* was filming & released, so almost a decade older than Robinson's character is supposed to be at the time the film takes place. The author suspects that part of his casting was because they needed an older actor with the kind of gravitas that you describe as opposed to some of his younger counterparts in Hollywood.

8. Rebecca Rubin, "'Black Panther' Crosses $1 Billion at Global Box Office," *Variety*, March 10, 2018, http://variety.com/2018/film/news/black-panther-billion-global-box-office-1202723326/.

9. Dennis Bingham, *Whose Lives Are They Anyway?: The Biopic as Contemporary Film Genre* (New Brunswick, NJ and London: Rutgers University Press, 2010), 10.

10. As Bingham points out, this narrative structure is perhaps mostly applicable to male-centered biopics whereas women-led stories exhibit significantly different concerns in large part because of the tension that surrounds women's positioning in the public sphere. Bingham views the differences as stark enough to use it as categorization device in his study. See *Whose Stories Are They Anyway?*.

11. Amen Oyibọke, "Chadwick Boseman Always Starring in Biopics Emphasizes Hollywood's Frustrating Lack of Black Stories," *Bustle*, October 27, 2017, https://www.bustle.com/p/chadwick-boseman-always-starring-in-biopics-emphasizes-hollywoods-frustrating-lack-of-black-stories-2951443. See also, Kara Brown, "Why Does Hollywood Keep Casting Chadwick Boseman in Biopics?" *Jezebel*, December 17, 2015, https://jezebel.com/why-does-hollywood-keep-casting-chadwick-boseman-in-bio-1748584019.

12. The Tonight Show Starring Jimmy Fallon, "Chadwick Boseman Surprises Black Panther Fans While They Thank Him," Youtube Video, 5:47, February 28, 2018, https://www.youtube.com/watch?v=expKmfdoo28&t=1s.

13. Ibid.

14. Ibid.

15. These actors can boast an impressive slate of roles in biopics and other historical films even if their consistent casting in such roles still evidences a limited range of parts for black actors who want to work regularly: Don Cheadle: *Rebound: The Legend of Earl "The Goat" Manigault* (Eriq La Salle, 1996), *Rosewood* (John Singleton, 1997), *The Rat Pack* (Rob Cohen, 1998), *Hotel Rwanda* (Terry George, 2004), *Talk to Me* (Kasi Lemmons, 2007), *Miles Ahead* (Don Cheadle, 2015); Jamie Foxx: *Ali* (Michael Mann, 2001), *Ray* (Taylor Hackford, 2004), *Jarhead* (Sam Mendes, 2005), *The Soloist* (Joe Wright, 2009); Chiwetel Ejiofor: *Amistad* (Steven Spielberg, 1997), *Talk to Me* (Lemmons, 2007), *American Gangster* (Ridley Scott, 2007), *Endgame* (Pete Travis, 2009), *Savannah* (Annette Haywood-Carter, 2013), *Phil Spector* (David Mamet, 2013), *12 Years a Slave* (Steve McQueen, 2013), *Come Sunday* (Joshua Marston, 2018), *The Boy Who Harnessed the Wind* (Ejiofor, 2019); Halle Berry: *Queen* (1993), *Race the Sun* (Charles T. Kanganis, 1996), *Why Do Fools Fall in Love* (Gregory Nara, 1998), *Introducing Dorothy Dandridge* (Martha

Coolidge, 1999), *Frankie and Alice* (Geoffrey Sax, 2010); Will Smith: *Ali* (Mann, 2001), *The Pursuit of Happyness* (Gabriele Muccino, 2006), *Concussion* (Pete Landesmen, 2015). Interestingly Terrance Howard, who first played the character of Rhodey in *Iron Man* (2008), also has a strong pedigree in black biopics: *The Jacksons: An American Dream* (Karen Arthur, 1992), *The O.J. Simpson* (Jerrold Freedman, 1995), *The King of the World* (John Sacred Young, 2000), *Boycott* (Clark Johnson, 2001), *Ray* (Taylor Hackford, 2004), *Pride* (Sunu Gonera, 2007), *Winnie Mandela* (Darrell Roodt, 2011), *Red Tails* (Anthony Hemingway, 2012), and *The Butler* (2013).

16. Evans played Johnny Storm, "The Human Torch" in both *The Fantastic Four* (Tim Story, 2004) and *The Fantastic Four: Rise of the Silver Surfer* (Story, 2007) whereas Jordan played the same character in the much-maligned attempt to reboot the series, *Fantastic Four* (Josh Trank, 2015). Ryan Reynolds had three less than laudable appearances in superhero movies, *Blade Trinity* (David S. Goyer, 2004), *X-Men Origins: Wolverine* (Gavin Hood, 2009), and *Green Lantern* (Martin Campbell, 2011) before finally gaining critical and box office success with Marvel's more recent *Deadpool* films (Tim Miller, 2016; David Leitch, 2018).

WORKS CITED

Anderson, John. "Thurgood Marshall Gets the Superhero Treatment in New Biopic." *America*, October 12, 2017. https://www.americamagazine.org/arts- culture/20 17/10/12/thurgood-marshall-gets-superhero-treatment-new-biopic.

Bingham, Dennis. *Whose Lives Are They Anyway?: The Biopic as Contemporary Film Genre*. New Brunswick, NJ and London: Rutgers University Press, 2010.

Brown, Kara. "Why Does Hollywood Keep Casting Chadwick Boseman in Biopics?" *Jezebel*, December 17, 2015. https://jezebel.com/why-does-hollywood-keep-castin g-chadwick-boseman-in-bio-1748584019.

Coggan, Devan. "*Marshall* is a Superhero Origin Story for the Legendary Civil Rights Lawyer: EW Review." *Entertainment Weekly*, October 13, 2017. https://ew .com/movies/2017/10/13/marshall-review/.

Oyiboke, Amen. "Chadwick Boseman Always Starring in Biopics Emphasizes Hollywood's Frustrating Lack of Black Stories." *Bustle*, October 27, 2017. https ://www.bustle.com/p/chadwick-boseman-always-starring-in-biopics-emphasizes-hollywoods-frustrating-lack-of-black-stories-2951443.

Rubin, Rebecca. "Black Panther Crosses $1 Billion at Global Box Office." *Variety*, March 10, 2018. http://variety.com/2018/film/news/black-panther-billion-global -box-office-1202723326/.

Shanna. "'Marshall' Feels Like a Historical Superhero Origin Story." *MTR Network*, June 22, 2017. https://www.mtrnetwork.net/news/marshall-feels-like-historical-su perhero-origin-story/.

Sullivan, John. "'Marshall' is a New Kind of Superhero Story." *SMU Daily Campus*, October 11, 2017. http://www.smudailycampus.com/ae/marshall-is-a-new-kind-of -superhero-story.

The Tonight Show Starring Jimmy Fallon. "Chadwick Boseman Surprises Black Panther Fans While They Thank Him." YouTube Video, 5:47. February 28, 2018. https://www.youtube.com/watch?v=expKmfdoo28&t=1s.

Wakeman, Gregory. "Why the 'Superhero Origin' Story of Thurgood Marshall is 'Important,' but Still Entertaining." *Metro*, October 12, 2017. https://www.metro.us/entertainment/movies/marshall-superhero-josh-gad-chadwick-boseman.

Zack, Jessica. "Marvel Superhero Boseman Plays Real-Life Hero Thurgood Marshall." *San Francisco Chronicle*, October 7, 2017. https://www.sfchronicle.com/movies/article/Marvel-superhero-Boseman-plays-real-life-hero-12252735.php.

FILMS

All Eyez on Me. Directed by Benny Boom. United States: Summit Entertainment, 2017.

The Amazing Spiderman 2. Directed by Marc Webb. United States: Sony Pictures Releasing, 2014.

Ant-Man. Directed by Peyton Reed. United States: Walt Disney Studios Motion Pictures, 2015.

Avengers. Directed by Joss Whedon. United States: Walt Disney Studios Motion Pictures, 2012.

Bird. Directed by Clint Eastwood. United States: Warner Bros., 1988.

Black Panther. Directed by Ryan Coogler. United States: Walt Disney Studios Motion Pictures, 2018.

Betty and Coretta. Directed by Yves Simoneau. United States and Canada: Lifetime, 2013.

The Butler. Directed by Lee Butler. United States: The Weinstein Company, 2013.

Captain America: Civil War. Directed by Anthony Russo and Joe Russo. United States: Walt Disney Studios Motion Pictures, 2016.

Captain America: The First Avenger. Directed by Joe Johnston. United States: Paramount Pictures, 2011.

Captain America: The Winter Solider. Directed by Anthony Russo and Joe Russo. United States: Walt Disney Studios Motion Pictures, 2014.

Catwoman. Directed by Pitof. United States: 20th Century Fox, 2004.

Creed. Directed by Ryan Coogler. United States: Warner Bros., 2015.

Deacons for Defense. Directed by Bill Duke. United States: Showtime Home Entertainment, 2003.

Django Unchained. Directed by Quentin Tarantino. United States: The Weinstein Company, 2012.

Doctor Strange. Directed by Scott Derrickson. United States: Walt Disney Studios Motion Pictures, 2016.

Doctor Strange: In the Multiverse of Madness. Directed by Sam Raimi. United States: Walt Disney Studios Motion Pictures, 2022. *42*. Directed by Brian Helgeland. United States: Warner Bros., 2013.

Fruitvale Station. Directed by Ryan Coogler. United States: The Weinstein Company, 2013.
Get on Up. Directed by Tate Taylor. United States: Universal, 2014.
The Great Debaters. Directed by Denzel Washington. United States: Harpo Productions, 2007.
Guardians of the Galaxy. Directed by James Gunn. United States: Walt Disney Studios Motion Pictures, 2014.
Hurricane Season. Directed by Tim Story. United States: Dimension Films, 2009.
The Incredible Hulk. Directed by Louis Leterrier. United States: Universal Pictures, 2008.
Introducing Dorothy Dandridge. Directed by Martha Coolidge. United States: Home Box Office, 1999.
Iron Man. Directed by John Favreau. United States: Paramount Pictures, 2008.
The Jacksons: *An American Dream*. Directed by Karen Arthur. United States: The Stan Marguiles Company, 1992.
Just Mercy. Directed by Destin Daniel Cretton. United States: Warner Bros., 2019.
The Last King of Scotland. Directed by Kevin Macdonald. United Kingdom and Germany: Fox Searchlight Pictures, 2006.
Malcolm X. Directed by Spike Lee. United States and Japan: Warner Bros., 1992.
Marshall. Directed by Reginald Hudlin. United States: Open Road Films, 2017.
Notorious. Directed by George Tillman Jr. United States: Fox Searchlight Pictures, 2009.
Panther. Directed by Mario Van Peebles. United Kingdom and United States: Gramercy Pictures, 1995.
Queen of Katwe. Directed by Mira Nair. United States: Walt Disney Studios Motion Pictures, 2016.
The Rosa Parks Story. Directed by Julie Dash. United States: CBS, 2002.
Thor. Directed by Kenneth Branagh. United States: Paramount, 2011.
Thor: Ragnarok. Directed by Taika Waititi. United States and Australia: Walt Disney Studios Motion Pictures, 2017.
Twelve Years a Slave. Directed by Steve McQueen. United States and United Kingdom: Fox Searchlight Pictures & Entertainment One Films, 2013.
What's Love Got to Do with It. Directed by Brian Gibson. United States: Buena Vista Pictures Distribution, Inc., 1993.
X-Men. Directed by Bryan Singer. United States: 20th Century Fox, 2000.
X-Men: Days of Future Past. Directed by Bryan Singer. United States, United Kingdom, and Canada: 20th Century Fox, 2014.
X-Men: The Last Stand. Directed by Brett Ratner. United States, United Kingdom, and Canada: 20th Century Fox, 2006.
X2: X-Men United. Directed by Bryan Singer. United States: 20th Century Fox, 2003.

Chapter 5

Let Ayo Have a Girlfriend

Resisting Black Lesbian Erasure on Twitter

Sarah E. S. Sinwell

In 2017, when it was announced that Marvel would be releasing Ryan Coogler's *Black Panther* in February 2018, fans were excited that two of the titular character's bodyguards, Ayo and fellow female warrior Okoye, would get together as Ayo and Aneka do in the comics. Roxane Gay and Yona Harvey's spin-off series of *Black Panther* entitled *World of Wakanda* portrayed a love story between Ayo and Aneka, two members of the Dora Milaje, an elite force of female bodyguards for the Black Panther. Though a rough cut of the film portrayed a flirtatious scene between Ayo and another guard, Okoye (played by Danai Gurira), the scene did not make it into the final version of the film. In fact, when a Marvel spokesperson reached out to clearly state that the nature of that relationship between Danai Gurira's Okoye and Florence Kasumba's Ayo in *Black Panther* would not be romantic, this Black lesbian erasure from *Black Panther* sparked outrage among fans of the comic books. Seen as a "missed opportunity" among fans of the comic books to include queer characters within the Marvel universe, these fans of *Black Panther* turned to Twitter to encourage Marvel to #LetAyoHaveAGirlfriend.[1]

Social movements on Twitter function as a contradictory space for political and social advocacy: both facilitating online activism and cultivating online harassment and bullying. Questioning ideas of normative gender, race, and sexuality, this chapter investigates how the Twitter campaign to #LetAyoHaveAGirlfriend is promoting more inclusive and diverse representation in popular media. In an effort to create more racial and sexual visibility online, media fans have taken to Twitter with hashtags like #RepresentationMatters, #WeNeedLGBTQStories, #GiveCaptainAmericaABoyfriend, and #MakeReyAsexual.[2] Creating communities not only of media fandom but also support for both LGBTQIA+ communities and communities of color, these hashtags are also enabling media fans to speak to corporations like Marvel and Disney about issues of diversity and inclusion. At the same time, the #RecastBatwoman and #RallyforRose Twitter campaigns in 2018 exemplify both instances of cyberbullying (#RecastBatwoman) and cyber support (#RallyforRose). In the context of these campaigns, celebrities such as Ruby Rose and Kelly Marie Tran were forced to exit Twitter and other social media amid a backlash over their casting as the first openly lesbian superhero and the first woman of color to have a lead in a *Star Wars* film.

Pushing up against the whiteness and heteronormativity of corporate-sponsored media culture, the campaign to #LetAyoHaveAGirlfriend draws attention not only to the absence of people of color and LGBTQIA+ characters within contemporary media more generally but also to alternative possibilities for inclusive media representation. As a means of discovering the gendered, raced, and sexualized geography of these campaigns, this chapter will map out the cultural language of this Twitter hashtag. At the same time, by (re)defining race, gender, and sexuality within the larger cultural zeitgeist of such franchises as Marvel's *Black Panther*, this essay will argue that these Twitter campaigns advocate for more diversity in contemporary media. Reimagining media representation via these pluralities and intersections enables us to rethink the ways in which identity is constructed in relation to gender, race, and sexuality and creates a space for more inclusive stories within popular culture.

HASHTAG CAMPAIGNS, FANDOM, AND QUEER VISIBILITY

Following the Occupy Wall Street protests in 2011, Eric Augenbraum of *The Guardian* coined the term "hashtag activism" to refer to the new online social movements, such as #OccupyWallStreet and #ArabSpring, that appeared on Twitter at that time.[3] Though he argued that hashtags could be seen as "the birth of a new form of technology-based social movement," he also questioned whether these forms of activism would be as effective as marches, rallies, and protests.[4] With the advent of online social networking sites, the public sphere has shifted from a literal space within communities to a virtual world encouraging larger scale community involvement. Online platforms, such as Facebook, Twitter, and Instagram, transgress the boundaries of how social movements function, raise awareness, and create a public forum where the nature of public participation constantly shifts and is redefined.

In this way, as communication scholar Mark Tremayne has pointed out, "Twitter has emerged as a popular organizing and communication tool for protestors around the world" (2014, 110) including the Tunisian Revolution of 2010–2011, the Egyptian Revolution of 2011, and *Occupy Wall Street* in 2011.[5] The Black Lives Matter hashtag (#BlackLivesMatter or #BLM) from 2013 and the Breonna Taylor hashtag (#SayHerName) from 2015 participate in this hashtag activism by raising awareness about police violence and brutality against people of color. Following the death of George Floyd in 2020, these hashtags have had a resurgence of popularity as issues of racial injustice and systemic racism plague both the United States and the globe. The popularity of Twitter in supporting and maintaining these protest movements worldwide points to the power of social media. In this vein, Twitter has proven to be particularly significant as a means of creating Black and LGBTQIA+ online social movements, protests, and communities. To this end, this chapter addresses such questions as: How can Black and LGBTQIA+ identities be articulated on Twitter? How do fans use hashtags to create a space for their own identities? How does hashtag activism enable possibilities for more representation of Black and LGBTQIA+ communities within popular media such as Marvel and Disney?

As media scholars Abigail De Kosnik and Keith Feldman have noted in *#identity: Hashtagging Race, Gender, Sexuality, and Nation*,

> Ever since, Augenbraun's concept has been applied by participants and supporters, as well as critics, to the practice of raising awareness, fostering a sense of collectivity, and expressing solidarity in relation to political causes via hashtags on Twitter (and other media platforms that make use of hashtags, such as Facebook, Tumblr, and Instagram).[6]

Following this use of hashtags, "Black Twitter" has become an especially noteworthy mode of online participation on Twitter, referring to the phenomenon of African Americans launching trending hashtags such as #BlackLivesMatter, #Ferguson, and #onlyintheghetto.[7] Though many critics have noted that these Twitter users should not be seen as a homogenous group, nor representative of all African Americans, this phenomenon has become a widely studied means of analyzing race, gender, and diversity in contemporary social media.[8] Though not homogeneous, Black Twitter often functions as a separate "universe" within Twitter such that trends can be very different than "non-Black" Twitter. As noted by De Kosnik and Feldman, "Through hashtag after hashtag, Black twitter raised awareness of the prevalence and danger of racism and sexism occurring throughout the United States."[9] In this way, they argue that "new media" is a concept and discourse that simultaneously disavows and stages the ongoing, daily renewal of identity and difference."[10]

This is particularly significant when addressing the gendered, raced, and sexualized identities of online fandoms. As feminist scholars Catherine

Driscoll and Melissa Gregg have noted in "Convergence Culture and the Legacy of Feminist Cultural Studies," the "structuring imperatives of labour and gender" are essential to discussions of new media and convergence cultures.[11] In fact, they argue, "The bottom line of convergence culture is that participation has become something media industries must engage with since consumers are already using existing technologies to break up and reformulate media texts for reasons of their own."[12] At the same time, as digital media scholar Tiziana Terranova argues, "free labor" is "a feature of the cultural economy at large."[13]

The free labor of Marvel and *Black Panther* fans who post on the #LetAyoHaveAGirlfriend hashtag on Twitter creates a space for both Black and LGBTQIA+ representation within these superhero franchises, while at the same time, it also speaks to alternative forms of fandom within the larger fan community. As film and media scholar Suzanne Scott notes in *Fake Geek Girls*, "it is precisely because of the convergence culture industry's gendered depathologization and affirmation of *certain* fans and *certain* fan practices that we must reinvest in and reimagine fan studies' commitment to studying female audiences and feminist modes of fannish resistance."[14]

As feminist media scholars Kaitlynn Mendes, Jessica Ringrose, and Jessalynn Keller have pointed out in their analysis of feminist digital activism and the #MeToo movement, social media platforms serve as a means of dialogue, network, and organizing against contemporary sexism, misogyny, and homophobia. This chapter follows in their footsteps by studying "the public's willingness to engage with *resistance* and *challenges to* sexism, patriarchy and other forms of oppression via feminist uptake of digital communication."[15] This form of resistance via social media and Twitter campaigns also enables online communities to learn about and challenge accepted tropes about race, gender, and sexuality within popular culture. For instance, the use of memes and gifs in these social media campaigns enables both the critique and the re-writing of these narratives, allowing traditional tropes to be inverted and transformed as a means of incorporating more diversity and inclusivity within the Disney and Marvel franchises. The use of digital and hashtag activism enables the possibility of creating community across disparate geographies and transnational locations. At the same time, it also creates an online space for sharing Black and LGBTQIA+ stories and resisting the norms of heteronormative and patriarchal culture.

Numerous media and queer theory scholars from Mary Gray (2009) to Christopher Pullen (2014), to Eve Ng and Julia Levin Russo (2017), have pointed out the ways in which queer youth and queer fans have utilized social media and digital activism to resist gender oppression and homophobia.[16] For instance, in her discussion of feminist digital activism, communication scholar Hester Baer writes,

Digital platforms offer great potential for broadly disseminating feminist ideas, shaping new modes of discourse about gender and sexism, connecting to different constituencies, and allowing creative modes of protest to emerge. The example of hashtag feminism makes clear how the increased use of digital media has altered, influenced, and shaped feminism in the twenty-first century by giving rise to changed modes of communication, different kinds of conversations, and new configurations of activism across the globe, both online and offline.[17]

It is these changing modes of communication, conversation, activism, and protest that this chapter will be investigating.

Since 2010, over 60,000 people have shared their "It Gets Better Stories," a social media initiative to prevent queer youth from committing suicide, in an attempt to remind the next generation of LGBTQ youth that hope is out there (ItGetsBetter.org). As film and media scholar Mark Hain notes in "We Are Here for You: The It Gets Better Project, Queering Rural Space, and Cultivating Queer Media Literacy," this campaign "documents an alternative history, telling a collective story of enduring and overcoming adversity, as communicated by a multicultural, multiperspectival, intergenerational, and international range of voices."[18] This need to make these invisible stories of the LGBTQIA+ community visible extends to a desire to see queer representation not only in online spaces such as Twitter but also in more popular media texts such as those created by Disney and Marvel. In the case of #LetAyoHaveAGirlfriend, members of the queer community are engaging with media representation as a means of promoting queer visibility on film and on Twitter.

The #LetAyoHaveAGirlfriend campaign is not the first time that the LGBTQIA+ community has utilized Twitter to resist homophobia. For instance, the "Bury Your Gays" trope was created in response to the killing off of lesbian characters on series like The CW's *The 100* (2014–present).[19] Additionally, fans of the characters of Brittany and Santana on *Glee* (Fox, 2009–2015) created a Twitter storm that generated enough mainstream attention to will their queer relationship "into canon."[20] Thus, by creating a space for voicing these demands for positive and complex representations of queer characters, Twitter has become a fertile arena for resisting both sexism and heteronormativity. Via the hashtag #LetAyoHaveAGirlfriend, feminist and LGBTQIA+ communities are attempting to transform common (and heteronormative) conceptions about which media texts are appropriate and available within the superhero canon.

The GLAAD 2016 Overview of Findings also points to the lack of LGBTQIA+ characters within contemporary media. "Of the 126 releases GLAAD counted from the major studios in 2015, 22 (17.5%) contained characters identified as lesbian, gay, bisexual, or transgender."[21] In addition, only 8.5 percent of these characters identified as Black or African American. Thus, there is a push for not only the mere presence of LGBTQIA+ and Black characters in the media but also for allowing those characters to be as psychologically complex and complicated as their straight White counterparts. This absence of Black LGBTQIA+ representation has led to multiple other Twitter campaigns that encourage companies, such as Disney and Marvel, to include Black and queer characters within their franchises. Campaigns such as #RepresentationMatters, #WeNeedLGBTQStories, #GiveElsaAGirlfriend, #GiveCaptainAmericaABoyfriend, and #MakeReyAsexual are a call to action from fans to recognize diversity and difference within the Disney and Marvel canon.[22]

Thus, the #LetAyoHaveAGirlfriend Twitter campaign is an attempt to continue in the vein of the "It Gets Better Project" and other online social movements by resisting the status quo and providing more Black and queer representations within the media. However, advocating for the representation of racial difference and queerness within the media becomes particularly difficult in the face of the family-friendly, gender-conforming, heteronormative Disney machine.[23] In light of this, it is all the more powerful to examine how the #LetAyoHaveAGirlfriend campaign (a) reframes stories and histories of racial and sexual identities, (b) creates a space for Black lesbians within Marvel and Disney media, (c) comments upon the intersectionality (or lack thereof) of the superhero genre.

BLACK PANTHER, RACIAL HISTORIES, AND RESISTANCE

Writing of *Black Panther*'s depiction of an African utopia and arguing for a reimagining of the ways in which sexuality also constructs racial difference and vice versa, critical race scholar Andrew Carrington "interrogates how race consciousness and colonial legacies inform the discourses of desire operating within the text."[24] To this end, Carrington argues for the need for Black queer visibility and re-envisions the ways in which these identities have been represented in the popular imagination through the concept of *desiring blackness*.[25] For Carrington, desiring blackness draws attention to the intersections between blackness and queerness while also creating a space for how interpretation and the production of meaning impact these texts. Within the context of fandoms, Black and LGBTQIA+ audiences of *Black Panther* insist upon representing Black lesbian identity within the film precisely because of its presence within comic book canon.

While homosexuality was seen as an affront to "African values" in the postcolonial era, in *Black Panther*, these forms of difference create a space for rethinking and reimagining African pasts and futures.[26] This blending of the traditional and modern extends to the film's representation of both race and sexuality.[27] Providing this afro-futurist alternative of reality both acknowledges the precolonial African past, while at the same time denying its present.[28] Within Ta-Nehisi Coates's *Black Panther* 2016 comic books, the all-female elite bodyguards Aneka and Ayo are not only given a lesbian relationship, but they are also portrayed as mutineers who have reclaimed their power in defiance of the Black Panther.[29] These intersections between blackness, power, and queerness reinscribe value onto these "Otherized" characters. As Carrington writes, "the terms black and queer also prove imprecise but evocative as descriptors for the text's utopian orientation to modernity and its multiple geographies."[30] While the comic books' investment in these terms is multilayered and problematic, the fans' investment via the #LetAyoHaveAGirlfriend Twitter campaign positions Black lesbian identity in an in-between space, one that is constantly vacillating between its hyper-awareness of racial and sexual difference and its erasure.

Through these Twitter fandoms and hashtags, *Black Panther* fans also participate in (re)producing cultural meaning and (re)creating alternative imaginaries for Black queer representation. At the same time, the desire to incorporate a politics of inclusion within the Marvel and *Black Panther* franchises also speaks to the complexity of the relationships between fandoms and the media and convergence cultures industries. As media scholar John Fiske argues, fandom is a space of "constant struggle between fans and the industry, in which the industry attempts to incorporate the tastes of the fans, and the fans to 'excorporate' the products of the industry."[31] In fact, film and media scholar Derek Johnson coined the term "fan-tagonism" to describe "ongoing, competitive struggles between both internal factions and external institutions to discursively codify the fan-text-producer relationship according to their respective interests."[32] Addressing these interrelationships between the fans and industries, the #LetAyoHaveAGirlfriend Twitter campaign speaks to the ways in which fans both respond to and influence current media texts.

As communication and media scholars Annemarie Navar-Gill and Mel Stanfill write, "Regardless of the degree to which queer fan hashtag campaigns are successful in provoking industrial reflection, however, their careful coordination shows many fans are aware of industrial discourses about the value of social media, the affordances of platforms they employ, and current best practices in social media marketing."[33] Thus, when fans of *Black Panther* took to Twitter to resist the erasure of Black lesbians from the Marvel canon, this also led to a direct response from Marvel's spokespeople. This complicates the relationship between fans and the industry even further as fans are able to "talk back" to the industry via these social media campaigns.³⁴ In fact, other Twitter campaigns, such as #MakeReyAsexual and #GiveElsaAGirlfriend, have elicited responses from Disney as well.³⁵ This dialectical relationship between the fans and industries also points to the ways in which fans' responses on social media may also create a space for marginalized identities. As fan scholar Alexis Lothian writes,

> To look queerly at fannish temporalities is to attend to moments in which they refuse narratives of development and progress by which particular moments in media and LGBT history are seen as passing into irrelevance; reconfigure norms of gender and sexuality; and use the affective technology of fannish love to build spaces that both reproduce and subvert dominant economies."³⁶

Thus, I argue that the #LetAyoHaveAGirlfriend campaign creates a space for Black lesbians within Marvel media and self-reflexively comments upon the intersectionality (or lack thereof) of the superhero genre.

FANDOM, RACE, AND LESBIAN IDENTITY: ANALYZING THE #LETAYOHAVEAGIRLFRIEND CAMPAIGN

The #LetAyoHaveAGirlfriend Campaign started in 2017 following the announcement of the release of Marvel's *Black Panther*. Reports at early screenings of *Black Panther* showed a possible romantic relationship between T'Challa's female bodyguards Ayo and Aneka. As noted in *Pink News*, "And these hopes were encouraged by reports that an early screening of the film featured *Walking Dead* star Danai Gurira's Okoye staring at Ayo flirtatiously as the two danced."³⁷ Following these accounts of fan outrage over the erasure of these characters' sexual identities, a Marvel spokesperson reached out to clearly state that "the nature of the relationship between Danai Gurira's Okoye and Florence Kasumba's Ayo in *Black Panther* is not a romantic one."³⁸

In 2015, though President of Marvel Studios Kevin Feige "promised that 'in the next decade or sooner' one of its films will feature an LGBT character,"³⁹ and despite the presence of Black lesbians Ayo and Aneka within the Marvel canon, Ryan Coogler's 2018 film did not enable those characters to relay even the possibility of romance. As Pink News reporter Joshua Jackson writes, "Many Marvel supporters pointed out that there are not many more organic ways to include LGBT characters like Ayo than to simply include them with their original sexuality."⁴⁰ This erasure of Black lesbian identities serves as a reminder of Suzanne Scott's concern about boundary-policing practices based on race, class, gender, sexuality, etc. within fandoms, while at the same time, it also draws attention to the limits of the Marvel industrial machine.⁴¹

Eve Ng uses the concept of "queer contextuality" to explain how media industries engage with these narratives, arguing that it "informs how viewers assess (1) the validity of reading queerness in a text, (2) the political and economic feasibility (particularly in regard to studio and network financial considerations) of having a canonical LGBT narrative, and (3) the quality of the canonical LGBT narratives that are produced."[42] The #LetAyoHaveAGirlfriend campaign insists upon the inclusion of Ayo and Okoye's lesbian relationship precisely because of its existence within the canon.[43]

For instance, many Twitter users of the #LetAyoHaveAGirlfriend hashtag pointed out the ways that Marvel erased Black lesbianism from the canon.[44] Other Twitter users pointed out that even the fans themselves are participating in the erasure of queer women and queer people of color from the franchise. For example, one Twitter user posted, "y'all love erasing representation don't ya? im tired of y'all #LetAyoHaveAGirlfriend." Whereas many fans were willing to post on the #GiveCaptainAmericaABoyfriend hashtag, those who posted in favor of the #LetAyoHaveAGirlfriend hashtag contended that because the characters were both Black and lesbian, they were less likely to be represented (or even hashtagged) than their White male counterparts.

In fact, as many film and media critics, including Alfred L. Martin, Jr., Rukmini Pande, Kristen Warner, and Mel Stanfill have pointed out, much of fan culture discourses revolve around masculinity, heteronormativity, and whiteness.[45] As Martin argues, "The desire for visibility, particularly in spaces that have typically been inhospitable to racialized bodies, drives many Black people's fandom."[46] In the case of #LetAyoHaveAGirlfriend, many fans are self-aware of these absences and erasures, drawing attention to the need to acknowledge the straightwashed, whitewashed, and male-washed nature of these campaigns.[47] While, Other fans place the blame on the industry itself, debating the nature of the risk-averse Marvel universe.[48]

As Navar-Gill and Stanfill have argued, the fans' familiarity with the industry and how it functions in relation to social media and online networking also impacts the ways in which fans engage with media texts and their many histories and futures.[49] For example, many Twitter users post articles from *Vanity Fair*, *Comic Book Now*, and other magazines and encourage Marvel to take risks with their storytelling and representation. Twitter campaigns such as #LetAyoHaveAGirlfriend are attempting to create a space for Black and LGBTQIA+ communities to (re)imagine themselves, their (hi) stories, and their experiences and share them with the larger fan community. In these campaigns, the intersections between race and sexuality are (re) envisioned as a means of creating a social movement and a network of public visibility. At the same time, by defining Black LGBTQIA+ identity within the larger cultural zeitgeist of such franchises as *Black Panther*, these Twitter campaigns are a means of further promoting Black and queer visibility. Reimagining Black and queer sexualities within the Marvel canon enables us to rethink the ways in which blackness and queerness are constructed in relation to media franchises and creates a space for LGBTQIA+ "coming out" online.

NOTES

1. Daniel Reynolds, "Don't Forget Roxane Gay (and Queer Superheroes), Hollywood," *The Advocate*, February 15, 2018, https://www.advocate.com/media/2018/2/15/dont-forget-roxane-gay-and-queer-superheroes-hollywood.

2. #MakeReyAsexual refers to the character of Rey in *Star Wars: The Force Awakens* (J.J. Abrams, 2015).

3. Eric Augenbraun, "Occupy Wall Street and the Limits of Spontaneous Street Protest," *The Guardian*, September 29, 2011, https://www.theguardian.com/commentisfree/cifamerica/2011/sep/29/occupy-wall-street-protest.

4. Augenbraun, "Occupy Wall Street and the Limits of Spontaneous Street Protest."

5. Mark Tremayne, "Anatomy of Protest in the Digital Era: A Network Analysis of *Twitter* and Occupy Wall Street," *Social Movement Studies* 13, no. 1 (2014): 110.

6. Abigail De Kosnik and Keith Feldman, "Introduction: The Hashtags We've BeenForced to Remember," in *#identity: Hashtagging Race, Gender, Sexuality, and Nation,* eds. Abigail De Kosnik and Keith Feldman (Ann Arbor: University of Michigan Press, 2019), 5. Journalist Eric Augenbraun coined the term "hashtag activism" when writing about the Occupy Wall Street protests for *The Guardian* in 2011. See Augenbraun, "Occupy Wall Street and the Limits of Spontaneous Street Protest."

7. See Andre Brock, "From the Blackhand Side: Twitter as Cultural Conversation," *Journal of Broadcasting and Electronic Media* 56, no. 4 (2012): 529–549 and Abigail De Kosnik and Keith Feldman, eds., *#identity: Hashtagging Race, Gender, Sexuality, and Nation* (Ann Arbor: University of Michigan Press, 2019).

8. See Brock, "From the Blackhand Side: Twitter as Cultural Conversation," 529–549 and Sarah Florini, "Tweets, Tweeps, and Signifyin': Communication and Cultural Performance on 'Black Twitter,'" *Television and New Media* 15, no. 3 (2013): 223–237.

9. De Kosnik and Feldman, "Introduction: The Hashtags We've Been Forced to Remember," 7.

10. De Kosnik and Feldman, "Introduction: The Hashtags We've Been Forced to Remember," 11.

11. Catherine Driscoll and Melissa Gregg, "Convergence Culture and the Legacy of Feminist Cultural Studies," *Cultural Studies* 25, no. 4–5 (2011): 567.

12. Driscoll and Gregg, "Convergence Culture and the Legacy of Feminist Cultural Studies," *Cultural Studies*. 574.

13. Tiziana Terranova, "Free Labor," in *Digital Labor: The Internet as Playground*, ed. Trebor Scholz (New York and London: Routledge, 2012), 68.

14. Suzanne Scott, *Fake Geek Girls: Fandom, Gender, and the Convergence Culture Industry* (New York: New York University Press, 2019), 47.

15. Kaitlynn Mendes, Jessica Ringrose, and Jessalynn Keller, "#MeToo and the promise and pitfalls of challenging rape culture through feminist digital activism," *European Journal of Women's Studies* 23, no. 2 (2018): 236–246.

16. See Mary L. Gray, *Out in the Country: Youth, Media, and Queer Visibility in Rural America* (New York: New York University Press, 2009), Christopher Pullen, ed., *Queer Youth and Media Cultures* (New York: Palgrave MacMillan, 2014), and Eve Ng and Julie Levin Russo, "Envisioning Queer Female Fandom" [editorial], *Transformative Works and Cultures,* no. 24 (2017).

17. Hester Baer, "Redoing Feminism: Digital Activism, Body Politics, and Neoliberalism," *Feminist Media Studies* 16, no. 1 (2016): 18.

18. Mark Hain, "We Are Here for You: The It Gets Better Project, Queering Rural Space, and Cultivating Queer Media Literacy," in *Queering the Countryside: New Frontiers in Rural Queer Studies,* ed. Mary L. Gray, Colin R. Johnson, Brian J. Gilley (New York: New York University Press, 2016), 162.

19. Erin Waggoner, "Bury Your Gays and Social Media Fan Response: Television, LGBTQ Representation, and Communitarian Ethics," *Journal of Homosexuality* 65, no. 13 (2017): 1877–1891.

20. Ng and Russo, "Envisioning Queer Female Fandom."

21. "Overview of Findings," GLAAD, https://www.glaad.org/sri/2016/overview.

22. See Mia Galuppa, "#GiveElsaAGirlfriend to 'Finding Dory': The Online Push for LGBT Characters in Animated Movies," *The Hollywood Reporter,* June 2, 2016, https://www.hollywoodreporter.com/news/finding-dory-frozen-lgbt-characters-898354.

23. See Henry Giroux and Grace Pollack, *The Mouse that Roared: Disney and the End of Innocence* (Roman and Littlefield, 2010); Carmen Lugo-Lugo and Mary Bloodsworth-Lugo, "'Look Out New World, Here We Come'? Race, Racialization, and Sexuality in Four Children's Animated Films by Disney, Pixar, and Dreamworks," *Cultural Studies <=> Critical Methodologies* 9, no. 2 (2009): 166–178; and Craig McGill, "'This Burning Desire is Turning Me to Sin': The Intrapersonal Sexual Struggles of Two Disney Singing Villains," *Queer Studies in Media & Popular Culture* 3, no. 1 (2018): 27–49.

24. Andrew Carrington, "Desiring Blackness: A Queer Orientation to Marvel's *Black Panther*, 1998-2016," *American Literature* 90, no. 2 (2018): 221.

25. Carrington, "Desiring Blackness."

26. Carrington, "Desiring Blackness," 237.

27. See Tim Posada, "Afrofuturism, Power, and Marvel Comics's *Black Panther*," *Journal of Popular Culture* 52, no. 3 (2019): 625–644 and Robert A. Saunders, "(Profitable) imaginaries of Black Power: The popular and political geographies of *Black Panther*," *Political Geography* 69 (2019): 139–149.

28. Carrington, "Desiring Blackness," 244.

29. Ta-Nehisi Coates, writer, and Chris Sprouse, penciller, *Black Panther*, no. 1 (New York: Marvel Comics, 2016).

30. Carrington, "Desiring Blackness," 235.

31. John Fiske, "The Cultural Economy of Fandom," in *The Adoring Audience: Fan Culture and Popular Media,* ed. Lisa K. Lewis (New York and London: Routledge, 1992), 38.

32. Derek Johnson, "Fan-tagonism: Factions, Institutions, and Constitutive Hegemonies of Fandom," in *Fandom: Identities and Communities in a Mediated World*, eds. Jonathan Gray, Cornell Sandvoss, and C. Lee Harrington (New York: New York University Press, 2017), 287.

33. Annemarie Navar-Gill and Mel Stanfill, "'We Shouldn't Have to Trend to Make You Listen': Queer Fan Hashtag Campaigns as Production Interventions," *Journal of Film and Video* 70, no. 3–4 (Fall/Winter 2018): 90.

34. See Henry Jenkins, *Textual Poachers: Television Fans and Participatory Culture* (New York and London: Routledge, 2012) and *Convergence Culture: Where Old and New Media Collide* (New York: New York University Press, 2008).

35. See Maria Cavasutto, "Idina Menzel Responds to Campaign to Give 'Frozen's' Elsa a Girlfriend," *Variety*, May 23, 2016, https://variety.com/2016/film/news/idina-menzel-give-elsa-a-girlfriend-frozen-sequel-1201781433/; Mia Galuppa, "#GiveElsaAGirlfriend to 'Finding Dory': The Online Push for LGBT Characters in Animated Movies," *The Hollywood Reporter*, June 2, 2016, https://www.hollywoodreporter.com/news/finding-dory-frozen-lgbt-characters-898354; and Bill Bradley, "'Frozen' Director Gives Glimmer Of Hope Elsa Could Get A Girlfriend," *Huffington Post*, February 26, 2018, https://www.huffingtonpost.com/entry/frozen-director-elsa-girlfriend_us_5a9388c5e4b01e9e56bd1ead.

36. Alexis Lothian, "Sex, Utopia, and the Queer Temporalities of Fannish Love," in *Fandom: Identities and Communities in a Mediated World*, eds. Jonathan Gray, Cornell Sandvoss, and C. Lee Harrington (New York: New York University Press, 2017), 239.

37. Josh Jackman, "Marvel's lesbian 'erasure' from Black Panther film sparks fan outrage," *Pink News*, April 21, 2017, https://www.pinknews.co.uk/2017/04/21/marvels-lesbian-erasure-from-black-panther-film-sparks-fan-outrage/.

38. Jackman, "Marvel's lesbian 'erasure' from Black Panther film sparks fan outrage."

39. Sarah Charleton, "Marvel boss reveals a film 'will feature an LGBT character' in future," *Pink News*, June 30, 2015, https://www.pinknews.co.uk/2015/06/30/marvel-boss-reveals-a-film-will-feature-an-lgbt-character-in-future/.

40. Jackman, "Marvel's lesbian 'erasure' from Black Panther film sparks fan outrage."

41. Scott, *Fake Geek Girls*.

42. Eve Ng, "Between Text, Paratext, and Context: Queerbaiting and the Contemporary Media Landscape," *Transformative Works and Cultures*, no. 24 (2017).

43. See Alexander Doty, *Flaming Classics: Queering the Film Canon* (New York and London: Routledge, 2000).

44.
marvel: we want to be faithful to the source material ayo: canonically gay marvel: i cant read suddenly i dont know #LetAyoHaveAGirlfriend

marvel 2015: lgbtq stories will happen when it's ~organic marvel 2017: adapting Ayo but no room for queer story #LetAyoHaveAGirlfriend

I'm ready to fight for #LetAyoHaveAGirlfriend because she already has one in the comics, so please @MarvelStudios don't erase that.

> #LetAyoHaveAGirlfriend STOP ERASING CANON QUEER RELATIONSHIPS AND CHARACTERS
>
> Roses are red Wakanda is rad But let's remind @MarvelStudios Queer erasure is bad #LetAyoHaveAGirlfriend

45. See Alfred L. Martin, Jr., "Fandom while Black: Misty Copeland, *Black Panther*, Tyler Perry and the Contours of US black fandoms," *International Journal of Cultural Studies* 22, no. 6 (2019): 747–753; Mel Stanfill, "Doing Fandom, (Mis)doing Whiteness: Heteronormativity, Racialization, and the Discursive Construction of Fandom," *Transformative Works and Cultures*, no. 8 (2011); Kristen Warner, *The Cultural Politics of Colorblind TV Casting* (New York and London: Routledge, 2015); and Rukmini Pande, *Squee from the Margins: Fandom and Race* (Iowa City, IA: University of Iowa Press, 2018).

46. Martin, "Fandom while Black," *International Journal of Cultural Studies*, 750.

47.
> can like half of the fandom just admit they don't actually care about real rep if it's not their white m/m ship #LetAyoHaveAGirlfriend
>
> @ MCU, stop forcing heterosexual ships and let the existing LGBT+ ships be brought to life in your portrayals! #LetAyoHaveAGirlfriend
>
> y'all been petitioning for cap to get a boyfriend but now that there's a black gay woman thats canon u don't care? #LetAyoHaveAGirlfriend
>
> remember when yall cared about rep when it came to your white m/m ship you could fetishise? its your time to shine #LetAyoHaveAGirlfriend
>
> Not anymore... so please speak out!! Make #LetAyoHaveAGirlfriend bigger than the cap hashtag. Ayo shouldnt be straightwashed.

48. When it comes to bringing LGBT representation to a broader audience, they call it "a risk." But isn't it their responsibility to elevate the standards and change people's perceptions? #LetAyoHaveAGirlfriend

> @Marvel if you're going to adapt a LESBIAN CHARACTER you can't just omit the fact that she's lesbian honey #LetAyoHaveAGirlfriend
>
> @MarvelStudios can bring a dead white man back to life but not let a canon lgbt character show interest in a woman? #LetAyoHaveAGirlfriend

49. Navar-Gill and Stanfill, "We Shouldn't Have to Trend to Make You Listen," *Journal of Film and Video*, 90.

WORKS CITED

Augenbraun, Eric. "Occupy Wall Street and the Limits of Spontaneous Street Protest." *The Guardian,* September 29, 2011. https://www.theguardian.com/commentisfree/cifamerica/2011/sep/29/occupy-wall-street-protest.

Baer, Hester. "Redoing Feminism: Digital Activism, Body Politics, and Neoliberalism." *Feminist Media Studies* 16, no. 1 (2016): 17–34.

Booth, Paul. *Digital Fandoms: New Media Studies*. New York: Peter Lang, 2010.

Bradley, Bill. "'Frozen' Director Gives Glimmer of Hope Elsa Could Get A Girlfriend." *Huffington Post*, February 26, 2018. https://www.huffingtonpost.com/entry/frozen-director-elsa-girlfriend_us_5a9388c5e4b01e9e56bd1ead.

Brock, Andre. "From the Blackhand Side: Twitter as Cultural Conversation." *Journal of Broadcasting and Electronic Media* 56, no. 4 (2012): 529–549.

Carrington, Andre. "Desiring Blackness: A Queer Orientation to Marvel's *Black Panther*, 1998-2016." *American Literature* 90, no. 1 (2018): 221–250.

Cavasutto, Maria. "Idina Menzel Responds to Campaign to Give 'Frozen's' Elsa a Girlfriend." *Variety*, May 23, 2016. https://variety.com/2016/film/news/idina-menzel-give-elsa-a-girlfriend-frozen-sequel-1201781433/.

Charleton, Sarah. "Marvel boss reveals a film 'will feature an LGBT character' in future." *Pink News*, June 30, 2015. https://www.pinknews.co.uk/2015/06/30/marvel-boss-reveals-a-film-will-feature-an-lgbt-character-in-future/.

Coates, Ta-Nehisi, writer, and Chris Sprouse, penciller. *Black Panther*, no. 1. New York: Marvel Comics, 2016.

Cokely, Carrie. "'Someday My Prince Will Come:' Disney, the Heterosexual Imaginary, and Animated Film." In *Thinking Straight: The Power and Paradox of Heterosexuality*, edited by Chrys Ingraham, 167–181. New York and London: Routledge, 2004.

Chun, Wendy. "Race and/as Technology: or How to Do Things to Race." *Camera Obscura* 70, no. 1 (2009): 7–34.

Doty, Alexander. *Flaming Classics: Queering the Film Canon*. New York and London: Routledge, 2000.

Driscoll, Catherine and Melissa Gregg. "Convergence Culture and the Legacy of Feminist Cultural Studies." *Cultural Studies* 25, no. 4–5 (2011): 566–584.

Fiske, John. "The Cultural Economy of Fandom." In *The Adoring Audience: Fan Culture and Popular Media*, edited by Lisa K. Lewis. New York and London: Routledge, 1992.

Florini, Sarah. "Tweets, Tweeps, and Signifyin': Communication and Cultural Performance on "Black Twitter."" *Television and New Media* 15, no. 3 (2013): 223–237.

Galuppa, Mia. "#GiveElsaAGirlfriend to 'Finding Dory': The Online Push for LGBT Characters in Animated Movies." *The Hollywood Reporter*, June 2, 2016. https://www.hollywoodreporter.com/news/finding-dory-frozen-lgbt-characters-898354.

Giroux, Henry and Grace Pollack. *The Mouse that Roared: Disney and the End of Innocence*. Rowman and Littlefield, 2010.

GLAAD. "Overview of Findings." https://www.glaad.org/sri/2016/overview.

Gray, Mary L. *Out in the Country: Youth, Media, and Queer Visibility in Rural America*. New York: New York University Press, 2009.

Hain, Mark. "We Are Here for You: The It Gets Better Project, Queering Rural Space, and Cultivating Queer Media Literacy." In *Queering the Countryside: New Frontiers in Rural Queer Studies*, edited by Mary L. Gray, Colin R. Johnson, Brian J. Gilley, 161–180. New York: New York University Press, 2016.

Jackman, Josh. "Marvel's lesbian 'erasure' from Black Panther film sparks fan outrage." *Pink News*, April 21, 2017. https://www.pinknews.co.uk/2017/04/21/marvels-lesbian-erasure-from-black-panther-film-sparks-fan-outrage/.

Jenkins, Henry. *Convergence Cultures: Where Old and New Media Collide.* New York: New York University Press, 2008.
Jenkins, Henry. *Textual Poachers: Television Fans and Participatory Culture.* New York and London: Routledge, 2012.
Johnson, Derek, "Fan-tagonism: Factions, Institutions, and Constitutive Hegemonies of Fandom." In *Fandom: Identities and Communities in a Mediated World*, edited by Jonathan Gray, Cornell Sandvoss, and C. Lee Harrington. New York: New York University Press, 2017.
Kosnik, Abigail De, and Keith Feldman, eds. *#identity: Hashtagging Race, Gender, Sexuality, and Nation.* Ann Arbor: University of Michigan Press, 2019.
Kosnik, Abigail De, and Keith Feldman, "Introduction: The Hashtags We've Been Forced to Remember." In *#identity: Hashtagging Race, Gender, Sexuality, and Nation*, edited by Abigail De Kosnik and Keith Feldman, 1–19. Ann Arbor: University of Michigan Press, 2019.
Lothian, Alexis. "Sex, Utopia, and the Queer Temporalities of Fannish Love." In *Fandom: Identities and Communities in a Mediated World*, edited by Jonathan Gray, Cornell Sandvoss, and C. Lee Harrington. New York: New York University Press, 2017.
Lugo-Lugo, Carmen and Mary Bloodsworth-Lugo. "'Look Out New World, Here We Come'? Race, Racialization, and Sexuality in Four Children's Animated Films by Disney, Pixar, and Dreamworks." *Cultural Studies <=> Critical Methodologies* 9, no. 2 (2009): 166–178.
Marwick, Alice and Danah Boyd. "To See and Be Seen: Celebrity Practice on Twitter." *Convergences* 17, no. 11 (2011): 139–158.
Martin, Jr., Alfred L. "Fandom while Black: Misty Copeland, Black Panther, Tyler Perry and the Contours of US Black Fandoms." *International Journal of Cultural Studies* 22, no. 6 (2019): 747–753.
McGill, Craig. "'This Burning Desire is Turning Me to Sin': The Intrapersonal Sexual Struggles of Two Disney Singing Villains." *Queer Studies in Media & Popular Culture* 3, no. 1 (2018): 27–49.
Mendes, Kaitlynn, Jessica Ringrose, and Jessalynn Keller. "#MeToo and the Promise and Pitfalls of Challenging Rape Culture through Feminist Digital Activism." *European Journal of Women's Studies* 23, no. 2 (2018): 236–246.
Monaghan, Whitney. *Queer Girls, Temporality, and Screen Media.* London: Palgrave Macmillan, 2016.
Navar-Gill, Annemarie and Mel Stanfill. ""We Shouldn't Have to Trend to Make You Listen": Queer Fan Hashtag Campaigns as Production Interventions." *Journal of Film and Video* 70, no. 3–4 (Fall/Winter 2018): 85–100.
Ng, Eve. "Between Text, Paratext, and Context: Queerbaiting and the Contemporary Media Landscape." *Transformative Works and Cultures*, no. 24 (2017).
Ng, Eve, and Julie Levin Russo. "Envisioning Queer Female Fandom" [editorial]. *Transformative Works and Cultures*, no. 24 (2017).
Pande, Rukmini. *Squee from the Margins: Fandom and Race.* Iowa City, IA: University of Iowa Press, 2018.
Posada, Tim. "Afrofuturism, Power, and Marvel Comics's *Black Panther*." *Journal of Popular Culture* 52, no. 3 (2019): 625–644.

Pullen, Christopher, ed. *Queer Youth and Media Cultures*. New York: Palgrave MacMillan, 2014.

Reynolds, Daniel. "Don't Forget Roxane Gay (and Queer Superheroes), Hollywood." *The Advocate*, February 15, 2018. https://www.advocate.com/media/2018/2/15/dont-forget-roxane-gay-and-queer-superheroes-hollywood.

Saunders, Robert A. "(Profitable) Imaginaries of Black Power: The Popular and Political Geographies of *Black Panther*." *Political Geography* 69 (2019): 139–149.

Scott, Suzanne. *Fake Geek Girls: Fandom, Gender, and the Convergence Culture Industry*. New York: New York University Press, 2019.

Stanfill, Mel. "Doing Fandom, (mis)doing Whiteness: Heteronormativity, Racialization, and the Discursive Construction of Fandom." *Transformative Works and Cultures*, no. 8 (2011).

Terranova, Tiziana. "Free Labor." In *Digital Labor: The Internet as Playground*, edited by Trebor Scholz. New York and London: Routledge, 2012.

Tremayne, Mark. "Anatomy of Protest in the Digital Era: A Network Analysis of Twitter and Occupy Wall Street." *Social Movement Studies* 13, no. 1 (2014): 110–126.

Waggoner, Erin. "Bury Your Gays and Social Media Fan Response: Television, LGBTQ Representation, and Communitarian Ethics." *Journal of Homosexuality* 65, no. 13 (2017): 1877–1891.

Warner, Kristen. *The Cultural Politics of Colorblind TV Casting*. New York and London: Routledge, 2015.

Warner, Kristen. "In the Time of Plastic Representation." *Film Quarterly* 71, no. 2 (Winter 2017): 32–37.

Warner, Michael. "Introduction." In *Fear of a Queer Planet: Queer Politics and Social Theory,* edited by Michael Warner. Minneapolis: University of Minnesota Press, 1993.

FILMS AND TELEVISION

The 100. Created and Produced by Jason Rothenberg. Aired March 19, 2014, on The CW.

Black Panther. Directed by Ryan Coogler. United States: Walt Disney Studio Motion Pictures, 2018.

Glee. Created and Produced by Ryan Murphy. Aired March 19, 2009, on Fox.

Star Wars: The Force Awakens. Directed by J.J. Abrams. United States: Walt Disney Studio Motion Pictures, 2015.

The Walking Dead. Created and Produced by Frank Darabont. Aired October 31, 2010, on AMC.

Chapter 6

"Tell Me a Story Baba"
Black Panther *and Wakanda's Foreign Policy in the Age of Neoliberalism*

Clarence Lusane

Black Panther is one of the most important and impactful movies of our time.[1] It stands out for many reasons not the least of which is its popularity. *Destroy the Comics* website editor Suni Muni estimated, using box office sales and dividing by average ticket prices domestically and in individual countries, that more than 175 million saw the film in 2018 just in theaters.[2] By the end of 2018, the movie took in more than $1 billion including $700,426,566 in domestic box office and $1,347,597,973 in international box office receipts.[3] These figures do not include DVD and Blue-ray sales nor streaming revenue that are also significant. *Black Panther* became the highest grossing superhero movie of all time.[4] According to *Variety*, the film was the "fifth highest-grossing movie ever" in the United States.[5] Following the tragic August 2020 cancer-related death of Chadwick Boseman, who played the role of the Black Panther, the film topped both Amazon and Apple's sales charts.[6]

Beyond the numbers, the film is visually stunning, brilliantly performed, and aesthetically precise. It held special meaning for people of African descent who have endured decades of Hollywood films that have denigrated or stereotyped Africa and African people. As film scholar and Loyola Marymount University professor Jennifer Williams argues, the Afrofuturist film was a qualitative rebuke of superhero movies by centralizing people of African descent in position of authority, agency, excellence, and vision. She writes, notably in *Foreign Policy* magazine, "To reimagine colonization from the position of the historically colonized is a brave new world of science fiction."[7] It was an act of artistic decolonialization. Few cultural or political events have received such celebratory outpouring of the global Black community as *Black Panther*. One thinks of the release of Nelson Mandela in 1990 from prison, setting the path to end Apartheid in South Africa or the election of Barack Obama as the first U.S. president of color in 2008.

The film tells a multitude of stories about race, gender, state authority, democracy, family, and, yes, global politics. From an international relations perspective, the filmmakers raise a question that is at the very center of the film's narrative arc: What should be the foreign policy of a technologically, all-powerful, yet secretive Black nation? The tension between key characters, shaped by racial, ideological, and even familial issues, focuses on the resolution of this concern.

BLACK PANTHER AND THE NEOLIBERAL REALITY

The prologue to the film sets up this narrative direction. It begins with the old king's brother, N'Jobu (Sterling K. Brown) who is living in Oakland, California, talking to his son, N'Jadaka, (Seth Carr):

N'Jadaka: Baba.
N'Jobu: Yes, my son.
N'Jadaka: Tell me a story.
N'Jobu: Which one?
N'Jadaka: The story of home.[8]

N'Jobu tells the creation story of how Wakanda was blessed with vibranium, a substance found in an extraterrestrial meteorite that crashed to earth, and how it built the nation into an advanced society steeped in African traditions. This is consistent with the comic books for the most part.[9] N'Jobu next tells his son that Wakanda must protect itself by keeping isolated:

N'Jadaka: "And we still hide Baba?
N'Jobu: "Yes."
N'Jadaka: "Why?"[10]

There is no answer.

The film locates itself in the contemporary era and, therefore, exists in the very real world of global neoliberalism. In the 1930s, in the middle of the Great Depression, economist John Maynard Keynes, in his now classic work, *The General Theory of Employment, Interest and Money,* called for state intervention to save market economies on the brink of total collapse including in the United States.[11] In exchange for labor peace and stability, governments expanded labor rights, developed massive social service policies and programs, such as unemployment payments and social security, and built national healthcare systems (with the United States being a notable exception). For half a century, this bargain shaped domestic and global economic and political relations. Keynesianism, as it became known, witnessed increasing democratic rights as labor unions and popular social movements pushed for more benefits.

However, there was always a counter-movement to this trend: neoliberalism. The theory and ideology of neoliberalism, as articulated by its founders in the late 1930s, called for liberating the economy from regulation, political constraints, and any other forms of state-determined monetary control.[12] It advocated for unrestrained market relations to determine not only the nature of the economy but in other social, cultural, and political areas as well. By the 1970s, political and economic crises in Chile, Argentina, and elsewhere provided conditions for a transition where welfare state programs, regulations, and democratic guardrails came under attack and in many instances, figuratively and literally, were overthrown. Democratically elected leftist president Salvador Allende was toppled in a United States-backed military coup in Chile on September 11, 1973, an iconic date that was perhaps as globally impactful as that same date twenty-eight years later. Shortly after Allende's violent ouster, conservative trained economists from the University of Chicago took control of the economy. Writer Naomi Klein calls this and other similar political calamities and how they were exploited *disaster capitalism* and details how they were taken advantage of to impose neoliberal policies that otherwise would have been unacceptable.[13]

The twenty-first-century global world in which the *Black Panther* occurs is one where social cushions have been disappearing, worker's rights have been compromised, climate death is looming, social justice marginalized, wealth inequality is growing, democracy is eroding, right-wing movements are surging, and racial equality deprioritized. The United States and global uprisings of 2020, which saw protests in every state and dozens of nations in response to the murders of unarmed Black individuals, but also racial and economic inequality overall, reflected the embrace of *Black Panther* and its positive, uplifting blackness. Nearly all human relations have become commodified, transactional, and financialized. As writer George Monbiot argues, neoliberalism is the "ideology at the root of all our problems."[14] In his classic work on neoliberalism, David Harvey defines it as

> a theory of political economic practices that proposes that human well-being can best be advanced by liberating individual entrepreneurial freedoms and skills within an institutional framework characterized by strong private property rights, free markets, and free trade. The role of the state is to create and preserve an institutional framework appropriate to such practices.[15]

This is a formula to benefit the infamous "one percent," not the masses or majority of working people. New technologies and the fall of the Soviet Union and other communist states facilitated the speed by which the theory and practice of market fundamentalism and marketization became hegemonic. As with other conservatives, neoliberals are not against the state but want to employ state mechanisms and power to advance ruling class interests.

The implementation of this thesis victimized, initially, the developing world, especially Africa and the Americas, through the policies of the International Financial Institutions (World Bank, International Monetary Fund, World Trade Organization, etc.), rapacious transnational corporations, and bilateral and multilateral agreements. Narratives of corruption, malfeasance, dictatorial leadership, and incompetence against developing states masked the systemic nature of the thievery of neoliberalism and its proponents. The neoliberalism menu included privatization, tax cuts for those who did not need them, budget cuts, and erosion of services accompanied by a rhetoric of personal responsibility and individualism. Wealth moved upward and developing nations and their people suffered.[16] As the U.S. House of Representatives Committee on the Budget reported, 83 percent of the benefits of the Trump-GOP 2017 tax cuts went to the top 1 percent further enriching the already wealthy.[17]

While arguably progress has been made globally against extreme poverty, there is no debate that wealth distribution is criminally skewed to the very few. Oxfam reported in 2018 that "26 people owned the same as the 3.8 billion people who make up the poorest half of humanity."[18] *Vox* reported, "The richest 147 billionaires in the world control about 1 percent of global wealth," or, to widen the aperture, "42 million people, or 0.8 percent of the world's population, have net worth in excess of $1 million. That group—roughly the global 1 percent exposed and targeted by the *Occupy Wall Street Movement*—controls 44.8 percent of the world's wealth."[19] According to *Bloomberg News*, owned by billionaire Michael Bloomberg, one of three billionaires who ran for U.S. president in 2020, the richest 500 individuals in the world increased their wealth in 2019 by $1.2 trillion to their portfolio.[20] Such was the fortune of the 0.001 percent.[21] As the Institute for Policy Studies points out, the super-rich "have benefited enormously from a system of tax, trade, and regulatory rules tipped in favor of wealth holders at the expense of wage earners."[22] These policies include regressive tax rates, untaxed capital gains, legal loopholes that reduce tax liability, and allowing wealth to be hidden in offshore tax and financial shelters.

Neoliberalism also required racism though not in the form of chattel slavery or de jure segregation. In the twenty-first century, racism is primarily exercised through race-neutral, but disproportionately race-impacting policies. Areas as diverse as criminal justice, education, health care, and affordable housing, for the most part, no longer have explicit racial barriers, but in practice, policies result in outcomes that privilege Whites over communities of color. Neoliberalism's retreat from redistributive social policies ensures that inclusionary remedies will be underfunded if funded at all. In addition, the racialization of immigrants and non-Christian religions convinces White populations to support neoliberal policies they believe pushback against social welfare agendas that benefit those they view as undeserving.[23]

While neoliberalism is never explicitly debated in the film, the struggles and debates over whether and how Wakanda should interact with the rest of the world occurs within these boundaries. Choices made in the end by King T'Challa (nee the Black Panther) do not fundamentally challenge the status quo, and arguably further some of its most pernicious narratives and tropes of global neoliberalism.

THE WAKANDA DILEMMA

African nations in Hollywood films, whether fictional or not, are generally portrayed as poor, violent, desperate, and dependent nations (*Blood Diamond, Hotel Rwanda, District 9*), or, at best, are mildly successfully but small and irrelevant players on the global stage (*Coming to America*). Quite often, African people are background (*Out of Africa, The African Queen*) or being White-saved from their fellow murderous citizens (*Tears of the Sun, The Last King of Scotland*).

In the *Black Panther*, the fictional nation of Wakanda is an anomaly. For centuries, it had been able to develop economically and technologically due to the discovery of vibranium, a super metal with magical powers that fell to earth hundreds of years ago. The capital city of Wakanda, and one can presume other cities, is as modern and advanced as any in the world. Innovations in medicine, transportation, science and other fields are on view for all to see. The film does, however, depict areas where basic farming is dominant and notes that one tribe, the Jabari, decided to voluntarily live a more traditional, pastoral lifestyle.

Modern technology, however, has not created a democracy in Wakanda. The nation is a monarchy ruled by a king with traditions that only barely seem to touch democratic input. Importantly, the decision about the nation's foreign policy is not a democratic one debated by elected officials, citizen lobbying, or a free press. It is ultimately a unilateral decision by the king with limited discussion with his family, inner circle, and advisory council.

Wakanda deliberately lets the world think, as one White newscaster states in *Captain America: Civil War*, that it is "one of the poorest nations" on the planet. According to Marvel's *Black Panther: The Ultimate Guide*, Wakanda is located in east Africa, one of the most impoverished regions in the world. In the comics, Wakanda's geography shifts at times, but it is surrounded by several fictional nations: Niganda, Canaan, Azania, and Hohanna.[24] However, in *Captain America: Civil War*, Wakanda is shown on a map to be near Lake Turkhana, a very real lake that crosses the borders of Kenya and Ethiopia. This would also likely have Wakanda border South Sudan and Uganda as well. According to the UN Human Development report, with the exception of Kenya, these nations rank at the very low end globally regarding poverty and other social indices. In 2019, the bottom nineteen countries on the United Nations Human Development Index were all in sub-Saharan Africa.[25] In a region notoriously destitute, Wakanda is somehow able to hide its wealth and modernity. It has also escaped the so-called "resource curse," the thesis that developing nations with immense natural resources often fail to grow or take advantage of their good fortune to benefit the whole nation and all the people in it.[26]

But the false notion that Africa in general is poor and hopelessly violent is left to stand. In fact, many nations on the continent have been responsible and judicious in making use of Africa's richness in natural resources and seen improvements and stability in their economies, and substantial growth in democratic policies and institutions. Poverty remains high but is driven by external factors as well as domestic ones. Africa's wealth is stolen and expropriated by foreign sources far more than squandered by local forces. One report by a group of international Non-Governmental Organizations (NGOs) found that while Africa receives $162 billion in income from the outside, such as remittances, loans, and foreign aid, more than $202 billion is taken out via loan payments, transnational corporate profits, and illegal trade and fishing among other methods, resulting in a net outflow of $41 billion.[27]

The dilemma faced by the King T'Challa (Chadwick Boseman) in *Black Panther* is to determine what should be the posture of Wakanda in the aftermath of an intense and traumatizing conflict with one of its own, a descendant of royalty in fact. N'Jadaka/Killmonger (Michael B. Jordan) grew up in America but wants to return to Wakanda to not only claim (or rather fight for) the throne but to use the nation's advance weaponry to overthrow global White power and free Black people around the world. Should the nation become more engaged in global affairs, as the king's former partner, Nakia (Lupita Nyong'o), also suggests albeit substantially differently than Killmonger? Or, in the tradition of the ancestors, remain an autarky, isolated and self-dependent?

The film rejects answering this question directly and instead sets up a debate that offers two options to the self-imposed isolationism that is no longer viable after the events in the film: a radical Pan-Africanism model—think Marcus Garvey or Malcolm X—or a more moderate, conventional internationalist model—think Barack Obama. Wakandan-descendant, U.S.-raised N'Jakaka/Erik Killmonger advocates an extremist approach that stands in opposition to King T'Challa's argument for a more globally but ideologically reserved engagement.[28] Both models ultimately reject T'Challa's "Wakanda First" isolationist nationalism that has defined the nation for centuries. The king eventually decides on a conventional model that does not clearly or explicitly challenge the fundamental principles and dictates of neoliberalism.

To make this argument in the film required critical changes in the comic book narrative. This included rewriting N'Jadaka/Killmonger's identity and history; linking Killmonger and his father to the revolutionary radicalism of the Black Panther Party; downplaying Wakanda/Black Panther's foreign interventions or seeing them as rouge; and having T'Challa reject the isolationist teachings and practices of his ancestors. These are huge narrative rifts and readers of the comic will immediately recognize the changes.

WAKANDIAN–AMERICAN TENSIONS

In the *Black Panther* comics, N'Jadaka was kidnapped from Wakanda by the White villain Ulysses Klaue; in the film, N'Jobu was sent to the United States on a mission, met an African American woman presumably in Oakland, California, and they had a child, N'Jadaka.

This is a decisive and necessary change because the filmmakers needed, in some part, an African American "voice" to make the criticism that Wakanda had failed in its responsibility to use its technology and power to help other people of African descent. His mixed nationality provides him the basis to articulate a radical Black internationalism rooted in African American politics as expressed by a long line of Black leaders from Martin Delaney and W. E. B. Du Bois to Angela Davis and Gerald Horne as countless other scholars and activists.[29] N'Jadaka is first cousin to King T'Challa, a relationship that tradition-bound Wakanda cannot erase or ignore. It is notable though that there are no other significant African American voices in the film. Other than Black children playing and perhaps Killmonger's girlfriend, Linda (Nabivah Be), who he coldly murdered, African Americans are erased from the film's discourses even as a White Americans CIA operative, Everett Ross (Martin Freeman), plays a key role. The mixed-nationality Killmonger is the only African American perspective foregrounded in the film.

Yet, in contrast to the comics, the filmmakers indirectly and symbolically, but clearly link Killmonger to the Black Panther Party for Self-Defense (BPP) of the 1960s and 1970s. Although principally thought of for their domestic politics, the BPP operated internationally as well and advocated for a radical, socialist world bred by the writings of Mao Tse Tung, Che Guevara, and Frantz Fanon.[30] The film made this connection in at least four different ways.

First, in the film, N'Jobu and N'Jakada are located in Oakland, CA, the birthplace of the BPP. This breaks with the comic narrative where N'Jadaka was kidnapped and taken to New York City. The only logical explanation for this change is to chain-link the story to the BPP. Perhaps coincidentally, it should be mentioned that Michael B. Jordan, who plays N'Jadaka/Killmonger, is famous for his lead role in *Fruitvale Station* (2013) which takes place in Oakland and is a real-life story about the Transit Police murder of Oscar Grant, a young African American man. Both films were directed by Ryan Coogler, who is also from Oakland.

Second, one of the most famous posters of the Black Power era is of Panther leader Huey Newton sitting in a large wicker chair wearing the Panther's iconic Black beret and Black jacket. He has a rifle in his right hand and an African spear in his left. The chair is on a leopard-skin type rug and two African-like items are on either side of Newton. This poster is in the apartment of N'Jobu and Killmonger.

Third, just in case any sharp-eyed viewer missed the brief image of the poster, T'Challa's throne in Wakanda, and, importantly, his way of sitting in it, strongly resembles Newton's chair and pose. Side-by-side images of Newton and T'Challa zoomed across the internet as countless viewers immediately recognized the similar imagery.

Fourth, Panther imagery also manifest in the movie's promotion. As the film was being released, for example, Jordan appeared on the cover of the March 2018 *British GQ* wearing a Black beret and Black leather jacket. The capture under the picture reads, "RISE UP: *Black Panther* star Michael B Jordan Fights the Power," a slogan identified with the Black Power Movement and the Black Panther Party.[31] The connection is specious.

BLACK PANTHER VS. THE BLACK PANTHER PARTY

The Black Panther character was introduced in July 1966 about three months before the actual Black Panther Party was formed in Oakland, California, in October of that year. The founding of the Black Panther character and comic was in large part driven by market forces. According to Jack Kirby, one of the key artists and editors at Marvel Comics at the time, and the co-creator of the Black Panther character:

> I came up with the Black Panther because I realized I had no blacks in my strip. I'd never drawn a black. I needed a black. I suddenly discovered that I had a lot of black readers. My first friend was a black! And here I was ignoring

them because I was associating with everybody else. It suddenly dawned on me—believe me, it was for human reasons—I suddenly discovered nobody was doing blacks. And here I am a leading cartoonist and I wasn't doing a black.[32]

It should be noted that Kirby makes no reference to the politics of the period. Although the Black Panther Party did not exist, the Black Power movement and more militant positions were emerging and challenging the dominance of the Civil Rights Movement.[33] It is doubtful that Kirby or Marvel were in sync with the politics of Black nationalism. Kirby's original name for the character—Coal Tiger—and the featuring of the Black Panther in a comic entitled *Jungle Action Featuring the Black Panther*—were cringe-worthy and certainly did not reflect an enlightened perspective on contemporary Black politics or Africa.[34]

Stan Lee, the other co-creator and a driving force in the comic world, had perhaps a more political motive in mind. Lee claims about the origins of the character, "One thing I felt was that there were not enough black superheroes so I created the Black Panther."[35] He would speak out more forcefully against racism going forward. In a now iconic article from 1968, Lee wrote, "Bigotry and racism are among the deadliest social ills plaguing the world today. But, unlike a team of costumed super-villains, they can't be halted with a punch in the snoot, or a zap from a ray gun. The only way to destroy them is to expose them—to reveal them for the insidious evils they really are."[36] As worthy as Lee's condemnation of racism may be, however, there was a commercial incentive that drove the creation of the "Black Panther" character and later comic series.

The formation of the Black Panther Party for Self-Defense in October 1966 was spurred by the political reality of the harassment and murder of Black people in Oakland by the police and the general surge of activism of the Civil Rights Movement and Black Power Movement.[37] The party would quickly grow into a national and even international organization. In response to its militancy and call for revolution, it found itself at war with local, state, and federal law enforcement. Shootouts, mass arrests, and high-profile trials became the face of the party for most obscuring the community programs, such as free breakfast for children and free clothing for the poor, and efforts at mass political education.[38]

Marvel Comics became politically skittish about the organization after the Black Panther Party developed into a national political force. At one point, in 1972, in *Fantastic Four* No. 119, the Black Panther character announced that he had changed his name to the Black Leopard. His explanation, when asked by the Thing why the name change, was "I contemplate a return to your country, Ben Grimm [the Thing], where the latter term has political connotations. I neither condemn nor condone those who have taken up the name—but T'Challa is a law unto himself. Hence, the new name—a minor point, at best, since the panther is a leopard."[39] By 1972, the Black Panther Party had become world famous for its militancy, had been designated America's number one domestic security threat, and been involved in a number of violent confrontations with local and state police around the country. Much of its leadership including founding members Huey Newton, Bobby Searle, and others were dead, imprisoned, out on bail, or in exile. These political circumstances generated deep consternation and worries for the comic book giant and as Marvel writer Roy Thomas stated, the company was "concerned that we'd become identified with that group."[40] Fans protested and the name was quietly changed back to the Black Panther.

While comic book Killmonger only wanted power in Wakanda, film Killmonger advocated for a global revolution similar to the real Black Panthers. Killmonger argued that African Americans were oppressed as did the Black Panthers who viewed the status of Blacks as colonialized. But distinct from Killmonger, the Panthers (or at least their leadership) identified themselves as Marxists who studied and were aligned with the views of Mao Tse Tung, Kim Il Sung, Fidel Castro, Ho Chi Minh, Kwame Nkrumah, and Frantz Fanon. They wanted unity of oppressed people regardless of race and made alliances with radicals of all colors. Former Black Panther Kathleen Cleaver argued, "Although its membership was exclusively Black, the Black Panther Party emphasized 'power to the people' far more than Black power and sought to unify the anti-imperialist movements and organizations."[41] In the United States, they formed working relations with Latinos (Brown Berets and Young Lords), Asians (Red Guards), and Whites (Young Patriots).[42]

They were explicitly opposed to the nationalist thinking of the era and would have dissented from the Blacks-only view held by Killmonger and the isolationist view of the leaders of Wakanda. Panther leaders traveled to Vietnam, North Korea, Cuba, and Algeria among other anti-imperialist nations building alliances and expressing solidarity.[43] The Black Panthers saw themselves as socialist and anticapitalists and supportive of global working class unity. Their global view was less the Pan-Africanism of Marcus Garvey or W. E. B. Du Bois and more Frantz Fanon, Amilicar Cabral, and Claudia Jones.[44]

In the film, there is nothing to indicate that either T'Challa or Killmonger were anticapitalist let alone in opposition to its contemporary manifestation: neoliberalism. While decrying the oppression of Black people in the United States and globally, the filmmakers also seem to accept the assumptions of the global economic order, that is, contemporary global problems can be resolved through international cooperation without a fundamental economic and political restructuring.

Killmonger's extremist solution—blow up the world—fails on many levels. His power would be that of a dictator not a democrat. Upon meeting T'Challa and his inner circle, including family members, he states, "I want the throne. Y'all sitting up here comfortable. Must feel good. There's are about 2 billion people all over the world who look like us but their lives are a lot harder. Wakanda has the tools to liberate them all." This is an indiscriminate violent foray that dismisses a role for the very people who are to be liberated. He advocates no system of government that resembles anything close to democracy. In an echo to Huey Newton's most famous work, Killmonger's "Revolutionary Suicide" would destroy half the world to save it.[45]

BLACK PANTHER, THE BLACK PANTHERS, AND THE CIA

In the film, a CIA agent is presented almost as comic relief—T'Challa's brilliant scientist sister Shuri (Letitia Wright) hilariously calls him a "colonizer"—but also, inexplicitly, as heroic and a friend of Wakanda and T'Challa. In a battle with Killmonger, CIA agent Everett Ross takes a bullet for Nakia. After he is wounded, he is flown back to Wakanda and his life is saved by the nation's advanced medical technologies. Later, under instructions from Nakia and Shuri, Ross shoots down the planes launched by Killmonger taking weapons out of Wakanda. All of this adds up to Ross being not just a personal friend of T'Challa but a savior of the world against Wakandian weaponry.

There is no mention or reference to the real and deadly role that the CIA played in Africa for decades. In 1961, it was involved in the plot that led to the capture and murder of progressive Congolese president Patrice Lumumba. In 1962, the CIA was involved in providing information to the South African Apartheid government that helped lead to the capture of African National Congress leader Nelson Mandela and others. That arrest and conviction kept Mandela in prison for twenty-seven years. In 1966, the CIA and other U.S. intelligence forces actively engaged in the overthrow of Ghanaian president and continental leader Kwame Nkrumah.[46] In the 1970s, the CIA supported the anticommunist group UNITA and its murderous rampage against people in Angola.[47] While some U.S. officials appropriately admonished Russia for interfering in the 2016 election, the CIA has a long history of intervening in elections across the world including in virtually every election in Africa during the Cold War period.[48]

U.S. law enforcement and intelligence agencies also targeted the BPP. The FBI's Counter-Intelligence Program (COINTELPRO) monitored the organization, created dissention within through spies and informants, and sowed conflict between the Panthers and other organizations. The CIA tracked Panther activities on a global scale and attempted to have other states refuse to house them.[49]

DOWNPLAYING WAKANDA/BLACK PANTHER'S FOREIGN INTERVENTIONS

In another departure from the comics, the film excludes the global activism of the Black Panther, who is actually quite vigorous in attacking racism outside of Wakanda including in the U.S. South and South Africa. In the series *Jungle Action Featuring the Black Panther*, the Black Panther travels to Georgia with his girlfriend at the time, Monica Lynne, and ends up clashing with and defeating the Ku Klux Klan. Lynne goes to investigate the death of her sister, a journalist who had been looking into corruption and the involvement of the local Klan. The Black Panther has several encounters with some far-right White supremacists as well as the Klan including being captured at one point and placed on a flaming cross. He escapes and beats the Klan in that encounter.[50]

He also takes the fight to Apartheid South Africa and to a South African-like nation, Azania that borders Wakanda. T'Challa's step-mother is kidnapped and held in South Africa for many years. The king believes she is dead, and when he finds out that she is alive, he goes there to rescue her. The series provides an opportunity to criticize the Apartheid regime. In other words, the Black Panther's struggle against racism in other countries was not as noninterventionist as Killmonger argues or that T'Challa wanted. Even in the movie, *Black Panther* opens with Nakia leading a covert rescue operation of young African girls from a Boko Haram type of group. Boko Haram is a dangerous terrorist group located in northeast Nigeria that exploded to world infamy in 2014 when it kidnapped nearly 300 young girls in a raid on the town of Chibook. The girls were to be sold as slaves or enslaved to Boko Harem fighters. The hashtag, #bringthegirlshome, became a global call by human rights, feminist, and antiterrorist activists.[51] T'Challa intervenes in the middle of the operation to inform Nakia, his former romantic partner, that his father had died and he would like her to return for the transition ceremony. He seems disinterested in the operation, so it is not clear if Nakia has gone rouge. She tells him, "You ruined my mission," which implies that she wanted to do more than just rescue the girls. The Black Panther easily vanquishes the kidnappers and Nakia orders the girls and one captured boy to go home. Before they leave, Okoye (Danai Gurira), leader of the king's security squad the Dora Milaje, tells them "You will never speak of this day."

Regardless of whether Nakia has T'Challa's blessing for the mission, as a member-state of the United Nations, Wakanda is obligated to implement the principle known as "responsibility to protect," which Nakia is seeking to carry out. The UN requires that states not only protect their own people but that the international community "also has the responsibility to use appropriate diplomatic, humanitarian and other peaceful means . . . to help protect populations from genocide, war crimes, ethnic cleansing and crimes against humanity."[52]

Wakanda, for reasons that are never fully explained, has agents globally. When King T'Chaka confronts his brother at the beginning of the film, N'Jobu is stunned to find that his colleague, who is helping him plan the distribution of vibranium-enhanced weapons, is actually Wakandian and not African American. T'Chaka tells his brother he should not be surprised because the kingdom has spies all over the world. It is never stated clearly what these spies are up to, but it seems reasonable to conclude that stopping the unauthorized distribution of vibranium is high on the list.

THE WAKANDAN STATE

Wakanda was received as a utopian paradise by many. The joy of seeing an African nation presented as an advanced society that outshines every other nation left little room for a more critical dissection of the nature of the Wakandan state. A tribal council exists but King T'Challa determines the executive, judiciary, and legislative functions of the state. This also includes foreign policy.

At the film's beginning, Wakanda is a proud autarky, an economic and politically self-sufficient state that requires little, if anything, from outside the nation. No true autarky exists today including the oft-cited nation of North Korea that engages in trade with China, Russia, and a few other nations despite its claim of total independence. But, unlike Wakanda, North Korea is economically deprived with credible evidence of periods of mass starvation and other basic needs largely unmet.

The events of the film's narrative—Nakia's push for international engagement, the struggle with Killmonger, T'Challa' reflections on King T'Chaka's death and his discussion with his father in the Ancestral Plane—convince T'Challa to ultimately break with the past. This decision moves forward without debate. In a speech before the United Nations, T'Challa states:

> Wakanda will no longer watch from the shadows. We cannot. We must not. We will work to be an example of how we, as brothers and sisters on this earth,

should treat each other. Now, more than ever, the illusions of division threaten our very existence. We all know the truth: more connects us than separates us. But in times of crisis the wise build bridges, while the foolish build barriers. We must find a way to look after one another, as if we were one single tribe.

Despite the obvious swipe at Donald Trump's xenophobia border partition, this speech is more Barack Obama than Fidel Castro. This is not anticapitalist or anti-imperialist. He is not calling for a redistribution of wealth or an equal seat at the table for all. Collective action in the form of #BlackLivesMatter or Occupy Wall Street is not the play here. Calling out unaccountable, greedy global corporations, brutal autocratic states, and the scrounge of global wealth inequality is not the path chosen by the king.

T'Challa's slam against Trumpism and its anti-immigrant, Islamophobic racism—"the foolish build barriers"—is safe and more in line with a global community that has resisted the rise of authoritarian leaders and movements including the racism they embody. Yet, more must be said and done. It is critical that bad behavior by states and political leaders are called out by name and held accountable. Democratic and human rights activists have denounced Philippine's president Rodrigo Duterte's murderous antidrug campaign, Saudi Arabia's vicious killing of *Washington Post* journalist Jamal Khashoggi, Egypt's Abdel Fattah el-Sisi jailing and torture of political enemies and journalists, and the killing of Afro-Brazilian politician and human rights activist Marielle Franco. At the same time, liberal democracies have not been excluded from the more brutal excesses of the far right as seen in the U.S. child separation policy against asylum seekers, the Brexit campaign that used xenophobia to win support, and attacks against Muslims from Indian prime minister Narendra Modi's administration.

CONCLUSION

Nakia is the voice of global outreach and political change in Wakanda. She pursues her own "foreign policy," which includes covert intervention, and pushes back against the argument that foreign aid or international engagement will hurt the nation.

Nakia: I found my calling out there. I've seen too many in need just to turn a blind eye. I can't be happy here knowing that there's people out there who have nothing.
T'Challa: What would you have Wakanda do about it?
Nakia: Share what we have. We could provide aid and access to technology and refuge to those who need it. Other countries do it, we could do it better.

T'Challa: We are not like other countries, Nakia. If the world found out what we truly are, what we possess, we could lose our way of life.
Nakia: Wakanda is strong enough to help others and protect ourselves at the same time.[53]

Nakia's "calling" is progressive and influential. In the end, a skeptical T'Challa concedes and begins to take steps to end Wakanda's isolation. In Oakland, Wakanda opens the Wakanda International Outreach Center.

Ultimately, the film settles on a solution that is conventional and safe. It does not identify the source of global oppression, poverty, concentrated wealth, and rising authoritarianism, all rooted in the ideology of neoliberalism. Instead, it points to neglect, ignorance, and lack of caring. Furthermore, the most dangerous threat to Wakanda is not autocratic, race-baiting, or antidemocratic leaders like U.S. president Donald Trump, UK Prime Minister Boris Johnson, Russian president Vladimir Putin, China's Xi Jinping, or Brazilian president Jair Bolsanaro, or unaccountable transnational corporations. The number one villain is an extremist Black man willing to violently blow up the world and kill millions. Killmonger's views are not debated in Wakanda in a free press or in public venues. His brief tenure in power is brutal, cruel, and destructive. His defeat by his cousin and his plan defeated by a CIA operative is welcome.

On the global stage, Wakanda has reached a new standing and commitment to some level of internationalism, respect for international norms, and a charitable approach to foreign assistance. Starting with the Center in Oakland, making amends with African Americans seems to be high on the list. But real and qualitative change will come from addressing the economic and political framework that marks the current era and oppresses working people in the developed and developing world.

NOTES

1. This analysis is primarily focused on the events and narrative of the film rather than a comparison of the differences between it and the comic series except where necessary to explain the politics of the movie. The comic series developed over decades with many different writers and often conflicting storylines from previous versions. There is some common consensus history, however, that is important to reference along the way.

2. "How many people watched Black Panther? Is it worth watching?" *Quora,* 2018, https://www.quora.com/How-many-people-watched-Black-Panther-Is-it-worth-watching.

3. "Black Panther," *The Numbers,* accessed February 20, 2021, https://www.the-numbers.com/movie/Black-Panther#tab=summary. Also updated on IMDb website:

"Black Panther," *IMDb*, accessed February 20, 2021, https://www.imdb.com/title/tt1825683/.

4. Rebecca Rubin, "'Black Panther' Surpasses 'The Avengers' as Highest-Grossing Superhero Movie of All Time," *Variety*, March 25, 2018, https://variety.com/2018/film/box-office/black-panther-surpasses-avengers-highest-grossing-superhero-movie-1202735863/.

5. Rubin, "'Black Panther' Surpasses 'The Avengers.'"

6. Scott Campbell, "Black Panther Surges In VOD Sales Following Chadwick Boseman's Death," *We Got This Covered*, August 2020, https://wegotthiscovered.com/movies/black-panther-experiences-huge-surge-vod-sales-chadwick-bosemans-death/; and Bruce Haring, "'Black Panther' Surges On Amazon And Apple Charts In Wake Of Chadwick Boseman Death," *Deadline*, August 30, 2020, https://deadline.com/2020/08/black-panther-surges-on-amazon-apple-charts-1203027107/.

7. Jennifer Williams, "Wakanda Shakes the World," *Foreign Policy*, April 1, 2018, https://foreignpolicy.com/2018/04/01/wakanda-shakes-the-world/.

8. Transcribed from the film's dialogue by author.

9. In the comics, it is noted that vibranium also has some dangerous side effects such as turning people into monsters and its strongest powers are restricted to a secret priesthood.

10. Transcribed from the film's dialogue by author.

11. John Maynard Keynes, *The General Theory of Employment, Interest, and Money* (New York: Harcourt, Brace & World, 2016).

12. See John Eatwell and Murray Milgate, *The Fall and Rise of Keynesian Economics* (New York: Oxford University Press, 2011) for a discussion of the transition by neoliberal economists who looked back to Keynes in the middle of the 2008 global economic crisis.

13. Naomi Klein, *Shock Doctrine: The Rise of Disaster Capitalism* (New York: Metropolitan Books/Henry Holt, 2007).

14. George Monbiot, "Neoliberalism—The Ideology at the Root of All Our Problems," *The Guardian*, April 15, 2016, https://www.theguardian.com/books/2016/apr/15/neoliberalism-ideology-problem-george-monbiot.

15. David Harvey, *A Brief History of Neoliberalism* (New York: Oxford University Press, 2005), 2.

16. See Ernst Wolff, *Pillaging the World: The History and Politics of the IMF* (Marbury, Germany: Tectum Verlag, 2014); and Joseph E. Stiglitz, *Globalization and Its Discontents Revisited: Anti-Globalization in the Era of Trump* (New York: W.W. Norton & Company, 2018).

17. "Hearing: 2017 Tax Law—Impact on Budget and American Families," *Committee on the Budget, U.S. House of Representatives*, February 27, 2019, https://budget.house.gov/legislation/hearings/2017-tax-law-impact-budget-and-american-families-1.

18. "5 shocking facts about extreme global inequality and how to even it up," *Oxfam*, 2018, https://www.oxfam.org/en/5-shocking-facts-about-extreme-global-inequality-and-how-even-it.

19. In 2011, weeks of protests against income and wealth inequality occurred around the United States and globally. The movement became known as "Occupy

Wall Street" because the initial demonstrations and encampments began in Zuccotti Park located near Wall Street in New York City. "Occupied" camps were setup in other cities in the United States. Dylan Matthews, "Are 26 billionaires worth more than half the planet? The debate, explained. It's complicated!" *Vox*, January 22, 2019, https://www.vox.com/future-perfect/2019/1/22/18192774/oxfam-inequality-report-2019-davos-wealth.

20. In addition to businessman and former mayor Bloomberg, California hedge fund manager Tom Steyer and President Donald Trump also ran for president in 2020. See Tom Metcalf and Jack Witzig, "World's Richest Gain $1.2 Trillion as Bezos Keeps Crown," *Bloomberg News*, December 27, 2019, https://www.bloomberg.com/news/articles/2019-12-27/world-s-richest-gain-1-2-trillion-as-kylie-baby-s-harks-prosper.

21. Metcalf and Witzig, "World's Richest Gain"; and Sarah Ruiz-Grossman, "Wealth of World's 500 Richest People Grew 25% This Year," *HuffPost*, December 27, 2019, https://www.huffpost.com/entry/world-richest-wealth-income-inequality_n_5e06915de4b0843d360653ad.

22. Chuck Collins and Josh Hoxie, *Billionaire Bonanza: The Forbes 400 and the Rest of Us* (Washington, DC: Institute for Policy Studies, 2017), 6.

23. Michael Tesler, "Trump Voters Think African Americans Are Much Less Deserving Than 'Average Americans,'" *HuffPost*, last modified December 20, 2017, https://www.huffpost.com/entry/trump-voters-think-africa_b_13732500.

24. Stephen Wiacek, *Black Panther: The Ultimate Guide* (New York: Penguin Random House, 2018), 48–49.

25. "Human Development Report 2019," *United Nations Development Program*, 2019, 302-303, http://hdr.undp.org/en/content/human-development-report-2019.

26. See Macartan Humphreys, Jeffrey D. Sachs, and Joseph E. Stiglitz, eds. *Escaping the Resource Curse* (New York: Columbia University Press, 2007).

27. "Honest Accounts 2017: How the World Profits from Africa's Wealth," *Global Justice Now*, May 2017, 3, https://www.globaljustice.org.uk/resources/honest-accounts-2017-how-world-profits-africas-wealth.

28. Huey P. Newton, *Revolutionary Suicide* (New York: Writers and Readers, 1995).

29. Keisha N. Blain and Tiffany M. Gill, eds., *To Turn the Whole World Over: Black Women and Internationalism* (Urbana, IL: University of Illinois Press, 2019); Brent Hayes Edwards, *Practice of Diaspora: Literature, Translation, and the Rise of Black Internationalism* (Cambridge, MA: Harvard University Press, 2003); Minkah Makalani, *In the Cause of Freedom: Radical Black Internationalism From Harlem to London, 1917-1939* (Chapel Hill: University of North Carolina Press, 2011); and H.L.T. Quan, ed., *Cedric J. Robinson On Racial Capitalism, Black Internationalism, and Cultures of Resistance* (London: Pluto Press, 2019).

30. Alexander C. Cook, ed., *Mao's Little Red Book: A Global History* (Cambridge: Cambridge University Press, 2013); and Frantz Fanon, *Wretched of the Earth* (New York: Grove Press, 2004).

31. *British GQ* (cover), March 2018.

32. Gary Growth, "Jack Kirby Interview," *The Comic Journal*, May 23, 2011, http://www.tcj.com/jack-kirby-interview/.

33. Stokely Carmichael, *Black Power: The Politics of Liberation in America* (New York: Random House, 1967).

34. Micah Peters, "The Evolution of Marvel's 'Black Panther,'" *The Ringer*, February 14, 2018, https://www.theringer.com/pop-culture/2018/2/14/17012374/marvel-black-panther-comics-history.

35. See *With Great Power: The Stan Lee Story,* dir. Terry Dougas, Nikki Frakes, Will Hess. United States: 1821 Pictures, 2010.

36. Lee Moran, "Stan Lee's 1968 Column Denouncing Racism 'Plaguing the World' Goes Viral Again," *HuffPost*, November 13, 2018, https://www.huffpost.com/entry/stan-lee-racism-bigotry-1968-column_n_5bea8299e4b0caeec2bd1bc5.

37. It is of note that two films involving the history of the Black Panthers have been recently released: Netflix's *The Trial of the Chicago Seven* (2020) and HBO's *Judas and the Black Messiah* (2021).

38. See Joshua Bloom and Waldo E. Martin Jr., *Black against Empire: The History and Politics of the Black Panther Party* (Berkeley, CA: University of California Press, 2016); Kathleen Cleaver and George Katsiaficas, *Liberation, Imagination, and the Black Panther Party: A New Look at the Black Panthers and their Legacy* (London and New York: Routledge, 2001); and Donna Murch, *Revolution in Our Lifetime: A Short History of the Black Panther Party* (New York: Verso Books, 2020).

39. Roy Thomas, *Fantastic Four*, No. 119, Marvel Comics, 1972.

40. Peters, "The Evolution of Marvel's 'Black Panther'."

41. Kathleen Cleaver, "Back to Africa: The Evolution of the International Section of the Black Panther Party (1969-1972)," in *The Black Panther Party [Reconsidered]*, ed. Charles E. Jones (Baltimore, MD: Black Classic Press, 1998), 212.

42. Cleaver, "Back to Africa," 230–231.

43. Jennifer B. Smith, *An international history of the Black Panther Party* (New York: Garland, 1999); and Sean L. Malloy, *Out of Oakland: Black Panther Party internationalism during the Cold War* (Ithaca: Cornell University Press, 2017).

44. Fanon, *Wretched of the Earth*; Amilcar Cabral, *Revolution in Guinea: Selected Texts* (New York: Monthly Review Press, 1969); and Carole Boyce Davies, *Left of Karl Marx: The Political Life of Black Communist Claudia Jones* (Durham: Duke University Press, 2007).

45. Huey Newton, *Revolutionary Suicide* (New York: Penguin Books, 2009).

46. Madeleine G. Kalb, "The C.I.A. and Lumumba," *New York Times*, August 2, 1981, https://www.nytimes.com/1981/08/02/magazine/the-cia-and-lumumba.html; Emmanuel Gerard and Bruce Kuklick, *Death in the Congo: Murdering Patrice Lumumba* (Cambridge, MA: Harvard University Press, 2015); Stephen R. Weissman, "What Really Happened in Congo: The CIA, the Murder of Lumumba, and the Rise of Mobutu," *Foreign Affairs* 93, no. 4 (July/August 2014): 14–24; Aislinn Laing, "Retired CIA Agent Confirms U.S. Role in Nelson Mandela's 1962 Arrest," interview by Kelly McEvers, *All Things Considered*, NPR, May 16, 2016, audio, https://www.npr.org/2016/05/16/478272695/retired-cia-agent-confirms-u-s-role-in-nelson-mandelas-1962-arrest; Rupert Cornwell, "CIA's involvement in arrest of Nelson Mandela is a classic example of US mistaking nationalism for communism,"

Independent, May 16, 2016, https://www.independent.co.uk/news/world/americas/cia-s-involvement-arrest-nelson-mandela-classic-example-us-mistaking-nationalism-communism-a7032816.html; and Seymour Hersh, "CIA Said to Have Aided Plotters Who Overthrew Nkrumah in Ghana," in *Dirty Work 2: The CIA in Africa*, eds. Ellen Ray et al. (Secaucus, NJ: Lyle Stuart Inc., 1980), 159–162.

47. Pete Brewton, *The Mafia, CIA & George Bush* (New York, NY: S.P.I. Books, 1992); and William Minter, "The US and the War in Angola," *Review of African Political Economy*, no. 50 (March 1991): 135–144.

48. Philip Agee and Louis Wolf, eds., *Dirty Work: The CIA in Western Europe* (Secaucus, NJ: Lyle Stuart, Inc., 1978).

49. Ward Churchill and Jim Vander Wall, *Agents of Repression: The FBI's Secret Wars Against the Black Panther Party and the American Indian Movement* (Boston, MA: South End Press, 1988); Ward Churchill and Jim Vander Wal, *COINTELPRO Papers: Documents from the FBI's Secret Wars Against Dissent in the United States* (Cambridge, MA: South End Press, 2002); and Nelson Blackstock, *COINTELPRO: The FBI's Secret War on Political Freedom* (New York: Vintage Books, 1976).

50. See *Jungle Action Featuring the Black Panther*, No. 19, 20, 21, and 24, Marvel Comics, 1972-76.

51. See *#BringBackOurGirls: Addressing the threat of Boko Haram*, United States Congress (Washington: U.S. Government Publishing Office, 2015); Hilary Matfess, *Women and the War on Boko Haram: Wives, Weapons, Witnesses* (London: Zed Books, 2017); Alexander Thurston, *Boko Haram: The History of an African Jihadist Movement* (Princeton: Princeton University Press, 2018); Caroline Varin, *Boko Haram and the War on Terror* (Santa Barbara, CA: Praeger, 2016); and Samuel T. Whitlock, ed., *Boko Haram: The Emerging Nigerian Terrorist Threat* (New York: Nova Publishers, 2014).

52. "United Nations Office on Genocide Prevention and the Responsibility to Protect," United Nations, https://www.un.org/en/genocideprevention/about-responsibility-to-protect.shtml.

53. Transcribed from the film's dialogue by author.

WORKS CITED

"5 shocking facts about extreme global inequality and how to even it up." *Oxfam*, 2018. https://www.oxfam.org/en/5-shocking-facts-about-extreme-global-inequality-and-how-even-it.

Agee, Philip, and Louis Wolf, eds. *Dirty Work: The CIA in Western Europe*. Secaucus, NJ: Lyle Stuart, Inc., 1978.

"Black Panther." *IMDb*, accessed February 20, 2021. https://www.imdb.com/title/tt1825683/.

"Black Panther." *The Numbers*, accessed February 20, 2021. https://www.the-numbers.com/movie/Black-Panther#tab=summary.

Blackstock, Nelson. *COINTELPRO: The FBI's Secret War on Political Freedom*. New York: Vintage Books, 1976.

Blain, Keisha N., and Tiffany M. Gill, eds. *To Turn the Whole World Over: Black Women and Internationalism*. Urbana, IL: University of Illinois Press, 2019.

Bloom, Joshua, and Waldo E. Martin Jr. *Black against Empire: The History and Politics of the Black Panther Party*. Berkeley, CA: University of California Press, 2016.

Brewton, Pete. *The Mafia, CIA & George Bush*. New York, NY: S.P.I. Books, 1992.

British GQ (cover), March 2018.

Cabral, Amilcar. *Revolution in Guinea: Selected Texts*. New York: Monthly Review Press, 1969.

Campbell, Scott. "Black Panther Surges in VOD Sales Following Chadwick Boseman's Death." *We Got This Covered*, August 2020. https://wegotthiscovered.com/movies/black-panther-experiences-huge-surge-vod-sales-chadwick-bosemans-death/.

Carmichael, Stokely. *Black Power: The Politics of Liberation in America*. New York: Random House, 1967.

Churchill, Ward, and Jim Vander Wall. *Agents of Repression: The FBI's Secret Wars Against the Black Panther Party and the American Indian Movement*. Boston, MA: South End Press, 1988.

Churchill, Ward, and Jim Vander Wall. *COINTELPRO Papers: Documents from the FBI's Secret Wars Against Dissent in the United States*. Cambridge, MA: South End Press, 2002.

Cleaver, Kathleen. "Back to Africa: The Evolution of the International Section of the Black Panther Party (1969-1972)." In *The Black Panther Party [Reconsidered]*, edited by Charles E. Jones, 212, 230–231. Baltimore, MD: Black Classic Press, 1998.

Cleaver, Kathleen, and George Katsiaficas. *Liberation, Imagination, and the Black Panther Party: A New Look at the Black Panthers and their Legacy*. London and New York: Routledge, 2001.

Collins, Chuck, and Josh Hoxie. *Billionaire Bonanza: The Forbes 400 and the Rest of Us*. Washington, DC: Institute for Policy Studies, 2017.

Cook, Alexander C. Cook, ed. *Mao's Little Red Book: A Global History*. Cambridge: Cambridge University Press, 2013.

Cornwell, Rupert. "CIA's involvement in arrest of Nelson Mandela is a classic example of US mistaking nationalism for communism." *Independent*, May 16, 2016. https://www.independent.co.uk/news/world/americas/cia-s-involvement-arrest-nelson-mandela-classic-example-us-mistaking-nationalism-communism-a7032816.html.

Davies, Carole Boyce. *Left of Karl Marx: The Political Life of Black Communist Claudia Jones*. Durham: Duke University Press, 2007.

Eatwell, John, and Murray Milgate. *The Fall and Rise of Keynesian Economics*. New York: Oxford University Press, 2011.

Edwards, Brent Hayes. *Practice of Diaspora: Literature, Translation, and the Rise of Black Internationalism*. Cambridge, MA: Harvard University Press, 2003.

Fanon, Frantz. *Wretched of the Earth*. New York: Grove Press, 2004.

Gerard, Emmanuel, and Bruce Kuklick. *Death in the Congo: Murdering Patrice Lumumba*. Cambridge, MA: Harvard University Press, 2015.

Growth, Gary. "Jack Kirby Interview." *The Comic Journal*, May 23, 2011. http://www.tcj.com/jack-kirby-interview/.

Haring, Bruce. "'Black Panther' Surges on Amazon and Apple Charts in Wake of Chadwick Boseman Death." *Deadline*, August 30, 2020. https://deadline.com/2020/08/black-panther-surges-on-amazon-apple-charts-1203027107/.

Harvey, David. *A Brief History of Neoliberalism*. New York: Oxford University Press, 2005.

"Hearing: 2017 Tax Law—Impact on Budget and American Families." *Committee on the Budget, U.S. House of Representatives*, February 27, 2019. https://budget.house.gov/legislation/hearings/2017-tax-law-impact-budget-and-american-families-1.

Hersh, Seymour. "CIA Said to Have Aided Plotters Who Overthrew Nkrumah in Ghana." In *Dirty Work 2: The CIA in Africa*, edited by Ellen Ray et al., 159–162. Secaucus, NJ: Lyle Stuart Inc., 1980.

"Honest Accounts 2017: How the World Profits from Africa's Wealth." *Global Justice Now*, May 2017. https://www.globaljustice.org.uk/resources/honest-accounts-2017-how-world-profits-africas-wealth.

"How many people watched Black Panther? Is it worth watching?" *Quora*, 2018. https://www.quora.com/How-many-people-watched-Black-Panther-Is-it-worth-watching.

"Human Development Report 2019." *United Nations Development Program*, 2019. http://hdr.undp.org/en/content/human-development-report-2019.

Humphreys, Macartan, Jeffrey D. Sachs, and Joseph E. Stiglitz, eds. *Escaping the Resource Curse*. New York: Columbia University Press, 2007.

Jungle Action Featuring the Black Panther, Marvel Comics, 1972–1976.

Kalb, Madeleine G. "The C.I.A. and Lumumba." *New York Times*, August 2, 1981. https://www.nytimes.com/1981/08/02/magazine/the-cia-and-lumumba.html.

Keynes, John Maynard. *The General Theory of Employment, Interest, and Money*. New York: Harcourt, Brace & World, 2016.

Klein, Naomi. *Shock Doctrine: The Rise of Disaster Capitalism*. New York: Metropolitan Books/Henry Holt, 2007.

Laing, Aislinn. "Retired CIA Agent Confirms U.S. Role in Nelson Mandela's 1962 Arrest." Interview by Kelly McEvers. *All Things Considered*. NPR, May 16, 2016. Audio. https://www.npr.org/2016/05/16/478272695/retired-cia-agent-confirms-u-s-role-in-nelson-mandelas-1962-arrest.

Makalani, Minkah. *In the Cause of Freedom: Radical Black Internationalism from Harlem to London, 1917-1939*. Chapel Hill: University of North Carolina Press, 2011.

Malloy, Sean L. *Out of Oakland: Black Panther Party Internationalism during the Cold War*. Ithaca: Cornell University Press, 2017.

Matfess, Hilary. *Women and the War on Boko Haram: Wives, Weapons, Witnesses*. London: Zed Books, 2017.

Matthews, Dylan. "Are 26 billionaires worth more than half the planet? The debate, explained. It's complicated!" *Vox*, January 22, 2019. https://www.vox.com/future-perfect/2019/1/22/18192774/oxfam-inequality-report-2019-davos-wealth.

Metcalf, Tom, and Jack Witzig. "World's Richest Gain $1.2 Trillion as Bezos Keeps Crown." *Bloomberg News*, December 27, 2019. https://www.bloomberg.com

/news/articles/2019-12-27/world-s-richest-gain-1-2-trillion-as-kylie-baby-sharks-prosper.

Minter, William. "The US and the War in Angola." *Review of African Political Economy*, no. 50 (March 1991): 135–144.

Monbiot, George. "Neoliberalism—The Ideology at the Root of All Our Problems." *The Guardian*, April 15, 2016. https://www.theguardian.com/books/2016/apr/15/neoliberalism-ideology-problem-george-monbiot.

Moran, Lee. "Stan Lee's 1968 Column Denouncing Racism 'Plaguing the World' Goes Viral Again." *HuffPost*, November 13, 2018. https://www.huffpost.com/entry/stan-lee-racism-bigotry-1968-column_n_5bea8299e4b0caeec2bd1bc5.

Murch, Donna. *Revolution in Our Lifetime: A Short History of the Black Panther Party*. New York: Verso Books, 2020.

Newton, Huey. *Revolutionary Suicide*. New York: Writers and Readers, 1995.

Newton, Huey. *Revolutionary Suicide*. New York: Penguin Books, 2009.

Peters, Micah. "The Evolution of Marvel's 'Black Panther.'" *The Ringer*, February 14, 2018. https://www.theringer.com/pop-culture/2018/2/14/17012374/marvel-black-panther-comics-history.

Quan, H.L.T., ed. *Cedric J. Robinson On Racial Capitalism, Black Internationalism, and Cultures of Resistance*. London: Pluto Press, 2019.

Rubin, Rebecca. "'Black Panther' Surpasses 'The Avengers' as Highest-Grossing Superhero Movie of All Time." *Variety*, March 25, 2018. https://variety.com/2018/film/box-office/black-panther-surpasses-avengers-highest-grossing-superhero-movie-1202735863/.

Ruiz-Grossman, Sarah. "Wealth of World's 500 Richest People Grew 25% This Year." *HuffPost*, December 27, 2019. https://www.huffpost.com/entry/world-richest-wealth-income-inequality_n_5e06915de4b0843d360653ad.

Smith, Jennifer B. *An international history of the Black Panther Party*. New York: Garland, 1999.

Stiglitz, Joseph E. *Globalization and Its Discontents Revisited: Anti-Globalization in the Era of Trump*. New York: W.W. Norton & Company, 2018.

Tesler, Michael. "Trump Voters Think African Americans Are Much Less Deserving Than 'Average Americans.'" *HuffPost*, last modified December 20, 2017. https://www.huffpost.com/entry/trump-voters-think-africa_b_13732500.

Thomas, Roy. *Fantastic Four*, No. 119. Marvel Comics, 1972.

Thurston, Alexander. *Boko Haram: The History of an African Jihadist Movement*. Princeton: Princeton University Press, 2018.

"United Nations Office on Genocide Prevention and the Responsibility to Protect." United Nations. https://www.un.org/en/genocideprevention/about-responsibility-to-protect.shtml.

Varin, Caroline. *Boko Haram and the War on Terror*. Santa Barbara, CA: Praeger, 2016.

Weissman, Stephen R. "What Really Happened in Congo: The CIA, the Murder of Lumumba, and the Rise of Mobutu." *Foreign Affairs* 93, no. 4 (July/August 2014): 14–24.

Whitlock, Samuel T., ed. *Boko Haram: The Emerging Nigerian Terrorist Threa*t. New York: Nova Publishers, 2014.

Wiacek, Stephen. *Black Panther: The Ultimate Guide*. New York: Penguin Random House, 2018.

Williams, Jennifer. "Wakanda Shakes the World." *Foreign Policy*, April 1, 2018. https://foreignpolicy.com/2018/04/01/wakanda-shakes-the-world/.

Wolff, Ernst. *Pillaging the World: The History and Politics of the IMF*. Marbury, Germany: Tectum Verlag, 2014.

#BringBackOurGirls: Addressing the threat of Boko Haram. United States Congress. Washington: U.S. Government Publishing Office, 2015.

FILMS

The African Queen. Directed by John Huston. United States: United Artists, 1951.

Black Panther. Directed by Ryan Coogler. United States: Walt Disney Studios Motion Pictures, 2018.

Blood Diamond. Directed by Edward Zwick. United States: Warner Bros. Pictures, 2006.

Captain America: Civil War. Directed by Joe Russo and Anthony Russo. United States: Walt Disney Studios Motion Pictures, 2016.

Coming to America. Directed by John Landis. United States: Paramount Pictures, 1988.

District 9. Directed by Neill Blomkamp. New Zealand, United States, South Africa: Sony Pictures, 2009.

Fruitvale Station. Directed by Ryan Coogler. United States: The Weinstein Company, 2013.

Hotel Rwanda. Directed by Terry George. *United States: United Artists, 2004.*

The Last King of Scotland. Directed by Kevin Macdonald. United Kingdom and Germany: Fox Searchlight Pictures, 2006.

Out of Africa. Directed by Sydney Pollack. United Stats: Universal Pictures, 1985.

Tears of the Sun. Directed by Antoine Fuqua. United States: Sony Pictures, 2003.

With Great Power: The Stan Lee Story. Directed by Terry Dougas, Nikki Frakes, Will Hess. United States: 1821 Pictures, 2010.

Chapter 7

The Underground Railroad as Afrofuturism

Enslaved Blacks That Imagined Freedom, Future, and Space

dann j. Broyld

The superhero film *Black Panther*, based off the Marvel Comic and distributed by Walt Disney, premiered in 2018 and rose to be one of the highest grossing motion pictures of all time, showcased the concept of Afrofuturism. Its Black director Ryan Coogler and Black cast starring Chadwick Boseman as T'Challa created a cultural phenomenon at theaters around the world, particularly among those of the African Diaspora. The philosophy of Afrofuturism, which is, put simply, the intersections of race and technology to visualize the future, relates directly to the fictional nation of Wakanda and the real "Underground Railroad" with its "conductors" and "passengers."[1] In fact, *Black Panther*'s climax, the final fight between T'Challa and his antagonist Killmonger (Michael B. Jordan) transpired on an actual underground railroad with trains dashing by, sought to evoke a familiar historical reference.[2] This prompted my thoughts about the real Black-led "Underground Railroad," named after the newest transportation advancement, and how this network was the enactment of early Afrofuturism for enslaved people in the American South.

After all, being outed and othered as a slave was alienating and the toil robotic. Escaping slavery brought imagination to life, and at times must have felt like "magical realism," and the American North, Canada, Mexico, Africa, Europe, and free Caribbean islands were otherworldly and science fiction-like, in contrast to where they ascended. For running away, involved fighting alien technologies like the telegraph, unknown to little known letters and words, advertisements sought to recapture, countering a formidable adversary that used modernity as its tools, and imagining spaces where they could innovate, flourish, and invoke the cultures of the African Continent. Fugitive enslaved Blacks, casted as "illegal aliens," employed the North Star to take flight to what seem to be nirvana or galaxies away a "Free State," the "Promised Land" Canada, or other outer spaces of slavery. Just as Futurological inquiry was initially met with "suspicion, wariness, and hostility," so too was the Underground Railroad in the pre-antebellum.[3] Also, the Railroad divorced the "long-lasting marriage of transportation and oppression" transforming it into a liberation force.[4]

This chapter will employ the lens of Afrofuturism to reimagine the "Underground Railroad" concept and those seeking freedom by flight, detailing what imagination, tactical codes and deception, the dynamic journey North or to other locations, and faith and fantasy of future, took to even attempt to flee. Black enslavement was as terrifying as any exotic fictional tale, but it happened to real humans. In fact, Josiah Henson, also known as "Uncle Tom," titled one of his narratives *Truth Stranger Than Fiction* and Peter Bruner titled his *A Slave's Adventures Toward Freedom. Not Fiction, But the True Story of a Struggle*. The objective is to connect the Underground Railroad with *Black Panther* to show how enslaved people with the conviction of a free future were Afrofuturist. Afrofuturism is current and on trend and it is historical and reflective of the Underground Railroad practitioners and general runaways. They engaged with inventions such as Eli Whitney's Cotton Gin and like others of their day were fascinated or had "railroad fever" and "future shock" with the Iron Horses racing through the nation moving people and commodities at a rapid pace predominately in the industrial futuristic American North.[5] The chapter will also examine the questions of: Were enslaved Blacks Afrofuturists? How can Afrofuturism be used to grasp the tangible Underground Railroad network and its attached American mythology? How does the Railroad comprehensively mix modernity, fairytale, and actual movement of Black fugitives? And how does the Underground Railroad and the technology used by Blacks to liberate themselves in the past compare to those displayed in *Black Panther?*

The Underground Railroad and Afrofuturism pair well together. Stories told by African-born enslaved people about the Middle Passage to the "New World" must have sounded like Sun Ra's tale of being teleported to Saturn or Elijah Muhammad of the Nation of Islam's extraterrestrial "mother plane" composed of spheres within spheres described by biblical prophet Ezekiel.[6] Slave soundtrack "Swing Low, Sweet Chariot" was re-conceptualized by George Clinton and Parliament-Funkadelic's "Mothership" lifting Blacks out of oppression.[7] "General" Harriet Tubman the "Moses" and Joan of Arc of her people would fit in with *Black Panther*'s Dora Milaje a team of special force women who protect Wakanda.[8] Tubman would also suit the character type of *Matty's Rocket* by cartoonist Tim Fielder. Slavecatcher Ridgeway of Colson

Whitehead's alternate history novel is the adversary that fugitives sought to sidestep.[9] They looked to the heavens or constellations for guidance. Hence, the solar eclipse that was a "sign" that convinced Nat Turner to rebel. The Negro Spirituals or "Sorrow Songs" of Blacks crafted out of necessity are dotted with coded messaging of the Negro grapevine that reflect Psychedelic Funk which was developed in the 1960s and 1970s when outer space was being conceptualized as an escape from social and political bigotry on earth.[2] Visual artists like Renee Cox have empowered the Black body and aesthetic, and *Black Panther* costume designer Ruth E. Carter utilized traditional African dress with futuristic nods. Cox and Carter, like many others, speak to the struggle Blacks fought to gain control over themselves and their attire under the horrors of enslavement. In all, Afrofuturists force its audiences to grapple with the notion that "if you can create a new vision of the future, you can create a new vision of the past" as professor and artist D. Denenge Akpem asserted.[10]

AFROFUTURISM DEFINED FOR THE HISTORICAL AND MYTHOLOGICAL RAILROAD

The term "Afrofuturism" was developed in North America and subsequently spread throughout the African Diaspora. It was coined in the early 1990s by author and cultural critic Mark Dery in an interview he conducted with semiotician Samuel Delany, writer and critic Greg Tate, and Africana Studies professor Tricia Rose later titled "Black to the Future."[11] It helps to define the musical and cultural production of individuals such as Sun Ra and George Clinton and sci-fi writers like Samuel L. Delany, Octavia Bulter, Charles Saunder, and Steve Barnes.[12] Their works displayed the intersection between African Diaspora cultures and technology. Afrofuturism can loosely be defined "as a way of imagining possible futures through a black cultural lens" and it acts as a means "to encourage experimentation, reimagine identities, and activate liberation."[13] Thereby, it's befitting of the Underground Railroad. It has emerged to encompass metaphysics, cosmology, and speculative philosophy. A key factor is that it challenges Eurocentric motifs and asks critical questions of alienation, racism, sexism, and a wealth of exploitive "isms." Afrofuturism also interrupted mainstream and canonized science fiction, liberating Blacks from nonexistence and background positions. Dery stated that the genre was a "Boys Club. Girls, keep out. Blacks and Hispanics and the poor in general, go away."[14]

Afrofuturists view race, as professor and medical-ethics advocate Dorothy Roberts does, as a "fatal invention," but not a "default biological category;" it has real historical, social, and political ramifications.[15] They also assess "race as technology" and as artist John Jennings explained "everything is a type of technology" meaning that race is machinery constructed and institutionalized as a mechanism to entangle and oppress Black people.[16] Media and Cultural Critic Beth Coleman highlighted "race as technology recognizes the proper place of race not as a trait but as a tool—for good or for ill." She expounded "the mechanism of race . . . is not a metal or wood contraption, but rather a thing that functions systematically." Indeed, race has "tool-like properties" which manifest via groups, governments, practices, and laws that deemed Blacks super or sub-human, but not quite fully human hence the calls for human rights and "Black Lives Matter."[17]

To deconstruct the "race as technology" apparatus is a matter of combating internal and external forces that "deliberately rubbed out" or unplugged Blacks from their motherboard, and to rewire thoughts and actions into circuit breakers of change and new spaces. The philosophy of Afrofuturism is applicable to slavery, because it was engineered to produce cash crops at the expense of "alien abductees" or Black bodies in a colonial, capitalistic, and systematic way via the Triangular Trade. However, the Underground Railroad proves that Blacks were technologist themselves, able to counter the technicalities and logistics legislated against them. In other words, Blacks were not primitive or backward and they could compute. Afrofuturists tackle notions of "recovery" and "draw power from the futures they endorse" much like the fugitive runaway.[18] Afrofuturism rewrites the African narrative revealing the "hidden transcript" of resistance and adding a Black empowerment spin to the plot.

The origins of the name Underground Railroad are conspicuous. It is believed that the name came from fugitive slave Tice Davids of Kentucky who fled in 1831 by swimming the Ohio River with his master in close pursuit. He reached the shore of Ripley, Ohio a hotbed of fugitive activity and after being unable to find Davids, as legend has it, the owner declared that he "must have gone off on an underground railroad."[19] Whatever the case, running away was the pessimism and optimism for an imaginary future of freedom. All the tropes of the railroad were employed: from "tracks," "stations," or "depots" to "conductors," "agents," and "station masters." Escaped enslaved individuals were titled "passengers," "cargo," and "freight;" they traveled with "tickets" and stopped at "terminals" on "Freedom Trails" that were funded by "stockholders." The then modern "techie terms" were transposed from their original meanings to coded messages or double talk aimed at transporting Blacks to new spaces outside of enslavement zones. Historically, the Underground Railroad has been clouded with misconceptions and stories of secret quilts, nonexistent hidden passageways and doors, Canadian "Promise Land" discourse, and early oral histories that were retold overtime without validation.[20]

Nonetheless, the traditional notions that the Underground Railroad was a well-organized network of devoted conductors, with secret codes and symbols, put forth by Wilbur H. Siebert between 1896 and 1951 in several volumes, has given way to the modern understanding of its fragmented character, a critique that started with Larry Gara in the 1960s.[21] The Railroad was strongest in areas like Cincinnati, Detroit, Philadelphia, Boston, and Rochester, but it did not help Blacks through the most hazardous section of their voyage, the slaveholding South. The aid, fugitives received, was often from Black allies instead of self-sacrificing White abolitionists who ran a modest risk for assisting. It was the fugitives, not the abolitionists, who played the key role in engineering their own escape and risked the gravest repercussions. Due to the limited nature of the Underground Railroad, fugitives had to rely heavily on themselves and Black communities for successful travel—that was the organized conspiracy. Still Southerners believed their own mythology that it was the abolitionists and not the enslaved themselves, who were generating the fugitive runaway crisis. They deemed that Blacks were too "stupid" to make it to the American North, Canada, or otherwise on their own recognizance. It had to be those damn abolitionist Yankees or sailors causing Blacks to run away. Whites essentially reckoned "their Negros were happy" and did not possess the technical skills to flee, or did they.

FUTURE FREEDOM AND SUPERHERO-LIKE

Enslaved Blacks dreamed and planned futures of freedom and used technology to "teleport" them to spaces where they could live emancipated and seek equality. The very act of writing a slave narrative was done as Harry Smith of Kentucky explained "with the full intention of enlightening the public and future generations on the subject of slavery."[22] Smith was enslaved for fifty years before being freed via the 1863 Emancipation Proclamation. He moved to Indiana and Michigan in the aftermath and possessed the outlook "to have his history written for future generations to read."[23] Even in bondage, Frederick Douglass explained, "I longed to have a future—a future with hope in it" and added, "I formed many a plan for my future, beginning and ending in the same determination . . . to find some way of escape from slavery." He ended *My Bondage and My Freedom* with stating "I shall labor in the future, as I have labored in the past, to promote the . . .elevation of the free colored people."[24] The word "future," though difficult to envision and "thoughts of grandeur," was a part of the Black lexicon and fortitude. It gave them the opportunity to ponder the what-ifs and what is out there? These futurologists and technocrats' present circumstances were not their conclusion or future, but the world they desperately desired could still be defined in the mind and accomplished with time.

William Wells Brown of Kentucky, eager to break the chains binding him, explained, "the trials of the past were all lost in hopes for the future. The love of liberty . . . had been burning in my bosom for years." Brown's obsession with running away only increased in time. "My escape to a land of freedom now appeared certain," he asserted on the eve of his getaway "and the prospects of the future occupied a great part of my thought." Once in the American North, Brown, a committed futurist, worked on Lake Erie steamboats that ushered Blacks to Canada and later wrote the novel *Clotel*, considered to be the first crafted by an African American.[25] For Rev. Charles Thompson faith and future aided him to survive enslavement in the Lower South. The minister explained, "my meditations sustained me through all my trials and hardships, and I plodded my weary way along with God in my heart and bright hopes for the future." He believed in *Hebrews* that "faith is the substance of things hoped for, the evidence of things not seen."[26] Nonetheless, before future "grandeur," the stark journey to "the outer spaces of slavery" had to be undertaken and this tested Blacks in every way imaginable.

All enslaved people that ran away were brave, but some displayed such staggering gall and liberty from mental slavery in the course of fleeing that it is frankly legendary. For these individuals to "act as if" emancipation was won when they were still in bondage and traveling in the South is extraordinary. They were not just running from being beaten or sold, these Blacks had a philosophical perspective for example on God-given "unalienable" rights, Enlightenment ideas, and a critique of unpaid labor. Also, the manner in which they fled [made clear that/highlighted that/reinforced that] [they] possessed." Also how do you possess shock as a runaway? That doesn't seem to align with the other adjectives. For the majority of escapees, sweaty palms, racing hearts, and instances of nervous actions were an innate and human part of the passage, but some like Harriet Tubman and Henry "Box" Brown, seemed to be superhero-like and possessed the weaponry or superpower of conviction. Others like Charles Ball, Henry Bibb, Moses Roper, Venture Smith, and a half dozen more used in the title of their slave narratives the word "Adventures" which was not to belittle their enslavement but rather to highlight the uncertainties they experienced and oddities they witnessed, and outright power it took to take flight.[27]

The aspect that fascinates people about Harriet Tubman is her audacity to outright insist upon being free in the time that she did. A Black petite enslaved woman, some five-foot-tall, disabled by a blow to the head, but still a notorious runaway, who with confidence in God, went back into the American South to save others. Characteristics deemed "weak," Tubman redefined and employed them with might, while trampling Victorian-era stereotypes. Just because Tubman was illiterate, even in freedom, did not make her a fool. The theory of multiple intelligence reveals that she could read people, landscapes, and astronomy which were the skill-sets she needed to undermine captivity. Philadelphia abolitionist William Still reported of Tubman that "The idea of being captured by slave-hunters or slave-holders, seemed never to enter her mind. She was apparently proof against all adversaries."[28] These types of testimonies, though perhaps fabricated to a degree, add to the legacy of Tubman as a direct-action protagonist that took courageous steps to lead people to greater liberty. Also, Tubman believed the future could be now (i.e., the mid-1800s) and engaged social networks, modern medians of the "transportation revolution," and the wired Niagara Falls Suspension Bridge to move across the American–Canadian border.[29] Just the act of running away was heroic and miraculous, but those such as Tubman seemed to possess superhero-like abilities or they experienced/engaged in superhero-like exploits.

Others invoked the same spirit and embraced the colloquialism and aphorism of "fake it 'til you make it." This saying was part performance, therapy, and liberation Afrofuturism to initially "fake" to eventually transition faith and fantasy into a tangible reality. This is reflected in *Black Panther*: it seems that this tension, the present and an imagined future, the role Wakanda could have played in forging a different future for other African nations (thinking of Nakia rescuing the kidnapped girls) is displayed here. The "faking" allowed for survival of enslavement and all of its abuses, but the "making it" asserted the fortitude and tenacity of escaping bondage and seeking to flourish in universal rights, liberties, and immunities, though these elements, vividly visualized and pursued, had not yet materialized.

Henry Bibb explained that after taking passage on a steamboat "I then walked as gracefully up [the] street as if I was not running away ... my object was to go to Canada."[30] The courage that Bibb acted with made him appear as a freedman going about his business. Even the bravery of traveling by daylight instead of at night exemplified a type of innocence as most runaways preferred the cover of night. John W. Lindsey was on a steamboat bound for Pittsburgh when a Black cook asked him if he was free. Lindsey told the man that he "had heard of a man in Maryland who got rich by minding his own business and that he would find it for his own interest to attend to his own affairs."[31] Although Lindsey reacted with a humorous tale, this was a serious matter. Anyone could betray a fugitive in exchange for a slave-catcher's reward, so maintaining a level of secrecy was key—but some were overcome with moxie.

When caught in the act of escaping, William A. Hall responded with boldness. Hall was asked if he was a runaway, he replied sarcastically, "No—I am walking away." When he was asked for his pass to prove his legal status, he answered back, "Do you suppose men need a pass in a free country." When the questioning continued, "I suppose you run away—a good many fugitives go through here, and do mischief," Hall playing freedman explained, "I am doing no mischief—I am a man peaceable, going about my own business; when I am doing mischief, persecute me—while I am peaceable, let no man trouble me."[32] Such actions embody the notion of W. E. B. Du Bois's "Unapologetic Blackness" to forcefully insist upon what was rightfully theirs without reluctance or total fear of the cost.[33] This shook the anxiety fantasy of Whites to think that enslaved Blacks were not simply unintelligent "Sambos" (the Uncle Remus, Jim Crow, and Uncle Tom figures who represented the childlike, faithful, submissive, and superstitious enslaved) but rather "Nats" (named after Nat Turner and represented enslaved persons cosmetically obedient, who were revengeful, bloodthirsty, cunning, treacherous, and savage) capable of intelligently raging against the machine of the "peculiar institution."[34]

USAGE OF TECHNOLOGY

It took technical thought and technology for many Blacks to travel toward liberty lines. Their usage of the railroad, steamboat, and other means of escape made them science lovers and techies, especially when it moved them to freedom faster, but the Black "inner geek" could not totally be revealed because it was illegal to read and write and displays of intelligence were met with punishment.[35] Some Blacks became literate anyway, and others used multiple intelligence means to escape bondage including survival skills and the reading of landscapes. The antennas of Blacks were keen to the instruments and agents of movement and change. Fugitive usage of technology required improvisation and adaptability; otherwise capture was the outcome. The travel of fleeing Blacks was not cookie-cutter simply moving from point A to B. For instance, many Blacks exited trains and ships early to avoid recapture or stayed off of main streets and utilized the "geography of resistance" to sidestep trouble.[36] Moreover, a compass was a great asset, a score of Blacks knew how to use them; however, the North Star or sailors were just as an effective alternative and guiding light. The want to modernize was quite ubiquitous, though Blacks were considered static and unsophisticated, that was until they were gone and unfound. The irony about this all is Africans have had long-standing contributions to science and astronomy in the "Old World" that were interrupted by slavery, but not entirely severed or irreparable in the "New World." There are therefore many parallels to Wakanda and its use of high-end technology due to vibranium.

The most widely used navigational tool was the astrological body of the North Star. "My only guide was the *north star*," explained blacksmith James W. C. Pennington of Maryland; "by this I knew my general course northward, but at what point I should strike Pennsylvania, or when and where I should find a friend I knew not."[37] The North Star (Polaris), the Black "supernova," located on the end of the Little Dipper's handle (Ursa Minor) is the brightest in the constellation points. A portion of Blacks understanding of the stars was passed down. Africans had centuries-old knowledge of the stars. There are also other messages of knowledge in Black Panther— indigenous knowledge—to T'Challa and his father or to the tending of the "heart shaped flower" (see chapter 18 by Paul Karolczyk about "The Other Worlds of *Black Panther's* Purple Heart-Shaped Herb" in this volume).

Dr. Jarita Holbrook, who studied astrophysics and co-edited *African Cultural Astronomy*, simply explained that "there is a history of black people looking at the sky," which was common for cultures throughout the world but "the nature of racism is one where they expect Africans to have done nothing."[38] As if Benjamin Banneker's Almanacs did not contain information on the rising and setting of the sun, the age and motion of the moon, knowledge of the planets above, and other astronomical calculations. In *Black Panther*, African indigenous knowledge was passed down to T'Challa from his father. For instance, the older generation passed down the understanding of the heart-shaped herb so it could aid the next generation.[39]

If the North Star was not visible, informed travelers found other means to forage their way out of bondage. Solomon Mosley and Jesse Happy in the late 1830s both escaped from Kentucky to British Canada by using their masters' horses.[40] Although, it was great to ride the horse of flesh and blood, as more trains crisscrossed the nation Blacks modernized and sought the horse of steam and iron. William Parker, of the 1851 Christiana, Pennsylvania revolt, found his way to the North by following railway tracks from Baltimore to York, Pennsylvania.[41] Later, Parker used the line of the New York Central Railroad to get to Rochester, New York, and boarded a steamer to Canada.[42] Fugitives looked to get off their feet and zoom to the next stage of the journey. Isaac Williams of Virginia *en route* to Canada explained "We watched as the trains came in through the day to see where the depot was, as we wished to get on the track for Philadelphia."[43] Fugitives desired to ride on the locomotive; it was metal magic and invoked surrealism.[44] Blacks praised developments in transportation because they could usher them out of bondage and into new liberated lives with rapidity.[45] "The train was moving at a very high rate of speed for that time of railroad travel," Douglass explained during his escape from Maryland and travels through Delaware "but to my anxious mind, it was moving far too slowly. Minutes were hours, and hours were days during . . . my flight."[46]

Slavery was a Stone Age and fugitives wanted to be "Black Jetsons" to push their people and the nation ahead to be better, faster, inclusive, progressive, and efficient. The steam-powered trains and steamboats might as well have been spaceships and spacecrafts—Blacks would take an UFO up out of captivity. In fact, Sci-fi has a subgenre called "Steampunk" that the Underground Railroad and Afrofuturism fits comfortably into. It employs steam-power technology from the old American "Wild West" and the Victorian Eras as framework to tell alternative stories about the explosion of invention and exploration. This subgenre of "retrofuture" features elegant brick homes, elaborate carriages, "stylish" clothing including the corset, pocket watch, top hat, and petticoat, and the general aristocratic Victorian era behavior all fueled and fashioned by the technological developments of "steam."[47] This timeframe also played host to the Underground Railroad and Blacks that had good use for combustion engines. Scholar John Michael Vlach explained that locomotives "with such inspirational names as Rocket, Racer, Hercules, or Giant suggested the unparalleled power of the train."[48] Using these vehicles demonstrated that Blacks could keep pace with the "hi-tech" world of the nineteenth century. Fugitives grasped that traveling by foot, horse, and sailboat were analog, though they did not totally rule them out, but they desired digital "steam" speeds to stay ahead and competitive with their pursuers. Tech was a part of fugitive's travel plans and nimbleness. They were praised, divine devices that could bring deliverance from the arms of slaveholders.

Fugitives were "commodities" worth a great deal of money thereby they were pursued aggressively by White local law enforcement or slave catchers and their bloodhounds. People considered inferior and non-human in fact brilliantly exploited technology and science as they sought liberation. And as in the film, technology can be a tool for good or for exploitation in the wrong hands. Science and invention open up possibility in Wakanda as the film emphasizes. Shuri and T'Challa used futuristic technology, spacecraft, and vibranium that paralleled the steampower, Railroads, and Underground Railroad of the past.

Also, fugitives needed tactic, technology, and weaponry to counter their antagonist. Runaways avoided dogs by rubbing red onion or spruce pine on the soles of their shoes or scattering pepper or spices over the grounds they employed.[49] This retarded the ability of hounds to successfully sniff out escapees, but these ploys were not a cure-all, they only brought fugitives valuable time to get ahead.[50] The Black fugitive gizmos and gadgets to run did not have flash and flare, sheer effectiveness was the goal. Samuel R. Ward simply explained, "the well-trained bloodhound [is]—a dog educated like an American, and by an American, to hate and worry a Negro."[51] Unquestionably, dogs were employed as repressive machinery of bondage and tools or extensions of their masters to tear flesh from bones. Moreover, slave possession of firearms was a crime punishable by death in Southern states; still fugitives usually carried a gun, a knife, or at least makeshift weaponry for defense on their journey out of slavery. Whites were not the only ones that believed in self-defense against the tyrant with revolver or rifle and the right to safeguard their liberty.

OUTER SPACES OF SLAVERY

For Blacks in the American South anyplace without slavery must have sounded and felt like outer space.[52] They would willingly inhabit those places if given the opportunity—the American North, Canada, Africa, Europe, or otherwise. "Slave holders sought to impress their slaves," Douglass explained, "with a belief in the boundlessness of slave territory and their own limitless power."[53] When Blacks in bondage grasped that there were spaces where they could live "free" or in the "safety" of a rival Empire, it became the brand-new world they sought. Slaveholders also attempted to brainwash Blacks to think that places where slavery had been abolished were untrue, too far, post-apocalyptic, or equally as bad as the American South. Some fugitives dreamed of Canada, others wanted to reach Africa or Haiti, and a number of Blacks wondered to several places attempting to find greater latitude in the "outer spaces of slavery."

Inhabiting places without slavery was the cosmos and fugitives had to some degree time-traveled when abiding within them. These spaces had "evolved" passed the static slave-labor South. Blacks praised these regions and nations for their legal emancipation, despite them being racially coarse, segregated, and alienating. They navigated these newfound galaxies avoiding the Black holes and finding the stars. The outright ownership of Black bodies was low to none in these spaces. Blacks realized as Sun Ra explained "Space is not only high, it's low. It's the bottomless. There's no end to it."[54] The bigotry and segregation for instance in the American North did not cease once they arrived. Racism was a transcending sentiment and having the right to vote was rare outside of New England. The racial and political tension in the North was overshadowed by the brutality of the South, yet it cannot be understated. For example, from 1834 to 1841 in New York, Ohio, and Pennsylvania alone some six race riots took place.[55] The millions of German and Irish immigrants flooding into the urbanizing North fueled even more clashes as each "undesirable" European group competed with Blacks for cheap labor positions and often found themselves cramped into nearby slums. Still fugitives reasoned the "bottomlessness" of space or being as historian Steven Hahn explained "slaves at large" in the North was better than being Southern human "merchandise."[56]

Fugitive Andrew Jackson left Kentucky after more than twenty years of bondage. He was hotly pursued on his northward journey but managed to settle in Illinois then Wisconsin. Jackson explained,

> I am sometimes asked, how we learn the way to the free States? My answer is, that the slaves know much more about this matter than many persons are aware. They have means of communication with each other, altogether unknown to their masters, or to the people of the free states—even the route of some who have escaped is familiarly known to the more intelligent ones.

This underscored the "Negro grapevine" and silent sabotage that was happening just beneath the surface in the slave community. They felt justified in reaching "outer space" like the Israelites that fled from captivity in Egypt. "If it was right for the revolutionary patriots to fight for liberty," Jackson concluded, "it was right for me."[57] With Biblical and philosophical vindication as well as coded data, runaways were ready to blast off.

Some Blacks ironically found the outer spaces of slavery right within the American South. After all it was the goal of Blacks to reshape the boundaries of slavery, so it was abolished in every space. A score in the Deep South acquired freedom by losing themselves in the free Black communities of cities like New Orleans and Charleston. Enslaved people found safety in the remote areas of the Great Dismal Swamp, which borders Virginia and North Carolina, as well as the Florida Everglades.[58] Bands of maroon societies congregated in these areas, while the Sea Islands of the Carolinas, Georgia, and Northern Florida were also options. In addition, escaped enslaved people sometimes entrusted Native American groups, such as the Seminoles, to provide sanctuary and protection.[59] Other enslaved people in the South employed an "absentee" run off status, in which they left for a few days or weeks hiding out in the greater regional area, only to return later when the situation might be more favorable. A larger number of Blacks in the Deep South, though it was fleeting, utilized this runaway model.[60]

However, for the majority entry to the "outer spaces of slavery" required venturing out of the South and crossing regional, national, or imperial borders which offered a new set of circumstances. Black fugitives headed south to the border of Mexico or to the Caribbean islands via southern maritime routes. In the Upper South, particularly in Maryland, Virginia, and Kentucky, Blacks employed the American North and British Canada. The majority of Black runaways did not remain where they initially ran, they moved around in space. For instance, William and Ellen Craft were confronted with the question of staying in the American North or going to Canada or Europe once they reached Philadelphia. They discussed with local leading abolitionists their intentions but were advised to go to Boston instead. Abolitionists assured the Crafts that it was nearly impossible to be taken back into slavery from there. They listened to the recommendation and set out for Boston, settled and found employment in the city, but after the passage of the Fugitive Slave Act of 1850, their owner sent agents to capture them. With the help of the Boston Vigilance Committee, the Crafts eluded the catchers and made their way to Maine, then Canada, and eventually to England, where they remained until after the Civil War.[61]

A score of Blacks just wanted to inhabit Africa, the Mother Continent, which was visualized as a Wakanda-like space. Africa was conceived to have the reparative nurture, values, creativity, ethnic diversity, and tech potential to heal what Western society bothered. William Webb, born in Georgia and enslaved in Mississippi as a hired-hand to several owners, fled during the Civil War to Union lines. "I have a great idea about Africa," Webb explained. "I think that it is the land the Bible speaks of as flowing with milk and honey." He asserted, "I often think that before the end of time, the colored people will return again to their own country [continent], and I think there will be a great light shown to them in the future." He maintained ties of affection with the homeland and in freedom he had a Back-to-Africa attitude. Webb also expressed the desire of Blacks "to learn the sciences of the earth" and he spoke of "a ray of light streaming through the land [. . .] showing the colored people they have some true friends."[62] This was not hollow-headed jibber jabber, it was a heightened realization of origins, lineage, and Afrofuturism. He was never able to reach Africa, but perhaps the most important thing he did was to contemplate it, as others lived out his vision.

The long arc from slavery to attempting to reverse the Atlantic Slave Trade was difficult but became a tangible reality for a score of Blacks. It embodied the Afrofuturism pillar to recover the past and to cite the cultures of the Continent. Blacks that set out for Africa hoped to escape being "aliens," however they had been detached from the motherboard, and untangling the threads of the Middle Passage was technically impossible. Still, in the "outer spaces of slavery" runaways searched in the midst of modernity for a sense of belonging—no matter what planet they landed on. Cora, the main character in Colson Whitehead's *The Underground Railroad,* captured the sentiment of the fugitive best when she explained, "anywhere, anywhere but where you are escaping from…find the terminus or die on the tracks."[63] Runaways simply wanted a new world order that was otherworldly.

OUTRO

In all, equating the Underground Railroad and Afrofuturism is boundary-pushing, but it does not over reach. Is not the point of scholarship, as sociologist Alondra Nelson explained, to engage "speculation, experimentation, and abstraction"?[64] Both the Underground Railroad and Afrofuturism rescue Blacks from the stereotype of being technophobes and asserts that they could keep pace with technoculture if they are not hi-tech hijacked.[65] Black techno-thrillers solved the ultimate algorithm—slavery, a calculated subtraction that did not figure them into the equation. The Underground Railroad has more meaning than the metaphorical. Enslaved people were not void of technology or simply primitive unskilled labor they were driven by the chronicles of progress. Contrary to the mainstream and stereotypical thought Blacks were curious. They looked to take advantage of technology as a tool to make their getaways less troublesome and quicker. By wearing "low-tech" masks, they were able to discreetly decipher complex codes and usher themselves to the "outer spaces of slavery."

By looking at the Underground Railroad as Afrofuturism, the understanding of the imaginative mind of the enslaved can be grasped. In the depths of slavery, Black fugitives had the ability to recognize a free future was possible and that they could be "teleported" through modern technology. This makes them some of the most inventive, astute, and cutting-edge modernist of their time. Blacks had the least resources and were the most resourceful with the little clandestine information and tools they could muster up, maximizing steam and other man-made mechanisms to carry them away from the clutch of bondage. Black runaways considered uneducated, unskilled, backward, and shiftless, among many other things, outthought, maneuvered, and managed to ride modern transportation to transform and invent the futures their slaveholding pursuers wanted to switch off. However, Blacks were state-of-the-art and light-years ahead of what was expected, but worked on a covert frequency as not to alarm owners of their exodus. The fugitive acknowledged that the point of slavery was to technically unplug and power down their abilities to be technocrats. Like in the past, the present, and future "digital divide" is a continuum and means to keep Blacks uninformed, miseducated, and as a technological underclass which renders less autonomy. The Black fugitive, unquestionably underground geeks and nerds, were archetypes for Afrofuturism. *Black Panther*'s final fight between T'Challa and Killmonger takes place on an underground railroad paying homage to Black fugitives' prototype of Afrofuturism.

NOTES

1. Ytasha L. Womack, *Afrofuturism: The World of Black Sci-Fi and Fantasy Culture* (Chicago, IL: Lawrence Hill Books, 2013); and R. Anderson and C.E. Jones,

eds., *Afrofuturism 2.0: The Rise of Astro-Blackness* (Lanham, MD: Lexington Books, 2017).

2. Christopher Lebron, "'Black Panther' Is Not the Movie We Deserve," *Boston Review*, February 17, 2018, http://bostonreview.net/race/christopher-lebron-black-panther; Carvell Wallace, "Why 'Black Panther' Is a Defining Moment for Black America," *The New York Times Magazine*, February 12, 2018, https://www.nytimes.com/2018/02/12/magazine/why-black-panther-is-a-defining-moment-for-black-america.html.

3. Kodwo Eshun, *More Brilliant Than the Sun: Adventures in Sonic Fiction* (New York, NY: Penguin Random House, 1998).

4. C. D. Bhimull, *Empire in the Air: Airline Travel and the African Diaspora* (New York, NY: New York University Press, 2017), 67.

5. Fredric Jameson, "Progress Versus Utopia; or Can We Imagine the Future?" *Science Fiction Studies* 9, no. 2 (July 1982): 151; A.M. Carrington, *Speculative Blackness: The Future of Race in Science Fiction* (Minneapolis, MN: University of Minnesota Press, 2016).

6. R.D.G. Kelley, *Freedom Dreams: The Black Radical Imagination* (Boston, MA: Beacon Press, 2003); Ruth Mayer, ""Africa As an Alien Future": The Middle Passage, Afrofuturism, and Postcolonial Waterworlds," *American Studies* 45, no. 4 (2000): 555–566.

7. Keith Harriston, "Forty Years Later, George Clinton's Mothership is Still Landing," *The Undefeated*, October 2, 2017, https://theundefeated.com/features/forty-years-later-george-clintons-mothership-is-still-landing/.

8. Robyn C. Spencer, "Black Feminist Meditations on the Women of Wakanda (Spoiler Alert)," *Medium*, February 21, 2018, https://medium.com/@robyncspencer/black-feminist-meditations-on-the-women-of-wakanda-5cc79751d9cd.

9. Colson Whitehead, *The Underground Railroad: A Novel* (New York, NY: Doubleday, 2016).

10. Womack, *Afrofuturism*, 154.

11. Mark Dery, *Flame Wars: The Discourse of Cyberculture* (Durham, NC: Duke University Press, 1994).

12. Erik Steinskog, *Afrofuturism and Black Sound Studies: Culture, Technology, and Things to Come* (New York, NY: Palgrave Macmillan, 2017); Paul Youngquist, *A Pure Solar World: Sun Ra and the Birth of Afrofuturism* (Austin, TX: University of Texas Press, 2016); John F. Szwed, *Space Is the Place: The Lives and Times of Sun Ra* (New York, NY: Da Capo Press, 1998).

13. Ingrid LaFleur, "Visual Aesthetics of Afrofuturism - TEDx Fort Greene Salon," *YouTube*, September 25, 2011, https://www.youtube.com/watch?v=x7bCaSzk9Zc; Womack, *Afrofuturism*, 9.

14. Dery, *Flame Wars*, 188.

15. Dorothy Roberts, *Fatal Invention: How Science, Politics, and Big Business Re-create Race in the Twenty-first Century* (New York, NY: The New Press, 2012); Womack, *Afrofuturism*, 27–28.

16. Henry Louis Gates Jr., ed., *Black Literature and Literary Theory* (New York, NY: Routledge, 1984), 59–80.

17. Beth Coleman, "Race as Technology," *Camera Obscura* 24, no. 1 (May 2009): 184–185, 189–190, 199, https://doi.org/10.1215/02705346-2008-018.

18. R. Latham, *Science Fiction Criticism: An Anthology of Essential Writings* (Bloomsbury Academic, 2017), 459–460.

19. David W. Blight, ed., *Passages to Freedom: The Underground Railroad in History and Memory* (New York, NY: HarperCollins, 2006), viii–xi.

20. Jacqueline L. Tobin, Raymond Dobard, and Maude S. Wahlman, *Hidden in Plain View: A Secret Story of Quilts and the Underground Railroad* (New York, NY: Anchor Books, 2000); Karolyn Smardz Frost, *I've Got A Home in Glory Land: A Lost Tale of the Underground Railroad* (New York, NY: Rarrar, Straus and Giroux, 2007); Sharon A. Roger Hepburn, "Following the North Star: Canada as a Haven for Nineteenth-Century American Blacks," *Michigan Historical Review* 25, no. 2. (Fall 1999): 91–126; Nancy Kang, "'As If I Had Entered a Paradise': Fugitive Slave Narratives and Cross-Border Literary History," *African American Review* 39, no. 3 (Fall 2005): 431–457; Boulou de b'Beri, Nina Reid-Maroney, and Handel K. Wright, *The Promised Land: History and Historiography of the Black Experience in Chatham-Kent's Settlements and Beyond* (Toronto, ON: University of Toronto Press, 2014).

21. Larry Gara, *The Liberty Line: The Legend of the Underground Railroad* (Lexington: University of Kentucky Press, 1961); Larry Gara, "The Underground Railroad: Legend or Reality?" *Proceedings of the American Philosophical Society* 105, no. 3 (June 27, 1961): 334–339.

22. Harry Smith, *Fifty Years of Slavery in the United States of America* (Grand Rapids, MI: West Michigan Printing Co., 1891), 5–6.

23. Smith, *Fifty Years of Slavery,* 5–6.

24. Frederick Douglass, *My Bondage and My Freedom* (New York: Miller, Orton & Mulligan, 1855), 95, 153, 405.

25. William Wells Brown, *Narrative of William W. Brown, an American Slave. Written by Himself* (London: C. Gilpin, 1849), 90, 92, 96, 103–108; William Wells Brown, *Clotel; or, The President's Daughter* (London, England: Partridge & Oakey, Paternoster Row, 1853).

26. Charles Thompson, *Biography of a Slave; Being the Experiences of Rev. Charles Thompson, a Preacher of the United Brethren Church, While a Slave in the South. Together with Startling Occurrences Incidental to Slave Life* (Dayton, OH: United Brethren Publishing House, 1875), 79; Hebrews 11:1–6, King James Version.

27. See C. Ball, *Slavery in the United States: A Narrative of the Life and Adventures of Charles Ball, a Black Man, Who Lived Forty Years in Maryland, South Carolina and Georgia, as a Slave Under Various Masters, and was One Year in the Navy with Commodore Barney, During the Late War* (New York: Published by John S. Taylor, 1837); Henry Bibb, *Narrative of the Life and Adventures of Henry Bibb, An American Slave, Written by Himself* (New York: Author, 1849); P. Bruner, *A Slave's Adventures Toward Freedom. Not Fiction, But the Ture Story of a Struggle* (Oxford, OH, 1918); T.H. Jones, *Experience and Personal Narrative of Uncle Tom Jones; Who Was for Forty Years a Slave. Also the Surprising Adventures of Wild Tom, of the Island Retreat, a Fugitive Negro from South Carolina* (Boston: Published

by H. B. Skinner, 185?); N. Love, *Life and Adventures of Nat Love, Better Known in the Cattle Country as "Deadwood Dick," by Himself; a True History of Slavery Days, Life on the Great Cattle Ranges and on the Plains of the "Wild and Woolly" West, Based on Facts, and Personal Experiences of the Author* (Los Angeles, CA: s.n, 1907); P. Neilson, *The Life and Adventures of Zamba, an African Negro King; and His Experience of Slavery in South Carolina. Written by Himself. Corrected and Arranged by Peter Neilson* (London: Smith, Elder, 1847); M. Roper, *A Narrative of the Adventures and Escape of Moses Roper, from American Slavery* (Philadelphia: Merrihew & Gunn., 1838); M. Roper, *Narrative of the Adventures and Escape of Moses Roper, from American Slavery. With an Appendix, Containing a List of Places Visited by the Author in Great Britain and Ireland and the British Isles; and Other Matter* (Berwick-upon-Tweed: Published for the author and printed at the Warder Office, 1848); V. Smith, *A Narrative of the Life and Adventures of Venture, a Native of Africa: But Resident above Sixty Years in the United States of America. Related by Himself* (New- London, [CT]: Printed by C. Holt, at The Bee-office, 1798); V. Smith, *A Narrative of the Life and Adventures of Venture, a Native of Africa, but Resident Above Sixty Years in the United States of America. Related by Himself. New London: Printed in 1798. Reprinted A. D. 1835, and Published by a Descendant of Venture. Revised and Republished with Traditions by H. M. Selden, Haddam, Conn., 1896* (Middletown, CT: J. S. Stewart, 1897); R. Voorhis, *Life and Adventures of Robert, the Hermit of Massachusetts: Who Has Lived 14 Years in a Cave, Secluded from Human Society: Comprising, an Account of his Birth, Parentage, Sufferings, and Providential Escape from Unjust and Cruel Bondage in Early Life, and His Reasons for Becoming a Recluse* (Providence, RI: Printed for H. Trumbull, 1829); P. Wheeler, *Chains and Freedom: Or, The Life and Adventures of Peter Wheeler, a Colored Man Yet Living. A Slave in Chains, a Sailor on the Deep, and a Sinner at the Cross* (New York: E. S. Arnold & Co., 1839).

28. William Still, *The Underground Railroad* (1872; repr., New York, NY: Arno Press, 1968), 540; Janell Hobson, "Between History and Fantasy: Harriet Tubman in the Artistic and Popular Imaginary," *Meridians* 12, no. 2 (2014): 50–77, doi:10.2979/meridians.12.2.50; and M.G. Hill, ed., *Black Bodies and Transhuman Realities: Scientifically Modifying the Black Body in Posthuman Literature and Culture* (Lanham, MD: Lexington Books, 2019).

29. G.R. Taylor, *The Transportation Revolution, 1815-1860* (New York, NY: Harper & Row, 1951); H.N. Scheiber and Stephen Salsbury, "Reflections on George Rogers Taylor's 'The Transportation Revolution, 1815-1860': A Twenty-Five Year Retrospect," *The Business History Review* 51, no. 1 (Spring 1977): 79–89; G.P. De T. Glazebrook, *A History of Transportation in Canada* (New Haven, CT: Yale University Press, 1938).

30. Bibb, *Narrative of the Life and Adventures of Henry Bibb*, 50.

31. Benjamin Drew, *The Refugee: Or the Narratives of Fugitive Slaves in Canada* (New York, NY: John P. Jewett and Company, 1856), 53; d.j. Broyld, "Justice was Refused Me, I Resolved to Free Myself:" John W. Lindsay Finding Elements of American Freedom's in British Canada, 1805-1876, *Ontario History* CIX, no. 1 (Spring 2017): 27–59.

32. Drew, *The Refugee*, 222.

33. W.E.B. Du Bois, "The Prize Fighter," *The Crisis* 8, no. 4 (August 1914).

34. J.W. Blassingame, *The Slave Community: Plantation Life in the Antebellum South* (New York, NY: Oxford University Press, 1979), 223–248.

35. R. Eglash, Race, "Sex, and Nerds: From Black Geeks to Asian American Hipsters," *Social Text* 20, no. 2 (2002): 49–64; L. Kendall, ""White and Nerdy": Computers, Race, and the Nerd Stereotype," *Journal of Popular Culture* 44, no. 3 (June 2011): 505–524.

36. C.J. LaRoche, *Free Black Communities and The Underground Railroad: The Geography of Resistance* (Urbana, IL: University of Illinois Press, 2014); M. Schoolman, *Abolitionist Geographies* (Minneapolis, MN: University of Minnesota Press, 2014).

37. J.W.C. Pennington, *The Fugitive Blacksmith or Events in the History of James W.C. Pennington*, 3rd ed. (London: Charles Gilpin, 1850), 15.

38. J. Holbrook, R. Thebe Medupe, and Johnson O. Urama, eds., *African Cultural Astronomy: Current Archaeoastronomy and Ethnoastronomy Research in Africa* (New York, NY: Springer, 2008); Womack, *Afrofuturism*, 92–94.

39. B. Rusert, "The Science of Freedom: Counterarchives of Racial Science on the Antebellum Stage," *African American Review* 45, no. 3, Special issue: On Black Performance (Fall 2012): 33–64; C. Cerami, *Benjamin Banneker: Surveyor, Astronomer, Publisher, Patriot* (John Wiley & Sons, 2002).

40. Frost, *I've Got A Home in Glory Land*, 239–246; David Murray, "Hands Across the Border: The Abortive Extradition of Solomon Moesby," *The Canadian Historical Review of American Studies* 30 (2000): 186–209; R.J. Zorn, "Criminal Extradition Menaces the Canadian Haven for Fugitive Slaves, 1841-1861," *Canadian Historical Review* 38 (December 1957): 284–294.

41. Fergus M. Bordewich, *Bound for Canaan: The Epic Story of the Underground Railroad, America's First Civil Rights Movement* (New York, NY: Amistad, 2006), 327.

42. *Frederick Douglass' Paper*, September 25, 1851; February 7, 1853.

43. Drew, *The Refugee*, 66.

44. Wakanda and its transportation system has developed an advanced flying technology, allowing its inhabitants to "escape" the real world into the future by being transported in a portal to their own country.

45. It is also important that Shuri and T'Challa reveal the spacecraft at the end of the film, showing the Black youth in Los Angeles that their technology is superior to the American way of life.

46. Frederick Douglass, *Life and Times of Frederick Douglass: His Early Life as a Slave, His Escape from Bondage, and His Complete History to the Present Time* (Hartford, CT: Park Publishing Co, 1881), 199.

47. Julie Anne Taddeo and Cynthia J. Miller, eds., *Steaming into a Victorian Future: A Steampunk Anthology* (Lanham, MD: Scarecrow, 2013); Margaret Rose, "Extraordinary Pasts: Steampunk as a Mode of Historical Representation," *Journal of the Fantastic in the Arts* 20, no. 3 (77) (2009): 319–333.

48. D.W. Blight, ed., *Passages to Freedom: The Underground Railroad in History and Memory* (New York, NY: HarperCollins, 2006), 98.

49. Isaac D. Williams and William F. Goldie, *Sunshine and Shadow of Slave Life. Reminiscences as told by Isaac D. Williams to "Tege"* (East Saginaw MI: Evening News Printing and Binding House, 1885), 10.

50. John Hope Franklin and Loren Schweninger, *Runaway Slaves: Rebels on the Plantation* (New York, NY: Oxford University Press, 2000), 162.

51. S.R. Ward, *Autobiography of a Fugitive Negro: His Anti-Slavery Labours in the United States, Canada, and England* (London: John Snow, 1855), 163–164.

52. Michelle Lee White, "Aftrotech and Outer Spaces," *Art Journal* 60, no. 3 (Autumn 2001): 90–104.

53. J. Stauffer, *Giants: The Parallel Lives of Frederick Douglass and Abraham Lincoln* (New York, NY: Twelve, 2008), 46.

54. Ramzi Fawaz, "Space, that Bottomless Pit: Planetary Exile and Metaphors of Belonging in American Afrofuturist Cinema," *Callaloo* 35, no. 4 (Fall 2012): 1103–1122.

55. L. Kerber, "Abolitionists and Amalgamators: The New York City Race Riots of 1834," *New York History* 48 (1967): 28–39; M. Feldberg, *The Turbulent Era: Riot and Disorder in Jacksonian America* (New York, NY: Oxford University Press, 1980).

56. Steven Hahn, *The Political Worlds of Slavery and Freedom* (Cambridge, MA: Harvard University Press, 2009), 1–54.

57. Andrew Jackson, *Narrative and Writings of Andrew Jackson, of Kentucky; Containing an Account of His Birth, and Twenty-Six Years of His Life While a Slave; His Escape; Five Years of Freedom, Together with Anecdotes Relating to Slavery; Journal of One Year's Travels; Sketches, etc. Narrated by Himself; Written by a Friend* (Syracuse, NY: Daily and Weekly Star Office, 1847), 13–15.

58. Irwin D.S. Winsboro, and Joe Knetsch, "Florida Slaves, the 'Saltwater Railroad' to the Bahamas, and Anglo-American Diplomacy," *Journal of Southern History*, 79 (February 2013): 51–78; William H. Alexander, Cassandra L. Newby-Alexander, and Charles H. Ford, eds., *Voices from Within the Veil: African Americans and the Experience of Democracy* (Newcastle, UK: Cambridge Scholars, 2008), 85–112.

59. Hahn, *The Political Worlds of Slavery and Freedom,* 26; Sylviane A. Diouf, *Slavery's Exiles: The Story of the American Maroons* (New York, NY: New York University Press, 2016).

60. Franklin and Schweninger, *Runaway Slaves,* 98–101.

61. William Craft, *Running a Thousand Miles for Freedom; or the Escape of William and Ellen Craft from Slavery* (London: William Tweedie, Strand, 1860), 81, 89–92.

62. William Webb, *The History of William Webb, Composed by Himself* (Detroit, MI: Egbert Hoekstra, 1873), 74–77.

63. Whitehead, *The Underground Railroad,* 304.

64. Howard Rambsy II, "Beyond Keeping It Real: OutKast, the Funk Connection, and Afrofuturism," *American Studies* 52, no. 4, The Funk Issue (2013): 205–206;

Alondra Nelson, "Afrofuturism: Past-Future Visions," *Color Lines* (Spring 2000): 34–37.

65. Constance Penley, and Andrew Ross, *Technoculture* (Minneapolis, MN: University of Minnesota Press, 1991); Debra Benita Shaw, *Technoculture: The Key Concept* (New York, NY: Berg, 2008).

WORKS CITED

Alexander, William H, Cassandra L. Newby-Alexander, and Charles H. Ford, eds. *Voices from Within the Veil: African Americans and the Experience of Democracy.* Newcastle, UK: Cambridge Scholars, 2008.

Anderson, Reynaldo, and Charles E. Jones, eds. *Afrofuturism 2.0: The Rise of Astro-Blackness.* Lanham, MD: Lexington Books, 2017.

Bauer, Raymond A., and Alice H. Bauer. "Day to Day Resistance to Slavery." *The Journal of Negro History* 27, no. 4 (October 1942): 388–419.

Bhimull, Chandra D. *Empire in the Air: Airline Travel and the African Diaspora.* New York, NY: New York University Press, 2017.

Bibb, Henry. *Narrative of the Life and Adventures of Henry Bibb, An American Slave, Written by Himself.* New York: Author, 1849.

Blassingame, John W. *The Slave Community: Plantation Life in the Antebellum South.* New York, NY: Oxford University Press, 1979.

Blight, David W., ed. *Passages to Freedom: The Underground Railroad in History and Memory.* New York, NY: HarperCollins, 2006.

Bolster, W. Jeffrey. *Black Jacks: African American Seamen in the Age of Sail.* Cambridge: Harvard University Press, 1997.

Bordewich, Fergus M. *Bound for Canaan: The Epic Story of the Underground Railroad, America's First Civil Rights Movement.* New York, NY: Amistad, 2006.

Bould, Mark. "The Ships Landed Long Ago: Afrofuturism and Black SF." *Science Fiction Studies* 34, no. 2 (2007): 177–186.

Brown, Henry Box. *Narrative of Henry Box Brown, Who Escaped from Slavery, Enclosed in a Box 3 Feet Long and 2 Wide. Written from a Statement of Facts Made by Himself.* Boston, MA: Brown and Stearns, 1849.

Brown, Henry Box. *Narrative of Henry Box Brown, Written by Himself.* Manchester: Printed by Lee and Glynn, 1851.

Brown, Henry Box. Introduction by Richard Newman & Forward by Henry Louis Gates, Jr. *Narrative of Henry Box Brown, Written by Himself.* New York, NY: Oxford University Press, 2002.

Brown, William Wells. *Clotel; or, The President's Daughter.* London, England: Partridge & Oakey, Paternoster Row, 1853.

Brown, William Wells. *Narrative of William W. Brown, an American Slave. Written by Himself.* London: C. Gilpin, 1849.

Broyld, dann j. "Fannin' Flies and Tellin' Lies: Black Runaways and American Tales of Life in British Canada Before the Civil War." *American Review of Canadian Studies* 44, no. 2 (April 2014): 169–186.

Broyld, dann j. "'Justice was Refused Me, I Resolved to Free Myself:' John W. Lindsay Finding Elements of American Freedom's in British Canada, 1805-1876." *Ontario History* CIX, no. 1 (Spring 2017): 27–59.

Bruner, Peter. *A Slave's Adventures Toward Freedom. Not Fiction, But the Ture Story of a Struggle*. Oxford, OH, 1918.

Carrington, Andre M. *Speculative Blackness: The Future of Race in Science Fiction*. Minneapolis, MN: University of Minnesota Press, 2016.

Cerami, Charles. *Benjamin Banneker: Surveyor, Astronomer, Publisher, Patriot*. John Wiley & Sons, 2002.

Coleman, Beth. "Race as Technology." *Camera Obscura* 24, no. 1 (2009): 177–207.

Craft, William. *Running a Thousand Miles for Freedom; or the Escape of William and Ellen Craft from Slavery*. London: William Tweedie, Strand, 1860.

De b'Beri, Boulou, Nina Reid-Maroney, and Handel K. Wright. *The Promised Land: History and Historiography of the Black Experience in Chatham-Kent's Settlements and Beyond*. Toronto, ON: University of Toronto Press, 2014.

Dery, Mark. *Flame Wars: The Discourse of Cyberculture*. Durham, NC: Duke University Press, 1994.

Douglass, Frederick. *Life and Times of Frederick Douglass: His Early Life as a Slave, His Escape from Bondage, and His Complete History to the Present Time*. Hartford, CT: Park Publishing Co., 1881.

Douglass, Frederick. *My Bondage and My Freedom*. New York: Miller, Orton & Mulligan, 1855.

Drew, Benjamin. *The Refugee: Or the Narratives of Fugitive Slaves in Canada*. New York, NY: John P. Jewett and Company, 1856.

Eglash, Ron. "Race, Sex, and Nerds: From Black Geeks to Asian American Hipsters." *Social Text* 20, no. 2 (2002): 49–64.

English, Daylanne K., and Alvin Kim. "Now We Want Our Funk Cut: Janelle Monáe's Neo-Afrofuturism." *American Studies* 52, no. 4, The Funk Issue (2013): 217–230.

Eshun, Kodwo. "Further Considerations on Afrofuturism." *CR: The New Centennial Review* 3, no. 2, Globalicities: Possibilities of the Globe (Summer 2003): 289–289.

Eshun, Kodwo. *More Brilliant Than the Sun: Adventures in Sonic Fiction*. New York, NY: Penguin Random House, 1998.

Fawaz, Ramzi. "Space, that Bottomless Pit: Planetary Exile and Metaphors of Belonging in American Afrofuturist Cinema." *Callaloo* 35, no. 4 (Fall 2012): 1103–1122.

Feldberg, Michael. *The Turbulent Era: Riot and Disorder in Jacksonian America*. New York, NY: Oxford University Press, 1980.

Franklin, John Hope, and Loren Schweninger. *Runaway Slaves: Rebels on the Plantation*. New York, NY: Oxford University Press, 2000.

Frost, Karolyn Smardz. *I've Got A Home in Glory Land: A Lost Tale of the Underground Railroad*. New York, NY: Rarrar, Straus and Giroux, 2007.

Gara, Larry. *The Liberty Line: The Legend of the Underground Railroad*. Lexington: University of Kentucky Press, 1961.

Gara, Larry. "The Underground Railroad: Legend or Reality?" *Proceedings of the American Philosophical Society* 105, no. 3 (June 27, 1961): 334–339.

Gates, Henry Louis, ed. *Black Literature and Literary Theory*. New York, NY: Routledge, 1984.

Glazebrook, G. P. De T. *A History of Transportation in Canada*. New Haven, CT: Yale University Press, 1938.

Hahn, Steven. *The Political Worlds of Slavery and Freedom*. Cambridge, MA: Harvard University Press, 2009.

Hall, Stephen G. "To Render the Private Public: William Still and the Selling of 'The Underground Rail Road.'" *The Pennsylvania Magazine of History and Biography* 127, no. 1 (January 2003): 35–55.

Harriston, Keith. "Forty Years Later, George Clinton's Mothership is Still Landing." *The Undefeated*, October 2, 2017. https://theundefeated.com/features/forty-years-later-george-clintons-mothership-is-still-landing/.

Henson, Josiah. *Truth Stranger Than Fiction. Father Henson's Story of His Own Life*. Boston, MA: John P. Jewett, 1858.

Hepburn, Sharon A. Roger. "Following the North Star: Canada as a Haven for Nineteenth-Century American Blacks." *Michigan Historical Review* 25, no. 2. (Fall 1999): 91–126.

Holbrook, Jarita, R. Thebe Medupe, and Johnson O. Urama, eds. *African Cultural Astronomy: Current Archaeoastronomy and Ethnoastronomy research in Africa*. New York, NY: Springer, 2008.

Hobson, Janell. "Between History and Fantasy: Harriet Tubman in the Artistic and Popular Imaginary." *Meridians* 12, no. 2 (2014): 50–77. doi:10.2979/meridians.12.2.50.

Howe, Samuel Gridley. *The Refugees from Slavery in Canada West: Report to the Freedman's Inquiry Commission*. Boston, MA: Wright and Potter, 1864.

Jackson, Andrew. *Narrative and Writings of Andrew Jackson, of Kentucky; Containing an Account of His Birth, and Twenty-Six Years of His Life While a Slave; His Escape; Five Years of Freedom, Together with Anecdotes Relating to Slavery; Journal of One Year's Travels; Sketches, etc. Narrated by Himself; Written by a Friend*. Syracuse: Daily and Weekly Star Office, 1847.

Jacobs, Harriet A. *Incidents in the Life of a Slave Girl. Written by Herself*. Boston: Published for the Author, 1861, c1860.

Jameson, Fredric. "Progress Versus Utopia; or Can We Imagine the Future?" *Science Fiction Studies* 9, no. 2, Utopia and Anti-Utopia (July 1982): 147–158.

Kang, Nancy. "'As If I Had Entered a Paradise': Fugitive Slave Narratives and Cross-Border Literary History." *African American Review* 39, no. 3 (Fall 2005): 431–457.

Kelley, Robin D.G. *Freedom Dreams: The Black Radical Imagination*. Boston, MA: Beacon Press, 2003.

Kelley, Sean. "'Mexico in His Head': Slavery and the Texas-Mexico Border, 1810-1860." *Journal of Social History* 37, no. 3 (Spring 2004): 709–723.

Kendall, Lori. "'White and Nerdy': Computers, Race, and the Nerd Stereotype." *Journal of Popular Culture* 44, no. 3 (June 2011): 505–524.

Kerber, Linda. "Abolitionists and Amalgamators: The New York City Race Riots of 1834." *New York History* 48 (1967): 28–39.

LaRoche, Cheryl Janifer. *Free Black Communities and The Underground Railroad: The Geography of Resistance*. Urbana, IL: University of Illinois Press, 2014.

Latham, Rob. *Science Fiction Criticism: An Anthology of Essential Writings*. Bloomsbury Academic, 2017.

Lebron, Christopher. "'Black Panther' Is Not the Movie We Deserve." *Boston Review*, February 17, 2018, http://bostonreview.net/race/christopher-lebron-black-panther.

Manning, Patrick. *The African Diaspora: A History Through Culture*. New York, NY: Columbia University Press, 2010.

Mayer, Ruth. "'Africa As an Alien Future': The Middle Passage, Afrofuturism, and Postcolonial Waterworlds." *American Studies* 45, no. 4, Time and the African-American Experience (2000): 555–566.

Murray, David. "Hands Across the Border: The Abortive Extradition of Solomon Moesby." *The Canadian Historical Review of American Studies* 30 (2000): 186–209.

Nelson, Alondra. "Afrofuturism: Past-Future Visions." *Color Lines* (Spring 2000): 34–37.

Pease, Jane H., and William H. Pease. *Bound with Them in Chains: A Biographical History of the Antislavery Movement*. Westport, CT: Greenwood Press, Inc., 1972.

Penley, Constance, and Andrew Ross. *Technoculture*. Minneapolis, MN: University of Minnesota Press, 1991.

Pennington, James W.C. *The Fugitive Blacksmith or Events in the History of James W.C. Pennington*. 3rd ed. London: Charles Gilpin, 1850.

Rambsy II, Howard. "Beyond Keeping It Real: OutKast, the Funk Connection, and Afrofuturism." *American Studies* 52, no. 4, The Funk Issue (2013): 205–216.

Rasheedah Phillips. *Black Quantum Futurism: Theory & Practice*. AfroFuturist Affair, 2015.

Roberts, Dorothy. *Fatal Invention: How Science, Politics, and Big Business Re-create Race in the Twenty-first Century*. New York, NY: The New Press, 2012.

Robbins, Hollis. "Fugitive Mail: The Deliverance of Henry "Box" Brown and Antebellum Postal Politics." *American Studies* 50, no. 1/2 (Spring/Summer 2009): 2–25.

Rose, Margaret. "Extraordinary Pasts: Steampunk as a Mode of Historical Representation." *Journal of the Fantastic in the Arts* 20, no. 3 (77) (2009) 319–333.

Rusert, Britt. *Fugitive Science: Empiricism and Freedom in Early African American Culture*. New York, NY: New York University Press, 2017.

Scheiber, Harry N., and Stephen Salsbury, "Reflections on George Rogers Taylor's 'The Transportation Revolution, 1815-1860': A Twenty-Five Year Retrospect." *The Business History Review* 51, no. 1 (Spring, 1977): 79–89.

Schoolman, Martha. *Abolitionist Geographies*. Minneapolis, MN: University of Minnesota Press, 2014.

Scott, James C. *Domination and the Arts of Resistance: Hidden Transcripts*. New Haven: Yale University Press, 1990.

———. *Weapons of the Weak: Everyday Forms of Peasant Resistance.* New Haven: Yale University Press, 1985.

Seraile, William. "The Brief Diplomatic Career of Henry Highland Garnet." *Phylon* 46, no. 1 (1st Qtr., 1985): 71–81.

Shadd, Mary Ann. *A Plea for Emigration or Notes of Canada West in Its Moral, Social, and Political Aspect: Suggestions Respecting Mexico, W. Indies and Vancouver's Island, For the Information of Colored Emigrants.* Detroit, MI: George W. Pattison, 1852.

Shaw, Debra Benita. *Technoculture: The Key Concept.* New York, NY: Berg, 2008.

Siebert, Wilbur H. *The Underground Railroad from Slavery to Freedom: A Comprehensive History.* New York, NY: Dover Publications, 2006.

Silverman, Jason A. *Unwelcome Guests: Canada West's Response to American Fugitive Slaves.* Millwood, NY: Associated Faculty Press, Inc., 1985.

Smith, Harry. *Fifty Years of Slavery in the United States of America.* Grand Rapids, MI: West Michigan Printing Co., 1891.

Spencer, Robyn C. "Black Feminist Meditations on the Women of Wakanda (Spoiler Alert)." *Medium*, February 21, 2018, https://medium.com/@robyncspencer/black-feminist-meditations-on-the-women-of-wakanda-5cc79751d9cd.

Stauffer, John. *Giants: The Parallel Lives of Frederick Douglass and Abraham Lincoln.* New York, NY: Twelve, 2008.

Steinskog, Erik. *Afrofuturism and Black Sound Studies: Culture, Technology, and Things to Come.* New York, NY: Palgrave Macmillan, 2017.

Still, William. *The Underground Railroad.* 1872. Reprint, New York, NY: Arno Press, 1968.

Szwed, John F. *Space Is the Place: The Lives and Times of Sun Ra.* New York, NY: Da Capo Press, 1998.

Taddeo, Julie Anne, and Cynthia J. Miller, eds. *Steaming into a Victorian Future: A Steampunk Anthology.* Lanham, MD: Scarecrow, 2013.

Taylor, George Rogers. *The Transportation Revolution, 1815-1860.* New York, NY: Harper & Row, 1951.

Thompson, Charles. *Biography of a Slave; Being the Experiences of Rev. Charles Thompson, a Preacher of the United Brethren Church, While a Slave in the South. Together with Startling Occurrences Incidental to Slave Life.* Dayton, OH: United Brethren Publishing House, 1875.

Tobin, Jacqueline L, Raymond Dobard, and Maude S. Wahlman. *Hidden in Plain View: A Secret Story of Quilts and the Underground Railroad.* New York, NY: Anchor Books, 2000.

Van Veen, Tobias C., and Reynaldo Anderson. "Future Movements: Black Lives, Black Politics, Black Futures—An Introduction." *Topia: Canadian Journal of Cultural Studies* 39 (Spring 2018): 5–21.

Wallace, Carvell, "Why 'Black Panther' Is a Defining Moment for Black America." *The New York Times Magazine*, February 12, 2018, https://www.nytimes.com/2018/02/12/magazine/why-black-panther-is-a-defining-moment-for-black-america.html.

Walton, Jr., Hanes, Ronald Clark, James Bernard Rosser, and Robert L. Stevenson. "Henry Highland Garnet Revisited Via His Diplomatic Correspondence: The

Correction of Misconceptions and Errors." *The Journal of Negro History* 68, no. 1 (Winter, 1983): 80–92.

Ward, Samuel Ringgold. *Autobiography of a Fugitive Negro: His Anti-Slavery Labours in the United States, Canada, and England.* London: John Snow, 1855.

Washington, Booker T. *Up from Slavery: An Autobiography.* Garden City, NJ: Doubleday, 1901.

Webb, William. *The History of William Webb, Composed by Himself.* Detroit, MI: Egbert Hoekstra, 1873.

Wells, H.G., and Taylor Anderson, eds. *The Future of America: A Search After Realities.* 1906. Reprint, CreateSpace Independent Publishing, 2017.

White, Michelle-Lee, Keith Piper, Alondra Nelson, Arnold J. Kemp, and Erika Dalya Muhammad. "Aftrotech and Outer Spaces." *Art Journal* 60, no. 3 (Autumn 2001): 90–104.

Whitehead, Colson. *The Underground Railroad: A Novel.* New York, NY: Doubleday, 2016.

Williams, Isaac D, and William F. Goldie. *Sunshine and Shadow of Slave Life. Reminiscences as told by Isaac D. Williams to "Tege."* East Saginaw MI: Evening News Printing and Binding House, 1885.

Winsboro, Irwin D.S., and Joe Knetsch. "Florida Slaves, the 'Saltwater Railroad' to the Bahamas, and Anglo-American Diplomacy." *Journal of Southern History* 79 (February 2013): 51–78.

Womack, Ytasha L. *Afrofuturism: The World of Black Sci-Fi and Fantasy Culture.* Chicago, IL: Lawrence Hill Books, 2013.

Youngquist, Paul. *A Pure Solar World: Sun Ra and the Birth of Afrofuturism.* Austin, TX: University of Texas Press, 2016.

Zorn, Roman J. "Criminal Extradition Menaces the Canadian Haven for Fugitive Slaves, 1841-1861." *Canadian Historical Review* 38 (December 1957): 284–294.

Zuberi, Nabeel. "Is This the Future? Black Music and Technology Discourse." *Science Fiction Studies* 34, no. 2, Afrofuturism (July 2007): 283–300.

FILMS

Black Panther. Directed by Ryan Coogler. United States: Walt Disney Studios Motion Pictures, 2018.

Chapter 8

The Evolution of the Dora Milaje

Wakanda's Greatest Warriors in Comics and Film

Joshua Truelove

The Dora Milaje, the warrior women and king's guard of Wakanda, grew famous after the theatrical release of *Black Panther* (directed by Ryan Coogler) in 2018. Toys, cosplays, and other forms of fandom became dedicated to the big screen portrayals of the Dora Milaje. Yet, the Dora Milaje have a deeper lore than the one that exists in the Marvel Cinematic Universe. The group debuted in Christopher Priest's 1998 *Black Panther* comic series and looked much different than the on-screen version of the group that is popular in American culture. The Dora Milaje in the comic were very representative of the "sex sells" culture and era of cynicism of the 1990s. The women were sexualized, looked like supermodels, and were described as promised future wives to the king of Wakanda. As the comics moved forward, and the Marvel films released, the characters became more adaptable to their current era. The comics introduced less sexualized characters in the early 2000s and 2010s. On screen, Ryan Coogler's *Black Panther* placed the Dora Milaje at the center of the story and featured the women as freedom fighters who were on equal standing with T'Challa and other men of Wakanda rather than sexualized trophy wives readers saw in many of the comics. By exploring the origins, background, characters, technology, and image of the Dora Milaje, this chapter argues that the Dora Milaje have a deeper history and lore than just the one expressed in the Marvel Cinematic Universe and that the women warriors of Wakanda have reflected and adapted to the eras in which they existed.

FROM "AMAZONIAN TEENAGE KARATE CHICKS" TO THE MIDNIGHT ANGELS

In 1966, comic book creators Stan Lee and Jack Kirby created a new character to join the Marvel universe. In *Fantastic Four #52*, the heroes known as the Fantastic Four arrived in the fictional African nation of Wakanda, where readers were introduced to a metal called vibranium, a fascinating new superhero landscape, and a "sensational" new superhero: the Black Panther.[1],[2] Readers soon learned the *Black Panther* T'Challa was King of Wakanda and had fighting abilities and access to advanced technologies that were found nowhere else on earth. As years passed, the Black Panther appeared in the story arcs of other famous superheroes such as *Captain America* and *Daredevil*.[3] In 1968, T'Challa made his debut as a member of a team of Earth's mightiest heroes, the Avengers, where he and the Avengers fought the Grim Reaper.[4] The Black Panther's popularity grew along with the number of appearances he made in comic book stories inside the Marvel universe.

In 1977, T'Challa finally starred in his own comic book series, *Black Panther #1*, where readers learned more about the Black Panther and the enchanting world of Wakanda.[5] As more years passed, and more Black Panther stories were written, Wakanda became its own little universe under Marvel's umbrella. The nation had its superhero in the *Black Panther*, but also had a copious number of friends and foes to its main character T'Challa. Kirby's *Black Panther* series was cancelled after fifteen issues, and the character did not receive his own arc again until Peter Gillis's 1988 four-part miniseries *Black Panther Volume Two*.[6] In 1998, the Black Panther again starred in his own comic series, this one much lengthier and more significant, Christopher Priest's *Black Panther Volume Three*.[7] Priest receives credit as the "man who made Black Panther cool," and it was his Black Panther story arc where readers were introduced to T'Challa's greatest allies yet: the Dora Milaje.[8]

In 1998, Christopher Priest's *Black Panther Volume Three #1* titled "The Client," debuted. Readers were introduced to a "cooler" version of the Black Panther, as T'Challa, "the client" of a new wise-cracking character named Everett Ross who narrated the story, is first seen walking out of a limousine and wearing a sharp suit, a stylish beard, sunglasses, and two women on his arms.[9] The women were dressed in red dresses and high heels, seeming as nothing more than T'Challa's trophy wives or simply his arm-candy.[10] As T'Challa fought a group of criminals, his female companions threw punches and kicks in his aide. Everett Ross described the women: "The girls were six feet tall and not quite LEGAL age. The client called them Dora Milaje, or 'adored ones,' and described them as the king's concomitants. A tribal thing—kind of wives in training."[11] The reader soon learned from Ross that these two Dora Milaje members were Okoye, T'Challa's "chauffer," and Nakia, his "personal aide."[12] In *Black Panther #2*, Ross further describes the Dora Milaje as "Amazonian teenage karate chicks from two Wakandan tribes."[13] In *Black Panther #3*, readers witnessed T'Challa having a negative reaction after being kissed by Nakia. Ross explained that the Dora Milaje were wives in training, promised to marry the King of Wakanda in order to keep peace between warring tribes.[14] T'Challa saw this marriage as purely ceremonial and had no intentions of even laying a hand on Nakia or any of the adored ones. Instead, he viewed the Dora Milaje as his king's guard. From the early introductions of the Dora Milaje in Priest's *Black Panther* story arc, the adored ones were much different than the women on the big screen in the Marvel Cinematic Universe (MCU). As opposed to shaved heads and body armor, the early renditions of Okoye and Nakia bore a striking resemblance to British Black supermodel Naomi Campbell and African American television actress and supermodel Tyra Banks.[15] The Dora Milaje were young, promised to the King of Wakanda and served as a type of secret service or king's guard.

The Dora Milaje are made up of hundreds of women from at least eighteen Wakandan tribes. Each tribe submits potential wives for the King. A Wakandan King who favored one bride-to-be risked dissent among Wakandan tribes, so the King is technically "married" to a woman from each tribe.[16] T'Challa, though, saw this tradition as purely ceremonial. For most Black Panther storylines, only a few of the members are central to the plot: Okoye, Nakia, Ayo, Aneka, and Queen Divine Justice. Okoye is the Dora Milaje's greatest warrior. Although the Dora Milaje in the comics are meant to serve as wives-in-training, Okoye happily accepted T'Challa's refusal of the tradition and serves as his personal bodyguard in both the comics and MCU. Nakia is also a great warrior but fell madly in love with T'Challa and could not accept his refusal of the wives-in-training tradition of the Dora Milaje. She attempted to kill T'Challa's true love, Monica Lynne, which led to T'Challa exiling her from Wakanda and her heel-turn under her new name: Malice.[17] Aneka was one of the leaders and trainers of the Dora Milaje, until she killed a Wakandan tribe leader due to his abuse of women. Aneka was imprisoned by the Dora Milaje, until Ayo broke her out, which lead to the now former Dora Milaje to form their own vigilante duo: the Midnight Angels. Finally, Queen Divine Justice: an African American activist from Chicago who learned of her Wakandan origins when T'Challa came to the United States to tell her and convince her to join the Dora Milaje. Queen Divine Justice then became a Dora Milaje while maintaining her role as an activist. These women were featured in the most important story arcs highlighting the Dora Milaje in the Marvel comics.

The first time readers met the Dora Milaje was in Christopher Priest's *Black Panther* 62-issue-run beginning in 1998. Priest took the Black Panther character and succeeded in his attempt to make him appealing to mainstream audiences.[18] In fact, Priest had the daunting task of rescuing the character. Priest recalled not being a fan of the Black Panther as a child, and that he mostly remembered finding T'Challa "incredibly dull" and "getting his ass kicked a lot."[19] It became Priest's, and the artists, duty to establish the *Black Panther* as a hero who can stand his own with the likes of *Spider-Man* and *Captain America*. To do so, Priest often isolated T'Challa from Wakanda and brought the character into the United States. In addition, Priest believed that T'Challa did not make a great fit with the Avengers and explained that he had to "shoehorn" Marvel references into his comics, because he was supposed to.[20] So, he expanded and explored the world of Wakanda enough for the nation to be its own universe and have its own villains, heroes, and sidekicks: most notable, the Dora Milaje.

Priest's 62-issue-arc was full of stories about the Black Panther's run-ins with the supernatural, the *Avengers*, and villains like Erik Killmonger. Accompanying T'Challa on his investigations, fights, and his constant struggle of having his own personal actions heavily affect the people of an entire nation were his most trusted Dora Milaje—Okoye and Nakia. Okoye mostly served as his most loyal bodyguard. Throughout Priest's stories, she symbolized virtue and loyalty as she always stood by T'Challa's side. Okoye's personality never fully shined in Priest's comics, but her role as T'Challa's subservient protector proved to be an important one, particularly in the White Tiger storyline where T'Challa suffered from an aneurism and went into hiding. Okoye followed him, and the two discovered a New York City cop named Kevin "Kasper" Cole who wore a Black Panther suit he found while fighting as a vigilante. To decide if Kasper Cole was a proper Black Panther successor, T'Challa and Okoye tested his morality by seeing if he would leave his pregnant girlfriend for Okoye, due to his attraction to her.[21] Cole did not, but he also did not become the next Black Panther. Instead, he took on the moniker of the *White Tiger* and chose his own destiny. Okoye's role in the *White Tiger* plot was important, but her most significant role in Priest's arc was being the antithesis to Nakia.

LOVE, JUSTICE, AND ANGELS

Similar to Okoye, Nakia was introduced in Priest's arc as one of T'Challa's most trusted Dora Milaje. Readers soon learned, though, that Nakia did not accept T'Challa's refusal to make them his wives as Okoye did. She was in love with him, and hated his love interest, an African American woman named Monica Lynne. Nakia's love for T'Challa reached the point of infatuation. While he was under the influence of a hallucinogen, Nakia kissed T'Challa. The hallucination made him think he was kissing Monica Lynne. Once it wore off, he was shocked and angry with Nakia, but she was ecstatic.[22]

In another instance, Nakia jumped off a cliff into a shallow pool that T'Challa and Monica were sitting in to get his attention. T'Challa had to give her mouth-to-mouth resuscitation, and it was one of Nakia's proudest memories. As she recollected about this moment, she and Okoye were assigned to a mission to protect Monica. Nakia, the pilot of the aircraft they were flying, intentionally tried to get Monica killed once they were under attack. Nakia believed she successfully killed Monica and told T'Challa she was killed in battle. T'Challa, suspecting Nakia's infatuation with him played role in the supposed death of Monica Lynne, shunned Nakia from the Dora Milaje, her tribe, and all of Wakanda.[23] Nakia returned about twenty comic issues later under a new name: Malice. She sought revenge on T'Challa and aimed to kill all of the women in his life. She also developed a toxin designed to make any man fall in love with her, which she used on T'Challa. Eventually, T'Challa became free of the toxin's power, and faced Malice in a final showdown where she disappeared without a trace.[24] The character made her return in appearances throughout *Black Panther* as a reoccurring villain. The Marvel Cinematic Universe's *Black Panther* has only portrayed Nakia has T'Challa's ally and love interest thus far. With inevitable sequels in the works, and the unfortunate passing of Chadwick Boseman, it is safe to assume the women of Wakanda will be featured even more prominently, which could lead to Nakia's villainous turn to Malice and the introduction of more characters from the *Black Panther* comics, like Queen Divine Justice. Coogler has also expressed his interest in women-led sequels and spin-offs to Black Panther.[25]

The final significant member of the Dora Milaje in Priest's arc is Queen Divine Justice, also known as Ce'Athuana Asira Davin. "Asira Davin" is Wakandan for "the Peace of God," and Queen Divine Justice was meant to bring lasting peace to Wakanda.[26] Readers first met Queen Divine Justice under her American name, Chante' Giovanni Brown, while giving a speech to a small group of fellow residents of her Chicago neighborhood:

> It's fascism. It's a targeted fragmenting of the Afro-American community. The defecation of unchecked acquisitiveness and targeted, surgical destabilization of the tribal bond masked as corporate rightsizing and migration pattern shift. The remapping of Congressional districts, affirmative action's attrited deaths of a thousand cuts. When a sister gonna pilot the bumpin' space shuttle? Send the poor peeops to die in Kosovo so the drug money don't get disturbed—while, here at home, the manufacturing base continues to be decimated, shifted to the sun belt and Thailand. Michael Jordan sneakers gettin' sewn by dirty little mud

boys in Honduras workin' for 12 cents a day—everybody's drinking Sprite, everybody's got a gold card, everybody's John Wayne. Now here come the I.C.P. Blaring your cheery jingle, eliciting a pavlovian response from these innocent children—while trampling their dignity and self-esteem by dividing the have's from the have-nots![27]

Priest made it clear that Queen Divine Justice was an activist, whose mouth was as big of a weapon as her fists would soon become. The next time readers saw her, she talked the *Incredible Hulk* out of smashing Black men and into smashing police cars, and the two soon formed a humorous friendship.[28] Soon, T'Challa told Queen Divine Justice of her Wakandan origins. Her father was Damola, the chieftain of the Jabari tribe, who fled Wakanda with his family to Chicago to escape persecution from religious extremists. T'Challa came to Chicago to recruit her to the Dora Milaje, but she had been preparing for this role her whole life.[29] Queen Divine Justice became a prominent member of the Dora Milaje, fighting side-by-side with T'Challa and Okoye, bringing her own unique style with her, along with her sarcastic personality and her activism.

In 2016, acclaimed journalist and author Ta-Nahisi Coates became the lead writer for another Black Panther comics reboot: *Black Panther Volume Six*. Coates took on the project for multiple reasons. One reason is because he is simply a fan of *Black Panther*. More importantly, though, was his belief that superheroes are a modern version of Greek Mythology and that these legends of folklore need to be more diverse, because "if you're not at least grappling with diversity, then you're not depicting the world." Coates explained that as a child, *Spiderman* was his hero. With writing Black Panther, he hoped he could help "*Black Panther* to be some kid's *Spiderman*."[30] The Dora Milaje were featured prominently, but this series arc drastically changed their appearance to match the MCU's desexualized version of the adored ones, featuring shaved heads and body armor. Coates explained that his interpretation of the Dora Milaje intentionally changed them from being sexualized like they were in previous comics and to make their appearance and clothing more suitable and necessary for fighting.[31] He placed his stories in Wakanda more than Priest did, and the series popularity, along with the MCU, allowed for spinoff stories about different characters. In the six-part *World of Wakanda* series, Coates and author Roxane Gay, along with artist Alitha E. Martinez, created perhaps *Black Panther's* most progressive story to date. It focused on the Dora Milaje and placed readers into their headquarters. The story's main characters are Ayo, a Dora Milaje in training, and Aneka, who trained the women warriors of Wakanda. Ayo and Aneka fell in love and hid their relationship from the rest of the Dora Milaje due to Aneka's preference to keep it a secret.[32] By the end of the series, Aneka traveled alone to Kagara, the home of the chieftain Diya, "who torments the women and girls of his village without consequence."[33] Aneka found multiple women caged near his quarters, victims of his abuse. To bring the women the justice they deserved, Aneka killed Diya. On her return to the Dora Milaje headquarters, Aneka was imprisoned for the murder of a village chieftain. Ayo broke Aneka out of prison, making it so she could also never return to the Dora Milaje. The two women, in love, formed the *Midnight Angels*: a vigilante duo who travel the world to free oppressed women.[34]

THE SUCCESS STORY OF THE DORA MILAJE

The origins of the Dora Milaje started with Christopher Priest's 1998 comic book series, but their rising popularity is mostly due to the success of the MCU. Although vibranium had been mentioned in prior MCU films, the characters of the Black Panther universe had not been introduced until the thirteenth film of the blockbuster movie franchise, *Captain America: Civil War*. After a twelve-film build-up, the Avengers had been divided over the issue of security. The United Nations wanted to put restrictions on the Avengers, due to the destruction they were partially to blame for in previous battles. Tony Stark (Robert Downey, Jr.), also known as *Ironman*, dealing with Post Traumatic Stress Disorder from the destruction he helped cause, supported this idea. Steve Rogers (Chris Evans), also known as *Captain America*, believed the restrictions on the Avengers were an infraction against liberty and freedom, and that if the Avengers hands were tied, they would not be able to help everyone they potentially could. When Bucky Barnes (Sebastian Stan), the *Winter Soldier*, was framed for the murder of King T'Chaka of Wakanda, T'Challa sided with Tony Stark in the war between the *Avengers*. The Dora Milaje were not featured prominently in *Civil War*, but Ayo's (Florence Kasumba) one line was enough to show the strength of the adored ones. At T'Challa's side as he walked to his car to start looking for the Winter Soldier, they bumped into Natasha Romanoff (Scarlett Johansson), the *Black Widow*, who stood in their way. Up until this point, besides Wanda Maximoff (Elizabeth Olsen), who was new to the team and learning how to control her superpowers, Natasha had been the only female Avenger and the strongest woman in the MCU. Ayo simply told her, "Move. Or you will be moved."[35] The confidence of Ayo, and the apparent hesitation from Natasha, showed the strength of the Dora Milaje in their big screen debut.

After the success of *Civil War* and the increased demand for more *Black Panther* on screen, Ryan Coogler wrote and directed the first *Black Panther* solo movie. The movie centered around T'Challa's (Chadwick Boseman) challenges as the new King of Wakanda, his biggest one being his long-lost cousin Erik Killmonger (Michael B. Jordan) who demanded to take back what he believed was rightfully his, royalty and vibranium, which he planned to use to arm oppressed Black people across the world to revolt. Although combining different comic book variants of the Dora Milaje to create his own, Coogler's *Black Panther* placed the Dora Milaje at the center of the story in a much different and better way than Priest's comics did. No longer were the adored ones problematically young, sexualized, or promised to the King of Wakanda. Instead, they mostly served as the kingsguard to the King of Wakanda, had shaved heads and body armor suitable for battle, and had lives outside of their duty to protect and serve Wakanda. Like Priest's comics, the film heavily focused on Okoye (Danai Gurira) and Nakia (Lupita Nyong'o). Okoye is still portrayed as the greatest warrior in Wakanda, is relatively accurate to her character in the comics. She was loyal to T'Challa and Wakanda and served as a symbol of virtue in the story. Nakia's character is drastically differed from the comics, though. No longer a teenager infatuated with T'Challa, Nakia is represented as a grown woman who was T'Challa's legitimate love interest. Most noticeably, beyond her wearing the armor during the final battle of the film, Nakia is not a member of the Dora Milaje in the film. Instead, she served as a spy/aide to T'Challa and Wakanda and a social advocate.

In addition to their fighting ability, the film illustrated that the input from Okoye and Nakia is as valuable as T'Challa's. In the opening scene where T'Challa helped Nakia free a group of oppressed people, Nakia told T'Challa not to hurt one of the soldiers involved in the kidnapping of these people, because he was a boy, and T'Challa listened. Before jumping off his aircraft into the jungle, T'Challa told Okoye to stay on the ship. Okoye jumped off as well and saved T'Challa and Nakia from getting killed. She openly disobeyed his order with no consequences, proving she was as much in charge as he was. Okoye also showed in the film that Dora Milaje had lives outside of their duty and were leaders in their home. She was married to W'Kabi (Daniel Kaluuya) and successfully demanded he stop fighting on Killmonger's side in the final battle. Okoye and Nakia, to an extent, were leaders. When Killmonger threw T'Challa off the cliff during their fight, and T'Challa was assumed dead, it was Okoye and Nakia's ultimate decision to save T'Challa's life, fight by his side, and save Wakanda from Killmonger. In the final scene of the film, T'Challa gave the famous speech in front of the United Nations assembly where he stated that in times of crisis, the wise build bridges while the foolish build walls. By his side: Okoye and Nakia. This is significantly different from the display of female warriors as "trophy wives." Again, showing their roles as leaders and being central to the story of the Black Panther.[36]

OTHER COMIC BOOK ITERATIONS OF OKOYE'S LEADERSHIP AND *BLACK PANTHER*

Following *Black Panther*, and other MCU films, was the two-part ending to the first three phases of the MCU: *Avengers: Infinity War* and *Avengers: Endgame*. In *Infinity War*, Earth was invaded by an alien titan named *Thanos* (Josh Brolin). Hunting infinity stones, extremely powerful gems, *Thanos* believed once he had all six stones, he could save the universe's resources by eliminating half of all living species with the snap of his fingers. *The Avengers*, including T'Challa, teamed up to stop *Thanos* from getting all of the stones. They failed, and with the snap of his fingers, half of all living species in the universe turned to dust. Among them was T'Challa. By his side was Okoye, who watched in horror as he crumbled.[37] *Endgame*, which took place five years after the events of *Infinity War*, featured the surviving heroes teaming up to travel back in time to get the infinity stones before *Thanos* does to hopefully reverse the mass genocide he had accomplished.

An early scene in the film showed Natasha Romanoff telecommunicating with Avengers from across Earth and the universe through holograms. It had been five years, and the leader of Wakanda was now Okoye. The *Black Panther* was not replaced. Wakanda apparently did not have a new King. Instead, Okoye, the Dora Milaje's greatest warrior and T'Challa's closest confidant, was apparently now the leader of Wakanda. Our heroes were successful in getting the stones and reversing *Thanos*'s genocide. As all of the fallen Avengers returned from the dead in time for one final showdown with *Thanos*, T'Challa appeared with all of Wakanda's warriors at his back. At his side were Okoye and his sister Shuri, again illustrating Okoye's prominent role as not only T'Challa's personal bodyguard but a leader in the fight to save Earth and the universe. Endgame's film cover/poster is also significant. It shows all of the surviving Avengers after the events of Infinity War: *Ironman, Captain America, Black Widow, The Incredible Hulk, Thor, Ant-Man, Hawkeye, Captain Marvel, War Machine, Rocket Racoon*, and *Okoye*.[38] More than a Dora Milaje, warrior, and bodyguard, Okoye had become an Avenger.[39]

From Christopher Priest's *Black Panther* comic book run to *Avengers: Endgame*, the Dora Milaje have evolved at great length. Originally, they were inappropriately young to be so sexualized and promised to the King of Wakanda. In fact, it was rather tasteless. But, by the time readers met Queen Divine Justice, she represented a new type of Dora Milaje. She was an adult and she had a unique personality and life outside of being a servant to King and country. Coates's comic book arc, which is currently still running, ties closer in with the MCU. The women in the comics are treated with more respect from their writers and artists, and Ayo and Aneka even have an ongoing queer relationship as they escaped the Dora Milaje to become freedom fighting vigilantes called the Midnight Angels. The MCU changed almost everything but the names of the Dora Milaje. No longer sexualized, and now adults, the Dora Milaje in the films were warriors, leaders, and Avengers.

"MOVE, OR YOU WILL BE MOVED": THE DORA MILAJE IN BATTLE AND THEIR LASTING IMAGE

In prehistoric Wakanda, a meteor crashed composed of the mineral vibranium. For centuries, Wakandans mined the precious metal to make weapons, armor, and advanced technologies. Vibranium was also the cause for supernatural powers and sometimes magic/sorcery possessed by some Wakandans, due to a mysterious radiation. Of course, some vibranium found its way out of Wakanda, hence the creation of *Captain America's* famous shield and the arc in Tony Stark's chest which kept shrapnel out of his heart and kept him alive. But Wakanda is home to almost all of the vibranium on earth. When turned into weapons, it absorbs all vibration from soundwaves to kinetic shock.[40] In addition to the *Black Panther*, whose suit is made of vibranium, the Dora Milaje, being the greatest warriors in all of Wakanda, were usually the ones wielding weapons and armor made of vibranium and using advanced technologies in battle. In addition to the benefits of vibranium, the Dora Milaje were also skilled warriors, martial arts masters, and a well-organized militia.

Right from their introduction in Christopher Priest's comics, the Dora Milaje proved to be elite warriors skilled in the teachings of martial arts (see Wayne Wong's chapter in this volume). The specific martial arts knowledge they possess was never clearly laid out in the comic books, but the *Black Panther* film's fight choreography gave some hint at the fighting style utilized by the Dora Milaje. An article by blogger Michael Munro dove into the fighting styles used in the film, from T'Challa's battles with Erik Killmonger to the Dora Milaje's weapon-based fighting. Munro gave evidence that although most contemporary African martial arts do not use lethal weapons, the influence of staff fighting from the Suri tribes is evident in the film. Munro also illustrated the influence of Egyptian Khopesh fighting with sickle-swords.[41] Because the MCU films are canonized in Black Panther folklore, it is fair to say that the Dora Milaje's fighting techniques are those of ancient African martial arts.

A lot of the Dora Milaje's fighting style involved weapons, and they had access to a plethora of advanced technology and weaponry in Wakanda. Seen in comics and on film, the Dora Milaje's primary weapon were their vibranium spears. As mentioned, vibranium is so powerful that it absorbs all vibration. The spears, and any other combat weapons made from the precious metal, served as both offensive and defensive tools in battle which inflicted pain onto enemies and protected the Dora Milaje from strikes or gunfire. Also seen in the film were ring blades, used by Nakia in the fight against Killmonger. The ring blades, made of vibranium, create a forcefield within them to use against enemies. In addition to combat weapons, the Dora Milaje used vibranium-based technologies in combat and travel, such as technologically advanced aircrafts and "gel-filled slugs" or "mercy bullets" used to stun enemies instead of killing them.[42] The Dora Milaje's access to and use of technology and weapons was only part of their legacy as the greatest warriors of Wakanda. Their image and reputation as great fighters were more iconic than their vibranium-based weaponry.

In multiple instances, the Dora Milaje appeared in major battles as an emergency task force, the best fighters on the battlefield, and on par with demigods, metahumans, and aliens. In the six-part comic event Doomwar, the *Black Panther* T'Challa and his sister Shuri were joined by the X-Men, the Fantastic Four, and Deadpool in an attempt to save Wakanda from *Doctor Doom*—a villainous sorcerer in hunt of vibranium.[43] In the fifth issue of the series, Deadpool lead an attack against Doombots, artificial intelligence robot versions of Doctor Doom. T'Challa realized that Deadpool, a mutant whose body rapidly heals from any wound or injury and trained marksman, could not safely handle this job alone. So, T'Challa sent in his most dangerous assets to accompany Deadpool—the Midnight Angels. The issue ended with a powerful image of the women of the Midnight Angels entering the Doomwar.[44] These elite members of the Dora Milaje helped defeat *Doctor Doom*, and it appeared that the heroes would not have won Doomwar without them.

In the MCU, the Dora Milaje's legacy and image as the Wakanda's greatest fighters was stressed even more than it was in the comics. From the now famous "move, or you will be moved" line from Ayo to Natasha Romanoff in *Captain America: Civil War*, it was understood from the get-go that these women were to be feared and respected as warriors.[45] As the series moved into the *Black Panther* stand-alone film, the Dora Milaje's fighting was on full display. Viewers watched Okoye rip through armed militias in the jungle and crime lords in a casino with ease. In these particular instances, it almost appeared that Okoye was as good or better than T'Challa at fighting. In the final act of the film, when T'Challa returned to fight Killmonger, a small group of the Dora Milaje fought Killmonger together. The fight seemed to be going in the favor of the Dora Milaje, until Killmonger killed a member of the adored ones. A look of shock and horror appeared on the faces of the surrounding Dora Milaje as Killmonger did the seemingly impossible by killing a member of the Dora Milaje. Somehow, killing a member of the Dora Milaje was more shocking than Killmonger's earlier defeat of T'Challa.[46]

Other proof of the power of the Dora Milaje's fighting prowess was on full display in both *Avengers: Infinity War* and *Avengers: Endgame*. When *Thanos* and his minions arrived in Wakanda, it was Okoye and the Dora Milaje who came to the aide of T'Challa and the Avengers in the fight to save the universe. Of course, all of Wakanda's best warriors were in the film's final battle, as characters like M'Baku defended their homeland. Yet it was Okoye and the Dora Milaje who were more frequently shown in battle on screen.[47] In *Endgame*, after the Avengers had successfully brought everyone back to life who disintegrated from the face of the Earth in *Infinity War*, the Dora Milaje led by Okoye accompanied T'Challa, Shuri, and the Avengers in the fight to defeat *Thanos* for good. Okoye, now an Avenger, joined Shuri and the other women Avengers in a memorable moment where all the women from the film franchise teamed up together for a battle and cinematic shot that moviegoers will always remember. Here were Okoye and Shuri, a human warrior and a human scientist, on a level playing field with space warriors like *Gamora*, demigods like Valkyrie, mutants like the *Scarlet Witch*, and extraterrestrials like *Captain Marvel*. No superpowers. No gods. Just women trained in ancient African martial arts defending the fate of the universe alongside superheroes and against an alien Titan named *Thanos*.[48]

The Dora Milaje's martial arts skills, use of advanced technology and weapons, and legacy as great warriors combined to create an image of the adored ones which stood apart from the rest of the Marvel universe, both cinematically and in comic books. "Regular" human women without superpowers saved their country, the planet, and the universe on multiple occasions with the use of advanced technologies and ancient African martial arts. The Dora Milaje were often the strongest warriors on the battlefield, including ones with T'Challa, and when they were not, they were at least on the same level as metahumans, extraterrestrials, and demigods. The comics and films which portrayed the Dora Milaje in battle created an image of the elite group as some of, if not the, greatest warriors in the world who both lead heroes into battle and save the universe.

NOTES

1. Stan Lee and Jack Kirby, *Fantastic Four #52* (Marvel Unlimited: Marvel Comics Group, 1966), https://read.marvel.com/#/book/4657.

2. Lee and Kirby, *Fantastic Four #52*.

3. Stan Lee and Jack Kirby, *Captain America #100*, vol. 1 (Marvel Unlimited: Marvel Comics Group, 1968.), Marvel.com; Roy Thomas and Gene Colan, *Daredevil #69*, vol. 1 (Marvel Unlimited: Marvel Comics Group, 1970), Marvel.com.

4. Roy Thomas and John Buscema, *The Avengers #52*, vol. 1 (Marvel Unlimited: Marvel Comics Group, 1968), https://read.marvel.com/#/book/4219.

5. Jack Kirby, *Black Panther #1*, vol. 1 (Marvel Unlimited: Marvel Comics Group, 1977), https://read.marvel.com/#/book/634.

6. Peter Gillis and Denys Cowan, *Black Panther #1*, vol. 2 (Marvel Unlimited: Marvel, 1988), https://read.marvel.com/#/book/50795.

7. Christopher Priest and Mark Texeira, *Black Panther #1*, vol. 3, Marvel Knights (Marvel Unlimited: Marvel, n.d.), https://read.marvel.com/#/book/1520.

8. Abraham Riesman, "The Man Who Made Black Panther Cool," *Vulture*, January 22, 2018, https://www.vulture.com/2018/01/christopher-priest-made-black-panther-cool-then-disappeared.html.

9. Riesman. In this interview, Priest explained that the comic needed a "Chandler Bing" from Friends character to provide sarcastic insight and humor to the story.

10. In *Black Panther* (2018), the film ends with Nakia and Okoye standing by T'Challa's side not as "trophy wives," but as diplomats, as they addressed the rest of the world about sharing their abundance of the resource Vibranium.

11. Priest and Texeira, *Black Panther #1*.

12. Ibid.

13. Christopher Priest and Mark Texeira, *Black Panther #2*, Marvel Knights (Marvel Unlimited: Marvel, 1998), https://read.marvel.com/#/book/1527.

14. Christopher Priest and Mark Texeira, *Black Panther #3*, Marvel Knights (Marvel Unlimited: Marvel, 1999), https://read.marvel.com/#/book/1529.

15. Christopher Priest, "Adventures in the Funnybook Game - Chapter Eleven: Black Panther Series Commentary," *Digital Priest*, June 2001, http://digitalpriest.com/legacy/comics/panther/start.html.

16. Stephen "Win" Wiacek, *Black Panther: The Ultimate Guide* (New York: DK Publishing, 2018), 30–31.

17. A heel-turn is when a former hero becomes a villain.

18. Riesman, "The Man Who Made Black Panther Cool," *Vulture*.

19. Christopher Priest, "Adventures in the Funnybook Game: Chapter Nine: The Last Time Priest Discussed the Viability of Black Characters," *Digital Priest*, 2003, http://digitalpriest.com/legacy/comics/chips3.html.

20. Zack Smith, "Priest on Black Panther, Pt. 1: 'Everyone Kind of Forgot Who Panther Was'," *Newsarama*, February 15, 2008, https://www.newsarama.com/25496-priest-looks-back-at-black-panther.html.

21. Christopher Priest and Patrick Zircher, *Black Panther #62* (Marvel Unlimited: Marvel, 2003), 62.

22. Priest and Texeira, *Black Panther #3*.

23. Christopher Priest and Mark Bright, *Black Panther #11*, Marvel Knights (Marvel Unlimited: Marvel, 1999), https://read.marvel.com/#/book/1524; Christopher Priest and Mark Bright, *Black Panther #12*, Marvel Knights (Marvel Unlimited: Marvel, 1999), https://read.marvel.com/#/book/1526; Christopher Priest and Sal Velluto, *Black Panther #13* (Marvel Unlimited: Marvel, 1999), https://read.marvel.com/#/book/10296.

24. Christopher Priest and Sal Velluto, *Black Panther #31* (Marvel Unlimited: Marvel, 2001), https://read.marvel.com/#/book/10376; Christopher Priest and Sal

Velluto, *Black Panther #32* (Marvel Unlimited: Marvel, 2001), https://read.marvel.com/#/book/10377; Christopher Priest and Sal Velluto, *Black Panther #33* (Marvel Unlimited: Marvel, 2001), https://read.marvel.com/#/book/4562.

25. Megan McCluskey, "The Black Panther Director Is Interested in a Female Spinoff," *Time*, May 11, 2018, https://time.com/5274278/black-panther-female-spinoff/; Alanna Vagianos, "Ryan Coogler Would Love to See a Women of Wakanda Spinoff," *Huffington Post*, May 15, 2018, https://www.huffpost.com/entry/ryan-coogler-would-love-women-wakanda-spinoff_n_5af990f9e4b032b10bfcf692.

26. Marvel, "Queen Divine Justice Powers, Enemies, History," *Marvel Entertainment*, https://www.marvel.com/characters/queen-divine-justice.

27. Priest and Velluto, *Black Panther #13*.

28. Christopher Priest and Sal Velluto, *Black Panther #15* (Marvel Unlimited: Marvel, 2000), https://read.marvel.com/#/book/10357; Christopher Priest, Glenn Herdling, and Sal Velluto, *Black Panther #17* (Marvel Unlimited: Marvel, 2000), https://read.marvel.com/#/book/10363.

29. Christopher Priest and Jim Calafiore, *Black Panther #35* (Marvel Unlimited: Marvel, 2001), https://read.marvel.com/#/book/4564.

30. "Ta-Nehisi Coates Hopes 'Black Panther' Will Be Some Kid's 'Spider-Man,'" NPR.org, April 6, 2016, https://www.npr.org/sections/codeswitch/2016/04/06/473224606/a-reluctant-king-ta-nehisi-coates-takes-on-marvels-black-panther.

31. "Ta-Nehisi Coates Hopes 'Black Panther,'" NPR.org.

32. The book does not give a full explanation of why their relationship is kept secret, other than Aneka's preference for doing so.

33. Roxane Gay, Ta-Nehisi Coates, and Alitha Martinez, *Black Panther: World of Wakanda #4* (Marvel Unlimited: Marvel, 2017), https://read.marvel.com/#/book/44080.

34. Roxane Gay et al., *Black Panther: World of Wakanda #1* (Marvel Unlimited: Marvel, 2016), https://read.marvel.com/#/book/43189; Roxane Gay, Ta-Nehisi Coates, and Alitha Martinez, *Black Panther: World of Wakanda #2* (Marvel Unlimited: Marvel, 2016), https://read.marvel.com/#/book/43488; Roxane Gay, Ta-Nehisi Coates, and Alitha Martinez, *Black Panther: World of Wakanda #3* (Marvel Unlimited: Marvel, 2017), https://read.marvel.com/#/book/43743; Roxane Gay, Ta-Nehisi Coates, and Alitha Martinez, *Black Panther: World of Wakanda #4*; Roxane Gay and Alitha Martinez, *Black Panther: World of Wakanda #5* (Marvel Unlimited: Marvel, 2017), https://read.marvel.com/#/book/44270; Rembert Browne and Roberto Poggi, *Black Panther: World of Wakanda #6* (Marvel Unlimited: Marvel, 2017), https://read.marvel.com/#/book/44520.

35. Anthony Russo and Joe Russo, *Captain America: Civil War*, 2016.

36. *Black Panther*, directed by Ryan Coogler (United States: Walt Disney Studio Motion Pictures, 2018).

37. *Avengers: Infinity War*, directed by Anthony Russo and Joe Russo (United States: Walt Disney Studio Motion Pictures, 2018).

38. Played by Robert Downey, Jr. Chris Evans, Scarlett Johansson, Mark Ruffalo, Chris Hemsworth, Paul Rudd, Jeremy Renner, Brie Larson, Don Cheadle, Bradley Cooper, and Danai Gurira.

39. *Avengers: Endgame*, directed by Anthony Russo and Joe Russo (United States: Walt Disney Studio Motion Pictures, 2019).

40. Wiacek, *Black Panther: The Ultimate Guide*, 62–63.
41. Michael Munro, "The Way of the Wakandan Warrior and the Real Martial Arts of Africa," *Observation Deck*, February 17, 2018, https://observationdeck.kinja.com/the-way-of-the-wakandan-warrior-and-the-real-martial-ar-1823104915; Pedro Olavarria, "The Styles of African Martial Arts," *Vice, Fightland* (blog), November 18, 2014, http://fightland.vice.com/blog/the-styles-of-african-martial-arts.
42. Christopher Priest and Mike Manley, *Black Panther #9*, Marvel Knights (Marvel Unlimited: Marvel, 1999), https://read.marvel.com/#/book/1542.
43. Jonathan Maberry, *Doomwar #1* (Marvel Unlimited: Marvel, 2010), https://read.marvel.com/#/book/13886; Jonathan Maberry, *Doomwar #2* (Marvel Unlimited: Marvel, 2010), https://read.marvel.com/#/book/14111; Jonathan Maberry, *Doomwar #3* (Marvel Unlimited: Marvel, 2010), https://read.marvel.com/#/book/14374; Jonathan Maberry, *Doomwar #4* (Marvel Unlimited: Marvel, 2010), https://read.marvel.com/#/book/14755; Jonathan Maberry, *Doomwar #5* (Marvel Unlimited: Marvel, 2010), https://read.marvel.com/#/book/15067; Jonathan Maberry, *Doomwar #6* (Marvel Unlimited: Marvel, 2010), https://read.marvel.com/#/book/15497.
44. Jonathan Maberry, *Doomwar #5*. *Note: The Midnight Angels in this storyline are different than the future vigilante team created in the World of Wakanda series.
45. *Captain America: Civil War*, directed by Anthony Russo and Joe Russo.
46. *Black Panther*, directed by Ryan Coogler.
47. *Avengers: Infinity War*, directed by Anthony Russo and Joe Russo.
48. *Avengers: Endgame*, directed by Anthony Russo and Joe Russo.

WORKS CITED

Browne, Browne, and Roberto Poggi. *Black Panther: World of Wakanda #6*. Marvel Unlimited: Marvel, 2017. https://read.marvel.com/#/book/44520.

Gay, Roxane, and Alitha Martinez. *Black Panther: World of Wakanda #5*. Marvel Unlimited: Marvel, 2017. https://read.marvel.com/#/book/44270.

Gay, Roxane, Ta-Nehisi Coates, and Alitha Martinez. *Black Panther: World of Wakanda #2*. Marvel Unlimited: Marvel, 2016. https://read.marvel.com/#/book/43488.

———. *Black Panther: World of Wakanda #3*. Marvel Unlimited: Marvel, 2017. https://read.marvel.com/#/book/43743.

———. *Black Panther: World of Wakanda #4*. Marvel Unlimited: Marvel, 2016. https://read.marvel.com/#/book/44080.

Gay, Roxane, Ta-Nehisi Coates, Alitha Martinez, and Yona Harvey. *Black Panther: World of Wakanda #1*. Marvel Unlimited: Marvel, 2016. https://read.marvel.com/#/book/43189.

Gillis, Peter, and Denys Cowan. *Black Panther #1*. Vol. 2. Marvel Unlimited: Marvel, 1988. https://read.marvel.com/#/book/50795.

Kirby, Jack. *Black Panther #1*. Vol. 1. Marvel Unlimited: Marvel Comics Group, 1977. https://read.marvel.com/#/book/634.

Lee, Stan and Jack Kirby. *Captain America #100*. Vol. 1. Marvel Unlimited: Marvel Comics Group, n.d. Marvel.com.

———. *Fantastic Four #52*. Marvel Unlimited: Marvel Comics Group, 1966. https://read.marvel.com/#/book/4657.

Maberry, Jonathan. *Doomwar #1*. Marvel Unlimited: Marvel, 2010. https://read.marvel.com/#/book/13886.

———. *Doomwar #2*. Marvel Unlimited: Marvel, 2010. https://read.marvel.com/#/book/14111.

———. *Doomwar #3*. Marvel Unlimited: Marvel, 2010. https://read.marvel.com/#/book/14374.

———. *Doomwar #4*. Marvel Unlimited: Marvel, 2010. https://read.marvel.com/#/book/14755.

———. *Doomwar #5*. Marvel Unlimited: Marvel, 2010. https://read.marvel.com/#/book/15067.

———. *Doomwar #6*. Marvel Unlimited: Marvel, 2010. https://read.marvel.com/#/book/15497.

Marvel. "Queen Divine Justice Powers, Enemies, History." *Marvel Entertainment*. https://www.marvel.com/characters/queen-divine-justice.

Marvel. "Black Panther (1977) #1." *Marvel Entertainment*. Accessed October 2, 2019. https://read.marvel.com/#/book/634.

McCluskey, Megan. "The Black Panther Director Is Interested in a Female Spinoff." *Time*, May 11, 2018. https://time.com/5274278/black-panther-female-spinoff/.

Munro, Michael. "The Way of the Wakandan Warrior and the Real Martial Arts of Africa." *Observation Deck*, February 17, 2018. https://observationdeck.kinja.com/the-way-of-the-wakandan-warrior-and-the-real-martial-ar-1823104915.

Olavarria, Pedro. "The Styles of African Martial Arts." *Vice. Fightland* (blog), November 18, 2014. http://fightland.vice.com/blog/the-styles-of-african-martial-arts.

Priest, Christopher. "Adventures in the Funnybook Game - Chapter Eleven: Black Panther Series Commentary." *Digital Priest*, June 2001. http://digitalpriest.com/legacy/comics/panther/start.html.

Priest, Christopher, Glenn Herdling, and Sal Velluto. *Black Panther #17*. Marvel Unlimited: Marvel, 2000. https://read.marvel.com/#/book/10363.

Priest, Christopher and Jim Calafiore. *Black Panther #35*. Marvel Unlimited: Marvel, 2001. https://read.marvel.com/#/book/4564.

Priest, Christopher and Mark Bright. *Black Panther #11*. Marvel Knights. Marvel Unlimited: Marvel, 1999. https://read.marvel.com/#/book/1524.

———. *Black Panther #12*. Marvel Knights. Marvel Unlimited: Marvel, 1999. https://read.marvel.com/#/book/1526.

Priest, Christopher and Mark Texeira. *Black Panther #1*. Vol. 3. Marvel Knights. Marvel Unlimited: Marvel, 1998. https://read.marvel.com/#/book/1520.

———. *Black Panther #2*. Marvel Knights. Marvel Unlimited: Marvel, 1998. https://read.marvel.com/#/book/1527.

———. *Black Panther #3*. Marvel Knights. Marvel Unlimited: Marvel, 1999. https://read.marvel.com/#/book/1529.

Priest, Christopher and Mike Manley. *Black Panther #9*. Marvel Knights. Marvel Unlimited: Marvel, 1999. https://read.marvel.com/#/book/1542.

Priest, Christopher and Patrick Zircher. *Black Panther #62*. Marvel Unlimited: Marvel, 2003.

Priest, Christopher and Sal Velluto. *Black Panther #13*. Marvel Unlimited: Marvel, 1999. https://read.marvel.com/#/book/10296.
———. *Black Panther #15*. Marvel Unlimited: Marvel, 2000. https://read.marvel.com/#/book/10357.
———. *Black Panther #31*. Marvel Unlimited: Marvel, 2001. https://read.marvel.com/#/book/10376.
———. *Black Panther #32*. Marvel Unlimited: Marvel, 2001. https://read.marvel.com/#/book/10377.
———. *Black Panther #33*. Marvel Unlimited: Marvel, 2001. https://read.marvel.com/#/book/4562.
Priest, Christopher. "Adventures in the Funnybook Game: Chapter Nine: The Last Time Priest Discussed the Viability of Black Characters." *Digital Priest*, 2003. http://digitalpriest.com/legacy/comics/chips3.html.
Riesman, Abraham. "The Man Who Made Black Panther Cool." *Vulture*, January 22, 2018. https://www.vulture.com/2018/01/christopher-priest-made-black-panther-cool-then-disappeared.html.
Smith, Zack. "Priest on Black Panther, Pt. 1: 'Everyone Kind of Forgot Who Panther Was.'" *Newsarama*, February 15, 2008. https://www.newsarama.com/25496-priest-looks-back-at-black-panther.html.
"Ta-Nehisi Coates Hopes 'Black Panther' Will Be Some Kid's 'Spider-Man.'" *NPR.org*, April 6, 2016. https://www.npr.org/sections/codeswitch/2016/04/06/473224606/a-reluctant-king-ta-nehisi-coates-takes-on-marvels-black-panther.
Thomas, Roy and Gene Colan. *Daredevil #69*. Vol. 1. Marvel Unlimited: Marvel Comics Group, 1970. Marvel.com.
Thomas, Roy and John Buscema. *The Avengers #52*. Vol. 1. Marvel Unlimited: Marvel Comics Group, 1968. https://read.marvel.com/#/book/4219.
Vagianos, Alanna. "Ryan Coogler Would Love to See a Women of Wakanda Spinoff." *Huffington Post*, May 15, 2018. https://www.huffpost.com/entry/ryan-coogler-would-love-women-wakanda-spinoff_n_5af990f9e4b032b10bfcf692.
Wiacek, Stephen "Win". *Black Panther: The Ultimate Guide*. New York: DK Publishing, 2018.

FILMS

Avengers: Endgame, Directed by Anthony Russon and Joe Russo. United States: Walt Disney Studio Motion Pictures, 2019
Avengers: Infinity War. Directed by Anthony Russo and Joe Russo. United States: Walt Disney Studio Motion Pictures, 2018
Black Panther. Directed by Ryan Coogler. United States: Walt Disney Studio Motion Pictures, 2018.
Captain America: Civil War. Directed by Anthony Russo and Joe Russo. United States: Walt Disney Studio Motion Pictures, 2016.

Chapter 9

"The Prince Will Now Have the Strength of the Black Panther Stripped Away"

Reading Disability and Queerness in Killmonger

Dominique Young

Marvel Studios announced that the superhero film *Black Panther*, directed by Ryan Coogler, would make its debut in February 2018.[1] This set Black social media in an anticipatory Black joy whirlwind. As the release of the film approached, many Marvel comic fans, Marvel Cinematic Universe fans, and cosplayers were excited to witness the Wakandan universe projected on the big screen. Namely, Black people expressed unconfined joy for arguably the blackest moment in the history of contemporary Black cultural production. Black moviegoers anticipated the representation of an imagined, thriving Afro-Futurist nation in Africa that has never been colonized, whose main characters are represented primarily by renowned dark-skinned Black actors, and directed by a Black man, debuting during Black History Month. Social media commentators on Black Twitter expressed their excitement for the film using the hashtag #BlackPanther to share communal feelings of pride and joy and to express how the film resonated with them. Assemblages of tweets and pictures of moviegoers online confirmed the importance of representation of Black people in mainstream films. Although *Black Panther* is widely received by global Black audiences predominantly for its varying representations of blackness, at a cursory glance, this film excludes representations of disabled and queer Black people. However, I argue that the intersection of Disability Studies and Black Feminist framework in Sami Schalk's book *Bodyminds Reimagined: (Dis)ability, Race and Gender in Black Women's Speculative Fiction*, and Cathy Cohen's essays, "Deviance As Resistance" and "Punks, Bulldaggers, and Welfare Queens" allow us to read the film's antagonist, Erik Killmonger, as both a psychologically disabled and queer character.

When analyzed through Schalks' definitions of bodymind and disability metaphor, Killmonger, played by actor Michael B. Jordan, exemplifies a psychologically disabled person because of his subversion of Wakandan principles for a more radical, African American anti-colonial politic influenced by his racial oppression. His genealogy of deviance beginning with his upbringing in Oakland, California, and his scarification as a cartography of his politics as an elite sniper for the U.S. military also constructs him as a psychologically disabled character. Killmonger simultaneously represents a queer character because of the liminal space between insider/outsider, or Wakandan and African American that he exists within. In this chapter, I go beyond character representations of queerness and consider how the vibranium-infused herb in the narrative portrays another kind of queerness. In using Schalk's framework for my analysis, I highlight the ways in which an intersection of Black Feminism and Disability Studies allows for the possibility to read disability in this film. Schalk offers a theoretical framework for nuancing the representation of Black-disabled characters in Speculative Fiction. In the end, I encourage readers to consider how Schalk's theoretical framework offers new ways of thinking about the representation of psychological disability in the film.

SITUATING KILLMONGER WITHIN CINEMATIC REPRESENTATIONS OF BLACK MEN'S DISABILITY

Situating *Black Panther* in a discourse of other films that center Black men with psychological disabilities such as childhood trauma or Post Traumatic Stress Disorder after deployment in recent wars emphasizes the importance of Killmonger's character, a representational character that deviates from the controversial, regular supercrip representations commonly shown in media. In "Reevaluating the Supercrip," Sami Schalk discusses the importance of nuancing our understanding of the term supercrip, stating that "we must understand the supercrip as a narrative that produces a stereotype rather than as a static category that a character or person can fully be or embody."[2] Continuing, Schalk draws on the work of Amit Kama to distinguish between the regular supercrip, glorified supercrip, and superpowered supercrip.[3] When considering mainstream U.S. films over the past 30 years that depict Black men with disabilities, several come to mind. Some of these films include Mike Binder's 1994 *Blankman*, Frank Darabont's 1999 *Green Mile*, Mike Tollin's 2003 *Radio*, Taylor Hackford's 2004 *Ray*, Peter Berg's 2008

Hancock, Denzel Washington's 2016 *Fences,* and more recently David Leitch's 2019 *Hobbs & Shaw.*

With the exception of Gabriel (Michael T. Williamson) in *Fences* (dir. Denzel Washington, 2016), these films center Black men who represent different supercrip narratives, and reading Killmonger alongside and against these characters illuminates the potential for the intersection of Black Feminist Theory and Disability Studies that Sami Schalk outlines, to better understand Killmonger. Darryl Walker (Damon Wayans) in *Blankman* (dir. Mike Binder, 1994) represents the glorified supercrip when he is portrayed as an exceptional inventor that invents bulletproof clothing so that he can fight crime in his urban city after the grandmother is killed by the local mafia. When he presents his proposal for crime-fighting to the police, he is arrested for disturbing the peace and told to see a psychiatrist upon his release, marking him as a psychologically disabled character. John Coffey (Michael Clarke Duncan) in *Green Mile* (dir. Frank Darabont, 1999) represents the superpowered supercrip via his supernatural power to heal others through touch. In the film, he is deemed a psychological disabled man and he is on death row after he is wrongly convicted of raping and killing two White girls. However, his character representation is somewhat forgiven after he successfully heals the warden's White wife of a brain tumor. Likewise, in *Hancock* (dir. Peter Berg, 2008), John Hancock (Will Smith) represents the superpowered supercrip. Hancock possesses supernatural powers—flight and strength—to fight criminals in his city. His disability is marked by the convergence of his blackness, alcoholism, public infamy, and the prison term he serves (he serves a short prison term after a public relations specialist that he saves recommends that he goes to jail until the public sees that they need his help fighting crime, again). The convergence of these three factors pathologizes John and pushes him to the spatial margins of society, similar to how historically, people labeled disabled have been pathologized and institutionalized at the margins of society. James "Radio" Kennedy (Cuba Gooding Jr.) in *Radio* (dir. Michael Tollin, 2003) can best be characterized as a regular supercrip. James is a young man who is deaf, but does not possess supernatural powers like the aforementioned protagonists. Instead he represents an exceptional character when he is heralded as the ideal model of a "good neighbor" in the film. Ray (Jamie Foxx) in *Ray* (dir. Taylor Hackford, 2004) represents the glorified supercrip through his portrayal of musician, Ray Charles', "exceptional overcoming" of disability by showing how he overcame life hardships (including disability) and became an iconic American musician. Finally, Brixton (Idris Elba) in *Hobbs & Shaw* (dir. David Leitch, 2016) represents an evil superpowered supercrip after he is brought back to life via cybernetic technology that gives him superhuman strength, to takeover humanity. Situating Killmonger among these prominent Black men protagonists emphasizes Killmonger's importance to cinematic representations of Black men's disability.

READING KILLMONGER AS A PSYCHOLOGICALLY DISABLED CHARACTER

Reading Killmonger as a psychologically disabled character requires the reconceptualization of disability apart from medicalized notions of disability. Robert W. Cape Jr recognizes that reconceptualizing disability enables new ways of perceiving disability in the essay, "Disabled Hero, Sick Society: Sophocles' Philoctetes and Robert Silverberg's The Man in the Maze." Cape Jr. writes, "Most important—and enabling—has been the shift from defining disability in purely medical terms . . . to understanding it as a symbolic network of social practices and beliefs that define and impact all people."[4] Understanding disability as a symbolic network of social practices makes it possible to read the character of Killmonger as a psychologically disabled character. His lived reality and mission to invade Wakanda to use their resources to wage an anti-colonial war on the oppressive regimes—an agenda that directly conflicts with Wakanda's reality and intended use of their military power—constructs him as a psychologically disabled character. Specifically, I turn to Sami Schalk's theory of bodyminds and disability metaphor to extend my analysis of Killmonger. In her book, *Bodyminds Reimagined: (Dis)ability, Race, and Gender in Black Women's Speculative Fiction,* Schalk elaborates on the work of Margaret Price to define bodymind. Schalk writes,

> Bodymind is a materialist feminist disability studies concept from Margaret Price that refers to the enmeshment of the mind and body . . . The term bodymind insists on the inextricability of mind and body and highlights how processes within our being impact one another in such a way that the notion of a physical versus mental process is difficult, if not impossible to clearly discern in most cases.[5]

In other words, the bodymind character is a figure whose mental state so closely represents their corporeality that it is nearly impossible to separate the two. This definition is especially important to my analysis of Killmonger's scarification later on in this section. Another important term in my analysis is *disability metaphor*. In her book, Schalk says, "(Dis)ability, race, and gender often operate as mutually constitutive discourses that inflect texts even in the absence of explicit embodied representations of these categories. As a result, these concepts can be used as metaphors without negating their physical, mental, and social materiality."⁶ In this way, one can read disability as a metaphor for other kinds of violence experienced by characters as it pertains to race (specifically, blackness) and gender. Sami Schalk's term is important to my later analysis of Killmonger as a social deviant in the United States.

Killmonger's genealogy of deviance and representation as a bodymind character through his scarification presents him as a psychologically disabled character. Early in the movie, viewers learn that he resides in Oakland, California, with his father. Killmonger is also the child of a perceived sociopolitically deviant father (who is labeled a traitor to Wakanda) and presumably becomes an orphan soon after his father is killed, because of his mother's absence in the film. He commits grand larceny in London, kills his Black girlfriend and co-conspirator, and is charged with introducing ideological sickness into the world of Wakanda with this radical, anti-colonial politics that is informed by his experience as a Black man in the United States. Taken together, Killmonger is socially constructed as a psychologically disabled character throughout the film, and the remaining discussion in this section analyzes specific scenes to support my argument.

The beginning of the movie introduces a young Killmonger within a spatial deviance. The *mise-en-scene* captures Killmonger and his friends playing basketball against the backdrop of the housing project where he lives (0:01:53). One of the players dunks the ball into the self-made hoop followed by a 360-camera rotation. This rotation reveals that the young Black boys are not actually playing on a basketball court, instead, they are playing in an empty parking lot. Nearby, young Black girls play Double Dutch and all of the kids are unsupervised by adults. The parking lot is contained by metal gates and a quick camera shot of tree branches just above the gate appear to be barbed wire at first glance (0:01:56). The construction of this scene, firstly, acknowledges that Killmonger is a resident of a housing project in Oakland and his residency here portrays an urban space, one historicized as a site of crisis and criminality. In S*patializing Blackness: Architectures of Confinement and Black Masculinity in Chicago,* Rashad Shabazz effectively captures this notion of criminality. In the introduction, "Carceral Interstice: Between Home Space and Prison Space," Shabazz writes, "Housing projects are sites that have been infused with carceral power for decades. City planning, architecture, and the injection of security measures all contributed to enhance carceral power in the projects, transforming the projects into something between a prison and a home and linking them with the prison industrial complex (PIC).''⁷ Portraying young Killmonger in this housing complex situates him in the liminal space that Shabazz outlines—one between prison and home—and I argue that this liminal space relegates Killmonger to the margins of society where he is marked by deviance.

Furthermore, Killmonger exists within a paternal genealogy of deviance starting with his father, Prince N'Jobu, who simultaneously betrays Wakanda and works against the laws of his current setting in the United States. The scene where Killmonger plays basketball in the parking lot jumpcuts to the scene where N'Jobu and his assistant, Zuri (Forest Whitaker), are planning an attack (0:02:16). In his apartment, Prince N'Jobu's TV projects a live newsclip of a confrontation between local police and the Black community in 1992. He simulates an attack using a map and modules while machine guns are on the table. Suddenly, N'Jobu hears an approaching sound and instructs Zuri to "hide the straps" (guns) while he clears the simulation (0:02:32). King T'Chaka (N'Jobu's brother) arrives with two of his soldiers to confront him about his betrayal to Wakanda, before killing him for turning on Zuri. The jumpcut between the basketball game scene and this one catapults Killmonger within a paternal genealogical resistance where he later attempts to avenge N'Jobu and fulfill his plan to supply African Americans with vibranium for their resistance against the U.S. State.

This scene portrays N'Jobu's politics of anti-colonial deviance. I draw on Cathy Cohen's definition of deviance to support my argument. In the essay, "Deviance as Resistance: A New Research Agenda for the Study of Black Politics," Cohen captures how queer, poor, and, Black people are perceived as social deviants when they resist their oppressive environments. Cohen writes,

> An intentional deviance given limited agency and constrained choices sits at the center for this field of research. These individuals are not fully or completely defining themselves as outsiders nor are they satisfied with their outsider status, but they are also not willing to adapt completely, or to conform. The cumulative impact of such choices might be the creation of spaces or counter publics, where not only oppositional ideas and discourse happen, but lived opposition, or at least autonomy, is chosen daily. Through the repetition of deviant practices by multiple individuals, new identities, communities, and politics might emerge where seemingly deviant, unconnected behavior can be transformed into conscious acts of resistance that serve as the basis for a mobilized politics of deviance.[8]

N'Jobu's apartment represents the space where this "deviant" behavior is transformed into conscious acts of resistance (later carried out by Killmonger). His apartment illustrates an African American anti-colonial militancy: he has African art on the wall, he tunes in to the grassroots anti-colonial militancy represented on the news, he hides the vibranium-infused roots used to combat oppressive American systems in his apartment, and most importantly, his apartment is based in the same city where the Black

Panther Party was founded. This representation also illuminates his deviance, because he reflects the politics of the Black Panther Party—an organization that was demonized and deemed a permanent outsider by the U.S. State. The connection between his politics and that of the Black Panther Party is further represented after N'Jobu's betrayal is revealed.

King T'Chaka interrogates N'Jobu for stealing and supplying Americans with vibranium (0:05:00). When T'Chaka asks N'Jobu why he betrayed Wakanda by helping Ulysses Klaue steal the vibranium, N'Jobu says,

> I observed for as long as I could. Their leaders have been assassinated, communities flooded with drugs and weapons, they are overly policed and incarcerated. All over the planet our people suffer because they don't have the tools to fight back. With vibranium weapons they could overthrow every country and Wakanda could rule them all the right way. (1:05:53)

N'Jobu's assertion calls to mind the Black Panther Party politics. In *Black Against Empire: The History and Politics of the Black Panther Party,* Joshua Bloom and Waldo E. Martin Jr. quote Fred Hampton and write,

> We're being harassed constantly by the pigs, and they're arresting us as fast as they can on any kind of charge such as traffic violation, smoking on buses, carrying concealed weapons, just anything . . . But no matter how many of us they try to lock up, force underground or even kill, the vanguard of the people's revolution, the Black Panther Party, will still go on. We are servants of the people, and any people who launch attacks against the servants of the people are enemies of the people.[9]

Juxtaposing N'Jobu's quote with Fred Hampton's, it becomes clear that the film's diegetic space of Oakland is connected to past Oakland through N'Jobu's and Hampton's shared witnessing of over policing and disproportionate incarceration of African Americans, the harassment and suffering of African Americans at the hands of the U.S. State and their shared belief that a militant revolution offers the possibility of freedom. Situating N'Jobu in this context relates him to the Black Panther Party (perceived ant-citizens), and this illustrates his own perceived deviant politics that Killmonger later adopts as an adult. In sum, Killmonger stems from a paternal genealogy of deviance because of his spatial location in the housing projects of Oakland and his biological and social connection to his father's anti-colonial politics and betrayal of Wakanda that mirrors the anti-colonial politics of the Black Panther Party. In turn, Killmonger adopts these politics and introduces a perceived social sickness into the world of Wakanda, thus marking him as a psychologically disabled character.

Killmonger's representation of psychological disability is also shown through his scarification. I return to Sami Schalk's definition of the *bodymind* to read his scars as a cartography of his disability that is metaphorically represented by his politics. Before Killmonger kills his co-conspirator, Klaue, he demands that Klaue takes him to Wakanda. Klaue responds by telling him that he does not want to go there, and Killmonger kills the pilot of their escape helicopter (1:02:29). Klaue grabs Killmonger's girlfriend as a hostage and Killmonger kills her too, before shooting Klaue in the chest. Klaue attempts to dissuade Killmonger from going to Wakanda by showing the branding he received on his neck for sneaking into their borders. However, unbeknownst to Klaue, Killmonger is actually half Wakandan. He shows Klaue the scars on his arm and says, "I ain't worry 'bout no brand, check these out. Each one is for a kill" (1:03:20). Klaue responds, "You can scar yourself as much as you like, to them, you'll just be an outsider. You're crazy to think that you can walk in there" (1:03:26). Killmonger then reveals the Wakandan birthmark on his inner bottom lip and Klaue suddenly realizes that Killmonger's superhuman capabilities to kill is partly due to his biological connection to Wakanda. Killmonger's corporeal scars signify the number of people he has killed in his resistance, and this visible marker of his political ideology connects his body to his mind (or psychology) thus marking him as a bodymind character.

Later in the movie, Killmonger prepares to fight T'Challa for the throne and he again reveals a cartography of psychological illness and confirms himself as a bodymind character (1:16:50). After T'Challa has his powers stripped away for the ceremonial battle for the throne, he offers Killmonger a final chance to settle this dispute another way. Killmonger removes his shirt to reveal all of his scars and he responds, "I lived my entire life waiting for this moment. I trained, I lied, I killed, just to get here. I killed in America, Afghanistan, Iraq. I took life from my own brothers and sisters right here on this continent, and all this death just so I could kill you" (1:18:15). The aforementioned scene informs the viewer that the scars on his arm that that he partially revealed to Klaue are tallies for the number of people that he murdered as a Black Ops solider in the U.S. Army. In this scene, viewers see Killmonger's entire torso covered in scars for the first time and this emphasizes just how much pain he has inflicted on others and himself in the name of resistance, and simultaneously his torso represents a map of his kills. Moreover, his scars portray the steps he has taken to reach Wakanda and the oppressive ideologies he adopted as a Black Ops soldier working for the U.S. empire and, in this way, his scars are a disability metaphor for trauma that he has suffered as a Black man trying to survive in the United States. In this way, Killmonger's representation as a bodymind character whose scarification is a cartography of his psychological disability is emphasized in this scene.

While Killmonger succeeds the throne, he announces his plan to wage war on oppressive regimes around the world, and the film visualizes his psychological disability through specific camera shots and dialogue. I turn to Michael Berube's book, *The Secret Life of Stories: From Don Quixote to Harry Potter, How Understanding Intellectual Disability Transforms the Way We Read*, to support my argument that narrative strategies, such as the use of camera shots and dialogue, contributes to Killmonger's representation as a disabled character. Berube explains how deployment of disability goes beyond specific rendering of disabled characters. He writes, "Representations of disability are ubiquitous, yes, even or especially when you are not looking for them; but narrative *deployments* of disability do not confine themselves to representation. They can also be narrative strategies, devices for exploring vast domains of human thought, experience, and action."[10] As Killmonger approaches the throne, the camera is positioned upside down and rotates slowly to right-side up as he walks toward the throne (1:29:30). This rotating shot is a deployment of disability, a filmic/narrative strategy that metaphorically portrays the confusion, ideological turmoil, and psychological sickness that Killmonger brings to the Wakandan throne. This visual deployment of disability is supported by another visual narrative strategy (camera jumpcuts between characters) and the dialogue between Killmonger and the Wakandan tribe leaders.

After Killmonger officially sits on the throne, he proclaims,

> We got spies embedded in every nation on Earth, already in place. I know how colonizers think, so I will use their own strategy against them. We're going to send vibranium weapons out to our war dogs. They'll arm oppressed people all over the world so they can finally rise up and kill those in power, and their children, and anyone else who takes their side. It's time they know the truth about us. We're warriors! The world's gonna start over and this time we're on top! The sun will never set on the Wakanda empire. (1:30:13)

During Killmonger's monologue, the camera jumpcuts between him and the leaders of the Wakandan tribes. These shots capture a rift between the Wakandan tribes—W'Kabi looks at Killmonger admirably, M'Kathu (the elder of the border tribe) looks at Killmonger in shock, Okoye looks at Killmonger in disgust, and she looks at W'Kabi in disbelief, because he agrees with Killmonger (1:29:50–1:30:49). Their varying facial responses to Killmonger's plan captured in these jumpcuts represent the disruptiveness of Killmonger's non-normative reality (which marks him disabled in Wakanda). Following this visual rift between the tribes, Okoye challenges Killmonger's mission to arm oppressed people over the world. She says, "Wakanda has survived for so long by fighting when only *absolutely* necessary" (1:30:50).

W'Kabi retorts, "Wakanda survived in the past this way, yes. But the world is changing, General. Elders, it is getting smaller. The outside world is catching up and soon it will be conquerors or the conquered. I'd rather be the former" (1:30:55). This exchange between Okoye and W'Kabi further illustrates the turmoil that Killmonger's influence induced between the tribes by portraying a temporal rift in the Wakandan empire. Okoye wants to maintain the *past* tradition of fighting only when necessary, while W'Kabi outlines a worldly *futurity* that demarcates the conquerors and the conquered. This disharmony between the tribes and the temporal rift, captured through camera shots and dialogue, only happens when Killmonger takes the throne.

Much of Killmonger's disability is represented by other characters' perception of him and his individualistic agency. However, I posit that his individualistic and selfish mission still held the potential to liberate Black people and this potential also nuances his supercrip representation. Though Killmonger is met with much resistance during the civil war, he continues the mission despite the objection of T'Challa and Okoye. Cathy Cohen's essay "Deviance as Resistance" helps to conceptualize Killmonger's resilience as a counter normative politic to dominant ideology. Cohen examines the political potential of the perceived deviance of Black communities. She writes, "While I accept the warning of Dorian Warren that cumulative acts of individual agency are not the same as collective agency, I do believe that in this counter normative space exists the possibility of radical change, not only in the distribution of resources, but also definitional power, redefining the rules of normality that limit the dreams, emotions, and acts of most people."[11] Killmonger's mission represents this counter normative space. His mission quite literally held the possibility of radical change by distributing vibranium to arm oppressed Black people around the world and if his plan was successful, he may have possibly acquired definitional power to redefine the rules of normalcy. However, his counter normative politic, tainted with individualism and deviance, marks him as a character with "hatred in his heart" and therefore "unfit to be a king" as Okoye tells him during the civil war scene (1:43:45).

Though individualism underscores Killmonger's mission, I argue that the way he is represented in the film highlights his superpowered supercrip representation. Returning to Schalk's chapter, "Reevaluating the Supercrip," she mentions Disability Studies scholars' observation that supercrip representations focus on individual attitudes. She writes,

> Almost all discussions of supercrips focus on how these representations rely on concepts of overcoming, heroism, inspiration, and the extraordinary. Additionally, most scholarship also mentions how these representations focus on individual attitude, work, and perseverance rather than on social barriers,

making it seem as if all effects of disability can be erased if one merely works hard enough.[12]

Taking this observation of the supercrip into consideration, it becomes clear that the film's lacking visualization of Killmonger's oppressive life growing up in the United States contributes to the erasure of the social barriers that influence his character. While I acknowledge that the film portrays how the murder of his father hurt him as a boy, I posit that only showing this grievance and not his subsequent oppressive life growing up as a Black boy in Oakland indirectly labels his mission a personal vendetta when is actually working for the liberation of all Black people (though his plan is flawed). Moreover, I read this lack of representation as an ableist narrative strategy that categorizes Killmonger as a hate-filled, unfit king (as Okoye says). The discourse surrounding fit/unfit is closely tied to the discourse of ability/disability since, often, people labeled disabled are also considered unfit by society's standards. Okoye's (and the film's) labeling of Killmonger as an unfit character merely due to his "hate-filled" heart ignores the multiple oppressions that result in his character representation. In sum, Killmonger's scarification and the film's narrative strategy including camera shots, character perception, and lack of representation contribute to the making of his disability.

Arguably, Killmonger is not the only psychologically disabled character in the film represented by deviance, M'Baku and Klaue ostensibly represent this disability as well. I acknowledge that M'Baku can be perceived as psychologically disabled because of his conservative politics that counters the rest of Wakanda, and Klaue can be perceived as psychologically disabled for telling Americans about the true potential of Wakanda when no one outside of Wakanda knows this truth (or will believe him). In the case of M'Baku, he disagrees with the dominant ideology of Wakanda, but he agrees to live in the mountains in isolation. Also, though he challenges T'Challa for the throne, he does so within the ritual battle and even surrenders to continue to serve his tribe. During the civil war, he aligns himself with the original ideology of Wakanda and assists T'Challa in defeating Killmonger. Taken together, M'Baku's resistance falls within the rules of Wakanda, and this limitation to his resistance rejects an argument that he is psychologically disabled.

Klaue is perceived psychologically disabled when he informs Agent Ross of the true technological advancements of Wakanda that is under the guise of a poor, third-world country (0:56:00). However, Klaue's perceived psychological disability is recovered when Agent Ross is brought to Wakanda to be "healed" after getting shot for saving Nakia during Klaue's escape. Agent Ross witnesses and experiences firsthand the technological advancements of the nation of Wakanda when Princess Shuri uses vibranium to recover his injured spine and when he controls a vibranium-simulated aircraft to help defeat Killmonger during the civil war. Moreover, the viewers of the movie are implicated in Klaue's recovery of psychological disability, because we also serve as witnesses to his testimony about Wakanda, and therefore the representation of this disability is limited to a racialized and geopoliticized construction (of course Klaue still remains a physically disabled character because of the partial amputation of his arm). This geopoliticized limitation is later emphasized when W'Kabi later adopts Killmonger's principles and helps to spearhead the civil war. However, during the scene of the civil war where he is confronted by Okoye (his lover), he acknowledges the death and destruction that his ideology has caused to the nation of Wakanda, and he surrenders in favor of saving the nation. W'Kabi, a full Wakandan and citizen of the nation, contrasts to Killmonger—part Wakandan and a citizen of the United States—because he does not adopt an African American "by any means necessary" approach to liberation. Thus, social constructions of psychological disability represented by anti-colonial resistance are limited to the politics and geography of a U.S.-based resistance.

READING KILLMONGER AS A QUEER CHARACTER

Killmonger represents a queer character because he exists within and between a Wakandan and African American binary. His existence within and between these two binaries marks him as queer because he complicates socially constructed normative categories in the film. I turn to Cathy Cohen's definition of queer from her essay, "Punks, Bulldaggers, and Welfare Queens: The Radical Potential of Queer Politics?" Cohen writes,

> For many of us, the label "queer" symbolizes an acknowledgement that through our existence and everyday survival we embody sustained and multi-sited resistance to systems (based on dominant constructions of race and gender) that seek to normalize our sexuality, exploit our labor, and constrain our visibility. At the intersection of oppression and resistance lies the radical potential of queerness to challenge and bring together all those deemed marginal and all those committed to liberatory politics.[13]

I read Killmonger as a queer character, because he is positioned outside of the dominant constructed norm of what it means to be Wakandan. His Wakandan identity is initially challenged when King T'Chaka abandons him in Oakland to literally constrain his visibility, as Cohen says, from Wakanda. Killmonger's Wakandan identity is later refused by Queen Romanda (Angela Bassett). When the M'Kathu (Danny Sapani) says that Killmonger is within his rights to challenge T'Challa for the throne since he is the son of N'Jobu, the queen retorts, "He has no rights here!" (1:16:23). Her rejection of Killmonger is simultaneously a rejection of her family's truth and a rejection of his royal Wakandan bloodline. Though T'Challa accepts his challenge, the rest of the tribes are reluctant to trust him because they still perceive him as an outsider, though they know he is N'Jobu's son.

Similarly, Killmonger exists within and is positioned outside the category, African American. Killmonger embodies African Americanness via his socio-spatial positioning in Oakland, California, in the 1990s as the son of a (performative) African American revolutionary. Also, his social and cultural connection to the African American experience radicalizes him to become Killmonger. However, his mother's character is never introduced in the film, though I presume she is an African American woman. Moreover, we learn later in the film that Killmonger's father N'Jobu is murdered by his brother, T'Chaka, while Killmogner is just a boy. Killmonger has no other known African American relatives in the diegesis of the film, and as I have mentioned earlier in this chapter, his African American lived experience is not portrayed beyond his youth. Insofar as the diegesis of the film, Killmonger is the only known African American character that is part Wakandan, and this biological connection to Wakanda makes him distinct from the other African American characters in the film. I read Killmonger's genealogical refusal of strict Wakandan or African American categories as what Deleuze and Guattari might describe as a rhizome—his character biologically and spatially resists rootedness in the United States and Wakanda.[14] In sum, Killmonger's existence in this liminal category marks him as a queer character in the film.

QUEERING THE BLACK PANTHER

This section of my chapter extends my discussion on the narrative representation of queerness, this time with a focus on the birth of the Black Panthers in the film. T'Chaka, T'Challa, and Killmonger all become the Black Panther by ingesting the vibranium-infused herb. I want to draw attention to what is described as the heart-shaped herb by N'Boju (0:00:50). N'Jobu tells young Killmonger that the panther goddess led the first Black Panther to a plant containing the herb. The depiction of the first Black Panther approaching the plant reveals that the "heart-shaped herb" resembles the opening of a vagina and it is important to note that the Black Panther's power only comes from consuming this herb. I consider the process of becoming a Black Panther an act of birthing and I read this birth as a queer act that is informed by heteronormativity. It is a queer act because the herb, a visual metaphor for a female via its resemblance to a vagina, impregnates the male with superpowers. Moreover, the reversal of heteronormative reproduction marks the plant and Black Panthers as queer. While this process of birthing the Black Panther may seem radical at cursory glance, I posit that the limitation of this birthing process is underscored by heteronormativity because it requires a "female" and a "male" body to reproduce, although Wakanda is a fictional world capable of breaking these heteronormative constructions.

CONCLUSION

The release of *Black Panther* made film and Black cultural production history. Ranked as the most successful Black superhero film ever, *Black Panther's* success and resonance with a global Black audience solidifies the importance of representation for Black people. At cursory glance, the representation of blackness is limited, because it excludes representations of disabled and queer Black people. However, as I have argued using the theoretical frameworks developed in Sami Schalk's book *Bodyminds Reimagined* and Cathy Cohen's essays, "Deviance as Resistance" and "Punks, Bulldaggers, and Welfare Queens" Killmonger represents both a psychologically disabled and queer character. Killmonger's disability is represented through multiple factors in the film. First, the convergence of his spatial, paternal, and anti-colonial political deviance relegates him outside of the normative functions of Wakanda and the United States. Second, his representation as a bodymind character via his scarification and the film's narrative portrayal of his character contributes to his representational disability. Third, a comparative analysis between Killmonger, M'Baku, and Klaue highlights psychological disability as a racialized geopolitical manifestation in this film. Killmonger's queerness is represented by his existence within and between a Wakandan and African American binary and his narrative construction as a Black Panther. Disability Studies, Black Feminist theory, and Queer theory make it possible to illuminate various representations of blackness in the film that are rendered absent at cursory glance.

NOTES

1. This chapter was inspired by my Spring 2018 "Feminist Theories and Women's Movements: Genealogies" seminar. During this course, my presentation assignment was to read Dr. Sami Schalk's book, *Bodyminds Reimagined,* and put the book in conversation with a contemporary popular cultural artifact. I chose to put this book in conversation with the character Killmonger. What started out as a seminar presentation became a final paper and now a published article.

2. Sami Schalk, "Reevaluating the Supercrip," *Journal of Literary & Cultural Disability Studies* 10 (2016): 76, doi:10.3828/jlcds.2016.5.

3. Schalk, "Reevaluating the Supercrip," 79–81. Schalk defines the regular supercrip as a narrative that "focuses on a person or character with a disability who gains attention for 'mundane accomplishments, which because of their impairment are considered exceptionally successful.'" In contrast, Schalk defines the glorified supercrip narrative as a "representation of a person or character with a disability who, according to Kama, 'achieve[s] feats that even non-disabled persons rarely attempt.'" Finally, Schalk defines the superpowered supercrip as "primarily a fiction, television, or film representation of a character who has abilities or "powers" that operate in direct relationship with or contrast to their ability." The powers and abilities are not the result of effort, but of accident or luck.

4. Robert W. Cape Jr., "Disabled Hero, Sick Society: Sophocles' Philoctetes and Robert Silverberg's The Man in the Maze," in *Disability in Science Fiction: Representations of Technology as Cure,* ed. Kathryn Allan (New York: Palgrave Macmillan, 2013), 144.

5. Sami Schalk, *Bodyminds Reimagined: (Dis)Ability, Race, and Gender in Black Women's Speculative Fiction* (Durham, North Carolina: Duke University Press, 2018), 5.

6. Schalk, *Bodyminds Reimagined*, 25.

7. Rashad Shabazz, *Spatializing Blackness: Architectures of Confinement and Black Masculinity in Chicago* (Champaign, IL: University of Illinois Press, 2015), 57.

8. Cathy J. Cohen, "Deviance as Resistance: A New Research Agenda for the Study of Black Politics," *Du Bois Review: Social Science Research on Race* 1 (2004): 27.

9. Joshua Bloom and Waldo E. Martin, *Black against Empire: The History and Politics of the Black Panther Party* (Oakland: University of California Press, 2016), 230.

10. Michael Bérubé, *The Secret Life of Stories: From Don Quixote to Harry Potter, How Understanding Intellectual Disability Transforms the Way We Read* (New York: New York University Press, 2016), 2.

11. Cohen, "Deviance as Resistance," 38.

12. Schalk, "Reevaluating the Supercrip," 73.

13. Cathy J. Cohen, "Punks, Bulldaggers, and Welfare Queens: The Radical Potential of Queer Politics?," *GLQ: A Journal of Lesbian and Gay Studies* 3 (1997): 440.

14. Gilles Deleuze and Guattari Félix, *A Thousand Plateaus: Capitalism and Schizophrenia* (Minneapolis, MN: University of Minnesota Press, 1987).

WORKS CITED

Bérubé, Michael. *The Secret Life of Stories: From Don Quixote to Harry Potter, How Understanding Intellectual Disability Transforms the Way We Read.* New York: New York University Press, 2016.

Bloom, Joshua, and Waldo E. Martin. *Black against Empire: The History and Politics of the Black Panther Party*. Oakland: University of California Press, 2016.

Cape Jr, Robert W. "Disabled Hero, Sick Society: Sophocles' Philoctetes and Robert Silverberg's The Man in the Maze." In *Disability in Science Fiction: Representations of Technology as Cure,* edited by Kathryn Allan, 144. New York: Palgrave Macmillan, 2013.

Cohen, Cathy J. "Deviance as Resistance: A New Research Agenda for the Study of Black Politics." *Du Bois Review: Social Science Research on Race* 1 (2004): 27–45.

Cohen, Cathy J. "Punks, Bulldaggers, and Welfare Queens: The Radical Potential of Queer Politics?" *GLQ: A Journal of Lesbian and Gay Studies* 3 (1997): 437–465.

Deleuze, Gilles, and Guattari Félix. *A Thousand Plateaus: Capitalism and Schizophrenia*. Minneapolis, MN: University of Minnesota Press, 1987.

Schalk, Sami. *Bodyminds Reimagined: (Dis)Ability, Race, and Gender in Black Women's Speculative Fiction*. Durham, NC: Duke University Press, 2018.

Schalk, Sami. "Reevaluating the Supercrip." *Journal of Literary & Cultural Disability Studies* 10 (2016): 71–86. doi:10.3828/jlcds.2016.5.

Shabazz, Rashad. *Spatializing Blackness: Architectures of Confinement and Black Masculinity in Chicago*. Champaign, IL: University of Illinois Press, 2015.

FILMS

Black Panther. Directed by Ryan Coogler. United States: Walt Disney Studio Motion Pictures, 2018.

Blankman. Directed by Mike Binder. United States: Sony Pictures, 1994.

Fences. Directed by Denzel Washington. United States: Paramount Pictures, 2016.

The Green Mile. Directed by Frank Darabont. United States: Warner Bros., 1999.

Hancock. Directed by Peter Berg. United States: Sony Pictures Releasing, 2008.

Hobbs & Shaw. Directed by David Leitch. United States: Universal Pictures, 2019.

Radio. Directed by Mike Tollin. United States: Sony Pictures, 2003.

Ray. Directed by Taylor Hackford. United States: Universal Pictures, 2004.

Chapter 10

Only When She Wants To
Code-Switching in Black Panther
Paul Moffett

Black Panther (Ryan Coogler, 2018) evinces at its core what W. E. B. Du Bois called a "double-consciousness." Du Bois wrote that an African American "ever feels his twoness, an American, a Negro; two souls, two thoughts, two unreconciled strivings; two warring ideals in one dark body, whose dogged strength alone keeps it from being torn asunder. The history of the American Negro is the history of this strife—this longing to attain self-conscious manhood, to merge his double self into a better and truer self."[1] *Black Panther* presents, and it sees, Black identity both from two perspectives at once—from both what we might call an American perspective and an African one.

Black Panther's setting and perspective is African—it is set in the (fictional) sovereign African nation of Wakanda, its aesthetic is conspicuously (and beautifully) inspired by Ghanaian, Kenyan, Lesothan, and other African art and architecture. It is also a profoundly American film and its central themes concern not only the history of an African diaspora but specifically that history as it intersects with American history. Even the name of the country the action centers around is both satisfyingly African-sounding to American ears and also implicitly built on understanding African from the outside. The word "Wakanda" was a neologism when it was created for Black Panther comics by co-creators Stan Lee and Jack Kirby, but its etymology is not difficult to imagine. In Swahili, the prefix "wa" indicates a plural people. Americans in Swahili is "Wamerikani," Kenyans in Swahili is "Wakenya," and Ugandans is "Waganda." It seems very likely that Lee and/or Kirby first named "Wakanda" from "Waganda" or possibly from "Wakamba," the Swahili name for the Kamba people of southeastern Kenya. To a Swahili speaker, or even to someone with a rudimentary knowledge of Swahili, Wakanda is a mildly confusing name for a country, since the "wa" suggests that the noun that follows is both (1) plural and (2) personal. Wakanda's very name sounds like what it is: a vision of Africa primarily for Americans and by Americans.

We can see the same dynamic at play in the Wakandan characters' accents, which are likely to sound pleasingly African to American Anglophones, but which are reportedly distractingly inconsistent to a Ghanaian audience: "forced, vague and unconvincing, with heavily articulated consonants and a grab-bag of speech patterns from Nigeria, South Africa, and the Swahili-speaking countries of East Africa."[2] Although the issue of speech and language in *Black Panther* is my central focus, I want to stress that my emphasis on the American perspective of *Black Panther* is not necessarily a criticism, nor should it be surprising. Perhaps I am belaboring what should really be a fairly obvious point. *Black Panther* is a character created by Americans (Lee and Kirby), published in American superhero comics by an American comic book publisher (Marvel), adapted into a feature film by an American director (Ryan Coogler) with a screenplay by American screen writers (Ryan Coogler and Joe Robert Cole), starring an American actor (late Chadwick Boseman). It is an American film and its perspective on African identity is an African American one. This is part of what provides nuance to the film's themes, because the perspective of the film is in many ways more closely aligned to its ostensible villain, the American-born Erik Killmonger (Michael B. Jordan), than it is to the ostensible hero, the Wakandan-born T'Challa.

The double-consciousness Du Bois talks about it not a uniquely American understanding of Black identity. Frantz Fanon, political philosopher and psychiatrist, makes a similar argument in *Black Skin, White Masks* (1952), writing specifically about Black people in French colonies.[3] Fanon writes about Black people who are one thing among other Blacks but are perceived, treated, and therefore in social terms become something else in their interaction with Whites. As Fanon points out, minorities—where "minority" refers to any people excluded from the dominant culture—are required by the dominant culture to be doubled: to have two identities. They must be conscious of both the dominant culture and of their sub-culture. And moving from one context to another, from one social or cultural register to another, requires code-switching; sometimes in the literal linguistic sense and sometimes metaphorically.

CODE-SWITCHING

Strictly speaking, "code-switching" is a linguistic phenomenon which primarily manifests in bilingual language speakers. Linguist Barbara E.

Bullock defines code-switching as "the ability on the part of bilinguals to alternate effortlessly between their two languages."[4] We can distinguish between a number of modes of code-switching, which demonstrate different degrees of effortlessness but all of which demonstrate the ability to alternate between languages. Linguists distinguish between *intra-sentential* code-switching, in which the speaker switches between languages within a clause, and *inter-sentential* code-switching, in which the speaker switches between languages at clause boundaries. Most of the code-switching on display in *Black Panther* is *inter-sentential*. Characters display effortless bilingualism, but their alternation between languages occurs at clause boundaries—most typically characters in *Black Panther* will speak an entire line of dialogue in one language and then switch to another language only after another character has spoken. We might also point out that, especially as it applies to analysis of fiction, linguistic alternation that is not strictly categorized as code-switching is also of interest. Bullock and fellow linguist Almeida Jacqueline Toribio point out that "[e]ven monolinguals are capable of shifting between the linguistic registers and the dialects they command"[5] and distinguish this monolingual shifting from code-switching proper and labels it "style-switching."

My interest, in this chapter, is less in the mechanics of code-switching and how it functions, either in the real world or in *Black Panther,* than it is in the symbolic or metaphorical meaning of code-switching within this film. Indeed, a scripted film would be a poor research site for analysis of code-switching as it occurs in everyday speech, both because any script necessarily decreases the naturalism of speech, and also because the scriptwriters of *Black Panther* clearly and understandably prioritized audience comprehension over realistic speech patterns. Single words or fragments of speech naturalistically interspersed within the speech of the bilingual characters would make the movie more difficult for monolingual American audiences (which we have already established are the primary audience envisioned by the film) to understand and would make subtitling more difficult and intrusive.

For the purposes of this chapter, however, I am most interested in the intersections between code-switching and identity. As linguist Peter Auer points out, "the most straightforward link between identities and the alternating use of more than one language in discourse would be to treat the distinction between 'being bilingual' and 'being monolingual' in itself."[6] We will return briefly to this distinction, because within the imaginative context of *Black Panther,* I think there is a fruitful distinction to be made between the characters who signal fluid identities through their linguistic flexibility and those who do not. Auer goes on to say that the bilingual/monolingual distinction "is rarely adequate, however, because as a rule, 'bilingual/monolingual' is not a membership category."[7]

HOW MUCH DOES LANGUAGE USE CONSTITUTE IDENTITY (IN *BLACK PANTHER*)?

Language use is both constitutive of and reflective of identity, and it is both a marker of structure, that is, "constrained by people's (authentic) membership in social groups"[8] and by agency, "the social construction of personal, relational and social meanings in discourse."[9] To the degree that language use is constitutive of identity, it creates group identities based around language. That is, English speakers have a shared group identity with all other English speakers. Smaller dialectical idiosyncrasies constitute smaller identity groups. This is the context within African American English (AAE) which creates a shared identity between its speakers that is not held in common with other English speakers. The very example of AAE, however, illustrates its opposite. AAE is better understood as reflecting a shared identity than creating it; a case-in-point of Auer's assertion that "usually, code-switching stands for something else. It symbolizes identities beyond the linguistic fact."[10]

Director and co-screenwriter Ryan Coogler reportedly "wanted to make it a priority to use Xhosa[11] as much as possible"[12] in *Black Panther*. From one perspective, this desire to steep the movie in an African language is impressive. The *New York Times* article in which Coogler's intention is cited also quotes South African musician Namhla Mbawuli: "reinforces the importance of our culture, accepting our language and having pride in being Xhosa."[13] The use of isiXhosa symbolically includes real Africans in the fictional world of the film.[14] It is also a vital part of the multi-leveled world-building which makes *Black Panther* aesthetically successful. The point is not *realism*, per se, but immersive fiction. The architecture, the colors, the mythology, the music, the fabrics, and the language all feel of a piece and that creates a full and textured world. But the statement that Coogler wanted to "use Xhosa as much as possible" raises an obvious question: how much is possible?

The desire to use isiXhosa as much as possible is an obvious hyperbole. It would be trivial to double the isiXhosa spoken in the film, even considering both artistic and commercial concerns about American tolerance for subtitles. What the film does is not use isiXhosa as much as possible, but rather use it as much as desirable—that is, desirable by Coogler and the other filmmakers. Whatever the reasons for the use of isiXhosa in *Black Panther*—and its effects on tone, atmosphere, character, plot, and theme, the result is that we have characters who switch between English and isiXhosa, and those moments of code-switching are illuminating both taken one by one and also considered as a whole.

There are characters, like T'Challa and Okoye (Danai Gurira), who are literally bilingual and who speak two languages on screen (in this case, English and isiXhosa). Nakia (Lupita Nyong'o) speaks at least three languages on screen, adding Korean to English and isiXhosa. There are also several characters who are presumably bilingual but whom we only ever see speaking one language on screen, such as Ulysses Klaue (Andy Serkis), who only ever speaks English but who arguably reacts to isiXhosa as if he understands it. Finally, characters like Everett Ross (Martin Freeman) perform monolingualism both in their speech and in their comprehension. Ross cannot understand the other characters when they speak isiXhosa.

This linguistic fluidity is a metaphorical representation of each character's ability to shift between cultural and political contexts. Nakia, a Wakandan spy, speaks several languages because she is able—required by her vocation—to change her identity, or at least her outward manifestation of it. Her linguistic fluidity represents the fluidity of her identity in general. T'Challa speaks both English and isiXhosa because, although he is politically and ideologically rooted in Wakanda, he must be literally and ideologically understandable to American English-speaking audiences: He literally speaks their language. Within the context of the film, he switches between the two languages because of his internal conflict between isolationism and interventionism. He does not speak only isiXhosa because he wants the rest of the world—as represented by the English language—to understand him, and despite his occasional protestations, to the contrary, he feels a responsibility toward the world at large.

Okoye speaks proportionally more isiXhosa than T'Challa does because she is more representative of the isolationist ideology. When Okoye, T'Challa, and Nakia are in Busan, South Korea, on a mission to apprehend Klaue, Klaue's men recognize Okoye as Wakandan when she speaks isiXhosa: "Yeka [Stand down]."[15] Klaue and his men are expecting a Wakandan ambush and are on the lookout for Wakandans. The club is in South Korea and most of the club's patrons present as Asian—the mostly White Americans stand out on sight. But it is not skin color or any other visual signifier that reveals Okoye as Wakandan; it is her use of language, and more specifically her shift from English to isiXhosa that outs her. This shift is not a marker of Okoye's lack of mastery of English—she has been speaking English fluently up to then. Rather it is a symbolic moment that represents the continuity of her Wakandan identity even when she is in disguise. Immediately after Klaue's men recognize her as Wakandan because of her use of language, Okoye drops all semblance of concealment and uses her erstwhile disguise, her wig, as a weapon. Unlike the spy Nakia, Okoye cannot—and perhaps is unwilling to—fully conceal her identity

N'JOBU, CODE-SWITCHING, AND ACCENT

Language and accent are markers of identity in *Black Panther*. In a memorable moment early in the film, N'Jobu (Sterling K. Brown) abruptly changes from speaking in an American accent to speaking in the movie's Wakandan accent when the object of his address changes from the (presumed by him to be) American James (Denzel Whitaker) to the Wakandan guards and his brother King T'Chaka (Atandwa Kani). This moment of code-switching is both formative and indicative of N'Jobu's identity and functions with regard to at least three registers.

In the first place, N'Jobu's code-switching signals his identity to the Wakandans. He speaks like them to indicate that he is one of them. Presumably he is known by his brother King T'Chaka but not necessarily by the two members of the Dora Milaje (Shaunette Renée Wilson and Christine Hollingsworth) who act as bodyguards for T'Chaka. N'Jobu's way of speaking is one of three markers of his identity—the others being his name and the phosphorescent tattoo on his lower lip. N'Jobu's code-switching is unremarked upon and unasked for, and is therefore ironically signaled as the most authentic of his identity markers. That is not to say that there is any indication that N'Jobu is lying about his name or that his tattoo is forged, but that his linguistic self-representation is spontaneous. That spontaneity signals authenticity because a naïve reading of identity would suggest that the most spontaneous, unstudied, unselfconscious, unguarded behaviors are most indicative of real identity. If we interpret social identities and performances as deceptive masks that conceal the true inner self, then N'Jobu's spontaneous linguistic alteration reveals that he was "pretending" to be an American—that his American accent is a "fake" accent while his Wakandan accent is his "real" accent.

I said that his code-switching is *ironically* signaled as the most authentic of his identity markers. The irony lies in two places: first, that this naïve reading of the meaning of N'Jobu's spontaneous shift in accent does not correspond to what we know about code-switching, or even to the logic of identity and how it works. Although it is certainly possible to fake an accent, linguistic registers, even among monolinguals, are flexible and fluid. As linguist Penelope Eckert has argued, "authenticity implies stasis."[16] The concept of an authentic identity that corresponds to spontaneous utterances implies that identity cannot change and that N'Jobu's Wakandan accent is more authentic to his identity because his identity is immutable. But it is, or should be, self-evident upon interrogation that identities shift, that N'Jobu's experiences can and do change him. If language is constitutive of identity, then learning a language is symbolic of a changing identity. In the more specific register of linguistic code-switching, in theory code-switching suggests mastery of both linguistic registers. Neither of N'Jobu's accents is "fake," in other words. Both are authentic, but each is appropriate for different contexts.

The other irony, of course, lies in the metatextual reality that actor Sterling K. Brown is affecting a "fake" accent when he speaks as a Wakandan and that American accent is the one that is arguably less constructed. "Arguably," because N'Jobu's accent in this scene is not identical to Sterling K. Brown's usual way of speaking, and because if accent and linguistic register are constitutive of identity—especially of group identities—then one of Sterling K. Brown's most important identities in this moment is his professional identity as an actor, in which case his faux-African accent *is* constitutive of that identity.

As well as signaling his identity to the Wakandans, N'Jobu's code-switch also signals it to the audience of the film. The film begins with a narration from an unnamed and unidentified male voice, addressed by a younger voice as "Baba," and speaking in a Wakandan accent. When Sterling K. Brown's N'Jobu first appears on screen, speaking in an American accent, the audience is unlikely to—and discouraged from—making a connection between the two characters. We assume that the character is who he appears to be—an African American man. When he suddenly speaks with a Wakandan accent, it signals his dual or fluid identity to the audience as well as reconstructing the presumed lines of allegiance and conflict. I suspect that only a very astute audience member would recognize N'Jobu as the narrator of the opening section of the film, but even a naïve one will presume allegiance and shared collective identity based on a shared way of speaking. In N'Jobu's case, there is an immediate conflict of presumed identities.

The third and final register within which N'Jobu's code-switching signifies is a metatextual one and it is grounded in the fluidity of the change. N'Jobu's accent signifies his allegiance and his identity, both to the characters on the screen and to the audience. The fact that he can—that he does—change it signals that identity, both collective and personal, is a central theme of the film. N'Jobu's Wakandan identity is again threatened and undermined by the revelation that he has betrayed the country.

N'Jobu's fluid movement from one linguistic register to another is soon echoed by his friend "James," who changes his accent to reveal that he is Zuri (Forest Whitaker), also a Wakandan. The difference between N'Jobu's code-switching and Zuri's is that N'Jobu has been "radicalized" by his interaction with African Americans. His identity has shifted so that he identifies with Americans—his speech reflects a shift in his self-conception, and his shifting accent represents the continuity between his new identity and his old one. Although those two identities are in conflict, he is authentic in both. It's striking that N'Jobu has no "American" name (or at least, we are not told what his American name is, which is tantamount to him not having one), while Zuri

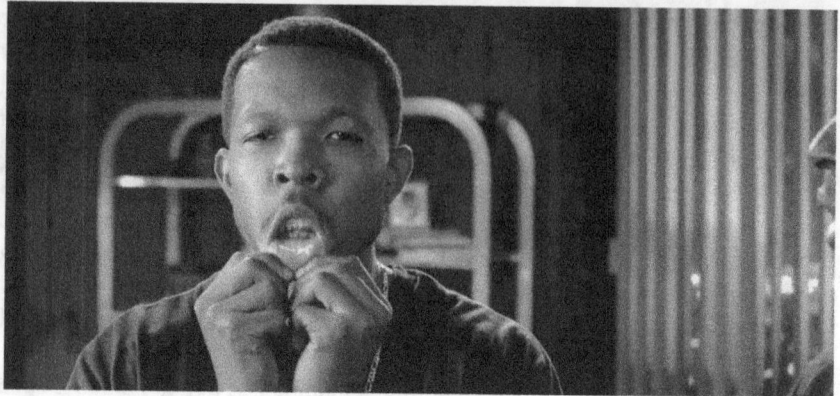

Figure 10.1 Zuri (First Whitaker) Reveals His Wakandan Ancestry by Showing the Tattoo on His Lower Lip. Screenshot taken by author.

takes on the identity of "James" while he is posing as an American. Zuri is in disguise as James, while N'Jobu has changed into the American-accented N'Jobu (see figure 10.1).

CODE-SWITCHING AND SUPERHERO SECRET IDENTITIES

The concept of the secret identity has been one of the central tropes of superheroes, ever since the creation of Superman, and inherited from the pulp-hero stories that inspired him, like *The Shadow*, and *Zorro*. Secret identities like Superman's alter-ego Clark Kent have fallen somewhat out of fashion in more recent superhero stories, however, and the Marvel Cinematic Universe of which *Black Panther* is a part has largely eschewed them. Captain America's identity as Steve Rogers is public knowledge within the interconnected film world of the MCU, as is Iron Man's identity as Tony Stark. Neither Thor nor Stephen Strange has an alter-ego, and Bruce Banner's identity as the Hulk is a thematic alter-ego but not a secret.

Black Panther's identity as King T'Challa, however, is more nuanced than any of these other examples. Within the fictional world of *Black Panther*, T'Challa's identity as the Black Panther is an open secret. Wakandans know T'Challa's dual identity, but generally speaking, the wider world does not. The film makes this explicit when Agent Ross (Martin Freeman) asks T'Challa "didn't I keep it under wraps that the king of a third-world country runs around in a bulletproof cat suit?."[17] T'Challa's identity as Black Panther is secret from the world, because Wakanda's true identity is secret from the world. As Black Panther is the personification of Wakanda's wealth and advanced technology.

Moreover, T'Challa's personal identity as an individual and his symbolic identity as Black Panther are potentially in conflict. He is a manifestation of Du Bois' idea of double-consciousness. He literalizes Fanon's metaphor of masks. But the film and its approach to linguistic code-switching provide us with a theoretical lens through which we can understand and even begin to reconcile the divided identities at play here. T'Challa's vacillation between individual and symbolic figure—whether that is the symbolic figure "Black Panther," a tropic character within the established genre of a superhero film or it is the symbolic political figure of "King"—is a kind of code-switching. Not only T'Challa's speech, but also his behavior, his posture, his actions and choices, all shift depending on whether he is acting as T'Challa or as Black Panther.

After T'Challa has successfully pursued and captured Klaue, and is presumably about to kill him, Klaue successfully stays his hand by making the connection between T'Challa and Black Panther public: "Mercy, King, Mercy!"[18] When Nakia tells T'Challa "Ilizwe likhangele [The world watches]"[19] she makes it clear that T'Challa's following actions are—and are appropriately—mediated by the fact of an audience. This moment collapses the convenient disparity between T'Challa's two personas that his secret identity provides. T'Challa-as-Black-Panther can resolve conflicts with personal violence—and arguably *must* do so, both within the internal logic of the genre of a superhero movie and also within the logic of his self-construction as a warrior-defender of his people. T'Challa shifts from the vengeful warrior guardian of his nation, "Black Panther," to a diplomatic and political actor who must consider the opinion of the global community. In other words, T'Challa code-switches from the "language" of a smaller sub-culture to the "language" of a broader, more universal context (see figure 10.2). We should note, too, though, that Nakia

Figure 10.2 None of King T'Challa's (Chadwick Boseman) Identities Is False—None Is a Trick. His powers get stripped at the outset of battle. Screenshot taken by author.

reproaches T'Challa in isiXhosa, not in English. Even while she is reminding him to behave in a manner appropriate to the world's attention, she is implicitly removing herself from that attention. Again, there is no indication at any point in the film that anyone outside of Wakanda can understand isiXhosa. So Nakia reinforces the sub-culture while reminding T'Challa of the broader culture that subsumes it. And the secret of T'Challa's identity as Black Panther dissolves, but the dual consciousness that comes of being part of Wakanda *and* part of the world does not. And as with N'Jobu's shifting identities, neither of T'Challa's identities is false—none is a trick. They are all authentic, even when they are in conflict with one another.

ONLY WHEN SHE WANTS TO

The Wakandan characters in *Black Panther* are able to—and required to—shift between the way they speak and act among each other. Nakia's use of isiXhosa to communicate with T'Challa in full view of an audience streaming the interaction on their smartphones but without their comprehension is one example of how isiXhosa functions in the film as a marker of community. Language functions as a barrier or a boundary line that demarcates inclusion in the community of Wakanda. We see this again, even more pointedly, when Okoye and T'Challa speak isiXhosa in front of Agent Ross, discussing their strategy while he cannot understand. Frustrated, Ross asks T'Challa of Okoye: "Does she speak English?" Okoye responds, in English, "when she wants to."[20] Okoye (and T'Challa) are both able to and required to switch between isiXhosa, which is symbolic of Wakandan identity and isolationism, and English, which is symbolic of globalism but also of interaction with the colonialist world. Okoye can deploy her Wakandan identity to exclude Ross but also "when she wants to" shift to function as a part of his world. Okoye, Nakia, T'Challa, and the other Wakandan characters, in other words, in their code-switching, and their flexible navigation of English *and* isiXhosa, have the facility and perspective that Ross has *and* an additional perspective. White American characters like Ross speak only English, while Black African characters must be everything the White characters are *and* something else.

The additional meaning of all of this, if we recall that *Black Panther* is above all an American film, not an African one, is that when it comes to the film's perspective on race, the Wakandans are symbolic representatives of the African side of "African American." But in the imagination of this film, even the African side of the hyphen is not whole. Even the Africans mostly speak English. And the presumed audience of the film does not understand isiXhosa any more than Agent Ross does. The subtitles simultaneously welcome an Anglophone audience into the Wakandan community since Anglophones do understand what Okoye and T'Challa are saying and they also make the demarcation explicit. Anglophones only understand the Wakandans when their experience is translated into English, and the lack of cultural fluidity is often mistakenly taken for a mark of superiority, as Ross assumes the superiority of the United States to Wakanda the "third world country."[21] In referring to Wakanda as "third world" Ross implicitly assumes, like the French United Nations ambassador (Tony Sears) at the end of the film, that Wakanda as a "nation of farmers"[22] has little to offer the rest of the world. The Anglophone audience is more included than Ross is, but not able to fully code-switch as Okoye and T'Challa are.

If the Wakandans—and if isiXhosa—symbolically represent the African side of "African-American," then that emphasizes the degree to which the Du Boisian double-consciousness persists. As Auer has pointed out, in conceptualizing code-switching as constitutive or representational of communal or ethnic or identity (he does not say racial identity, but I will), "the ethnically 'rich' language is used in addition to (alternating with) another language, which in itself cannot achieve the relevant kind of ethnic positioning of the speaker since it is neutralized by virtue of being used 'by everybody' (or at least by too many) in a given social field."[23] So, for example, in a classroom setting where educators advocate code-switching between AAE and so-called "Standard English," AAE gives the speaker an ethnic or racial position that Standard English does not. This theoretical framework suggests Standard English as neutral and AAE as loaded; AAE as specific and Standard English as general. Consequently, the effect of code-switching, at least framed in this way, is that since the language White children use coincides with Standard English, whiteness is racially neutral. It is the default from which other racial identities differentiate themselves.

And even in *Black Panther*, which is in so many ways a film about Africa, African Americans, and Blackness as an identity, the Wakandan characters—ostensibly citizens of a never-colonized African nation—speak English most of the time, even among each other. And while we can perhaps ignore or discount the omnipresence of English in Wakanda as a narrative or marketing necessity—it is easy to imagine that the studio anticipated too many subtitles as a barrier to commercial success—within the text the characters shift to be understood by the world and the world understands in English.

WHAT ABOUT KILLMONGER?

The notable complication to all of this seems to be Erik Killmonger (Michael B. Jordan). Killmonger is the only significant African American character in *Black Panther* (his girlfriend Linda [Nabiyah Be] is also American, but her role is very brief). Killmonger literalizes the metaphor of the African characters representing the African side of African American dual consciousness. His father, N'Jobu is Wakandan, and his mother, who is unnamed in the film, is American. Killmonger speaks only one line in isiXhosa: "Ndingu N'Jadaka, unyana ka-N'Jobu [I am N'Jadaka, son of N'Jobu.]"[24] In this moment, Killmonger—who despite the revelation is listed in the credits only as "Erik Killmonger" and is only referred to in dialogue as "N'Jadaka" once more throughout the run of the film—reveals his identity to the Wakandans, but not to the audience. The audience learned who Killmonger was when he revealed himself to—and killed—Klaue. T'Challa, too, already knows who Killmonger is. He recognizes a ring that Killmonger wears once he is abducted by Klaue from the interrogation room of Agent Ross. So, this lone moment of code-switching on Killmonger's part establishes his identity to the Wakandan Tribal council. He speaks ixiXhosa in response to a question in isiXhosa. Having established his identity, however, Killmonger abandons isiXhosa for English for the remainder of the film. Instead, he speaks conspicuously colloquial American English. While T'Challa's, Nakia's, and Okoye's code-switching are all constitutive of their divided or fluid identities, Killmonger's is utilitarian. He uses isiXhosa as a tool exactly as much as it is necessary, then drops it.

We should also note that Killmonger never speaks so-called "Standard English": the English of Agent Ross. Killmonger speaks in AAE from his first appearance—he speaks exactly the same way in the museum as he does in Wakanda. In the museum scene near the beginning of the film Killmonger appears at first to be an interested museum-goer, asking about the artifacts in the West Africa exhibit. Both before and after the reveal that he is there to rob the museum, Killmonger speaks in AAE. His agenda is secret, but not his identity. Killmonger does not code-switch because he, unlike T'Challa, Nakia, Okoye, and his father N'Jobu, has and prioritizes a unified identity. This is part of what makes Killmonger appealing, despite his crimes. He has an integrity that the other characters do not, in that his worldview is integrated, even single-minded.

DOUBLE CONSCIOUSNESS AND SCHIZOPHRENIA

For both Du Bois and Fanon, doubled existence is a bad thing—not in that engaging in double-consciousness is wrong of Black people but that the social circumstances that require it are harmful. Du Bois' conception of double consciousness is an articulation of African Americans as experiencing a sort of metaphorical, racial schizophrenia. Fanon, too, connects his articulation of the post-colonial Black subject with mental illness.

Is the conclusion, then, that code-switching, especially code-switching where linguistic registers are racialized[25] as they are in *Black Panther*, exacerbates racial schizophrenia through the divided selves of the characters on the screen? After all, "Du Bois's statement . . . illustrates blacks' 'longing' to resolve double consciousness, 'to merge his double self,' the American and black selves, into a unified identity that would be better than either could ever be alone, divided, unmerged."[26] If so, then Killmonger is a preferable, more idealized subject than T'Challa is. But the framing of the film makes unified identity villainous.

NOTES

1. W. E. B. Du Bois, *The Souls of Black Folk: The Oxford W. E. B. du Bois*, ed. Henry Louis Gates (Oxford: Oxford University Press, 2007), 3.

2. Tim McDonnell, "Ghanaian Fans Have One Nit To Pick But Otherwise Adore 'Black Panther,'" *NPR*, February 20, 2018, https://www.npr.org/sections/goatsandsoda/2018/02/20/ 587224592/ghanaian-fans-have-one-nit-to-pick-but-otherwise-adore-black-panther.

3. Frantz Fanon, *Black Skin, White Masks* (New York: Grove Press, 1967).

4. Barbara E. Bullock and Almeida Jacqueline Toribio, "Themes in the study of Code-Switching," in *The Cambridge Handbook of Linguistic Code-Switching* (Cambridge: Cambridge University Press, 2009), 1.

5. Bullock and Toribio, "Themes in the study of Code-Switching," 2.

6. Peter Auer, "A Postscript: Code-switching and Social Identity," *Journal of Pragmatics* 37, no. 3 (2005): 404.

7. Auer, "A Postscript," 404.

8. Nicholas Coupland, "The Authentic Speaker and the Speech Community," in *Language and Identities,* eds. Carmen Llamas and Dominic Watt (Edinburgh: Edinburgh University Press, 2010), 100.

9. Coupland, "The Authentic Speaker," 100.

10. Auer, "A Postscript," 404.

11. The amaXhosa people are Bantu ethnic group from Southern Africa. English-speakers most often refer to the language as "Xhosa," but native speakers refer to the language as "isiXhosa" and to the people as "amaXhosa." Except in quotations I will use "isiXhosa" as a noun to refer to the language, "amaXhosa" as a noun to refer to the people and "Xhosa" as an adjective.

12. John Egliton, "Wakanda Is a Fake Country, but the African Language in 'Black Panther' Is Real," *New York Times*, February 16, 2018, https://www.nytimes.com/2018/02/16/us/wakanda-black-panther.html.

13. Egliton, "Wakanda Is a Fake Country," *New York Times*.

14. The choice of isiXhosa over any other African language is largely a choice grounded in coincidence. Actor John Kani, who appears as T'Chaka in both *Black Panther* and its predecessor *Captain America: Civil War*, speaks isiXhosa, and

reportedly suggested that his character should speak that language in *Captain America: Civil War* (Eligon). That choice set a precedent that led to isiXhosa as the language of Wakanda.

15. *Black Panther*, directed by Ryan Coogler (United States: Walt Disney Studios Motion Pictures, 2018), film, 47:00.

16. Penelope Eckert, "Elephants in the Room: Sociolinguistics and Authenticity: An Elephant in the Room," *Journal of Sociolinguistics* 7, no. 3 (2003): 393.

17. *Black Panther*, directed by Ryan Coogler, 44:10.

18. *Black Panther*, directed by Ryan Coogler, 53:35.

19. *Black Panther*, directed by Ryan Coogler, 53:45.

20. *Black Panther*, directed by Ryan Coogler, 55:05.

21. *Black Panther*, directed by Ryan Coogler, 44:10.

22. *Black Panther*, directed by Ryan Coogler, 2:06:30.

23. Auer, "A Postscript," 405.

24. *Black Panther*, directed by Ryan Coogler, 1:15:30.

25. As Young writes, "Code switching is nothing if it ain't about race!" Vershawn Ashanti Young, "'Nah, We Straight': An Argument Against Code Switching," *JAC* 29, no. 1/2 (2009): 51.

26. Young, "'Nah, We Straight'," 52.

WORKS CITED

Auer, Peter. "A Postscript: Code-switching and Social Identity." *Journal of Pragmatics* 37, no. 3 (2005): 403–410.

Coupland, Nicholas. "The Authentic Speaker and the Speech Community." In *Language and Identities*, edited by Carmen Llamas, Dominic Watt, 99–112. Edinburgh: Edinburgh University Press, 2010.

Bullock, Barbara E., and Almeida Jacqueline Toribio. "Themes in the study of Code-Switching." In *The Cambridge Handbook of Linguistic Code-Switching*, edited by Barbara E. Bullock and Almeida Jacqueline Toribio, 1–17. Cambridge: Cambridge University Press, 2009.

Du, Bois, W. E. B. *The Souls of Black Folk: The Oxford W. E. B. du Bois,* edited by Henry Louis Gates. Oxford: Oxford University Press, 2007. *ProQuest Ebook Central.*

Eckert, Penelope. "Elephants in the Room: Sociolinguistics and Authenticity: An Elephant in the Room." *Journal of Sociolinguistics* 7, no. 3 (2003): 392–397.

Egliton, John. "Wakanda Is a Fake Country, but the African Language in 'Black Panther' Is Real." *New York Times*, February 16, 2018. https://www.nytimes.com/2018/02/16/us/wakanda-black-panther.html.

Lavan, Makeba. "To Whom Does Wakanda Belong?" *Africology: The Journal of Pan African Studies* 11, no. 9 (August 2018).

McDonnell, Tim. "Ghanaian Fans Have One Nit To Pick But Otherwise Adore 'Black Panther.'" *NPR*, February 20, 2018. https://www.npr.org/sections/goatsandsoda/2

018/02/20/ 587224592/ghanaian-fans-have-one-nit-to-pick-but-otherwise-adore-black-panther.

Young, Vershawn Ashanti. "'Nah, We Straight': An Argument Against Code Switching." *JAC* 29, no. 1/2 (2009): 49–76. JSTOR, www.jstor.org/stable/20866886.

FILMS

Black Panther. Directed by Ryan Coogler. United States: Walt Disney Studios Motion Pictures, 2018.

Captain America: Civil War. Directed by Anthony Russo and Joe Russo. United States: Walt Disney Studios Motion Pictures, 2016.

Chapter 11

The Dora Milaje in Real Life

A Continuing Legacy of African Warriors

Myron T. Strong, K. Sean Chaplin, and Giselle Greenidge

Afrofuturism's embrace of divine feminism—the idea that women themselves have complete agency over both their lives and choices that they make—was on full display in the movie *Black Panther*. From the beginning, the panther goddess Bast bestowed power to a shaman who became the first Black Panther and united Wakanda. This powerful female god symbolized that it is women who grants one power, and it is their essence that grants dominion. T'Challa is guided by the divine feminine, as the movie weaves a picture of powerful women decoupled from European ideas, significant and celebrated, past, present, and future. Women in the film are agents of change, and these powerful images reject many of the negative tropes of Black femininity too often associated with Africa and patriarchal religious traditions. The egalitarian nature of the relationships between men and women in *Black Panther* are, instead, portrayed as seamless and natural. Women choose the paths and guide the society. Specifically, the all-female warrior army sworn to protect the King of Wakanda, the Dora Milaje with the shaved and tattooed heads is a celebration women's power. These images reflect aspects of historical reality that is often suppressed or ignored.[1]

The Dora Milaje led by General Okoye (Dania Gurira), along with Shuri (Letitia Wright) and Nakia (Lupita Nyong'o), are the driving force of the movie. Nakia, who leaves T'Challa in order to rescue women in Nigeria, General Okoye who is head of the Dora Milaje and considered the most powerful warrior in Wakanda and even threatens to kill her partner if he does not yield to Wakanda, and Shuri, whose intelligence creates a path to use technology to free oppressed people around the world; their leadership is essential for the advancement of the people. Even though they are fictional, they represent the factual and long history of African women leadership as rulers and warriors. While many modern views of African women are framed with Eurocentric ideas about their roles and abilities, the Dora Milaje challenges these notions and bridges the fictional warrior force with the real traditions of African women.

These traditions are evident in all aspects of the movie language, culture, and even their armor which draws heavily from pan-African roots. The gold rings the warriors wear around their necks are known as "idzila" and come from the Ndebele tribe of South Africa. The deep red color of their armor draws from Maasai warriors from southern Kenya and northern Tanzania.[2] These artifacts are unapologetically African in form and tradition, and both honors the history of African women, while simultaneously challenging long-held misconceptions of Western scholars about the roles of women in pre-colonial Africa. African women are often framed in similar positions as European women, who in general held lower status than men in Europe. Women of pre-colonial Western Africa had a higher social status than women in Europe and Asia. Not that there were not roles but there was a much more fluid situation where women often had the freedom to own land and hold political positions.[3] While there were some patriarchies and patriarchal practices, such as patrilineal residence and patrilineal descent, there was not a dependency on men because women could be economically independent, carried out physical labor, exercised political power and shaped Africa that cannot be denied.

While some may view this as a romanticized view of the many Africa cultures, there is more than enough research that suggests that gender role ideology among Africans in all societies were more egalitarian and androgynous than in European societies.[4] There is a consensus among scholars that women held a higher social status and were more respected regardless of the social system that existed in the various African societies. So, while there is much debate over the extent Western African cultures were or were not patriarchal, the most reliable scholarship underscores profound differences between their practices and the European cultures.[5]

This chapter explores how these roles and others, specifically African women as warriors and leaders, are reflected through the Dora Milaje. Even as a fictional group, they represent a continuation of these traditions and show how Pan Africanism and collective memory is important to not only understanding Black identity but also how Blacks deal with both structural oppression while carving out meaningful powerful lives. Afrofuturism, specifically the divine feminism, allows us to center Black women in the study of Black experience and challenge Western misconceptions and stereotypes about Black women. The images of the Dora Milaje serve as a bridge between the past, present, and future of Black women's power.

ORIGINS OF DORA MILAJE

This portrayal of the Dora Milaje was not always a positive one, as a matter fact, their creation was rooted in stereotypical and gendered ways. The group first appears in 1998 in *Black Panther* Vol. 3, No. 1., written by Cristopher Priest. They were introduced as the "adored ones" protectors of the king. They were drawn in Eurocentric feminine ways with long, straight hair, red miniskirts, and high stiletto heels. They were segregated from both the royal family as well as other Wakandans. They trained in secret, isolated from others and outside of other members of the Dora Milaje, and spoke only to the king. Their marginalization can also be in seen in the language they spoke as they only spoke Hausa, a native African language not widely spoken in Wakanda. Nakia and Okoye, the characters played by Lupita Nyong'o and Danai Gurira, respectively, in the *Black Panther* movie were teens (even though they were not drawn to look much older) and T'Challa's chauffeur and his personal aide.[6] The group itself was envisioned as subservient wives-in-training to their king, and though T'Challa rejects the idea it sets up a paternal relationship to the Dora Milaje, including Nakia and Okoye.[7]

So, their portrayal was framed within the larger context of Black in comics, one that is negative, stereotypical, and flat. Not surprising because since the late nineteenth century, Blacks have frequently been portrayed negatively in mainstream comics. The negative images were in opposition to the modern expression emerging from Black churches and Masonic lodges.[8] Early images of Blacks in comics muted and stereotyped Blacks, however examining finding that images and racial discourse found in *Aya* gave a much more diverse and racially conscious image. In the 1930s, Black newspapers, comics showed Black in a positive light and featured characters, like Bootsie, in the *Dark Laughter* comic strip in the *Amsterdam News*.[9] The character Bootsie is embedded within a master plot of how Black Americans deal with everyday forms of racism and cultural exclusion that uses light-hearted comical satire with humorous strategies and tactics of coping and resistance.

The current iteration of the Dora Milaje is a direct reimaging of Ta-Nehisi Coates in the current *Black Panther* comic series started in 2016 and the short-lived six issue spinoff *World of Wakanda*. Though it was in *Black Panther* that began to show complex powerful women of the Dora Milaje, the portrayal in *World of Wakanda* was probably more significant. This was in part because it was written by two Black women, Roxane Gay and Yona Harvey, who focused on developing the characters and exploring the complexities of their lives. Representation matters, having individuals create content for characters who share a similar experience is important. These were Black women lead characters written by Black women writers. It follows the stories of two African women who are also lovers, Ayo and Aneka, and former members of the Black Panther's female security force.[10]

The main plot of the series focuses on how Ayo and Aneka form the Midnight Angels and break away from the king because warlords in other parts of the country are enslaving women and child. The king's reluctance to address these women in any immediate matter causes them to break. They defeat the warlord, free the women and child, and train them. They start their own country in Northern Wakanda free from tyranny. This was undoubtedly inspired by histories of women warriors in Africa. In the Niger and Chad regions and in the Hausa territory, women founded cities, led migrations, and conquered kingdoms. Women held formal leadership roles and were influential in decision-making patrilineages.[11] In fact there were so many women who had led the kingdom of Meroe that the outside world believed that it had never had a king (read male leader).[12]

The comic emphasizes the depiction of Black women as protectors, makes a powerful statement to the readers about the abilities and history of Black women in Africa, where Ayo and Aneka are located. They're framed as protectors who aren't afraid of challenging the government to do what is right. These images connect back to the divine feminism, which emphasizes that women have agency and control of their lives. Ayo and Aneka are in a lesbian relationship, and from their introduction in the first issue of Black Panther, they have supported, protected, and loved each other. While their relationship is not an issue in the comics, it certainly is powerful to readers, who are rarely exposed to homosexual couples in comics. The message from both is not only about loving who you love but choosing your own path. The comic emphasizes spirituality as a major theme. Characters in *World of Wakanda* refers to women spiritual guides, though the main do not directly, other characters, such as Shuri, are lead as a spiritual guide.

World of Wakanda reveals common themes that resonate with viewers and readers. These themes connected to a readership and their popularity has continued to grow. Looking at the presentation and representations of the Dora Milaje, the powerful presence is obvious and *Black Panther* director Ryan Coogler acknowledged that it had a major effect on his presentation in the movie.[13]

COLLECTIVE MEMORY

There are a lot of reasons that Black Panther was successful and continues to be one of the most popular comic mythologies. There is no denying that the framing of the continent of Africa through Wakanda sparked not only a renewed interest in Africa, but became a symbol of pride as Africa was complicated. Wakanda celebrated Pan Africanism, which connects Black people around the world. Its ability to embrace complex identities, relationships, egalitarianism, and even things non-Eurocentric beauty norms challenged Eurocentric ethics. One of the most powerful scenes in the movie happens when General Okoye goes undercover wearing a wig complaining that it was "ridiculous" and a "disgrace." The Dora Milaje challenging Eurocentric factors is no doubt significant. The ability of the audience, particularly Blacks, to connect with these powerful women was a testament to not only the challenges to European narratives of women but also their collective memory. African Americans have developed strong, resilient, and ever-changing concepts of self, partially based on African cultural and philosophical teachings.[14] Ideas like the Zulu *umuntu ngabantu* which translates to "a person is a person through other people" emphasizes that the collective cultural identity was important to Africans and subsequently African Americans.[15] W.E.B. Du Bois's concept of double consciousness can be applied to understand how group solidarity and cultural preservation of African Americans have maintained through the development of two identities, one that preserves ancestral culture and the other that is influenced by traditional dominant ideology, the historical oppression, and current racial injustices.[16] There has been a transmission of cultural and group history when he found that this was an important part of African American family from the time of enslavement of the Africans.[17] Despite the many elements and events that sought to diminish the sense of self and the sense of group, African Americans, as individuals and as a group, both remain strong without major fluctuation.[18]

HISTORY OF WOMEN WARRIORS

The Dora Milaje represents a long history of African women warriors and leaders, and their presentation contradicts long-held Western beliefs about African women. Western ethnographers have spread inaccurate information based on socialized assumptions and interpretations about African women. But truth is there is a long history of women warriors, conquers, and rulers in Africa. The Dora Milaje pulls from many aspects of pre-colonial African women, including the Kingdom of Dahomey (modern-day Benin), which had fearsome female warriors and powerful kings.

The role of women in pre-colonial Africa is long, varied, and significant, as evidenced in African legends and historical traditions; many African traditions chronicle their accomplishments, which are supported by the accounts of early travelers. While it would be incorrect to infer that all the social systems around gender in Africa were alike, there is some commonality between many of the cultures, as well as great variety. But part of the challenge that exists when studying any culture in Africa that has been colonized is acknowledging the way Western epistemology has affected the perspective of many of the scholars studying them. Western conceptual schemes and theories have become so widespread that almost all scholarship, even by Africans, utilizes them unquestioningly.[19] This is a major obstacle because it makes it difficult to understand the complexities and differences between cultures in Africa in comparison to Europe.[20] The author does acknowledge the limitation of all approaches writing that each one comes with their cultural and philosophical baggage, much of which becomes alien distortion when applied to cultures other than those from which they derive.

Scholars intentionally and unintentionally using a European paradigm have simplified complex relations between men and women. Western ethnographers bring those socialized assumptions about African women and this limits their interpretations.[21] This Indo-European paradigm tended to look at social systems in Africa as totalitarian systems of either matriarchy or patriarchy.[22] Much of the scholarship on the gender role ideology of pre-colonial Africa has been shaped by these Western European inaccuracies.[23] Europeans believed in a dichotomous idea that societies were either going to be patriarchal or matriarchal, and this caused them to study gender role ideology from a systematic point of view with built-in ethnocentric assumptions.[24] Once they began to look at African societies, these assumptions limited their understanding of the complexities of social systems within these societies. Subsequently, this lack of understanding led to a misrepresentation of pre-colonial Africa. European scholars assumed that men and women occupied similar statuses and roles that were in European society without taking the symbols, infrastructure, or influential cultural norms into account.[25] But, it would be unwise to generalize the Western European ideas of patriarchy and matriarchy, and subsequently apply them to Africa or vice versa.

Not to say that the European paradigms of gender were not complex, but generally speaking, they sought to classify females and males in a gender hierarchy, where men were the dominant group. European ideology of gender is based on the fact that physical bodies are always social bodies, so men and women are classified based on biology. This meant that women were confined to the domestic sphere with little or no political, economic, and social power because of biology.[26] This confinement represented a sexual division of labor that not only limited women to the domestic sphere but defined their role by household tasks and work.[27] There was an assumption that women were biologically unsuitable for roles other than domestic roles.[28] This was not a universal idea, which can easily be seen by examining pre-colonial Yoruban culture and communities in which the social category of "woman" did not exist.[29] Clarifying that even though the body was very important, it was not the basis of societal roles, social inclusions, and/or exclusions. It was not until the infusion of Western notions that the body began to have any social significance.

It is important to understand how these cultures differed because it helps to, in part, explain why the current gender role ideology among African Americans tends to be considered to be more egalitarian than traditional White gender ideology. In many of the cultures in Africa, systems of kinship, religion, and symbolism all affected how men and women were perceived and realized in a culture. For example, there is gendered symbolism behind the roles of the Jelgobe, a Fulani people who live between Mali and Upper Volta. There is a division of labor between men and women, where men are herdsmen responsible for the land and women are responsible for shelter, clothing, and food.[30] The division of labor does not imply hierarchal roles within what would appear to be a patriarchal social system under the European paradigm. It is instead a symbolic connection between the roles that women and men hold and interdependence on one another. So, in order to understand the gender role ideology and indeed the social structure, one has to examine the symbolic meaning behind the roles. Anthropologist Ifi Amadiume in *Reinventing Africa: Matriarchy, Religion and Culture* writes,

> There are consequently the parallels of the construction of woman's relationship with her nature in the sense of mother and child, and man's relationship with his nature in that of man and cow. From these derived a whole set of gendered symbolisms of binary opposition: female equals woman equals house, *wuro*, on the one hand, and male equals man equals bush, *ladde*, on the other. *Wuro* and *ladde* appear to constitute the basic paradigmatical structures of matriarchy and patriarchy.[31]

There is symbolic interaction between the male and female roles and the idea that one cannot exist without the other. This implies that there is not a gender hierarchy because every role was seen as essential and no role is seen as more important than the other. West African countries show a distinction in the tasks of men and women but not necessarily in the hierarchical structure.[32] The role of women in pre-colonial Africa was evident in African legends and historical traditions; many African traditions chronicle their accomplishments, which are supported by the accounts of early travelers.

Igbo culture is quite different than the Jelgobe. The Igbo lived in the rural village of Nnobi in Nigeria. Its system of kinship and gender are in binary opposition and are represented by *Obi* (ancestral family house) which is male and the *Mkpuke* (the matricentric unit mother and child compound) which is female. It has a matriarchal superstructure that derives from the idea that all the people come from a common mother, the goddess Idemili, the major Igbo god.[33] Igbo culture in Nigeria did not have a rigid structure of what was masculine and what was feminine. In Igbo culture, it was not only the norm for women to have gender roles that Europeans usually associated with men, but these women also held economic, social, and political power within their culture. Moreover, Igbo women displayed military prowess leading the fight against the British invasion of Nigeria in 1929. Researchers of the time universally recognized these women as "the most militant of women."[34]

CONCLUSION

Black Panther channeled much of the collective memory through imagery and imagination. The Dora Milaje represents a long legacy of African women rulers and warriors. They pull from legacies of the past while celebrating women in the present all the while showing a future that can be imagined through embracing the divine feminism. The divine feminine reckons back to gynocentric religions of the pre-colonial Africa. The Dora Milaje is a celebration of this history, both culturally and socially. It speaks to the necessity of Afrofuturism as a vehicle to challenge, change, and highlight those important aspects of being Black.

NOTES

1. Myron T. Strong and K. Sean Chaplin, "Afrofuturism and Black Panther," *Contexts* 18, no. 2 (Spring 2019): 59.

2. Rudy Veridiano, "To design costumes for 'Black Panther,' this artist drew on his Filipino upbringing," *NBC news*, March 6, 2018, https://www.nbcnews.com/news/asian-america/design-costumes-black-panther-artist-drew-his-filipino-upbringing-n852856.

3. Tarikhu Farrar, "The Queenmother, Matriarchy, and the Question of Female Political Authority in Precolonial West African Monarchy," *Journal of Black Studies* 27, no. 5 (1997): 584.

4. Beverly Guy-Sheftall, "African Feminist Discourse: A Review Essay," *Agenda: Empowering Women for Gender Equity*, no. 58 (2003); Ifi Amadiume, *Reinventing Africa: Matriarchy, Religion and Culture* (London: Zed Books, 1997); Ifi Amadiume, *Male Daughters, Female Husbands: Gender and Sex in an African Society* (London: Zed Books, 1987); Oyeronke Oyewumi, *Invention of Women: Making An African Sense Of Western Gender Discourses* (Minneapolis, MN: University of Minnesota Press, 1997); Emmanuel Akyeampong and Pashington Obeng, "Spirituality, Gender, Power in Asante History," in *African Gender Studies: A Reader*, ed. Oyeronke Oyewumi (New York: Palgrave Macmilan, 2005), 23–48.

5. Guy-Sheftall, "African Feminist Discourse," 32.

6. Christopher Priest, *Black Panther vol. 3 no. 1* (New York: Marvel, 1998), 1.

7. Jamie Broadnax, "Get to know the Dora Milaje, Black Panther's mighty women warriors," *Vox*, February 21, 2018, https://www.vox.com/culture/2018/2/21/17017234/black-panther-dora-milaje-wakanda-warriors.

8. Sylvia E. White and Tania Fuentez, "Analysis of Black Images in Comic Strips, 1915–1995," *Newspaper Research Journal* 18, no. 1–2 (January 1997): 72.

9. Brian Dolinar, "Humor Can Often Make Dents Where Sawed-Off Billiard Sticks Can't: The Bootsie Cartoons by Ollie Harrington," *Studies in American Humor* New Series 3, no. 14 (2006): 73–90.

10. Roxanne Gay and Yona Harvey, *World of Wakanda no. 1* (New York: Marvel, 2018), 1.

11. Norma J. Burgess, "Gender Roles Revisited: The Development of the "Woman's Place" Among African American Women in the United States," *Journal of African American Studies* 24, no. 4 (1994): 394.

12. David Sweetman, *Women Leaders in African History* (Nairobi, Nigeria: Heinemann Educational Books Ltd, 1984).

13. Sam Flynn, "Ryan Coogler Says 'Black Panther' Film Is 'Absolutely' Influenced by Ta-Nehsi Coates," *Heroic Hollywood*, July 25, 2016, https://heroichollywood.com/ryan-coogler-says-black-panther-absolutely-influenced-by-ta-nehisi-coates/.

14. Richard L. Allen, *The Concept of Self: A Study of African American Identity and Self-Esteem* (Detroit, MI: Wayne State University Press, 2001), 53.

15. Ibid., 47.

16. Ibid., 30.

17. Herbert George Gutman, *The Black Family in Slavery and Freedom, 1750-1925* (New York: Pantheon Books, 1976).

18. Ibid., 46.

19. Oyewumi, *Invention of Women*.

20. Ibid.

21. Josephine Beoku-Betts, "Western Perceptions of African Women in the 19th and 20th Centuries," in *Readings in Gender in Africa*, ed. Andrea Cornwall (Bloomington, IN: Indiana University Press. 2005), 21.

22. Amadiume, *Reinventing Africa*.

23. Ibid.

24. Ibid.

25. Cheikh Anta Diop, *Precolonial African American Africa: A Comparative Study of the Political and Social Systems of Europe and African American Africa, from Antiquity to the Formation of Modern States* (New York, NY: Lawrence Hill Books, 1987).

26. Oyeronke Oyewumi, *Invention of Women: Making an African Sense of Western Gender Discourses* (Minneapolis, MN: University of Minnesota Press, 1997).

27. Barbara Reskin and Irene Padavic, *Women and Men at Work* (Thousand Oaks, CA: Pine Forge Press, 1994).

28. Linda L. Lindsey, *Gender Roles: A Sociological Perspective,* 3rd ed. (Upper Saddle River, NJ: Prentice Hall, 2005), 3.

29. Oyewumi, *Invention of Women*.

30. Amadiume, *Reinventing Africa*.
31. Ibid., 38.
32. Burgess, "Gender Roles Revisited."
33. Amadiume, *Male Daughters, Female Husbands*.
34. Ibid., 13.

WORKS CITED

Akyeampong Emmanuel and Pashington Obeng. "Spirituality, Gender, Power in Asante History." In *African Gender Studies: A Reader*, edited by Oyeronke Oyewumi, 23–48. New York: Palgrave Macmilan, 2005.

Allen, Richard L. *The Concept of Self: A Study of African American Identity and Self-Esteem*. Detroit, MI: Wayne State University Press, 2001.

Amadiume, Ifi. *Male Daughters, Female Husbands: Gender and Sex in an African Society*. London: Zed Books, 1987.

Amadiume, Ifi. *Reinventing Africa: Matriarchy, Religion and Culture*. London: Zed Books, 1997.

Beoku-Betts, Josephine. "Western Perceptions of African Women in the 19th and 20th Centuries." In *Readings in Gender in Africa*, edited by Andrea Cornwall, 20–24. Bloomington, IN: Indiana University Press, 2005.

Broadnax, Jamie. "Get to know the Dora Milaje, Black Panther's mighty women warriors." *Vox*, February 21, 2018. https://www.vox.com/culture/2018/2/21/17017234/black-panther-dora-milaje-wakanda-warriors.

Burgess, Norma J. "Gender Roles Revisited: The Development of the "Woman's Place" Among African American Women in the United States." *Journal of African American Studies* 24, no. 4 (1994): 391–401.

Coates, Ta-Nehisi. *Black Panther no. 1*. New York: Marvel, 2016.

Diop, Cheikh Anta. *Precolonial African American Africa: A Comparative Study of the Political and Social Systems of Europe and African American Africa, from Antiquity to the Formation of Modern States*. New York, NY: Lawrence Hill Books, 1987.

Dolinar, Brian. "Humor Can Often Make Dents Where Sawed-Off Billiard Sticks Can't: The Bootsie Cartoons by Ollie Harrington." *Studies in American Humor* New Series 3, no. 14 (2006): 73–90.

Farrar, Tarikhu. "The Queenmother, Matriarchy, and the Question of Female Political Authority in Precolonial West African Monarchy." *Journal of Black Studies* 27, no. 5 (1997): 579–597.

Flynn, Sam. "Ryan Coogler Says 'Black Panther' Film Is 'Absolutely' Influenced by Ta-Nehsi Coates." *Heroic Hollywood*, July 25, 2016. https://heroichollywood.com/ryan-coogler-says-black-panther-absolutely-influenced-by-ta-nehisi-coates/.

Gay, Roxanne and Yona Harvey. *World of Wakanda*. New York: Marvel, 2018.

Gutman, Herbert George. *The Black family in slavery and freedom, 1750-1925*. New York: Pantheon Books, 1976.

Guy-Sheftall, Beverly. "African Feminist Discourse: A Review Essay." *Agenda: Empowering Women for Gender Equity*, no. 58 (2003): 31–36.

Oyewumi, Oyeronke. *Invention of Women: Making an African Sense of Western Gender Discourses*. Minneapolis, MN: University of Minnesota Press, 1997.

Priest, Christopher. *Black Panther vol. 3 no. 1*. New York: Marvel, 1998.

Reskin, Barbara, and Irene Padavic. *Women and Men at Work*. Thousand Oaks, CA: Pine Forge Press, 1994.

Strong, Myron T., and K. Sean Chaplin. "Afrofuturism and Black Panther." *Contexts* 18, no. 2 (2019): 58–59.

Sweetman, David. *Women Leaders in African History*. Nairobi, Nigeria: Heinemann Educational Books Ltd, 1984.

Veridiano, Rudy. "To design costumes for 'Black Panther,' this artist drew on his Filipino upbringing." *NBC news*, March 6, 2018. https://www.nbcnews.com/news/asian-america/design-costumes-black-panther-artist-drew-his-filipino-upbringing-n852856.

White, Sylvia E. and Tania Fuentez. "Analysis of Black Images in Comic Strips, 1915–1995." *Newspaper Research Journal* 18, no. 1–2 (January 1997): 72–85.

FILMS

Black Panther. Directed by Ryan Coogler. United States: Walt Disney Studios Motion Pictures, 2018.

Chapter 12

Echoes of the History of Black Utopian Visions, "Black Manhood," and Black Feminism in the Making of *Black Panther*

Dolita Cathcart

What does Josephine St. Pierre Ruffin, a radical abolitionist, feminist, and "race" leader in Boston, Massachusetts, have to do with Ryan Coogler's 2018 Marvel Studios' blockbuster film, *Black Panther*? Ruffin not only led radical Black elite women in Boston, but she embodied the tenets of ideal Black womanhood; she was both a Victorian era "lady" and a "race" leader. She is an example of the countless Black women and men in the early twentieth century, known to history and forgotten, who committed their lives to a near impossible vision of building a just nation. They were political, social, and class activists, writers, and artists of all types.

But what they imagined for themselves and for their country was ultimately utopian, because whether they were reformers or revolutionaries, they had to convince the majority of White Americans that Blacks and all women deserved first-class citizenship. Their struggles and utopian vision of America's past history is echoed throughout the film, *Black Panther*.

Elite and middle-class Blacks served as a bridge between Blacks and Whites, between the desires of Blacks for full inclusion and White fears of what full Black citizenship might ultimately mean to White identity development and power. Booker T. Washington, W. E. B. Du Bois, and William Monroe Trotter each represented and embodied different paths toward achieving manhood rights for themselves and for their constituencies. Their ideologies in the late nineteenth and early twentieth centuries on how to achieve equality can be traced in the characters of the two Black Panthers in the movie, cousins with diverging attitudes toward radical change, activism, and identity. William Monroe Trotter's approach toward achieving racial equality was based on Black elites leading the fight to protect Black rights. Trotter, the youngest of the three, ascribed to a more muscular approach than Du Bois. His constant and belittling attacks on Washington in his paper, the *Boston Guardian*, to his leadership and participation in a number of major protest actions in Boston, reflected the construct of the new masculinity of the early twentieth century. Trotter's racial ideology did away with the genteel and respectable methods of the past in favor of a more radical approach to combating racial discrimination, reminiscent of Erik Killmonger's (Michael B. Jordan) call for an armed struggle. Trotter's radicalism was similar to that of Josephine St. Pierre Ruffin who called for violent self-defense and the founding of a national Black organization to fight the Jim Crow South and North.

In Black America, those who believed moral suasion could end the reigning White supremacist ideologies of America's racist institutions were the first utopianists. They were political activists, enslaved and free, antebellum and postbellum. They were people who resisted their condition in both active and passive ways. Class, region, and gender affected the shape of their individual and collective utopian visions. In Black America, the arts were next, especially fiction, which allowed writers to experiment with Black history and culture in constructing new and better tomorrows. There were two major Black cultural nationalist movements. The Harlem Renaissance of the 1920s was a politicized art movement intending to prove Black capabilities to Whites in a bid to win first-class citizenship. The second was the Black Arts Movement (BAM) from 1965 to 1975. BAM was another cultural nationalist movement begun in Harlem by Amiri Baraka, or LeRoi Jones, who founded the Black Arts Repertory Theater. BAM used the arts to uncover Black culture and history in order to create a Black consciousness movement to awaken Black pride. *Black Panther* combines Black history and culture with a science-fiction twist, an Afrofuturist re-imagining of fabled Prester John, the king of a mythical powerful nation in Africa for which the Portuguese and other Europeans searched as they sought allies to defeat the Moors in the 1400s.[1]

Histories of the Black experience frequently, and understandably, focus on the dystopian aspects of over 400 years of Black struggle in North America. As important as this history is as a measure of humanitarian and just progress in the United States, Black Americans, in general, and Black activists, in particular, have exhibited an optimistic and resilient persistence in both imagining a better world and striving to make it so. In short, African Americans tend to construct utopian visions of a more just society somewhere in the future. Black Americans do so in the arts, in politics, and in the nexus of socio-political and economic praxis.

White skin privilege today does not offer much to undereducated Whites replaced by automation and robots, it only offers a past that barely elevated such folks from people of color. Blacks, on the other hand, have generally embraced the future because therein lies the transformative nature of a Black utopian vision, hope. The future would set them free. In the eyes of White nationalists, freedom and equality are a step backward and a possible reason why invoking empathy as a method to end racism may not change their hold on their myth of White superiority. Racism separates the vision of White supremacist utopian fiction where people of color seldom exist, from Black utopian fiction, which results in multiple Black and inclusive visions of utopia, from respectability to emigration and to science fiction.

The Black Lives Matter (BLM) protests of the 2020 election season are the culmination of centuries of protest, resistance, and struggle for equality and equity. One chant frequently heard at all BLM protests is that "all lives can't matter until Black Lives Matter!" This chant goes to the heart of the movement, to the pain and trauma Black lives experience in the United States. A trauma that sickens and kills Black babies, children, and adults. Police brutality and political indifference to Black lives was the underlying spark that ignited Black riots in the United States during and after the Civil Rights Movement of the 1960s. But the chant suggests something more; it suggests we are all connected. No other lives are safe from police brutality, from political indifference, and from the worse of a racialized corporate capitalist system built on principles created during the slave era in the United States that affects all working people until Black lives matter. What is allowed to happen to one group ultimately threatens other groups of people, a social entanglement not dissimilar to quantum entanglement theory, to borrow from quantum physicists, that shows we are all ultimately connected to one another. Social entanglement does not need a Large Hadron Collider to show just how connected we are to one another. We are not merely individuals unaffected by the totality of our shared histories; we are part of an inseparable whole. One only needs to look at healthcare delivery to understand just how connected we are.

Drug addiction in the United States has been linked to Black America for decades. This political linkage, politicized by Presidents Richard M. Nixon and Ronald Reagan, undergirds the mass incarceration of Black America. On the political side of this equation, racializing drug addiction has helped conservatives blame Black America for crime, poverty, drug addiction, and more. Blaming Black America for all of the nation's ills reduces the options for handling these issues in a racist society, particularly for addiction disorders. The problem is reduced to one of a collective moral failing, instead of looking at the disorder as a medical, social, and political problem. If drug addiction is seen as a moral failing, then the solution to this problem is hiring more police officers, militarizing police forces, building more prisons, and starving social programs that may actually help to address the problem and all of the underlying causes leading to addiction disorders. As horrendous a situation this is for Black and poor America with up to one-third of Black males entangled in the prison industrial complex mostly for nonviolent drug crimes, primarily for marijuana possession and use, for the last several years, it has been affecting the White middle class whose addiction frequently begins with surgery and ends with multiple prescriptions for opioids. White Americans, wealthy and poor, educated and undereducated, with and without college degrees are collaterally damaged, are dying, by what began as racist policies targeting people of color. The Covid-19 pandemic is another example. People of color and the poor are dying of the virus two to three times the rate of wealthier White America. The poor and people of color tend to work jobs that are considered essential in order for the rest of the country to enjoy their lives more safely. Poor and racist healthcare delivery kills those workers, but the virus kills others as well, like the elderly of all skin colors. It has destroyed our economy, traumatized school children, caused women to voluntarily leave the workforce to care for their children or parents, and like the opioid crisis, has lowered the life expectancy of American citizens. And to make matters worse, systemic racism in health care has made many Black Americans wary of the various vaccines that have been produced, which will affect all of our lives. All of the nation's "isms" constrains what could be possible in making America great, or at least better, for all.

Poor and racist healthcare delivery has definitely affected people of color more as a percentage of the population, but wealthier Whites also suffer from the conservative and racist ideology that created the problem. Former vice president Mike Pence and other conservative members of the House and Senate who were not complicit in the insurrection on January 6, 2021, certainly, if not briefly, learned that lesson when hundreds of mostly White males stormed the Capitol building looking to lynch Pence and others. His decades-long fidelity to White supremacist and radical Christian conservative principles, let alone his fawning fidelity to the former president, would not have saved him, the gallows were already built just outside of the Capitol building. He was saved by Eugene Goodman, a Black Capitol Police officer and former veteran who served in Iraq. Goodman diverted the crowd of insurrectionists away from the Senate chamber where Pence and others were hiding. Goodman was willing to sacrifice his life to save them and America. His sacrifice is another example of how frequently Black America has saved the nation from the fallen angels who would destroyed her. Black Americans were instrumental in winning the War of Independence, the Civil War, both World Wars, subsequent wars, the civil rights movement, and so much more.

There is no one Black superhero, but a myriad of heroes who have received little from their nation in return for their unceasing heroism.

Racist Whites' self-interest in the myth of White superiority serves as a foil to the struggle for freedom and equality in Black utopian fiction. Even Thomas Jefferson, who claimed not to support the idea of slavery, kept slaves because he needed the wealth their unpaid labor produced. Black women authors, in addition to addressing "race" in their novels, also addressed sexism in contrast to Paul Lawrence Dunbar, Charles Chestnutt, and James Weldon Johnson who remained moored to the ideal of Black respectability and patriarchy as a ticket out of racist discrimination to equality. Black literary dreams imagining the end of racism and sexism in the United States shifted to speculative fiction, potentially a better medium for such an intractable problem as racism.

Black Panther is a film of two utopias, one of an African nation not infected by the disorganization and destructive forces of a colonial past and the other is that of Erik Killmonger, Black Panther's cousin, whose backstory was that of Black Americans who lived a life defined by racism and discrimination. Whereas Black Panther T'Challa's (Chadwick Boseman) fictional nation of Wakanda resembled an African Tuskegee Institute, Killmonger's history was similar to Malcolm Little, later Malcolm X, whose father was allegedly killed by racist Whites and whose death resulted in his family's destruction and Malcolm Little's transformation into Malcolm X.

ECHOES OF BLACK LIBERATION HISTORY IN *BLACK PANTHER*

The film opens with a young Erik "Killmonger" Stevens, asking his father, the younger brother of the king of Wakanda and a spy for Wakanda, to tell him the story of Wakanda. His father, N'Jobu (Sterling K. Brown), relates Wakanda's cosmology starting with the comet laden with vibranium, a metal that transformed the land, plants, and animals that landed in what would become Wakanda. Five warring tribes finally found peace when a warrior shaman had a vision of a Panther, a vision that united four out of the five tribes. The fifth tribe, the J'Bari, decided not to join, but lived with the other four tribes in peace. The vibranium was a powerful metal that powered the nation and its technological advances, and a special herb that grew in Wakanda provided the superpower of the nation's future kings, the Black Panthers. Wakanda escaped the African continental history that affected African development by shielding its nation from view and pretending to be an undeveloped African nation of herders. Unbothered by the Arabic and Atlantic slave trades, the arms race catalyzed by the slave trade, European colonization and everything that followed, Wakanda was able to develop into the most advanced nation on the planet. But they did not protect their cousins on the continent. They did not protect their cousins in the diaspora as well. Theirs was a nation intent on their survival alone. Booker T. Washington's rhetoric suggests he would have favored the self-segregation that Wakandans traditionally followed. He preferred that Black Americans remain separate from White America and separately build their economic prosperity without engaging with Whites. William Monroe Trotter's history suggests more radical action, like Killmonger's approach. Like the fictional Killmonger, Trotter was an Ivy League graduate who demanded first-class citizenship. Trotter even illegally traveled to France in a bid to speak at the Treaty of Versailles about the condition of Blacks in America. He was rebuffed. W. E. B. Du Bois was somewhere in the middle, more like T'Challa, beginning in the Washington camp and ending up in Trotter's. Like T'Challa, Du Bois also became more radical over time. Erik asked his father "Why?" Why did Wakanda continue to hide from the world and not help change it for the better? Erik was born and lived in Oakland, California, the birthplace of the Black Panther Party. His father, Prince N'Jobu, sent to Oakland as a spy for Wakanda, became radicalized living as a Black man in America. His brother, King T'Chaka (John Kaui), the then current Black Panther, kills N'Jobu and abandons his nephew, Erik aka Killmonger aka N'Jadaka. Erik discovers his dead father with panther claw marks across his chest, and so continued his radicalization as a son of the diaspora.

Marvel Studios 2018 film, *Black Panther*, offers the viewer two diametrically opposed visions, and by the end choses a compromise of sorts. Wakanda would no longer be hidden and would not exact revenge on past colonizers and current racists. It is not a surprising position; Black Panther is, after all, a superhero in the *Marvelverse*. But there is also a suggestion that diasporic African descent peoples represented by Killmonger are too close to past and current suffering to offer a viable vision for the nation of Wakanda, its technology, and its peoples. They are too radicalized. Too angry. The suggestion is that there is a difference between Africans living in a majority Black state ruled by Blacks compared to Black Americans living on the margins of the American Dream.[2] The film has a number of issues. It rejects radicalism by presenting Killmonger as just that, a kill monger. He even kills his girlfriend to get at Klaue (Andy Serkis) so that he can enter Wakanda with Klaue's body, the man who killed the beloved former king, Killmonger's uncle, who killed Killmonger's father. The women of Wakanda are certainly better off than the dead girlfriend, but they are limited as well, they could never rule Wakanda because it requires a fight to the death. Otherwise, they could be warriors, spies, and scientists, but never the ruler of the nation. Josephine St. Pierre Ruffin, Ida B. Wells-Barnett, and other radicalized Black women activists of any century would have recognized this disconnect of women from the power men enjoyed. Their work was necessary and instrumental in the struggle for racial equality, but their gender relegated them to the back of the proverbial bus. Even in Wakanda, the patriarchy reigned supreme.

Modern Wakanda is a benevolent patriarchy, but limited in its vision as it holds onto its traditional ways. M'Baku (Winston Duke) makes this very clear when he criticizes T'Challa for letting a girl, T'Challa's sister, Shuri (Letitia Wright), create and control Wakandan technology. The tension between the traditional ways of Wakanda and those who want to change it is played out by a number of characters. Killmonger, of course, wants to use Wakandan power and technology to seek retribution. But there are others as well. Killmonger is not alone in wanting change. T'Challa's girlfriend, Nakia (Lupita Nyong'o), is a spy and a liberator of kidnapped children from a Boko Haram-type militia. T'Challa's brother, W'Kabi (Daniel Kaluuya), and his followers, side with Killmonger and is only brought to heel by his warrior wife, Okoye (Danai Gurira), which ends the short-lived revolution for control of Wakanda. The women are powerful in *Black Panther*, but under a glass ceiling nonetheless.

Wakanda and its kings appear to echo a mythical nation ruled by Prester John that was sought by Europeans from the 1200s to the 1700s. Europeans were in search of allies to fight the Moors and believed that Prester John, reputed to be brilliant with superhuman strength ruling a magical nation of Christians, could be just the ally they were seeking.[3] Prester John is even a Marvel Comic character appearing in several comics, including the *Fantastic Four*.[4] Though Prester John's nation was first believed to be somewhere in Asia, it was later assumed to be Ethiopia, a nation that isolated itself from the Moors, and everyone else as a result, in order to remain uncolonized by Moslems or Europeans. The Tuskegee Institute could also have served as a model for Wakanda. Though not physically hidden from sight, it did hide its true mission from racist Whites in Alabama, the education of teachers, doctors, and other professionals. The University was an isolated island surrounded by a sea of racist hatred and violence in Alabama, and it had its own spies in the form of supporters and journalists who worked for Washington across the nation. The Wizard of Tuskegee graduated many who went on to earn professional degrees, but success in the south meant maintaining a low profile. Radicalism was out of the question, and in Alabama, that meant maintaining the fiction of White superiority in all aspects of life. It meant ignoring the threats, the violence, the disrespect, and the constricted racialized life of living under the color line.

In contrast to Wakanda's decision to remain hidden and segregated from the world and their African cousins, N'Jobu, the king's younger brother, is sent to Oakland, California, as a spy for the fictional nation. Living as a Black man in the United States during the Reagan and Bush years radicalized N'Jubo in spite of his princely upbringing in Wakanda. He did not denigrate American-born Blacks as a way to separate himself from racist stereotypes of African Americans. He lived the racism of his American cousins. The audience is left imagining the discrimination that radicalized N'Jubo. Oakland in 1992 was the most-deadly city in California. Poor diverse communities purposefully ignored by lawmakers suffered the most in the 1980s and 1990s, feeding newly privatized prisons with their bodies. Additionally, in 1992, four Los Angeles police officers were filmed stopping and beating Rodney King, and were later found not-guilty of assault and of the use of excessive force when tried in majority White and conservative Simi Valley. Los Angeles erupted in a desperate cry for help and despair.

As the action shifts to the present day, King T'Chaka is assassinated at the UN by Klaue, the arms dealer who does not believe Wakanda should control Vibranium. The audience learns that N'Jobu is not the only one who disagrees with Wakanda's tradition of segregation. T'Challa's off-again on-again girlfriend, Nakia, carries out secret missions helping the powerless, in particular, young girls kidnapped by a Boko Haram type group. M'Baku, the J'Bari leader who fights T'Challa for the right to be the next king and loses, is also disgusted with Wakanda, but for different reasons. He is a conservative traditionalist that believes Wakanda lost its way. T'Challa could not protect his father, King T'Chaka, and his sister, Shuri, a "girl," directs and creates Wakandan technology. T'Challa wins, but not for long. Killmonger is set to make his play for the Kingdom by killing Klaue and bringing his body to Wakanda. Killmonger drags Klaue's body to Wakanda's border, and meets W'Kabi, T'Challa's brother. W'Kabi is also ready for change. He might also be jealous of his brother, the king, but he also appreciates Killmonger for killing Klaue, his father's killer. Killmonger fills W'Kabi in on his origin story off screen, and then enters the throne room, where he demands to fight T'Challa and replace him as king. It is not until Killmonger sits on the throne after he literally overthrows T'Challa (by throwing him off of a waterfall) that the viewer recognizes the scene. He is the spitting image of Huey Newton, cofounder of the Oakland, California, based Black Panther Party for Self-Defense, in the iconic photo of him sitting on the peacock throne. Killmonger exudes the same power and muscular masculinity of Newton in the iconic photo. T'Challa was just a man sitting on the same throne, Killmonger looked like so much more. But Killmonger's Wakandan followers do not yet know that Killmonger is a sociopath and a tyrant. He has killed so many people along the way their deaths are meaningless to him. He even kills his girlfriend in his effort to capture and kill Klaue. But the audience gets the message, Killmonger's path is the wrong one, he is not the hero, he is an enemy.

T'Challa, as he learns that his father killed his own brother and abandoned his nephew, is transforming, becoming politicized, and he begins to question Wakanda's traditional ways. Nakia tells him "I have seen too many in need to turn a blind eye... Share what we have." She believes that Wakanda is strong enough to survive and help others. T'Challa's brother does not want refugees in Wakanda, but he is willing to take his men to wage wars of freedom. He is unhappy that his father did not fight and unhappy that T'Challa was not strong enough to capture their father's killer. When T'Challa meets his father in the ancestor's land after drinking the magical herb that gives Black Panther his powers, his dead father greets him and tells him "It is hard for a good man to be king." Later, when Erik walks into the throne room to challenge T'Challa for the throne he intones: "You all, sitting up here comfortable, must feel good. It's about 2 billion people all over the world who looks like us, but their lives are a lot harder. Wakanda has the tools to liberate them all." T'Challa asks, "and what tools are those?" "Vibranium," Erik answers. T'Challa responds and says "it is not our way to be judge, jury, and executioner for people who are not our own." "Not your own!" Erik exclaims, "Didn't their lives start right here on this continent?"

But T'Challa is not a power-hungry tyrant. He does not want to be king of the world. He is a good man learning there are no easy answers and lots of unintended consequences. W'Kabi, on the other hand, sees that others are catching up to Wakanda's technological superiority and would rather be a conqueror than the conquered. The world is changing, and tradition will not keep Wakanda safe for much longer. Erik challenges T'Challa for the throne and wins, tossing T'Challa over the waterfall. T'Challa is found by members of the J'Bari tribe and brought to J'Bari lands, more dead than alive, but is brought back to the living after being given the magic herb. The herb first brings T'Challa back to the ancestor's lands where he has the chance to confront his father. It is there that T'Challa comes to the realization that the nation must change. That the father's brutal actions undergird the trouble the nation is now facing. It was the old king who radicalized Killmonger. Killmonger is the unintended consequence of the father's actions, and T'Challa must now fix the mess his father created.

Killmonger and T'Challa echo the centuries-long struggles of Black Americans in all of its diversity. Some wanted revolutionary change believing the nation could not be reformed. It had to be dismantled and built anew. Most, though, preferred reform, believing in the nation's experiment with democracy for which so many fought and died. In both cases, and in everything in between, these struggles were utopian at their core, at least for the last 400 years of American history. Utopian as these struggles were, the dream of a better world for all fed thousands of Black activists for hundreds of years, particularly the activism of Black women.

WOMEN IN THE STRUGGLE: JOSEPHINE ST. PIERRE RUFFIN

Dressed respectably in somber colors, petticoats, cloche hat, and White gloves, Josephine St. Pierre Ruffin sat sedately in the front meeting room of the League of Women for Community Service's (LWCS) clubhouse she founded in Boston's South End neighborhood. Located at 558 Massachusetts Avenue, the building housing the League of Women was the old Farewell mansion, a former stop on the Underground Rail Road that had sheltered fugitive slaves during the Antebellum Era. After World War I, the club purchased the building to provide services for poor Black women, men, and children in the city. The February 28, 1924, annual meeting began with the reading of annual reports and ended with the election of the club's executive officers.

The long day and February chill did not deter 128 of the 154 members from attending the meeting. The women discussed issues from the mundane to the poignant, like the assessed value of the League's building, a recent membership drive, and the numbers of local Black residents assisted by the League over the past year. Some members complained that their social welfare work among the poor was exhausting and never ending. There were simply too many Black residents who needed help, and too few dollars to help them. At age 82, Ruffin had heard it all before during her long tenure as a pragmatic leader who spent a lifetime addressing racial and gender discrimination. By one in the morning, the votes for the new leadership were finally tallied and the meeting was called to a close. Approximately two weeks later, on March 13, 1924, following a brief illness, Ruffin quietly passed away.[5] Ruffin's death ended an era of radicalized feminist race politics in Boston. Black, female, radical, and respectable, Ruffin, by the early twentieth century, turned to pragmatism, as she and other club members sought ways to help poor Blacks in Boston's growing Black slums. Ruffin's pragmatism, though, was constrained by the dwindling political options available to Black Americans at that time in both the city and the nation. Nonetheless, Ruffin continued to struggle to first halt and then to mitigate the effects of Jim Crow legislation nationally, and the attendant sensibilities locally, by organizing Black women in the battle for Black civil rights.

Like Nakia, Black women activists at the turn of the last century quietly struggled to make a difference in their communities across the nation without celebration or recognition. Black men were mostly dismissive of their efforts. The women's community work, necessary as it was to those they helped, just wasn't big or powerful enough. And the women's work, when celebrated like that of Ida B. Wells anti-lynching campaign, was threatening to male prerogatives. But in the south, advancements were made through the work of

Black women's clubs working with their White counterparts. Assistance to Black communities was also made through the many Black churches where the majority of the congregants were women who did most of the community outreach work. Black women kept their communities together, aiding those they could and working with Whites on occasion to make a difference. The same was true during the civil rights movements. Many a Black "Aunty" held sewing circles in their homes during the 1960s that were really voter registration meetings. Most of these women were risking their lives, their homes, and their livelihoods in the war against racism have been forgotten to history. But so were so many of the men as well. Trotter has only recently been rediscovered by historians, and Du Bois was rediscovered about two decades earlier. Washington, the accommodationist, was the only one of the three men that White historians cared to remember.

The fictional nation of Wakanda combines aspects of Booker T. Washington's Tuskegee Institute, and the kings of Wakanda echo that of Washington and Prester John. *Black Panther* eschews radicalism, as represented by the Panther's cousin, Erik "Killmonger" Stevens, for a more palatable hero, that of the Black Panther T'Challa, who is a cross between Booker T. Washington and Martin Luther King, Jr. If he liked peanuts, one might also throw in George Washington Carver, the Black scientist with which my grade school history books seemed obsessed. In other words, he is the "good negro," nonthreatening, not angry, and male.

BLACK AMERICAN UTOPIANISM

In 1619, twenty Africans were sold into slavery in Jamestown, Virginia. 400 years later, we are at a time when democracy and liberalism is under threat by those fearful of change. The desperate belief of too many in White superiority, climate change denial, sexism, heterosexism, and so much more may briefly soothe the shifting shoals of a White identity propped up by, what W. E. B. Du Bois described as, a psychological wage of whiteness. Du Bois wrote in *Black Reconstruction* that "[i]t must be remembered that the White group of laborers, while they receive a low wage, were compensated in part by a sort of public and psychological wage." Du Bois goes on to state how White laborers were rewarded: they could vote, the police came from their ranks, and they were more likely to be treated with respect relative to Black Americans.[6] What Du Bois enumerates in this passage is that poor Whites were marginally treated better than African Americans. That's it.

The traditional utopia of poor White Americans consisted of having Blacks around so that poor Whites had someone to which to feel superior. When this arrangement was threatened during the Civil Rights Movement of the 1960s, poor White supremacists no longer wanted Blacks in America. Black civil rights, feared many Whites, would thwart White entitlements and prove the myth of White supremacy. White Americans already faced this quandary during and after slavery. During slavery, proslavery White rhetoric declared slavery was better than freedom, because Blacks would not survive freedom. This resulted in states like Virginia and Maryland forcing out thriving free Black populations as a means of shielding themselves from the truth.[7] After the Civil War, Radical Reconstruction once again proved the lie of White supremacy, and that resulted in Jim Crow legislation and mass incarceration as a method to constrain Black progress and secure the myth of White supremacy for several more generations. But the 1960s were more troubling for White supremacists, because federal actions and television news programs showed how southern states maintained the myth of White superiority through state sanction terrorism of their Black citizens. By 1978, White supremacists had their own utopian text to follow as their bible for White nationalism, *The Turner Diaries*.[8] Written by William Luther Pierce, *The Turner Diaries*, promoted the idea of an inevitable race war of Whites against people of color, Jews, Hollywood liberals, and politicians. The book shaped modern White nationalism and inspired the 1995 Oklahoma City bombing by Timothy McVeigh, which resembled the fictional bombing of the FBI building in the novel. Whereas the novel directly inspired bombings, assassinations, lynchings, and other violence, the ideas in the novel also inspired mass shootings, like the Charleston Church massacre in South Carolina, on June 17, 2015.

The origins of utopian texts, offering visions of White utopias, begin with Plato's *Republic* (375BCE) and continued with Sir Thomas More's *Utopia* (1516), Francis Bacon's novel, *New Atlantis* (1627), Robert Owen (1800), Charles Fourier (1772-1837), Thomas Hobbes (1651), and in the United States, Emma Goldman's *Anarchism and Other Essays* (1910), Edward Bellamy's *Looking Backward* (1888), and Charlotte Perkins Gilman's, *Herland* (1915).[9] Suffice it to say, that few texts on utopian visions include the work of African Americans.[10] Blacks not only envisioned literary utopias but created them as well, like the Maroon societies of slave era Jamaica and Brazil, the Haitian Revolution, and the towns founded by and for African Americans in the United States. The first clearly defined Black literary utopian vision was written by Martin R. Delany in 1859, *Blake; or the Huts of America*.[11] Blake tells the story of Henry Blake who escapes from a plantation and travels throughout the United States, Canada, Cuba, and Africa. Blake is a pan-Africanist hoping to unite the enslaved and free to fight for their freedom in the Americas. Other Black authors also tried their hand at writing Black utopian fiction, like Francis Harper (1892), Pauline Hopkins (1902–1903), Edward A. Johnson (1904), and Richard Wright's 1954 anti-colonial and anti-utopian novel, *Black Power*, which examined the negative effects of colonialism on the colonized.[12]

Afrofuturism is subversive. It is a term coined by author, lecturer, and culture critic, Mark Dery, in his essay, "Black to the Future." It is expressed in multiple art forms and embodies centering the pan-African experience in the African diaspora through science fiction.[13] Marvel Studio's February 2018 film, *Black Panther*, with a budget of 200 million, made about 1.4 billion dollars during its theatrical release.[14] It was, in a word, a blockbuster. *Black Panther* is a subversive film. It overturns White constructs of art and of being Black in America. From the natural hairstyles to the strong, heroic, and very dark Black women who populate the film and to the diversity of the Black characters' roles, thoughts, and ideas of being. Movie goers were not only treated to the high production values of the film, the clothing, the cityscapes, and Shuri's (Wright) many inventions; they also received a history lesson of Africa and her colonization by Europeans. They learned the word, "colonizer," what Shuri called Everett K. Ross (Martin Freeman), the White CIA agent in the film. Most viewers learned more about the continent of Africa in the first few minutes of the film than they learned in school where the "country" of Africa was only the land where slaves came from. The film is subversive because it does not focus on the pain and trauma of the peoples of the African diaspora, it focused on strength, creativity, heroism, achievement, inventors, rulers, and creators. The world of *Black Panther* offers the young and old a vision of possibility, of what could have been had colonization not occurred, the Africa of imagination and not strife. Carvell Wallace of the *New York Times* writes,

> In a video posted to Twitter in December, which has since gone viral, three young men are seen fawning over the "Black Panther" poster at a movie theater. One jokingly embraces the poster while another asks, rhetorically: "This is what White people get to feel all the time?" There is laughter before someone says, as though delivering the punch line to the most painful joke ever told: "I would love this country, too."[15]

Speculative fiction, like utopian fiction, has predominantly been a White vision of the future, a future that is curiously without people of color. Afrofuturism is subversive and inclusive of all art forms. Wallace writes that "[t]he movement spans from free-jazz thinkers like Sun Ra, who wrote of an African past filled with alien technology and extraterrestrial beings, to the art of Krista Franklin and Ytasha Womack, to the writers Octavia Butler, Nnedi Okorafor and Derrick Bell, to the music of Jamila Woods and Janelle Monáe."[16] But overturning White constructs did not go unnoticed. The film premiered during Black History month in the middle of twice impeached

President Trump's single term in office. John Wenzel, of the *Denver Post*, wrote in February 2018 that:

> While some conservatives have decried the film as social-justice propaganda, and alt-right trolls have attempted to tank its online ratings, a loose coalition of artists, church leaders and educators are seizing it as rallying cry for racial justice in the age of renewed public racism ... online campaigns have mobilized in recent weeks to sink the Rotten Tomatoes and Internet Movie Database Ratings of the film, which are vulnerable to user-generated manipulation. Earlier this month, Facebook cracked down on an alt-right group called Down With Disney's Treatment of Franchises and Its Fanboys by taking the unusual step of deactivating their "Black Panther"-hating page, while some Twitter users have advocated for in-theater protests against what they see as liberal Hollywood propaganda.[17]

White supremacist pushback against the film is to be expected in the United States, but it did not stop the audiences from coming. Black Lives Matter Cofounder Patrisse Cullors writes about her experience seeing the film:

> I can't describe the feeling one gets when they see themselves represented. Although an accurate and multidimensional representation of black women is rare, when I have seen it, I've left a theater feeling that much more connected to my purpose. Whether it's on TV or on social media, young black girls have historically been represented through the white gaze. But this time Wakanda doesn't just highlight black cis men; it also gives room and space for black women, presented as complicated, brilliant, flawed people—and, most important, presented as superheroes.
>
> I think Black Lives Matter has contributed cultural ammunition to help fuel a movie like *Black Panther,* which can be seen as a necessary response to a trying time in our country. Because Wakanda isn't fiction; for so many of us, it's real life. This is why there are right-wing groups on social media boycotting the movie. Unfortunately, some people see black life and the celebration of it as a direct contradiction to American values. Instead there is an investment in the belief that Black people are to be feared and thus harmed and discriminated against. *Black Panther* is a celebration of black life and the global black diaspora, and it centers on a world where black people are in charge of their own destinies. The idea that black people—whether we're hanging out with our friends and family, on our block and in our communities—pose a threat to whiteness is a reflection of white fragility. It's the same white fragility that allowed for 45 to be voted into office.[18]

Conservative politics and White fragility result in a lack imagination. This lack of imagination in the United States has resulted in the creation of fictional futures not so different from the eras in which they had been written. A lack of imagination for the future plus fear resulted in White supremacists storming the U.S. Capitol on January 6, 2021, because White supremacists are still stuck in conservative visions of yesterday that inform their fears of tomorrow. Change is the only constant. It is the one thing we all can count on, but conservatism builds walls against the inevitable and in doing so, limits who can participate, create, and invent, and we all lose when that happens. But some of us are brave.

There are many other historical moments that address racism but adhere to the dominant cultural norm of the invisibility of women in the struggle. However, Josephine St. Pierre Ruffin, and many others, like the brave Ida B. Wells-Barnett, who faced death when she uncovered the truth of lynchings in the south, and the warrior, Harriet Tubman, the Moses of her people and so much more, took on the challenge of women's roles in the struggle for basic human rights. Nonetheless, passing the torch to the next generation of race leaders may not have been easy for Ruffin, a native Bostonian. She was born in 1842 to a White mother and multi-heritage father. Ruffin was an abolitionist, a journalist, a publisher, and a founder of the Black woman's club movement, the Boston chapter of the NAACP, a World War I Soldier's Comfort Unit, and the League of Women for Community Service. A Black woman with an eighth-grade education, the highest level of education a Black woman could attain in Boston during the time of her youth, she raised four children who all attended college, Hubert, a lawyer; Florida, an educator; Stanley, a politician and inventor, and George, a musician. Ruffin's fourth son, Robert, died in infancy. She assisted her husband, George Lewis Ruffin, the first Black American to attend Harvard Law School, to be elected to the Boston City Council, and to be appointed a Municipal Court Judge, in his political and judicial career in the city, as well as helped found the Massachusetts State Federation of Women's Clubs.[19] Her daughter, Florida Ruffin Ridley, in a letter to author, educator, and lecturer Hallie Quinn Brown, wrote: "This [club work] puts her not only as a pioneer in colored club work, but also as a pioneer in white."[20]

There were few real opportunities for educated Black women outside of teaching or working in their own organizations in the late nineteenth and early twentieth centuries. As a result, they had much more in common with poor Black women whose labor was concentrated in agricultural or domestic work. Though class divisions remained, their shared obstacles allied them to each other. Mary Church Terrell spoke of the strategic nature of allying with poor Black women. Since Whites ignored Black class stratification, wealthier Black women were invisible to Whites who stereotyped all Black women as sexually wanton. Terrell stated:

> they (black women) know that they cannot escape altogether the consequences of the acts of their most depraved sisters. They see that even if they were wicked enough to turn a deaf ear to the call of duty, both policy and self-preservation

demanded that they go down among the lowly, the illiterate and even the vicious, to whom they are bound by ties of race and sex, and put forth every possible effort to reclaim them.[21]

Terrell was calling for enlightened self-interest, a win-win situation that could benefit both middle-class and poor Black women. In 1894, enlightened self-interest was also what Fannie Williams called for in the *Women's Era* relative to Black women's political engagement following the model set by Black men:

> Must we begin our political duties with no better or higher conceptions of our citizenship than shown by our men when they were first enfranchised? Are we to bring any refinement of individuality to the ballot box? Shall we learn our politics from spoilsmen and bigoted partisans or shall we learn it from the school of patriotism and an enlightened self-interest?[22]

In one pro-suffrage editorial, Ruffin was clear that she did not believe women were inferior to men, and even lambasted those who believed the bible was an authority on woman's "place" in society.[23] Boston's Black elite women were likewise clear in their desire not to primarily uplift all Blacks generally but rather to uplift Black women in particular. They recognized women were different from men but did not accept that this difference made women incapable of acting in the public sphere. Black clubwomen wanted Black and White women to be active in the public sphere to make the country a more moral place for all.

By 1895, Ruffin was well aware of the failure of moral suasion alone to halt Jim Crow. Ruffin felt relatively safe in the North where, she wrote, "the spirit of the times is felt, but . . . [where] a Black man is a man." Ruffin was cognizant of the Jim Crow sensibilities that had already spread to Boston. Black protest did slow the progression of Jim Crow in the city, but not in the South. Southern Blacks, according to Ruffin, remained "powerless" against the overwhelming odds arrayed against them, and thus Black males could not fully realize their manhood. Their best hope, felt Ruffin, was to leave the South: "The time for resistance, wise resistance, has come," she wrote. "Our hope for creating public sentiment grows dimmer and dimmer, and patience and humility ceased to be virtues."[24]

Ruffin's earlier work with the Boston Kansas Relief Association for Black Migrants, an organization that helped Blacks leaving the South for Kansas, certainly affected her opinion as to what southern Blacks should do to defend themselves against White violence and discrimination. But the tone of her editorial shows a great sadness as well. She no longer believed Whites could be moved to honor Black citizenship or empathize with Black struggles. That special time that undergirded Black triumphalism at the conclusion of the Civil War was over by the end of the nineteenth century, but the hope it engendered continued to live on in the political activism of these women. Ruffin called for resistance, albeit "wise resistance," as an acknowledgment that Blacks, even Black elites, had lost patience with racist White retrenchment. What was "wise resistance" was left undefined by Ruffin who bridged two eras, one of great sacrifice and triumph and another of growing despair. Nakia (Nyong'o), Black Panther's on-again off-again girlfriend, echoes the frustration felt by Ruffin and her cohorts who were demanding that those who had so much more than others had a duty to rise up and fight against the White supremacists of her day. Ruffin, a Christian, believed that "to whom much is given, much will be required."[25] Nakia lived by the same code and tried repeatedly to convince T'Challa to believe the same. But T'Challa would not be moved until he temporarily lost everything to Killmonger when he became the next Black Panther.

Ruffin understood that respectability alone offered Black Americans few, if any, tangible benefits. In an editorial criticizing a racist speech given by a certain "Mr. Donald," an otherwise unidentified White guest attending the Tuskegee Institute's commencement ceremonies in June 1895, Ruffin wrote she did not expect an open protest from Tuskegee, as she would have expected had the speech been delivered in Boston, because Blacks in Boston would have immediately launched a protest.[26] Ruffin angrily condemned Donald's speech in her editorial. Necessary as it may have been, she was finding that the politics of respectability alone was proving insufficient in stemming the growth of anti-Black sentiments spurred by a racist revision of the nation's Reconstruction Era history and the desire for southern redemption. She believed something had to change, and change soon, if Jim Crow was to be halted and reversed. [27]

Ruffin linked the growth of Jim Crow sentiments in the North to the problems faced by the Black elite and the failure of the politics of respectability to protect elite and middle-class Blacks from discrimination. "It is useless to blind ourselves to the fact that our position grows worse; *we* progress in education, in character and in the acquisition of money, but while in some cases these *must* tell, they do not bring that universal respect that they should." The trappings of respectability had, for some ethnic Whites, allowed them to be accepted by the White middle class, but Blacks remained locked out. "As long as [he/she is] identified with the race," Ruffin continued, "the Negro is regarded and treated as an inferior except in individual cases."[28] And yet, it was in those "individual cases" among the Black elite that allowed for Black and White interaction, which resulted in their voices, again however faintly, being heard by the majority culture.

Boston's elite Blacks did not need to read tea leaves or consult with "Madame Cloud," a Boston spiritualist who regularly advertised in the *Women's Era*, to understand the effect of southern redemption on Black rights throughout the nation. Ruffin's concerns on the eve of the Jim Crow Era appeared to have no other solution than self-defense. "We must acknowledge that there is nothing left for us but to strike for ourselves," wrote Ruffin in 1895. "We have a few staunch friends, but only a few, and even public sentiment at its best is bored with us." Elite Blacks in Boston continued to press for federal intervention to halt the spread of Jim Crow, but their trust in the party of Lincoln was waning. "We can no longer wait for the problems to solve [themselves]," Ruffin continued. "Away with the doctrine of humility . . . . If extinction awaits us finally, let us go to meet it like men, not lie down for it to overtake us."[29] Ruffin was putting out a call for action. Liberation could only be won if all, men and women, were willing to face the consequences of demanding their full citizenship rights, rights, Ruffin believed, Black men had failed to protect. Nakia was also willing to risk her life to protect the rights of others in her efforts to address the discrimination, but in this passage Ruffin is sounding more like Killmonger than Nakia. Ruffin was fed up and wanted all Blacks to rise up and defend their rights.

LEGACY OF BLACK MEN'S RESISTANCE, PROTEST, AND FIGHT FOR "MANHOOD RIGHTS"

Three Black men dominated Black political expression during the early twentieth century. All three had links to Boston, but only one was born in the state. Two of the men lived and worked in the South, but the third never made it farther South than Washington, D. C. Booker T. Washington, W. E. B. Du Bois and William Monroe Trotter each affected the direction Black protest would take in the nation in the new century and the next, and each represented different Black "masculinities" at the time. Gender constructs were in flux at the turn of the century and were influenced by race, class, and the nation's burgeoning imperialism.[30] In Boston, much of the battle to determine which ideology would reign supreme took place between the pages of Trotter's newspaper, the *Boston Guardian*. Nationally, the three men and their competing ideologies struggled to define what "place" Blacks would inhabit in the country.

Segregation and southern disfranchisement constrained Black masculinity in the nation during the late nineteenth and early twentieth centuries. Military service, the last symbol of Black manhood, was seen as mitigating the otherwise "shrinking" terrain of public space for Black males. Jim Crow laws in the South and Jim Crow sensibilities in the North had already and were continuing to limit Black competition with Whites and limit Black advancement. As a result, the "self-made man" trope of the early twentieth century was denied Black males. Protecting Black manhood from the depredation of Jim Crow undergirded Black activism in the late nineteenth and early twentieth centuries. Manhood was necessary for expressing citizenship, which in turn determined who was eligible to vote, engage in politics, and serve in the military. Suffragists during the mid-nineteenth century challenged the androcentric construct of citizenship, as Black men and women challenged its racial exclusivity after the Civil War. Civil War veterans, according to historian Kristin Hoganson, were the "epitome of honor and the model of manly character" in the United States.[31] But the presence of Black veterans and the results of Radical Reconstruction threatened White male identity in the United States.

Booker T. Washington, W. E. B. Du Bois, and William Monroe Trotter pursued distinctly different strategies to achieve Black manhood, similar to the oppositional forces in reaching racial equality on a global scale, between T'Challa and Killmonger in *Black Panther*. In *Black Panther*, several manhood constructs are at play that offer the audience a refreshingly diverse view of masculinity. In the late nineteenth century, Black activists openly discussed manhood, manliness, and masculinities, while White Anglo-Saxon Protestants from the east coast were dismayed at the changes taking place in the old social order. Industrialization, immigration, Black males in the work force, unions, class strife, and the *New Woman* were all threatening to old, White gender constructs in the United States. White male eastern elites were seen as a major part of the problem, because many believed that wealthier White males were losing their edge in a changing world. Their insecurity regarding their own manliness undergirded the turn to American imperialism as an antidote to their flaccid masculinity on the international stage and at home. Future president, Teddy Roosevelt, extolled rugged individualism as his own antidote to having been sickly as a child and derided as a "Nancy Boy" by the press in New York. Roosevelt's insecurities led him to create the Rough Riders and to Whitewash the cowboy, leaving out Mexican American *Vaqueros* and the many Black cowboys of the West, let alone the Black Buffalo soldiers whose job was to "tame" the West. But in White supremacist America, only White men could be true men, because everyone else was deemed wanting, which was why African American activists kept talking about manhood and manhood rights. Meanwhile, Black women activists like Ruffin and others created the first national Black organization, the National Association of Colored Women (NACW), years before the Niagara Movement that was co-founded by Du Bois and Trotter, and the National Association for the Advancement of Colored People (NAACP) that Du Bois also helped to co-found.

Black Panther did not rely on just one vision of Black manhood. Each major male character expressed a type of masculinity. T'Challa represented the elite and educated version of masculinity with expressions of paternalism that the women in his life resisted. He, the heir to the throne and eldest son of the previous king, was bred to rule and serve Wakanda, sort of the "Prince William" of Wakanda. The "spare," T'Challa's younger brother, W'Kabi, was "Prince Harry" to T'Challa's "Prince William." He was free of the responsibilities of the heir apparent (and maybe a little jealous), and this freedom allowed him to consider alternatives to T'Challa's traditional ideas of Wakanda's future. Though not concerned with saving others, he was concerned about maintaining Wakanda's technological power at a time when other nations were slowly catching up. When W'Kabi sides with his cousin, Killmonger, it is W'Kabi's wife, Okoye, who brings him back to his senses. J'Bari, the king of the fifth tribe that is aligned with Wakanda, but not ruled by Wakanda, represents traditional male orthodoxy, a toxic masculinity that is dismissive of women and of the technology that disrupts his male-centered orthodoxy that privileges physical strength over anything else. Killmonger, though, represents a toxic masculinity that is born out of his struggles and traumas that is power hungry, narcissistic, misogynistic, and where everyone else is a tool for achieving his vision of redemption and vengeance. Ulysses Klaue, the South African gun-runner whose father was a Nazi war criminal, represents a White male construct of masculinity whose only interest is in securing more wealth and power regardless of who might be injured or killed. He assumes that his wealth will ultimately protect him from the chaos and destruction his gun running causes. He is a man without empathy and is clearly a sociopath. Everett, the White CIA agent, represents a positive White male construct whose sense of racial entitlement and cluelessness is evident every time Shuri calls him a colonizer, but he comes through in the end. The film offers its audience a number of masculinities to try on, but clearly favors T'Challa's version of manliness, of honor, of strength, and of reflection. T'Challa's ideological transformation regarding Wakanda's future in the world is not weakness, as a more toxic masculinity would conclude, it is his strength.

Booker T. Washington chose a path of least resistance in combating racial discrimination. Though his legacy is more complicated than that, he did accommodate White power by preferring segregation to first-class citizenship, similar to T'Challa's decision in the beginning of the film to maintain Wakanda's segregation from the rest of the world. Washington's politics of accommodation rejected the Black stratification model for one based on creating an economic niche for Blacks that would elevate Black workers to an indispensable position within American society, much like T'Challa's desire to maintain Wakanda's invisible and unique niche in the world. His model, though, denied recognition of the needs of women and elite and middle-class Blacks. Du Bois clearly represented the elite model, one that was articulated in his talented tenth thesis.[32] Du Bois believed Black advancement could only occur through the continuation of Black male respectability as derived through classical or liberal education. Additionally, Du Bois rejected accommodation to Jim Crow and believed Blacks had to act to protect the franchise and defeat segregation in order to achieve social, political, and economic equality. T'Challa was also a traditionalist, like Du Bois, and an elitist who disregarded his girlfriend's and brother's council regarding the future of the nation. Not surprisingly, Du Bois' 10 percent solution rested on elite Blacks serving as a vanguard for racial progress and leadership, as T'Challa's solution rested on his royal upbringing.

Trotter's activism also took on aspects of Black messianism, particularly after his wife, Geraldine "Deenie" Pindell Trotter, died of the Spanish Influenza in 1918.[33] Trotter's failed mission to storm the peace talks in France after World War I was as potentially successful a mission as John Brown's raid on Harper's Ferry. Of the three Black leaders, the younger Trotter hailed from Black aristocracy. Trotter was raised in relative wealth, in White neighborhoods in Boston, and attended Harvard College with members of the White aristocracy. As a result, Trotter came to expect that he too would be part of that pantheon of great and powerful Americans like his White classmates at Harvard. Trotter's turn to radicalism and his sense of mission reflected the collision of his optimistic expectations for his future with the realities of his racial position in the nation. Killmonger's back story echoes aspects of Trotter's personal history. Killmonger was of royal "blood" but without the entitlements of royalty. He attended the U.S. Naval Academy in Annapolis, MIT, and then joined the Navy Seals. One difference between Trotter and Killmonger is that Killmonger began his journey radicalized, and Trotter became radicalized when it became apparent to him that all of his college honors would not erase the stain of his skin color in the eyes of White America.

William Monroe Trotter grew up in predominantly White Hyde Park, the southern-most part of Boston. His school mates in Hyde Park were all White. William Trotter was the top student in his all-White classes and was elected president of his class, a history similar to Du Bois while a student in Great Barrington, Massachusetts. Trotter originally wanted to be a minister, but his father, James Trotter, thought the ministry was too limiting for his brilliant son and feared it would ultimately lead to William being segregated from Whites. James Trotter was a firm believer in integration and in competing directly with Whites as proof of self-worth. Trotter, after working for a year as a shipping clerk, entered Harvard in 1891 as a member of the class of 1895.[34] Trotter was not the first Black male to attend Harvard College

(Richard Greener, class of 1870, a civil rights activist in Washington, D.C., was the first). Trotter's father died during his freshman year at Harvard, so he worked while attending college. A brilliant student, Trotter was elected to *Phi Beta Kappa* during his junior year and graduated *magna cum laude* with an A.B. and an A.M. after his four-year course of study. Trotter was also fortunate to be taught by some of Harvard's more famous faculty at the time, George Santayana, William James, Francis Peabody, and others.[35]

Du Bois, like Trotter, grew up in a predominantly White section of Great Barrington, Massachusetts, located in the western part of the state. He was born on February 23, 1868, on Church Street in Great Barrington. His parents were Congregationalists of French, Dutch, and African ancestry.[36] Du Bois was an excellent student and an academic star in his high school. After earning an A. B. at Fisk University, Du Bois' biographer, David Levering Lewis, writes that Du Bois developed a Black consciousness. Fisk, a Black college, was Du Bois' first real opportunity to be surrounded by what he would later term the "talented tenth."[37] In Great Barrington, Du Bois stood out as an exemplary member of the "Black race." But at Fisk, Du Bois found others like himself, and there, surrounded by other talented Black Americans, Du Bois began to develop a thesis regarding the role of elite Blacks in Black America. Du Bois' Black consciousness was further developed during his summer breaks from college when he traveled throughout the South meeting the other 90 percent of the Black population: poor, rural Blacks, undereducated, and terrorized by Whites. After Du Bois graduated from Fisk, he was accepted as a junior at Harvard College, class of 1890. Du Bois continued at Harvard and received his Ph.D. in 1895, crossing paths frequently with the younger Trotter at elite Black social events in Boston with the Ruffin family and in Cambridge. Ultimately, Du Bois could not reconcile his own experiences with White America with Washington's accommodationist rhetoric. The 1903 publication of his book, *The Souls of Black Folk*, served as the beginning of Du Bois' public break with Washington.[38]

Booker T. Washington, born a slave on a Virginia plantation in 1856, was emancipated in 1863 by Lincoln's Emancipation Proclamation. His family moved to the free state of West Virginia shortly afterward where Washington worked in coal mines. Dreaming of a better life, Washington attended the Hampton Normal and Agricultural Institute (later Hampton University), and after a few years was chosen to lead a new industrial school, Tuskegee Normal and Industrial Institute (later Tuskegee University), in Tuskegee, Alabama, in 1881, at the age of 25. Tuskegee consisted of two unequipped buildings when Washington began, and by his death, boasted over 100 well-equipped buildings and an endowment of $2 million.[39] Tuskegee was a Black oasis in what was arguably the most racist state in the nation, Alabama. Washington's work was among the most discriminated class of Black

Americans in the country, the 90 percent of the Black population that lived in the south. Black men in the south were an endangered species, and as such, Washington, in order to survive and fulfill his dream, played it safe in the south. One could see a bit of Washington in Killmonger's earlier years in joining the Navy and attending MIT. Though it might appear Killmonger was playing it safe, he was really preparing himself to take on the establishment by using the establishment against itself. Washington made his plan clear in his Atlanta Exposition speech delivered at the Cotton States and International Exposition on September 18, 1895, what Du Bois would later label the "Atlanta Compromise." Washington stated that "In all things purely social we can be as separate as the fingers, yet one as the hand in all things essential to mutual progress."[40] But Washington said different things to different audiences, soothing White fears in the south while sounding more radical in the north. Though he ran Tuskegee in the South careful to not anger White supremacists, he also graduated many Black professionals that, over time, would have a more positive effect on the future of Black America.

The struggle among differing Black political ideologies for integration or self-segregation, nonviolent direct action and self-defense and revolution continued into the twentieth century with a variety of groups and individuals. The National Association for the Advancement of Colored People (NAACP) and the Congress of Racial Equality (CORE) represented more elite and educated Black Americans and sought reform. The Deacons for Defense, The Black Panther Party (BPP), and the Black Liberation Army (BLA) espoused a more muscular masculinity favoring self-defense or revolution. The Southern Christian Leadership Council (SCLC) and the Student Non-violent Coordinating Committee (SNCC) were also more reform oriented but willing to put their lives on the line in their struggle for equality and equity. SNCC would change over time, calling for Black power, kicking out White members, and essentially transforming into the Black Panther Party. All espoused differing approaches to achieving equality, justice, and manhood rights. *Black Panther*'s fictional nation of Wakanda appears to have borrowed more from Booker T. Washington's Tuskegee Institute in the beginning of the film, and then transforming into a cross between Martin Luther King, Jr.'s SCLC and the BPP by embracing integrating with the rest of the world and providing social programs for those left behind like what the BPPs provided in the communities where they were based, like Oakland, California. King, a Christian reverend, struggled to keep the Civil Rights Movement nonviolent. He was well aware of the power of Whites, and was ultimately a victim of White power. But even before he was assassinated, younger Black activists, particularly those outside of the south, had gotten tired of being arrested, beaten, and killed. Joined by Black veterans of the Vietnam war, many younger Black activists in the north became revolutionaries. Similar transformations would take place in Wakanda as well as the nation. Wakanda was split into three camps, one led by T'Challa, the second by Killmonger, and the third, the wildcard, by M'Baku. Wakanda would be saved from the sociopath, Killmonger, only if T'Challa's supporters and M'Baku and the J'Baris put aside their differences and come together to battle Killmonger and his supporters.

THE RESOLUTION OF OPPOSING IDEOLOGIES ON BLACK STRUGGLE

The final fight scene in *Black Panther* is a *Kumbaya* moment in the film. Shuri sets up Everett Ross, the CIA agent, or "Colonizer," as Shuri repeatedly calls him, to remotely fly a Wakandan plane to stop the export of Vibranium. The warriors, who were originally non-political because they served the throne, not any one person sitting on it, come to a change of heart and try to stop Killmonger. M'Baku and the rest of the J'Bari put aside their differences and arrive to do battle against Killmonger and his supporters. But T'Challa's brother is still intent on revolution as he rides his heavily armored giant rhinoceros into battle. He is finally stopped by his wife, the warrior, Okoye, who stands in his rampaging path. The rhino, no doubt familiar with Okoye, stops in its tracks and gives Okoye a friendly lick as well. This is the moment when all of the various fractions in Wakanda, all of their visions for tomorrow, coalesce, returning harmony to the land, and ending with T'Challa fatally stabbing Killmonger. T'Challa shows empathy for his cousin, Killmonger, and tells him he can be healed. But Killmonger is not interested in spending a life time in prison, otherwise he would have stayed in Oakland. He chooses death and asks T'Challa to "[b]ury me in the ocean with my ancestors that jumped from the ships, because they knew death was better than bondage."

T'Challa is now "woke." Though no revolutionary, he is no longer content with accommodating a world that treats too many with disdain. He doesn't believe in the path Killmonger chose, but he is awakened to the path Nakia, his girlfriend, chose to combat historical inequities. If the previous kings had more in common with Booker T. Washington, and Killmonger too much in common with a pre-Mecca Malcolm X, T'Challa decides to find a middle way that he hopes will maintain harmony. Martin Luther King's wokeness led him to a more inclusive ideology that included all poor people and the end of the Vietnam War. As threatening as King was to traditional White power in his campaign to end racialized discrimination, his antiwar stance and attempts to form a coalition of all suffering people in his Poor People's Campaign, was even more threatening to entrenched White power. Unfortunately, his death melted away the possibility of all marginalized people from coming together and, instead, led to the fragmentation of the movement and identity politics. T'Challa does not have all of the answers figured out by the end of the film, but he is alive and making changes. His first act is to build the first Wakanda International Outreach Center in Oakland, California, in the very building where Killmonger grew up and became radicalized. In the final scene, a little boy looks on as the Wakanda airship takes off and turns to T'Challa and asks, "who are you?" That will take the next *Black Panther* film for us to find out, even though Chadwick Boseman will not lead the way.

NOTES

1. See Matteo Salvadore, *The African Prester John and the Birth of Ethiopian-European Relations, 1402-1555* (New York: Routledge, 2017).

2. Jennifer V. Jackson and Mary E. Colthran, "Black Versus Black: The relationships among African, African American, and Caribbean Persons, *Journal of Black Studies* 33, no. 5 (May 2003): 576–604.

3. See Robert Silverberg, *The Realm of Prester John* (Athens, OH: Ohio University Press, 1996).

4. See Stan Lee and Jack Kirby, *Fantastic Four* vol. 1, no. 54 (Marvel Comics: September 1966); and "Prester John (Johann) (Earth-616)," *Marvel Database*, accessed December 1, 2019, https://marvel.fandom.com/wiki/prester_j ohn_(johann)_(earth-616).

5. Club Minutes, February 28, 1924, League of Women for Community Service, Harvard University, The Radcliffe Institute, Schlesinger Library; "Letter from Florida Ruffin Ridley to the author," in *Homespun Heroines and Other Women of Distinction*, ed. Hallie Q. Brown (New York: Oxford University Press, 1988), 153.

6. W. E. B. Du Bois, *Black Reconstruction in America: An Essay Toward a History of the Part which Black Folk Played in the Attempt to Reconstruct Democracy in America, 1860-1880* (New York: Harcourt, 1935), 700–710.

7. See Barbara J. Fields, *Slavery and Freedom on the Middle Ground: Maryland During the 19th Century* (New Haven, CT: Yale University Press, 1984).

8. William Luther Pierce, *The Turner Diaries* (National Vanguard Books, 1978).

9. Plato and Allen Bloom, *The Republic* (New York: Basic Books, [375 BCE] 1968); Sir Thomas More and Paul Turner (annotations), *Utopia* (Baltimore: Penguin Classics, [1516] 2003); Francis Bacon, *New Atlantis* (Kila, MT: Kessinger, [1627] 1992); Charles Fourier, *Design for Utopia: Selected Writings, Studies in the Libertarian And Utopian Tradition* (New York: Schocken, 1971); Thomas Hobbes, *Leviathan* (Baltimore: Penguin Books, [1651] 1968); Emma Goldman, *Anarchism and Other Essays* (New York: Mother Earth Publishing Association, 1910); Edward Bellamy and Matthew Beaumont, *Looking Backwards, 2000-1887* (Oxford: Oxford University Press, [1888] 2009); Charlotte Perkins Gilman and Ann Levine, *Herland* (New York: Pantheon Books, [1915] 1979).

10. Two exceptions are: Robin D.G. Kelley, *Freedom Dreams: The Black Radical Imagination* (Boston: Beacon Press, 2003); Wilson J. Moses, *Afrotopia: The Roots of African American Popular History* (New York: Cambridge University Press, 1998).

11. Martin R. Delany, *Blake; or, The Huts of America: A Corrected Edition*, ed. Jerome McGann (Cambridge: Harvard University Press, 2017).

12. See Francis Ellen Watkins Harper's, *Iola Leroy, or, Shadows Uplifted* (New York: Oxford University Press, [1892] 1988); Pauline Hopkins, *Of One Blood: or, The Hidden Self* (New York: Washington Square Press, [serialized from 1902-1903] 2004); Edward A. Johnson's, *Light Ahead for the Negro* (New York: AMS Press, [1904] 1975); and Richard Wright, *Black Power: Three Books from Exile: Black Power, the Color Curtain and White Man, Listen!* (New York: Harper Perennial Modern Classics, [1954] 2008).

13. Mark Dery, ed., *Flame Wars: The Discourse of Cyberculture* (Durham: Duke University Press, 1994).

14. Sarah Whitten, "'Black Panther' made more money at the box office than the other 7 best picture nominees combined," *CNBC.com*, January 22, 2019, https://www.cnbc.com/2019/01/22/black-panther-made-more-money-than-the-other-best-picture-nominees-.html.

15. Carvell Wallace, "Why 'Black Panther' is a defining moment for Black America," *New York Times Magazine*, February 12, 2018, https://www.nytimes.com/2018/02/12/magazine/why-black-panther-is-a-defining-moment-for-black-america.html.

16. Wallace, "Why 'Black Panther' is a defining moment for Black America."

17. John Wenzel, "The Black Panther movie, already a national flashpoint, becomes Colorado rallying cry," *The Denver Post*, February 16, 2018, https://www.denverpost.com/2018/02/16/black-panther-movie-colorado-rallying-cry/.

18. Patrisse Cullors, "'Black Panther' Reflects a Cultural Shift in Hollywood—and in America," *Glamour*, February 15, 2018, https://www.glamour.com/story/black-lives-matter-cofounder-black-panther-reflects-a-cultural-shift.

19. Brown, *Homespun Heroines*, 151. Brown was also president of the NACW in 1923. In 1924, she was the director of the Colored Women's Republican National Committee (see Noralee Frankel and Nancy S. Dye, eds, *Gender, Race, and Reform in the Progressive Era* (Lexington, KY: University of Kentucky Press, 1991), 156.) Also see Eleanor Flexner, *Century of Struggle: The Women's Movement in the United States* (Cambridge: The Belknap Press of Harvard University Press, 1975 [1969]), 189; Rayford W. Logan, *The Negro in American Life and Thought: The Nadir, 1877-1901* (New York: Dial Press, 1954), 236; "Elizabeth Fortson Arroyo, "Ruffin, Josephine St. Pierre, (1842-1924)" in *Black Women in America: An Historical Encyclopedia*, Vol. II, eds. Darlene Clark Hine, Elsa Barkley Brown, and Rosalyn Terborg-Penn (Indiana: University of Indiana Press, 1994), 994.

20. Brown, *Homespun Heroines*, 153.

21. Sharon Harley, "Mary Church Terrell: Genteel Militant," in *Black Leaders in the Nineteenth Century*, eds. Leon Litwak and August Meier (Urbana: University of Illinois Press, 1988), 311.

22. Fannie Williams, "Club Gossip," *Women's Era*, November 1894.

23. Josephine St Pierre Ruffin, "Editorial," *Women's Era*, September 1, 1894, 8.
24. Josephine St Pierre Ruffin, "Editorial," *Women's Era*, July 1, 1895, 13.
25. Luke 12:48.
26. Josephine St Pierre Ruffin, "Editorial," *Women's Era*, July 1,1895, 12.
27. Josephine St Pierre Ruffin, "Editorial," *Women's Era*, July 1, 1895, 12.
28. Josephine St Pierre Ruffin, "Editorial," *Women's Era*, July 1, 1895, 12–13.
29. Josephine St Pierre Ruffin, "Editorial," *Women's Era*, July 1, 1895, 13.
30. Kristin L. Hoganson, *Fighting for American Manhood: How Gender Politics Provoked the Spanish-American and Philippine-American Wars* (New Haven: Yale University Press, 1998), 3–18.
31. Hoganson, *Fighting for American Manhood*, 24.
32. W. E. B. Du Bois, *The Souls of Black Folk* (New York: Bantam Books, 1989 [1903]), 30–42; also see August Meier, *Negro Thought in America, 1880-1915: Racial Ideologies in the Age of Booker T. Washington* (Ann Arbor: University of Michigan Press, 1963), 171–255.
33. On Black messianism, see Wilson Moses, *Black Messiahs and Uncle Toms: Social and Literary Manipulations of Religious Myth*, rev. ed. (University Park: Pennsylvania State University Press, 1993), 1–16.
34. Maude Trotter Steward, "William Monroe Trotter," *Boston Guardian*, August 18, 1952, 5.
35. "Negroes at Harvard," Harvard Archives, Widener Library, Harvard University; *Record of Class of 1895*, Harvard Archives, Widener Library, Harvard University.
36. Lewis, *Biography of a Race*, 11–20.
37. Lewis, *Biography of a Race*, 73.
38. Lewis, *Biography of a Race*, see chapter 11; Du Bois, *The Souls of Black Folks*, see chapter 3, "Of Mr. Booker T. Washington and Others."
39. See Booker T. Washington, *Up from Slavery: An Autobiography* (Lexington: Tribeca Books, 2013 [1906]); and Thomas Aiello, *The Battle for the Souls of Black Folks: WEB DuBois, Booker T. Washington, and the Debate that Shaped the Course of Civil Rights* (Santa Barbara, CA: Praeger, 2016).
40. Washington, *Up from Slavery*, 9, 107.

WORKS CITED

Aiello, Thomas. *The Battle for the Souls of Black Folks: WEB DuBois, Booker T. Washington, and the Debate that Shaped the Course of Civil Rights*. Santa Barbara, CA: Praeger, 2016.

Arroyo, Elizabeth Fortson. "Ruffin, Josephine St. Pierre, (1842-1924)." In *Black Women in America: An Historical Encyclopedia*, Vol. II. edited by Darlene Clark Hine, Elsa Barkley Brown and Rosalyn Terborg-Penn. Indiana: University of Indiana Press, 1994.

Club Minutes, February 28, 1924, League of Women for Community Service, Harvard University, The Radcliffe Institute, Schlesinger Library.

Bacon, Francis. *New Atlantis*. Kila, MT: Kessinger, 1992.

Bellamy, Edward and Matthew Beaumont. *Looking Backwards, 2000-1887*. Oxford: Oxford University Press, 2009.

Brown, Hallie Q. *Homespun Heroines and Other Women of Distinction*. New York: Oxford University Press, 1988.

Cullors, Patrisse. "'Black Panther' Reflects a Cultural Shift in Hollywood—and in America." *Glamour*, February 15, 2018, https://www.glamour.com/story/black-lives-matter-cofounder-black-panther-reflects-a-cultural-shift.

Du Bois, W. E. B. *The Souls of Black Folk*. New York: Bantam Books, 1989 [1903].

Du Bois, W. E. B. *Black Reconstruction in America: An Essay Toward a History of the Part which Black Folk Played in the Attempt to Reconstruct Democracy in America, 1860-1880*. New York: Harcourt, 1935.

Delany, Martin R. *Blake; or, the Huts of America*, edited by Jerome McGann. Cambridge: Harvard University Press, 2017.

Dery, Mark, ed. *Flame Wars: The Discourse of Cyberculture*. Durham: Duke University Press, 1994.

Fields, Barbara J. *Slavery and Freedom on the Middle Ground: Maryland During the 19th Century*. New Haven, CT: Yale University Press, 1984.

Flexner, Eleanor. *Century of Struggle: The Women's Movement in the United States*. Cambridge: The Belknap Press of Harvard University Press, 1975 [1969].

Fourier, Charles. *Design for Utopia: Selected Writings, Studies in the Libertarian and Utopian Tradition*. New York: Schocken, 1971.

Goldman, Emma. *Anarchism and Other Essays*. New York: Mother Earth Publishing Association, 1910.

Gilman, Charlotte Perkins, and Ann Levine. *Herland*. New York: Pantheon Books, 1979.

Harley, Sharon. "Mary Church Terrell: Genteel Militant." In *Black Leaders in the Nineteenth Century*, edited by Leon Litwak and August Meier. Urbana: University of Illinois Press, 1988.

Harper, Francis Ellen Watkins. *Iola Leroy, or, Shadows Uplifted*. New York: Oxford University Press, 1988.

Hobbes, Thomas. *Leviathan*. Baltimore: Penguin Books, [1651] 1968.

Hoganson, Kristin L. *Fighting for American Manhood: How Gender Politics Provoked the Spanish-American and Philippine-American Wars*. New Haven: Yale University Press, 1998.

Hopkins, Pauline. *Of One Blood: or, The Hidden Self*. New York: Washington Square Press, 2004.

Jackson, Jennifer V., and Mary E. Colthran. "Black Versus Black: The Relationships among African, African American, and Caribbean Persons." *Journal of Black Studies* 33, no. 5 (May, 2003): 576–604.

Johnson, Edward A. *Light Ahead for the Negro*. New York: AMS Press, 1975.

Kelley, Robin D.G. *Freedom Dreams: The Black Radical Imagination*. Boston: Beacon Press, 2003.

Lee, Stan and Jack Kirby. *Fantastic Four* vol. 1, no. 54. Marvel Comics, September 1966.

Lewis, David Levering. *W. E. B. Du Bois: Biography of a Race, 1868-1919*. New York: Henry Holt and Company, 1993.

Logan, Rayford W. *The Negro in American Life and Thought: The Nadir, 1877-1901.* New York: Dial Press, 1954.

"Prester John (Johann) (Earth-616)." *Marvel Database*, accessed December 1, 2019. https://marvel.fandom.com/wiki/prester_john_(johann)_(earth-616).

Meier, August. *Negro Thought in America, 1880-1915: Racial Ideologies in the Age of Booker T. Washington.* Ann Arbor: University of Michigan Press, 1963.

More, Sir Thomas, and Paul Turner (annotations). *Utopia.* Baltimore: Penguin Classics, [1516] 2003.

Moses, Wilson J. *Black Messiahs and Uncle Toms: Social and Literary Manipulations of Religious Myth.* Rev. ed. University Park: Pennsylvania State University Press, 1993.

Moses, Wilson J. *Afrotopia: The Roots of African American Popular History.* New York: Cambridge University Press, 1998.

"Negroes at Harvard," Harvard Archives, Widener Library, Harvard University; *Record of Class of 1895*, Harvard Archives, Widener Library, Harvard University.

Pierce, William Luther. *The Turner Diaries.* National Vanguard Books, 1978.

Plato, and Allen Bloom. *The Republic.* New York: Basic Books, [375 BCE] 1968.

Salvadore, Matteo. *The African Prester John and the Birth of Ethiopian-European Relations, 1402-1555.* New York: Routledge, 2017.

Silverberg, Robert. *The Realm of Prester John.* Athens, OH: Ohio University Press, 1996.

Wallace, Carvell. "Why 'Black Panther' is a defining moment for Black America." *New York Times Magazine*, February 12, 2018. https://www.nytimes.com/2018/02/12/magazine/why-black-panther-is-a-defining-moment-for-black-america.html.

Washington, Booker T. *Up from Slavery: An Autobiography.* Lexington: Tribeca Books, 2013 [1906].

Wenzel, John. "The Black Panther movie, already a national flashpoint, becomes Colorado rallying cry." The *Denver Post*, February 16, 2018. https://www.denverpost.com/2018/02/16/black-panther-movie-colorado-rallying-cry/.

Whitten, Sarah. "'Black Panther' made more money at the box office than the other 7 best picture nominees combined." *CNBC.com*, January 22, 2019. https://www.cnbc.com/2019/01/22/black-panther-made-more-money-than-the-other-best-picture-nominees-.html.

Women's Era.

Wright, Richard. *Black Power: Three Books from Exile: Black Power, the Color Curtain and White Man, Listen!* New York: Harper Perennial Modern Classics, 2008.

FILMS

Black Panther. Directed by Ryan Coogler. United States: Walt Disney Studios Motion Pictures, 2018.

Chapter 13

Tradition, Purpose, and Technology

An Archaeological Take on the Role of Technological Progress in Black Panther

Shayla Monroe

Why did the story of an African nation with superior technology, the fantasy metal ore called *vibranium*, resonate with Black viewers around the world? In stark contrast to the trope of Africa as technologically stagnant, *Black Panther* (directed by Ryan Coogler, 2018) imagines an African country as the most technologically advanced nation-state on Earth. The nation is protected, bounded, and rendered invisible by an intelligent energy field at its borders. Wakandan weapons, such as small laser cannons, fire energy-based laser projectiles, and laser cannons are also outfitted on space-aged aircraft with highly advanced navigation systems. Viewers are shown that Wakanda's military capability is so far advanced beyond any other country, including the United States, that in Marvel's next installment of the *Avengers* series, Wakanda is presented as the *only* possible place in which the Avengers can mount a strategic defensive stand against supervillain, Thanos, and his massive extraterrestrial army.

This chapter covers three theoretical junctures between archaeology and Science and Technology Studies. As the plot of *Black Panther* goes forth, we are drawn into the technologically advanced world of Wakanda, while being reminded throughout the film's dialogue that a technologically advanced African nation is supposed to be read as an irony, if not an impossibility. I use this as a point of entry to discuss archaeology's role in global perceptions of Africa's relationship to technology. Wakanda's weapons, art, architecture, and other material forms take on a variety of African aesthetics and stylistic expressions. While this has been explored from a variety of disciplinary standpoints, I explain in this chapter how archaeology is uniquely situated to contextualize material expressions of ideology. Finally, and perhaps most importantly, the film depicts a sharp and violent disagreement over the orientation and usage of technology in Wakanda's political future. I will discuss the relationship between technological progressivism and technological conservatism, highlighting evidence from the archaeological record before discussing the modern iterations of each framework, adding time depth to present dialogues about technology, politics, and ethnic conflict.

Technologies are culturally constructed, socially constituted, and historically contingent.[1] Since the first humans (and even hominins) in Africa began to manipulate the material world, creating artifacts that were both a repository and a catalyst for cultural knowledge, social conflicts and dilemmas concerning technology have been with us. In Africa's archaeological record, this is illustrated in the contested and uneven spread of ironworking across the continent of Africa. In the fictional case of *Black Panther*, ancestral Wakandans discover a metal that can outperform the physical functions iron in the form of weapons and tools. If the decision to adopt the new metal were solely about mechanical properties, then all five tribes would have been in agreement about the use of *vibranium*. It is more believable, however, for a significant portion of a society to question the meaning and implications of coming to rely on a material from an unknown source (in this case a meteor). As in the film, real-life communities do not adopt new technologies blindly and unanimously.

This chapter approaches the intricate relationship between technological innovation and social conflict in the movie *Black Panther* from the perspective of anthropological archaeology. Technology plays a central role in defining the fictional Wakanda, a small African country that hides its advanced scientific developments from the world. Imminent technological change causes a rift between Wakandan ethnic factions, creating several ethical dilemmas for the new Wakandan king and title character, T'Challa (Chadwick Boseman). Conflicts over technology in *Black Panther* directly reflect patterns of technological change in Africa's archaeological record, as well as challenges faced by the African Diaspora as we encounter imminent technologies with the power to replicate inequality.

In the narrative of *Black Panther*, we see Wakanda's leadership, embodied by T'Challa, step back and consider alternative approaches to Wakanda's technological ethics as represented by M'Baku (Winston Duke) and Nakia (Lupita Nyong'o). As we watch T'Challa struggle with considering a new purpose and a new vision for tech innovation, we have to acknowledge that similar dialogues have not received due prominence in our American present. It is fitting that a film that wrestles with long-term issues concerning race and technology ends in Oakland, a historically Black enclave losing ground to a "phenomenal surge of evictions, buyouts, and tenant harassments" driven by Silicon Valley capita.[2] Wakanda's considerable technological resources are under the direction of T'Challa's younger sister, Princess Shuri (Letitia Writght), a genius inventor and wunderkind in the vein of Marvel's Tony Stark. Like Stark, Shuri represents the gifted genius that we can see worshipped in our own society such as Steve Jobs (founder of Apple), Gates (Microsoft's founder), Elon Musk (Tesla's founder), and Mark Zuckerberg (Facebook's CEO).

Beyond the exceptional functionality and performance of Wakandan technology, the style and aesthetics of Wakandan material culture appear to be more than just the result of individual artistic choices. In Wakanda, we see mechanical genius and craftsmanship combined with beauty, creativity, and imagination. The weaponry, tools, and even the AI system interface employed (named *Griot*) are oriented toward African aesthetics and sensibilities. We first meet the villain, Erik Killmonger (Michael B. Jordan), in a scene set in a British museum, he points out a decorative farming implement created in the metalworking style of Benin is actually a highly advanced Wakandan weapon. The museum docent dates the artifact to the seventh century, a fictional date that gives viewers a time depth for how long Wakandans have been working with *vibranium*. The hoe's style exemplifies the union of artistic expression and mechanical prowess present in Wakandan technology and in African metalworking more broadly.

In order to fully appreciate the visualization of Wakandan material culture on screen, one must disavow the way that modernist Western frameworks force a dichotomy between the artisan and the technician. Science and Technology academic Sheila Jasanoff implores us to "look behind the surface of machines, at the judgments and choices that shaped how lines were drawn between what is allowed and what is not."[3] Firearms as we have known them (handguns, pistols, rifles) are notably absent from Wakandan material culture. Even the laser canon attached to Klaue's (Andy Serkis) arm was not meant to be a weapon; he admitted that he modified it from a mining tool. Why is the absence of firearms significant? One of the most prolific, profound, and irreversible technological changes on the Africa continent was the introduction and dispersion of the gun. The proliferation in firearms in West Africa in the 1700s destroyed several indigenous centers of technological production, including the smithing towns of Bassar and Bengho in West Africa,[4] and caused an entropic increase in political disintegration via increasingly deadly warfare.[5] The point is that Wakandan designers would have been well aware of firearms, but they chose not to design rifles and handguns for cultural reasons unstated.

For those of us familiar with Siri, Alexa, and Cortana, *Black Panther* offers us a vision of an Artificial Intelligence interface created with a particularly African orientation. Princess Shuri (portrayed by Letitia Wright) is assisted in her laboratory complex by an Artificial Intelligence system called Griot (voiced by South African-born comedian, Trevor Noah). The term *griot* refers to several traditions of oral history keeping in Western Africa. Historically, *griot* traditions vary slightly from culture to culture, but they were commonly tasked with incredible feats of institutional memory, remembering king's lists and ethnic histories stretching back as many as sixteen generations, generally without the aid of written records. The ways that griots would recite these memories would vary between cultures, but the histories could be performed via oral presentation, poetry, or song. Griot is also, notably, male. Queer History writer Dejan Jotanovic asks in *Bitch Magazine* in 2019 whether "The Future is Fembot. Can We Change the Direction of Gendered AI?" He made the argument that tech innovators "feminize" AI interfaces so that they can be perceived as "compliant, passive, cleanse of authority and agency . . . the perfect servant."[6] Another point of comparison is Ironman's Jarvis, an AI interface highly reminiscent of an archetypal British butler. If Jotanovic is correct that the tech innovators have replicated female subservience within AI, it is worth considering that, as many functions as *griots* serve, they are never described or defined as "assistants."

The narrated prologue to the film describes an ethnic rift stemming from the initial discovery of a new metal ore, called *vibranium*. When the Five Tribes that make up the Wakanda go to war over the metal, T'Challa's ancestor Bashenga ingests the Heart-Shaped herb becomes the first Black Panther and unites the tribes under one polity that will share the precious metal. While one of the Five Tribes, the Jabari, refuse to adopt or use the metal that caused the conflict, the other four tribes flourish technologically and economically, building a wealthy, scientifically advanced society. An archaeological perspective on the impact of *vibranium* offers a way to explore (1) how cultures accommodate technological change after the introduction of new materials, (2) ethnic and intercultural tensions that arise with the adoption of new technologies/raw materials, and (3) how this these tensions were expressed in the non-fictional spread of metal ores across the African continent. The story explores the conflicting ideologies of *technological progressivism*, represented by the new king, T'Challa, and the four tribes of Wakanda that adopted the use of *vibranium*, and *technological conservatism*, characterized by the isolated Jabari tribe.

Archaeologists have long commented on social conflicts related to technological change in precolonial and colonial Africa. How closely does *Black Panther's* narrative reflect the real-life social and ethnic conflicts concerning the ancient mining and working of metal ores on the continent? As metalworking spread unevenly across geographic space, why did certain groups refuse to adopt new technologies? As social rifts over technology continue in the present day, who, within a given cultural community, has the most influence over assessing the potential harm of new technological processes and products?

I am trained as an anthropological archaeologist in the U.S. tradition, so I will draw upon both archaeological and broader anthropological theories to discuss the cultural motivators of technological change. Modernist, racialized narratives have been weaponized against Africans and the African Diaspora since the late 1700s, equating a perceived lack of advanced technology with a lack of contribution to human "progress."[7] Anthropology has studied technology systematically since the early nineteenth century[8] and archaeology discourse on technological progress in Africa has reflected (and influenced) the social attitudes of each era.

As archaeology developed into a discipline in the Victorian era, White supremacist attitudes influenced disciplinary interpretations of Africa's material record. The technologies that were attested in Africa, such as metal working, were portrayed as static and somehow more primitive than similar technological processes in Europe and Asia due to the associations of African metallurgy with magic.[9] As archaeologist Shadreck Chirikure demonstrates, "Going back to Hegel in the 1820s, African societies and technologies such as iron working were thought to be in a 'deep and perpetual slumber' without any advancement."[10]

Both archaeology and anthropology make methodological and theoretical contributions to social, cultural, and behavioral approaches to technology. However, archaeology documents an enormous database of variability and change throughout the whole of the human past.[11] The archaeological study of technology has focused on cultural processes through time by "the manufacture, use, modification, and discard of things that were made."[12]

The focus on technology in the film illustrates a central tenet of the anthropology of technology: technological innovation is culturally situated, culturally contingent, and adopted selectively.[13] Culture itself enables technology to come into being. Cultural structures influence perceptions of what needs to be made and by whom. When we argue that technology is culturally contingent, this is a response to older, conventional explanations of technology (and culture) as simplistic adaptations to the environment. People living in similar environments sometimes create homologous technology, but more often than not, people across cultures express unique technological needs and desires in similar environments.

HOW AND WHY DOES TECHNOLOGY CHANGE?

Inventions tend to represent the social systems in which they were created or used. The study of any realm of human behavior (from religion to enculturation, from communication to ideology) can benefit from the addition of a technological perspective.[14] Technology changes by means of invention, diffusion, and adoption, and all three of these processes are meaningfully embedded in the fabric of a given culture. Archaeologists see technological invention, change, and progress, not as inevitabilities, but the result of collective actions motivated by ideals, needs, and desires. Technologies that succeed and endure are technologies that can be adapted to changing societal needs and values.[15] Technology is often *so* embedded in all realms of human activity that it is not easily segregated as a unit of study.[16]

Thus, archaeologists have endeavored to find the best means to explore the values that go into the design, manufacture, and accessibility of a given technology. Archaeologists investigate why certain materials are chosen over others and employed in the making of artifacts, for example, flint vs. quartz, iron vs. stone, wood vs. antler. These choices are especially interesting in cases where it is clear that the maker was considering factors other than the mechanical properties of the material. An interesting dilemma can arise when artisans have an ideological attachment to one material even when a new material is shown to have superior mechanical qualities.

Archaeologists Richard R. Wilk argues that technology changes when the collective needs of a society change or expand. While Marxians and materialists would see the needs that drive tech innovation in capitalist societies as starkly different than the needs that drive tech innovation in non-market societies, Wilk argues that all societies, including traditional societies, have the capacity to experience needs so novel that they must be addressed technologically.[17]

METALS AND CONFLICT IN THE AFRICAN PAST

From the perspective of Africanist archaeology, it is highly significant that the *Black Panther* saga begins with a metal ore. Metals endure in the archaeological record and have been valuable in helping us understand class, trade, ethnic interaction, and gender relationships in both historic era and ancient Africa. The adoption of metallurgy occurred differently across Africa, and the variation by region provides important points of comparison concerning the cultural consequences of innovation and technology transfer. As the mining, smelting, and casting of metals spread gradually over Africa, iron production often coexisted with, rather than replaced, the use of stone tools.[18] The founders of Wakanda not only recognized *vibranium* as the raw material for metal, they valued *vibranium*'s properties as superior to those of other metals, which would lead me to believe they must have practiced metalworking themselves or witnessed metal production elsewhere. The presence of the Egyptian goddess Bast in the film hints at Wakanda's connection to the Nile Valley, where metalworking spreads north to south from 4000 to 2600 BC.[19] Based on archaeological chronologies of incipient metalworking in Wakanda's vicinity,[20] I might speculatively place the beginnings of Wakanda's vibranium industry between 4000 and 800 BC.

Once established, metallurgy was neither static nor homogenous throughout the continent. Local and regional developments demonstrate a richly varied history of innovation and cross-cultural borrowing.[21] The spread of iron across the southern part of the African continent is loosely associated with the spread of intensive agriculture. The use of metal created farming tools that were more efficient, leading to greater agricultural productivity. Archaeologist Chirikure argues that:

> Metal hoes and axes made it far easier to cultivate the land and to clear the vegetation which in turn opened up more land for cultivation.[22] The burning of the trees produced ash, which increased the fertility of the land. These activities resulted in increased yields, which made it easier to sustain growing populations.[23]

It must be noted, however, that all communities adopted metals to facilitate food production. Some Aksumites (modern-day Ethiopia) used stone tools for cultivation until the early first-millennium AD because possession of metal correlated with class. Indeed, both Gurage and Kondo hide workers in modern Ethiopia still to this day and prefer to process animal skins with lithic tools rather than blades made of metal.[24]

The spread of ironworking is also associated with changes in conflict and warfare. Metals produced weapons were deadlier and more efficient in general.[25] Like with farming tools, the spread of metal for weapons was selective and culturally contingent, as some groups had other preferences. Take for example, the ancient Nubians, known throughout their neighboring Egypt and the Mediterranean world for their prowess with the bow. One of the Egyptian names for Nubia, *Ta-Seti*, translates into the phrase "Land of the Bow."[26] The famed Nubian archers preferred to shoot stone-tipped or bone-tipped arrows, long after iron tips became popular in Egypt and elsewhere.[27] Despite its advantages, Egypt only fully embraced iron 700 BC, more than six centuries after its adversaries, neighbors and trading partners adopted it around the Mediterranean.[28] The Twenty Fifth Dynasty pharaohs were defeated by iron-armed Assyrians in 691 BC,[29] right as our fictive Wakandans have been working with vibranium for just over 100 years.

Ironworking requires the development of specialized communities of people skilled in the arts of metallurgy. Sometimes these communities formed as castes within communities; other times, metallurgists formed ethnic enclaves unto themselves. The fact that the adoption of metallurgy required a reorganization of a given society no doubt contributed to the fact that could not or would not adapt to the requirements of its manufacture. In the film and in the comics, one of the five tribes is called the Mining Tribe, and they are responsible for harvesting the ore of Wakandan *vibranium*.

In addition to enabling and constraining human possibilities, technology establishes rights and obligations among major social actors.[30] Sometimes, as in the case with African metalworking, the social obligations proposed are found to be unacceptable to the potential adopters. In such a case as these new obligations would compete with existing social needs, communities have ways of placing checks on individual desires through leveling mechanisms, implicit restraints, and repressive practices.[31]

In nineteenth-century West Africa, ironworking technology changed because West African iron production had to fit into the new Atlantic World economic/industrial system. David Livingstone, a Scottish geographer and missionary in the 1800s, commented that African iron was of a better quality when compared to that produced in Europe in the late nineteenth century.[32] Under for as long as indigenous metalworking technologies were effective, there was no need to change them in favor of alien ones. Chirikure argues that African technologies changed with nineteenth-century colonialism imposed a value system based on capitalism and Christianity while directing heavy assaults on local technological practices. Under those conditions, African metalworkers had little or no choice in the changes, whereas in the past, other sociopolitical or cultural factors would have influenced the forms and/or means of production.[33]

European players disparaged African technological trajectories while coveting and disrupting those trajectories at the same time, and this contradiction is brought into sharp relief by Wakanda's nemesis, Ulysses Klaue (played by Andy Serkis). Throughout the movie, Klaue slurs Wakandans as "savages" and repeatedly articulates the perceived distinction between who should or should not have access to the most advanced technology in the world. The narrative is powerful because it is designed to play on the globally internalized association of the myth of a "backwards Africa." While the story does serve as a foil for historically racist tropes about Africa's technological primitiveness, it also sits in direct dialogue with issues of race and technology in the United States.

TECHNOLOGICAL PROGRESSIVISM VERSUS TECHNOLOGICAL CONSERVATISM

The prevalence of metal and ores in creation myths across cultures on the African continent is echoed, profoundly, in *Black Panther*'s explanation of *vibranium* and its role in Wakanda's origins. As the prologue goes, the crash of a meteor to Earth deposits a metal ore called *vibranium* into Wakanda's environment. The Jabari tribe takes the conservative stance and rejects the usage of the new material. The Jabari are outnumbered by the other four tribes who, taking the progressivist stance, want to develop and use the new metal. Despite the Jabari tribe's defection, the use of *vibranium* goes on to have profound political, cultural, and economic impact of Wakanda's future.

The Jabari tribe may have been portrayed as adversaries to the Wakandan throne, but several aspects of their opting out deserve attention. First, they did not seem to suffer any political punishment for choosing to abstain from the use of *vibranium*. They were free to live out their lives for generations, according to their previous traditions. Second, they were free to challenge T'Challa's ascension to the throne through the tradition of ritual combat. They were not forbidden from participating in a seminal political process.

The ideology of technological progressivism assumes that technological change is a societal good in and of itself.[34] Futurist Gerd Leonhard describes technological progressivism as tending toward creating a future on blind optimism.[35] Indeed, *Black Panther* does not so much escape the trap of technology-as-panacea as it leans into it, demonstrated in the scene in which an injured CIA agent Everett Ross, played by Martin Freeman, asserts that "bullet wounds don't magically heal overnight." "They do here," T'Challa's younger sister, Princess Shuri (Letitia Wright) counters, "But not by magic, by *technology*." Shuri's response to Ross's presence offers a glance at Shuri's moral core. Shuri does not hesitate to save Ross, although one of the movie's most famous lines ("Oh, you scared me, colonizer!) reveals that Shuri has no illusions about Ross's innocence. When T'Challa first brings Ross to the lab, Shuri quips that she will have fun fixing "another broken white boy." We surmise that Shuri herself must have also been instrumental in treating Sam "Bucky" Barnes, a.k.a. The Winter Soldier, another injured character brought to Wakanda by T'Challa earlier in the MCU timeline. After pronouncing that he will live, Shuri tenderly touches the shoulder of an unconscious Ross, showing sympathy for an injured stranger. Shuri's optimism, that focuses on the human hardships that technological insights can overcome, drives proponents of technological progressivism to privilege the potential substantial benefits (like life-saving medical techniques) over concern that associated innovations can also be used to do harm.

The ideology of technological conservatism proposes a more cautious approach to the adoption of new technologies, in that technological invention upsets continuity, it changes who we are as well as how we live our lives on Earth, and that change is not always beneficial.[36]

Conservative and progressive stances in technology pivot around the awareness of unintended consequences. Progressivist views of unintended consequences tend to imply that is not possible or even necessary to forecast the negative consequences of new technology.[37] It also stands that the intentions behind technology's design, use, and distribution are not necessarily fixed to a specific moment in time. As human relationships to artifacts change through time, the meaning and function of those artifacts change. Just because the designer did not intend an artifact to be used toward a certain purpose, does not mean that the designer cannot benefit and further adapt the invention toward new uses (i.e., Facebook levering user data rather than just selling ads). As Jasanoff argues, however, somewhere within that trajectory of an artifact evolving new usage, new meanings, and new avenues to help or harm, citizens have to decide how inventors, manufacturers, and distributors will be held accountable for what they are or are not even willing to foresee.[38]

The objections of the Jabari mirror modern tensions over technological risk assessment. Jasanoff argues that practice of risk assessment in the United States values change over continuity, and subordinates concerns over long-term impacts to visible, short-term hazards.[39] Jasanoff defines *technological determinism* as considering technological invention to have "an unstoppable momentum, reshaping society to fit its insatiable demands."[40] In *Black Panther*, the technological innovation enabled by *vibranium* is as much an actor in this drama as any of the heroes. Even while treating the Jabaris' viewpoint with empathy, the ethos of the movie does not wholly divest from the hegemonic association of advanced technological progress with status, and more acutely, *legitimacy* on the international stage. Without *vibranium*, and the technological legacy it enabled, would Wakanda or any nation in the global south have the right to wield such international political influence?

THE ETHICS OF INVENTION AND DISTRIBUTION: NAKIA'S CRITIQUE

As we have seen with both ironworking and glass production in Africa, the introduction of new technology presents a given society with an array of ethical dilemmas. Who, within each society, is allowed to opine on these dilemmas and decide how new technologies are put to use? When a culture promotes the worship of technology as its own end, citizens are discouraged from interrogating the ethics that drive technological innovation.[41] In *Black Panther*, one of the principle ethical dilemmas concerning Wakandan technology is their state policy of political isolationism.

Nakia (Lupita Nyong'o), T'Challa's heroic and principled love interest, challenges T'Challa to put Wakanda's technology to a higher, greater purpose. We first see Nakia when the Dora Milaje track her down using a sophisticated positioning system in their aircraft. T'Challa enters the operation in order to extract Nakia from her undercover work with a Boko Haram style terrorist group. His goal is not to end the group's activities, but to invite Nakia to his ascension ceremony; his disbanding of the terrorist unit is all but incidental. Nakia has to stop T'Challa from shooting one of the terrorists, by pointing out that the potential victim was actually a child soldier. We see from Nakia's initial introduction into the story that the major barrier in Nakia and T'Challa's relationship is that they see Wakanda, and its place in the world, quite differently.

We also see Nakia challenge the general of the Dora Milaje, Okoye (Danai Gurira), who expresses loyalty to a throne rather than to the recently deposed T'Challa. What sets Nakia apart from the other main characters is a very specific human-first politic. Through that human-first politic, Nakia criticizes Wakanda's policies of inaction that refuse to take into account context or extenuation. Through Nakia's argument, we get a glimpse of the evolution and the negotiation of the moral philosophy driving Wakandan technological innovation.

From Wakanda's fictive vantage point, somewhere in the vicinity of Uganda, T'Challa could throw a stone in any direction of Wakanda's borders and locate social ills and suffering that might greatly benefit from Wakanda's resources. Princess Shuri's lab is a scientific wonderland, and her skills as a wunderkind physician are central to the plot of several Marvel movies. It is not wholly inappropriate to wonder what Princess Shuri has been doing to combat HIV/AIDS in eastern Africa. Infant mortality dropped globally and dramatically between 1990 and 2015, but rates in Africa remained five times higher than those in Europe according to the WHO.[42] If this is the Africa in which we situate Wakanda, then the implications of Wakanda's isolationism present a severe ethnical quandary. Indeed, the suffering a fictional Wakanda's isolationist stance would have ignored is easy for viewers to surmise,[43] but within the film, the only two characters who stand in opposition to these views are Killmonger and Nakia.

In protest of T'Challa's isolationist policy, dissent, Nakia vows to him that she will continue to work as an operative outside of Wakanda's borders. As much as the royal family loves and respects her, Nakia's arguments against Wakanda's isolationist policies have apparently gone unheeded. It is fortunate indeed that T'Challa happens to be in love with her so that she holds the king's ear; without that personal relationship, the viewers would see not only other argument against Wakanda's isolationist policies outside of Killmonger's. Killmonger's father, N'Jobu (played by Sterling K. Brown), was so driven by his conviction that Wakandan technology could deliver liberation for African Americans and the diaspora, he was driven to acts of sedition. The violence of Killmonger's own actions places his arguments against

Wakanda's isolationism in the mouth of a problematic messenger. Nakia's pleas offer a more reasoned, if more universally palatable, call to action.

Social anxieties around the potential harm of imminent technology are often ameliorated by institutional risk assessment. The problem with risk assessment, according to Jasanoff is that adverse consequences are dismissed as unfortunate human errors by people who are (1) socially and financially insulated from those affects and (2) stand to profit regardless of the negative consequence to others.[44] Meanwhile, the most vulnerable people get very little say at the inception of technological developments that may have negative consequences that affect them disproportionately. In other words, what Leonhard describes as "blind optimism"[45] of the most protected people in society helps them develop technologies that gamble with the futures of the most vulnerable.

Nakia's objections can also be seen as mirroring Jasanoff's argument that risk assessment, in its current iteration, subordinates justice for all members of society to the economic benefit and advantage of product developers.[46] *Technocracy* is a system of governance in which technology is managed and controlled by human actors, to the exclusion of those who do not have specialized technological knowledge and skills.[47] During the Renaissance, the concept of craftsmanship was subordinated to the exaltation of theoretical knowledge (a distinction rooted in the writings of Plato).[48] Anthropologist Timothy Ingold goes on to argue that the debasement of craft becomes one of the hallmarks of modernity.[49] The idea of theoretician as superior to the craftsperson becomes (according to Ingold) the basis of technocracy and technocratic policies.

How a culture envisions its future has great bearing on how people in that culture will assess the risk of new technologies.[50] I deliberately use the word culture instead of society, because in a multicultural society like the United States, it is not society as a whole that gets to weigh on the risks of new technologies. The power to determine what is too risky lies almost unilaterally in homogeneous cultural enclaves like Silicon Valley and centers of biotech research, like San Diego, and the right to weigh in on technological futures is deeply unequal along ethnic lines. This point ties into Shuri's vision for Oakland. In these communities, which are by and large culturally homogenous, frameworks like *transhumanism* congeal.[51] An extreme form of technological progressivism, transhumanism, is a "rush to the edge of the unknown" with a dogmatic disdain for the potential negative consequences.[52]

Imagining a real-world future with technology origination in service to distinctly African ethics and ideals, or at the very least, antiracist ideals, is not something that can be accomplished without a seat at the table where technologies are conceived; it will never happen if we are only allowed to assess them for possible risk after they are completed.

OPTING OUT: WHAT WE LEARN FROM THE JABARI

In addition to illustrating how the social implication of new technology can exacerbate ethnic tensions, the story of the Jabari also demonstrates the difficulty of choosing not to participate in certain technological changes, an action known in modern parlance as "opting out." From PredPol (an algorithmic software used by police to "predict" crime) to designer babies, there are strong, logical reasons for apprehension surrounding our current technological revolution.[53] Sociologist Ruha Benjamin explains how technologies such as PredPol harm neighborhoods through the ramifications of aggressive law enforcement and over-policing.[54] The rate of technological change is rapid accelerating; Moore's Law, a 1965 prediction that computers would increase in capability while their components shrink and their prices decrease in every two years, has expired.[55] Leonhard warns that a technological megashift is coming and that community fortunes will be heavily influenced by their levels of preparation. The firms, corporations, and entrepreneurs who expect to profit the most from the imminent megashift are largely unconcerned with the potential environmental, political, and social harm to the marginalized.[56] As tech innovators seek to exploit addictive behaviors and the desire for convenience to make human populations exceeding trackable, predictable, and ultimately "programmable," Leonhard argues that we must begin now to codify into law the human right to decline participation in intrusive technologies.[57]

Jasanoff argues that as an instrument of governance, technology rules us as much as laws do, and she documents the ways in which U.S. policy has not adequately addressed the failure of our tech visionaries to foresee, forecast, and forestall potential harm.[58] If populations are disturbed by the social consequences and implications of technological change, the only choice we have is hope that enough people will "opt out" to the extent that avoidance can shift the Invisible Hand. The frightening thing is that, as the Gun Debate makes clear every week, we have very little power to stop fellow citizens from creating, replicating, and distributing technologies that we fear may do us or our descendants harm. This dilemma goes back at least as far as the Iron Age.

TECHNOLOGICAL FUTURES AND THE AFRICAN DIASPORA: THE BATTLE FOR OAKLAND

Technology has been a tool, some would say unwittingly, for reproducing forms of oppression and domination. As the forms take new expressions, technological change often outpaces our efforts to develop language that describes and defends against these new expressions of inequality.[59]

Biotechnology, in particular, has already seen several researchers ring the alarm for the rise of biotechnologies that blatantly imperil people of impoverished backgrounds and racialized identities.[60] Assessing the potential harm of these technologies after they've been designed is not effective. As mentioned at the beginning of the chapter, technological innovation reflects a community's goals. We need a critical eye on the goals of tech innovation.

While some scholars are actively watching and warning of technologies with the potential to harm communities, other scholars are calling for an overhaul of the motivations that drive tech design from its inception. Leonhard proposes a proactive approach to shifting the values that drive technological innovation. CORE stands for Compassion and Creativity, Originality, Reciprocity and Responsibility, and Empathy. Leonhard's hope is that if technologies designed to profit from surveillance capitalism, predictive policing, or algorithmic bias were to be scrutinized in the design phase under the CORE rubric, designers would do better at catching potentially problematic inventions. Critical Information researcher Syed Mustafa Ali has a related rubric for reflexivity in his Decolonial Computing model, a "critical" project that interrogates who is doing computing, where they are doing it, and, thereby, what computing means both epistemologically (i.e., in relation to knowing) and ontologically (i.e., in relation to being).[61]

As Shuri and T'Challa declare their intention to build a technology center in Oakland, I hope that they are bringing all the lessons they so recently and painfully learned. I hope their technological prowess is balanced with ethical judgment. I hope that M'Baku's voice is heard, demanding that we routinely stop and think about what could be irreparably harmed or lost. I hope we hear the voice of Nakia, reminding us at every moment that a building bounded by technological utopia surrounded by suffering is a nightmare, and quite unacceptable. As the story of the Bay Area has proven, technological genius without the proper ethics in place is nothing but a tool for the reproduction of inequality. Where is our Nakia to challenge us on our values and the consequences of the tech innovations that make only some of us feel secure?

CONCLUSION

Here is an opportunity to compare the ethical dilemma in Wakanda to similar ethical dilemmas in the current technological trajectory of the United States. Scholars of science and technology studies, or STS, are in some disagreement with the some of the largest stakeholders in Silicon Valley as to what constitutes ethics in the realm of technology. Benjamin,[62] Leonhard,[63] Jasanoff,[64] and Ali,[65] among others, have demanded that Big Tech firms like Google,

Apple, and Facebook, to name a few, pay attention to how their technologies exacerbate and reproduce social inequality. When tech companies do pay attention to ethics, their orientation toward problems of racism and inequality are quite different: they answer inequality by proposing wider, more equal access to the technologies that they are already committed to creating. The aforementioned STS scholars are asking that tech companies think about how their innovations can cause problems for vulnerable communities; Tech answers that call by planning wider distribution to problematic technology, skipping over the reflection that is being asked of them and completely missing the point.

Added to the problem of inequality, in the conceptualization and creation of technology, is the pace at which our world is changing in irreversible ways. The problem, as Leonhard sees it, is that some technological revolutions are as pervasive as they are irreversible. Leonhard defines the Singularity as "the moment when computers finally trump and then surpass human brains in computer power" and then warns that this will only occur after we are "utterly dependent on machines in every aspect of our lives."[66] As impractical as it is to not own a cell phone or some sort of personal computing device, what are the chances that a U.S. citizen could find or keep a job if they did not want to employ those technologies? If and when opting out of technology is possible, the socioeconomic cost could be catastrophic.

Reflexivity is made more difficult by homogeneity; Big Tech has too few people in the room who are willing and able to question the validity of shared cultural assumptions. Timnit Gebru, a leading scholar the ethics around AI—and a Black woman—served the much-needed role of "Nakia" for Google until her contentious exit in December of 2020.[67] Gebru's concerns about AI language models containing troubling risk of harm, including racial bias, were forcibly dismissed, leading many people, including colleagues, peers, and members of Congress, to question whether companies such as Google can be trusted to successfully monitor their own ethics and recognize the ways in which their products can hurt marginalized people.[68] Thus, we step into the future carrying a conflict as old as iron and age-old questions about who might be harmed by the next wonderous new thing. Hopefully, the heroes of *Black Panther* remind us to proceed with caution, because genius must be guided by wisdom.

NOTES

1. Michael B. Schiffer, ed., *Anthropological Perspectives on Technology* (Albuquerque: University of New Mexico Press, 2001), 3.

2. Florian Opillard, "Resisting the politics of displacement in the San Francisco bay area: Anti-gentrification activism in the tech boom 2.0," *European Journal of American Studies* 10, no. 10–13 (2015): 1.

3. Sheila Jasanoff, *The Ethics of Invention: Technology and the Human Future* (New York: W. W. Norton & Company, 2016), 11.

4. Walter Rodney, *How Europe Underdeveloped Africa* (New York: Verso Trade, 2018).

5. Warren Whatley, "The Gun-slave Hypothesis and the 18th Century British Slave Trade," *Explorations in Economic History* 67 (2018).

6. Dejan Jotanovic, "The Future is Fembot. Can We Change the Direction of Gendered AI?," *Bitch Magazine. A Feminist Response to Pop Culture* 79 (Summer 2018): 32.

7. Chris Godsen, "Race and Racism in Archeology: Introduction," *World Archeology* 38, no. 1 (2006).

8. Schiffer, *Anthropological Perspectives on Technology*, 4.

9. Peter Schmidt, *Iron Technology in East Africa: Symbolism, Science, and Archaeology* (Bloomington: Indiana University Press, 1997); Shadreck Chirikure, *Metals in Past Societies: A Global Perspective on Indigenous African Metallurgy* (New York: Springer, 2015).

10. Chirikure, *Metals in Past Societies*, 159.

11. Schiffer, *Anthropological Perspectives on Technology*, 1.

12. Ibid., xi.

13. Ibid., Introduction.

14. Ibid.

15. Jasanoff, *The Ethics of Invention*, 32.

16. Schiffer, *Anthropological Perspectives on Technology*, 9.

17. Richard Wilk, "Toward an Archaeology of Needs," in *Anthropological Perspectives on Technology*, ed. Michael B. Schiffer (Albuquerque: University of New Mexico Press, 2001), 107–122.

18. Terry S. Childs and Eugenia W. Herbert, "Metallurgy and its Consequences," in *African Archaeology: A Critical Introduction*, ed. Ann Brower Stahl (Hoboken, NJ: Wiley-Blackwell, 2004), 276–300.

19. Chirikure, *Metals in Past Societies*, 17.

20. Chirikure, *Metals in Past Societies*, 17.

21. Ibid.

22. David Phillipson, *African Archaeology* (Cambridge: Cambridge University Press, 2005), 214

23. Chirikure, *Metals in Past Societies*, 127.

24. Phillipson, *African Archaeology*; Kathryn Weedman, "Gender and Stone Tools: An Ethnographic Study of the Konsoand Gamo Hideworkers of Southern Ethiopia," *Gender and Hide Production* 11 (2005): 175; Kathryn Weedman, "An Ethnoarchaeological Study of Hafting and Stone Tool Diversity Among the Gamo of Ethiopia." *Journal of Archaeological Method and Theory* 13, no. 3 (2006): 188–237; Kathryn Weedman Arthur, "Feminine Knowledge and Skill Reconsidered: Women and Flaked Stone Tools," *American Anthropologist* 112, no. 2 (2010).

25. Childs and Herbert. "Metallurgy and its Consequences."

26. Stuart Tyson Smith, *Wretched Kush: Ethnic Identities and Boundries in Egypt's Nubian Empire* (London; New York: Routledge, 2003); Timothy Kendall, "Egypt and Nubia," in *The Egyptian World*, ed. Timothy Kendall (London and New York: Routledge, 2007), 429–444.

27. Anthony John Arkell, "Iron in the Meroitic Ages," *Antiquity* 19, no. 76 (1945): 213–214; John Desmond Clark et al., "Interpretations of Prehistoric Technology from Ancient Egyptian and Other Sources: Part 1: Ancient Egyptian Bows and Arrows and Their Relevance for African Prehistory," *Paléorient* 2, no. 2 (1974); Bastien Jakob, "Holocene Lithic Industries in Nubia," in *Handbook of Ancient Nubia,* ed. Dietrich Raue (Berlin: De Gruyter, 2019), 239; and Carolyn Graves-Brown, "Flint and Forts: The Role of Flint in Late Middle-New Kingdom Egyptian Weaponry," in *Walls of the Prince: Egyptian Interactions with Southwest Asia in Antiquity*, ed. Timothy P. Harrison, Edward B. Banning, and Stanley Klassen (Leiden: Brill, 2015), 37–59.

28. Paul T. Craddock, "From Hearth to Furnace: Evidences for the Earliest Metal Smelting Technologies in the Eastern Mediterranean," *Paléorient* 26, no. 2 (2000): 151–165; Augustin F. C. Holl, "Metals and Precolonial African Society," in *Ancient African Metallurgy: The Sociocultural Context*, ed. Joseph O. Vogel (Walnut Creek: AltaMira Press, 2000).

29. Chirikure, *Metals in Past Societies*.

30. Jasanoff, *The Ethics of Invention*, 9.

31. Wilk, "Toward an Archaeology of Needs."

32. Shadreck Chirikure, "New Light on Njanja Iron Working: Towards a Systematic Encounter between Ethnohistory and Archaeometallurgy," *The South African Archaeological Bulletin* 61, no. 184 (2006).

33. Chirikure, *Metals in Past Societies*.

34. Jasanoff, *The Ethics of Invention*.

35. Gerd Leonhard, *Technology vs. Humanity: The Coming Clash Between Man and Machine* (London: Fast Future Publishing, 2016).

36. Jasanoff, *The Ethics of Invention*, 5.

37. Ibid., 23.

38. Ibid., 26.

39. Ibid., 36.

40. Ibid., 14.

41. Ibid; Leonhard, *Technology vs. Humanity*.

42. Jasanoff, *The Ethics of Invention*, 5.

43. Hayden Wilkinson, "The Moral Horror of Black Panther," *The Artifice*, January 13, 2019, https://the-artifice.com/black-panther-moral-horror/.

44. Jasanoff, *The Ethics of Invention*.

45. Leonhard, *Technology vs. Humanity*.

46. Jasanoff, *The Ethics of Invention*, 36.

47. Ibid., 19.

48. Timothy Ingold, "Beyond Art and Technology: The Anthropology of Skill," in *Anthropological Perspectives on Technology*, ed. Michael B. Schiffer (Albuquerque: University of New Mexico Press, 2001).

49. Ingold, "Beyond Art and Technology," 20.
50. Jasanoff, *The Ethics of Invention*, 35.
51. Lisa Ikemoto, "Race to Health: Racialized Discourses in a Transhuman World," *DePaul J. Health Care Law* 9, no. 2 (2005).
52. Leonhard, *Technology vs. Humanity*.
53. Ruha Benjamin, ed., *Captivating Technology: Race, Carceral Technoscience, and Liberatory Imagination in Everyday Life* (Durham, NC: Duke University Press, 2019).
54. Ibid.
55. David Rotman, "We're not prepared for the end of Moore's Law." *MIT Technology Review*, February 24, 2020, https://www.technologyreview.com/2020/02/24/905789/were-not-prepared-for-the-end-of-moores-law/.
56. Leonhard, *Technology vs. Humanity*.
57. Leonhard, *Technology vs. Humanity*.
58. Jasanoff, *The Ethics of Invention*, 8.
59. Jasanoff, *The Ethics of Invention*, 28.
60. Ikemoto, "Race to Health."
61. Syed Mustafa Ali, "A Brief Introduction to Decolonial Computing," *Association for Computing Machinery* 22, no. 4 (Summer 2016).
62. Benjamin, *Captivating Technology*.
63. Leonard, *Technology vs. Humanity*.
64. Jasanoff, *The Ethics of Invention*.
65. Ali, "A Brief Introduction to Decolonial Computing."
66. Leonhard, *Technology vs. Humanity*, 217.
67. Zoe Schiffer, "Timnit Gebru's team at Google is going public with their side of the story," *The Verge,* December 7, 2020, https://www.theverge.com/2020/12/7/22158501/timnit-gebru-team-google-public-statement-fired; Julia Carrie Wong, "More than 1,200 Google workers condemn firing of AI scientist Timnit Gebru," *The Guardian,* December 4, 2020, https://www.theguardian.com/technology/2020/dec/04/timnit-gebru-google-ai-fired-diversity-ethics.
68. Karen Hao, "Congress wants answers from Google about Timnit Gebru's firing," *MIT Technology Review*, December 17, 2020, https://www.technologyreview.com/2020/12/17/1014994/congress-wants-answers-from-google-about-timnit-gebrus-firing/.

WORKS CITED

Ali, Syed Mustafa. "A Brief Introduction to Decolonial Computing." *Association for Computing Machinery* 22, no. 4 (Summer 2016): 16–21.
Arkell, A. J. "Iron in the Meroitic Ages." *Antiquity* 19, no. 76 (1945): 213–214.
Arthur, Kathryn Weedman. "Feminine Knowledge and Skill Reconsidered: Women and Flaked Stone Tools." *American Anthropologist* 112, no. 2 (2010): 228–243.
Benjamin, Ruha, ed. *Captivating Technology: Race, Carceral Technoscience, and Liberatory Imagination in Everyday Life*. Durham, NC: Duke University Press, 2019.

Brown, J. "Early Iron Production." *Rhodesian Prehistory* 7 (1973): 3–7.
Chikwendu, V. E., P. T. Craddock, R. M. Farquhar, Thurston Shaw, and A. C. Umeji. "Nigerian Sources of Copper, Lead and Tin for the Igbo-Ukwu Bronzes." *Science and Archaeology* 30 (1989): 27–36.
Childs, S. Terry, and Eugenia W. Herbert. "Metallurgy and its Consequences." In *African Archaeology: A Critical Introduction*, edited by Ann Brower Stahl, 276–300. Hoboken, NJ: Wiley-Blackwell, 2004.
Chirikure, Shadreck. "New Light on Njanja Iron Working: Towards a Systematic Encounter between Ethnohistory and Archaeometallurgy." *The South African Archaeological Bulletin* 61, no. 184 (2006): 142–151.
Chirikure, Shadreck. *Metals in Past Societies: A Global Perspective on Indigenous African Metallurgy*. New York: Springer, 2015.
Clark, J. Desmond, James L. Phillips, and Preston S. Staley. "Interpretations of Prehistoric Technology from Ancient Egyptian and other Sources: Part 1: Ancient Egyptian Bows and Arrows and Their Relevance for African Prehistory." *Paléorient* 2, no. 2 (1974): 323–388.
Cline, Walter Buchanan. *Mining and Metallurgy in Negro Africa*. Menasha, WI: George Banta Publishing Company, 1937.
Craddock, Paul T. "From Hearth to Furnace: Evidences for the Earliest Metal Smelting Technologies in the Eastern Mediterranean." *Paléorient* 26, no. 2 (2000): 151–165.
Curtin, Philip D. "The lure of Bambuk gold." *The Journal of African history* 14, no. 4 (1973): 623–631.
Dobres, Marcia-Anne. "Meaning in the Making: Agency and the Social Embodiment of Technology and Art." In *Anthropological Perspectives on Technology*, edited by Michael B. Schiffer, 47–76. Albuquerque: University of New Mexico Press, 2001.
Ford, Richard Thompson. "Black Panther: An Afrocentric Ethical Fable." *The American Interest*, February 22, 2018. https://www.the-american-interest.com/2018/02/22/black-panther-afrocentric-ethical-fable/.
Godsen, Chris. "Race and Racism in Archeology: Introduction." *World Archeology* 38, no. 1 (2006).
Goody, Jack. "Technology, Tradition and the State in Africa." Cambridge: Cambridge University Press, 1971.
Gould, Richard A. "From Sail to Steam at Sea in the Late Nineteenth Century." In *Anthropological Perspectives on Technology*, edited by Michael Brian Schiffer, 193–213. Albuquerque: University of New Mexico Press, 2001.
Graves-Brown, Carolyn. "Flint and Forts: The Role of Flint in Late Middle-New Kingdom Egyptian Weaponry." In *Walls of the Prince: Egyptian Interactions with Southwest Asia in Antiquity*, edited by Timothy P. Harrison, Edward B. Banning, and Stanley Klassen, 37–59. Leiden: Brill, 2015.
Hao, Karen. "Congress wants answers from Google about Timnit Gebru's firing." *MIT Technology Review*, December 17, 2020. https://www.technologyreview.com/2020/12/17/1014994/congress-wants-answers-from-google-about-timnit-gebrus-firing/.
Holl, Augustin F. C. "Metals and Precolonial African Society." In *Ancient African Metallurgy: The Sociocultural Context*, edited by Joseph O. Vogel, 1–82. Walnut Creek: AltaMira Press, 2000.

Ikemoto, Lisa C. "Race to Health: Racialized Discourses in a Transhuman World." *DePaul J. Health Care Law* 9, no. 2 (2005): 1101.

Ingold, Timothy. "Beyond Art and Technology: The Anthropology of Skill." In *Anthropological Perspectives on Technology*, edited by Michael B. Schiffer, 17–31. Albuquerque: University of New Mexico Press, 2001.

Jakob, Bastien. "Holocene Lithic Industries in Nubia." In *Handbook of Ancient Nubia*, edited by Dietrich Raue. Berlin: De Gruyter, 2019.

Jasanoff, Sheila. *The Ethics of Invention: Technology and the Human Future*. New York: W. W. Norton & Company, 2016.

Jotanovic, Dejan. "The Future is Fembot. Can We Change the Direction of Gendered AI?" *Bitch Magazine. A Feminist Response to Pop Culture* 79 (Summer 2018): 30–33.

Kendall, Timothy. "Egypt and Nubia." In *The Egyptian World*, edited by Timothy Kendall, 429–444. London and New York: Routledge, 2007.

Lankton, James W., O. Akin Ige, and Thilo Rehren. "Early primary glass production in southern Nigeria." *Journal of African Archaeology* 4, no. 1 (2006): 111–138.

Leonhard, Gerd. *Technology vs. Humanity: The Coming Clash Between Man and Machine*. London: Fast Future Publishing, 2016.

Opillard, Florian. "Resisting the Politics of Displacement in the San Francisco Bay Area: Anti-gentrification Activism in the Tech Boom 2.0." *European Journal of American Studies* 10, no. 10–13 (2015).

Pfaffenberger, Brian. "Technical Ritual: Of Yams, Canoes, and the Delegitimation of Technology Studies in Social Anthropology." In *ESRC Seminar on Technology as Skilled Practice, University of Manchester*, vol. 18, 1995.

Phillipson, David W. *African Archaeology*. Cambridge: Cambridge University Press, 2005.

Rickard, Thomas Arthur. "The Primitive Smelting of Iron." *American Journal of Archaeology* 43, no. 1 (1939): 85–101.

Rodney, Walter. *How Europe Underdeveloped Africa*. New York: Verso Trade, 2018.

Rotman, David. "We're not prepared for the end of Moore's Law." *MIT Technology Review*, February 24, 2020. https://www.technologyreview.com/2020/02/24/905789/were-not-prepared-for-the-end-of-moores-law/.

Schiffer, Michael B., ed. *Anthropological Perspectives on Technology*. Albuquerque: University of New Mexico Press, 2001.

Schiffer, Zoe. "Timnit Gebru's team at Google is going public with their side of the story." *The Verge*, December 7, 2020. https://www.theverge.com/2020/12/7/22158501/timnit-gebru-team-google-public-statement-fired.

Schmidt, Peter R. *Iron Technology in East Africa: Symbolism, Science, and Archaeology*. Bloomington: Indiana University Press, 1997.

Shaw, Thurstan. *Igbo-Ukwu: An Account of Archaeological Discoveries in Eastern Nigeria*. London: Faber & Faber, 1970.

Smith, Stuart Tyson. *Wretched Kush: Ethnic Identities and Boundries in Egypt's Nubian Empire*. London; New York: Routledge, 2003.

Suchman, Lucy. "Building Bridges: Practice-based ethnographies of contemporary technology." In *Anthropological Perspectives on Technology*, edited by Michael B. Schiffer, 163–177. Albuquerque: University of New Mexico Press, 2001.

Thomas, Nicholas. *Entangled Objects: Exchange, Material Culture, and Colonialism in the Pacific*. Cambridge: Harvard University Press, 2009.
Walker, William H. "Ritual Technology in an Extranatural World." In *Anthropological Perspectives on Technology*, edited by Michael B. Schiffer, 87–106. Albuquerque: University of New Mexico Press, 2001.
Weedman, Kathryn. "Gender and Stone Tools: An Ethnographic Study of the Konsoand Gamo Hideworkers of Southern Ethiopia." *Gender and Hide Production* 11 (2005).
———. "An Ethnoarchaeological Study of Hafting and Stone Tool Diversity Among the Gamo of Ethiopia." *Journal of Archaeological Method and Theory* 13, no. 3 (2006): 188–237.
Whatley, Warren C. "The gun-slave hypothesis and the 18th century British slave trade." *Explorations in Economic History* 67 (2018): 80–104.
Wilk, Richard R. "Toward an Archaeology of Needs." In *Anthropological Perspectives on Technology,* edited by Michael B. Schiffer, 107–122. Albuquerque: University of New Mexico Press, 2001.
Wilkinson, Hayden. "The Moral Horror of Black Panther." *The Artifice*, January 13, 2019. https://the-artifice.com/black-panther-moral-horror/.
Winner, Langdon. "Do Artifacts have Politics?" *Daedalus* 109, no. 1 (1980): 121–136.
Wong, Julia Carrie. "More than 1,200 Google workers condemn firing of AI scientist Timnit Gebru." *The Guardian*, December 4, 2020. https://www.theguardian.com/technology/2020/dec/04/timnit-gebru-google-ai-fired-diversity-ethics.

FILMS

Black Panther. Directed by Ryan Coogler. United States: Walt Disney Studios Motion Pictures, 2018.
Avengers: Infinity War. Directed by Anthony and Joe Russo. United States: Walt Disney Studios Motion Pictures, 2018.

Chapter 14

Reflections on *Black Panther* and the Traditions of Third Cinema

Cynthia Baron

As the eighteenth Marvel Cinematic Universe movie and an addition to film and television depictions of Black superheroes from the 1970s forward, there certainly is value in studying *Black Panther* (Ryan Coogler, 2018) in relation to those media productions.[1] Because the film is based on Marvel Comics characters visualized by multiple artists for more than fifty years, Coogler's film also warrants analysis as one representation of the comic book characters and their world.[2] In addition, as coeditor Renée T. White points out, the film's use of science-fiction conventions to reimagine "the past, present, and futures of the African Diaspora" makes it useful to consider *Black Panther* in relation to Afrofuturist art, music, literature, and cinema.[3]

Narrowing the inquiry, this chapter explores aesthetic and thematic parallels linking *Black Panther* to international Third Cinema traditions, which have offered alternatives to corporate filmmaking and apolitical art cinema since the mid-twentieth century. "For an Imperfect Cinema," written in 1969 by Cuban filmmaker Julio García Espinosa, anchors the analysis of *Black Panther* and viewers' sometimes disparate ideas about the film's meaning and significance. Like "An Aesthetic of Hunger" by Glauber Roca (1965), "Towards a Third Cinema" by Fernando Solanas and Octavio Getino (1969), and "Problems of Form and Content in Revolutionary Cinema" by Jorge Sanjinés (1979), "For an Imperfect Cinema" is one of the key Third Cinema manifestos.[4]

Black Panther does not satisfy Espinosa's modernist vision that the "future lies with folk art" or his idealistic stance that Third Cinema should avoid the commercial "exhibitionism" of "getting shown in established theatres and circuits."[5] Yet the film vividly fulfills his vision that politically progressive departures from both mainstream and elitist cinema "above all show the process which generates the [social or political] problem."[6] For instance, *Black*

Panther gives ample credence to the rage that fills Killmonger/N'Jadaka (Michael B. Jordan), as T'Challa (Chadwick Boseman) repeatedly highlights the circumstances that led his abandoned cousin to formulate a militarist response to racial injustice. Furthermore, by using popular culture material to explore society's divergent responses to systemic racism, *Black Panther* exemplifies Espinosa's view that progressive films can use "whatever genre, or all genres" to create cinema that can "enjoy itself despite everything which conspires to negate enjoyment."[7] The contrasts and connections between Espinosa's ideas and *Black Panther*'s intertwined commercial status and political post-modernism prompt this essay to analyze opposing arguments about the film to better illustrate how *Black Panther* contributes to progressive Third Cinema traditions and ongoing cultural-aesthetic processes of re-imagining Blackness.

As will be discussed below, some viewers do not see *Black Panther* as a progressive text. Others think it even sustains right-wing ideas. More often, audiences see the film as revolutionary, since it puts Black experiences at the center of a mainstream movie, supplanting myths that sustain White male supremacy with decolonized images and sounds grounded in pan-African "myth and ritual."[8] Weighing the diverging assessments, the discussion considers questions about the film's progressive credentials and concludes that *Black Panther* fully responds to Espinosa's call for films made for people "who struggle," for films that explore the "problems and difficulties" they face as they seek to constructively transform their worlds.[9]

THIRD CINEMA AND OPPOSING VIEWS ABOUT *BLACK PANTHER*

What might it mean for a film to belong to Third Cinema? Filmmakers and theorists explain that Third Cinema aims to decolonize minds, contribute to the development of radical consciousness, frame local issues as part of international struggle, and move beyond "facile dichotomies such as traditional/modern, realist/modernist, modernist/postmodernist."[10] The films illuminate connections between historical-systemic factors and situations in the present. Images, sounds, and narrative elements draw on marginalized cultural traditions to create meaning for the oppressed and Diasporic people.

While not identical to Third World filmmaking, Third Cinema shares common ground with Third World liberation movements. Film theorists Ella Shohat and Robert Stam explain: "As a political coalition, the 'Third World' coalesced around the enthusiasm generated by anticolonial struggles in Vietnam and Algeria, and specifically emerged from the 1955 Bandung

Conference of 'non-aligned' African and Asian nations."[11] They note that the term "Third World" was coined by Alfred Sauvy, who saw "an analogy to the revolutionary 'third estate' of France—that is, the commoners, in contrast with the first estate (nobility) and the second (the clergy)."[12] In political terms, the Third World stands opposed to "the capitalist First World of Europe, the US, Australia, and Japan" and the "Second World" of socialist countries.[13] Subsequent formulations have highlighted the significance of "Fourth-World" Indigenous people across the globe and the "First World/Third World struggle [that] takes place not only *between* nations but also *within* them."[14]

The anticolonial thrust of the political coalition linking all marginalized people has inspired a demand for aesthetic expression grounded in popular, culturally specific traditions. Third Cinema proponents have sought to create films distinct from "big-budget commercial films (First Cinema)" and "independent, *auteur* films (Second Cinema)."[15] The left-leaning politics of Third Cinema leads its theorists to challenge commercial endeavors *and* art cinema designed to garner favor with elite critics. Criticizing finely crafted art films with neurotic characters isolated from social realities, Espinosa's "For an Imperfect Cinema" implores filmmakers to abjure safe, disinterested art to create engaged films for ordinary people "who think and feel and exist in a world which they can change."[16]

Recognizing *Black Panther*'s political dimensions, sociologist Renée T. White explains that it is "indebted to . . . Third Cinema."[17] Without referencing the tradition, other writers also identify Third Cinema principles in Coogler's film. Noting its rejection of "facile dichotomies," film critic Manohla Dargis finds that *Black Panther* "dispenses with familiar either/or divides, including the binary opposition that tends to shape our discourse on race."[18] Echoing the point that progressive films reveal the ways that social problems arise, film critic Devika Girish argues that *Black Panther* is a "truly unique" mainstream film, because it does not mask the dystopian reality of Black people "living in imprisonment and bondage" across the world.[19]

Other commentators cast doubt on connections between *Black Panther* and Third Cinema. Media studies scholar Tabassum "Ruhi" Khan questions the significance of T'Challa opening "a community center in an urban ghetto at the very site where [his] father committed fratricide."[20] To her, the action "represents a severe diminution of Killmonger's proposal, which is to demand a full-scale revolution of political-economic-cultural structures to redress racial injustices."[21] She finds that the film's failure to embrace Killmonger's approach is "one reason why postcolonial critics have been unconvinced by arguments hailing *Black Panther* as an example of Third Cinema."[22] To literary scholar Makeba Lavan armed struggle to "end global racial oppression" seems to be too bold an idea "even for a movie that appears to be an Afro-futurist manifesto."[23]

Lamenting the missed opportunity to show a "reconciliation between the African and African American family," Lavan highlights that the Wakandans have no interest in welcoming outsiders into their land and instead opt to bring Wakanda "to the world."[24] Khan argues that having "the choice to intervene in the struggle of Black liberation from the space of safety" makes Wakanda-like Western nations who have doled out aid "at their convenience."[25] Seeing the same parallel, humanities scholar George Faithful explains that in building the Outreach Center, "T'Challa seems to be in danger of developing an Afro-centric version of the 'white savior complex,' in which an outsider lacking first-hand local knowledge but flush with cash arrives hoping to make a difference."[26]

In Lavan's view, *Black Panther* is conventional, in that it makes Killmonger/N'Jadaka the problem.[27] Similarly, literary scholar Délice Williams argues that "*Black Panther* falls short [of being a progressive text] because it cloaks Killmonger in familiar and dangerous clichés of Black (American) gangsterism."[28] Media historian Julian C. Chambliss amplifies these objections, noting that despite the CIA's involvement in "torture, mass surveillance and endless war," *Black Panther* presents agent Everett Ross (Martin Freeman) as a positive figure and allows *him* to characterize Killmonger/N'Jadaka as a killer.[29] He argues that the narrative of a CIA agent "supporting a noble monarchy against a crazed African-American killer [simply] reframes long-held stereotypes about inner-city black youths."[30] Critics often associate this villainizing with Marvel Cinematic Universe formulas.[31]

Other authors agree that *Black Panther*'s commercial position puts it at odds with a progressive message. Journalist Vann R. Newkirk II notes that despite its "incredible gains in representation," *Black Panther* "is still a Marvel tentpole movie."[32] He remarks, the "major motivation of the enterprise is profit, [and so] the franchise lives and dies not with its commentary, but with the bottom line."[33] Chambliss sees the "gains in representation" as suspect, since they reflect "Marvel's print history, and as such, the goal is not social or political transformation so much as further market exploitation."[34]

Black Panther has also appealed to some right-leaning viewers. Humanities scholar Anthony Faramelli explains that Wakanda's decision "to hide from the world in order to protect its own citizens" and achieve "its utopian dream by sacrificing all other Africans . . . has made the film appealing to the political right."[35] He notes that for right-leaning Americans, "Wakanda's brand of nationalism is instantly recognizable as a version of Trump's 'America First' doctrine."[36] Right-leaning audiences also value Wakanda insofar as "it is a deeply patriarchal society" that reflects their ideas about domestic policies.[37] Historian Derek Charles Catsam illuminates these findings in his study of alt-right audiences who tried to "torpedo *Black Panther*'s 'Rotten Tomatoes' audience scores" and succeeded in causing its IMDB ratings to fall.[38] Initially criticizing *Black Panther* for depicting a fictional society that does not exist, alt-right audiences decided that Coogler had "secretly produced an homage to Donald Trump's America."[39] For them, the key points are that "Wakanda is intentionally isolated from the rest of the world, is strong on border security, has an invisible barrier . . . to keep outsiders out, is anti-globalist, and is racially homogenous."[40]

However, as Catsam explains, right-wing interpretations of the film require "cherry picking, intellectual calisthenics, and . . . ignorance of the traditions of African Nationalism, Black Power, and Black Consciousness, all three rivers from which *Black Panther* drinks deeply."[41] In addition, as the objections to the demonization of Killmonger/N'Jadaka indirectly reveal, the film generates sympathy for him (and his father), creating an open text that allows audiences to see the value of peaceful support for fellow Africans and members of the African Diaspora, as well the persuasive reasons for armed struggle. *Black Panther* thus aligns with Third Cinema films, whose purpose is not a simple "call for action, but rather an invitation to consider one alternative among many."[42] As film scholar Teshome Gabriel explains, in the course of weighing options, Third Cinema films reactivate decolonized "historical memories" that illuminate "the causes of conflict, of failure, and of difference."[43]

The idea that *Black Panther* falls outside of Third Cinema because it does not promote armed struggle directly conflicts with Espinosa's views. As he explains, "To analyze, in the traditional sense of the word, always implies a closed prior judgment [but to] show the process of a problem . . . is to submit it to judgment without pronouncing the verdict."[44] Throughout *Black Panther*, multiple characters debate the merits of global retribution and non-intervention. In addition, characters embrace different positions at different points. *Black Panther* also avoids a simple binary of armed struggle and isolation. Traditionalists like "T'Challa's mother, Ramonda (Angela Bassett), and Okoye (Danai Gurira), head of the king's women-only security unit," see value in sustaining the isolation that has protected them.[45] By comparison, Nakia (Lupita Nyong'o) holds "a more pan-African worldview" whereas for a time W'Kabi (Daniel Kaluuya) believes "Wakanda must use its might to remedy the world of evil."[46] Summarizing the film's rejection of simple judgments, film critic Christopher Orr writes, "The arguments *Black Panther* undertakes with itself are central to its architecture, a narrative spine that runs from the first scene to the last."[47]

It is true that audiences will not find "a race war at the center of a potentially billion-dollar property" produced in Hollywood.[48] Yet for Teshome Gabriel, Third Cinema is "not so much oppositional in the usual sense of the term, but simply more relevant politically and culturally to the milieu in which it is formed."[49] As he explains, there "can be several kinds of Third

Cinema depending on the prevailing social order."⁵⁰ As the ongoing efforts of "minorities and progressives in the West" reveal, in "regions where the major battles have moved into the cultural front," the "conjunction of cinema and struggle" requires the creation of empowering, re-imagined representations of marginalized people that "recover popular memory and activate it."⁵¹

Writing about Black independent cinema in the United States as one iteration of Third Cinema, Gabriel emphasizes that it is not "oppositional" or "reactive," but instead uses "new, emergent tendencies which are more difficult to categorize."⁵² This point is pertinent to *Black Panther*, which does not use alienating modernist aesthetic strategies to disrupt the ideological project of First Cinema, but instead creates a radical perspective from within commercial cinema by mobilizing enjoyable but political post-modernism. Highlighting the accessible nature of Third Cinema films, Jorge Sanjinés notes that in "revolutionary art we always encounter the stylistic mark of a people and the life-breath of a popular culture that embraces a whole community of men and women."⁵³ He explains, for Third Cinema filmmakers, the aim is to "arrive at the truth *through* beauty, and [that] this is what differentiates it from bourgeois art, where beauty is pursued even at the cost of lying" about cultural and material conditions.⁵⁴ Reflecting Third Cinema traditions, *Black Panther* offers a wondrous picture of Wakanda but emphasizes that it exists alongside the despair of oppressed people across the globe. It presents T'Challa as an admirable figure but allows Michael B. Jordan's nuanced portrayal to make the emotionally wounded boy N'Jadaka visible underneath Killmonger's hard surface. It frames T'Challa's father T'Chaka (John Kani) as a well-meaning man but clearly permits Sterling K. Brown's expressive performance as N'Jadaka's father N'Jobu to illuminate the compassion that drove him to violate Wakandan tradition.

The idea that *Black Panther*'s industrial position means that it primarily or exclusively supports the status quo, and so falls outside of Third Cinema traditions, ignores Espinosa's contrast between popular and mass art. As he explains, popular art reflects the "personal" tastes, values, and aspirations "of a people" whereas "mass art is art produced by a minority in order to satisfy the demand of a public reduced to the sole role of spectator and consumer."⁵⁵ In popular art, "the creators are at the same time the spectators and vice versa."⁵⁶ As many observers point out, *Black Panther*'s formal and thematic choices suggest that it is a film by and for historically disempowered people "who think and feel and exist in a world" they seek to change.⁵⁷

Thus, the film resonates with audiences concerned with social justice. While Newkirk suggests that *Black Panther* might simply be "a feature-length rumination on the message of many comic-book heroes, that with great power comes great responsibility," African American studies scholar Adilifu Nama asserts that Black superheroes are uniquely associated with "racial equality" and "racial justice."[58] Given this, the film has special importance for African Americans. Journalist Karen Good Marable notes, "Folks haven't been this excited about Africa in a film since Zamunda in 1988's *Coming to America*."[59] Ticket sales confirm this. In its opening weekend, "37 percent of ticket buyers for *Black Panther* in North America . . . were African-American. Caucasians made up 35% of the audience, while Hispanics made up 18%."[60] This is "very different from the demographic makeup for most superhero movies [that] tend to draw in audiences that are 15% African-American."[61]

Highlighting *Black Panther*'s depiction of an African society untouched by colonization, Marable explains that the film offers "a powerful counter-narrative to the literal and psychological violence Black people – particularly women and girls throughout the diaspora – endure daily."[62] Historian Marsha R. Robinson and cultural theorist Caryn Neumann propose that *Black Panther* "may be as significant in the near term in the United States as Alex Haley's *Roots* (1977)," the eight-part ABC miniseries based on Haley's best-selling book.[63] They suggest that it could even impact "global conversations about the complexities of slavery, colonialism, African diaspora relations, identity, and the social, gender and economic transformations now taking place in the fifty-five nations of the African Union."[64] These observations and others indicate that *Black Panther* reflects Third Cinema's aim to use popular culture forms to engage marginalized audiences, foster decolonized consciousness, connect past and present, and link local and global struggles.

BLACK PANTHER AND THIRD CINEMA IN THE UNITED STATES

Black Panther belongs to a tradition of filmmaking in the United States that is involved in "the First World/Third World struggle [that] takes place not only *between* nations but also *within* them."[65] Like its antecedents, *Black Panther* uses realistic and stylized strategies to create performance–sound–image collages that render the humanity of marginalized individuals and the realities of their group's collective history. It illuminates the emotional and spiritual connections within families and between men and women of color. While reaching a smaller audience, L.A. Rebellion films anticipate *Black Panther*, because they use Third Cinema principles and pan-African aesthetics to oppose mainstream cinema and elitist art cinema. Films by Charles Burnett, Haile Gerima, Julie Dash, and others reveal that this line of work consistently reflects popular, culturally specific, African American traditions. They feature aesthetic choices found in "Black expressive forms like jazz" and "novels by writers such as Toni Cade Bambara, Alice Walker, and Toni Morrison, which stop time to render audible and visible Black voices and characters that have been suppressed by centuries of Eurocentrism."[66]

Reflecting its Third Cinema politics, *Killer of Sheep* (Charles Burnett, 1978) does not lead audiences to "view people under the sociological lens of Blackness as lack."[67] Instead, it invites them to "spend sympathetic time with Black people in a narrative where the most significant meaning lies within *them, not* within the gaze of some idealized White observer."[68] The film shows the socio-economic pressures that create distance between the married couple and the sympathetic understanding that allows them to transcend, for a moment, the isolating, individual pain that they bear. Like other Third Cinema films, *Killer of Sheep* employs narrative, stylistic, and performance strategies rooted in "non-Western, or para-Western cultural traditions featuring other historical rhythms, other narrative structures, other views of the body, sexuality, spirituality, and the collective life."[69] Similarly, while *Black Panther* employs mainstream conventions (e.g., action sequences), aspects such as its set, costume, and hair design that reflect non-Western traditions that convey "not only the tribal diversity that exists within Wakanda but the diversity of black culture and identity as well."[70]

Bush Mama (Haile Gerima, 1979) is another precursor of *Black Panther*. It belongs to Third Cinema because it centers on "Black emotional experiences, which have been either disavowed or marginalized within dominant cinema's on-screen representation of Black people."[71] In place of a crass, dissolute welfare mother, the film presents Dorothy (Barbara O.) as a caring mother, loving wife, intelligent woman, and resilient human being. Johnny Weathers portrays T. C., Dorothy's gentle and considerate husband, who has returned from two tours of duty in Vietnam only to face unemployment and then imprisonment for a crime he did not commit. Like Dorothy, he is a person of gravity and sensitivity, and he shares Dorothy's transformational arc from tragically isolated individual to politically conscious member of the African Diaspora. In contrast to the Wakandans, Dorothy and T. C. exist in a world dominated by White supremacy, but their cultural and political journey anticipates the Wakandans' interest in engaging the Black Diaspora imagined community, which emerges from Nakia's humanitarian missions and the Wakandans' evolving encounters with Killmonger/N'Jadaka.[72]

Despite the state violence that shapes Dorothy and T. C.'s lived experiences, they remain a couple whose communication and loving connection transcends physical separation. Letters between them, conveyed through the performers' voiceover or direct address, illustrate the couple's growing political insights and their remarkable ability to communicate. The emotion embedded in the actors' vocal performance of the letters increases exposure to the characters' subjectivity and contributes to creating the "*humanized* representations" of marginalized people emblematic of Third Cinema.[73]

In *Black Panther*, transformation also emerges from people who communicate, with actors' performances conveying the characters' humanity. At the height of the battle that pits Wakandans fighting for Killmonger/N'Jadaka against Wakandans and Jabari loyal to T'Challa, there is a sudden pause as Okoye protects M'Baku (Winston Duke) from an assault by W'Kabi astride a rhino. Here, Danai Gurira reveals Okoye's resolve through the forceful qualities in her physical/vocal expression; a fleeting tremble in her voice and glistening in her eyes is all that betrays the sorrow Okoye feels in threatening her husband. In turn, Daniel Kaluuya conveys the complexity of W'Kabi's decision to surrender. The tilt of his head and furrowed brow suggests W'Kabi's stunned astonishment, yet he also wistfully asks, "Would you kill me, my love?" His quiet voice and careful articulation of the words express the melancholy that grows as he comes to understand the situation. As W'Kabi grapples with the weight of the moment, point-of-view shots suggest his emerging awareness that the internecine war has implications for him and his society. The powerful exchange between Okoye and W'Kabi exemplifies Third Cinema, because it makes ordinary people the agents of change (see figure 14.1.).

Moreover, the battle between the warring factions ends when members of the society stand down. The fact that the group, rather than a conventional hero, changes the course of events is another sign of *Black Panther*'s Third Cinema politics. As Sanjinés notes, the "presence of a collective protagonist, rather than an individual protagonist" is key to Third Cinema.[74] Change begins with Okoye protecting M'Baku, another regular member of the group, and it takes place with Okoye and W'Kabi surrounded by their peers. The peace they achieve illustrates the process by which people with different experiences and priorities find common ground. Okoye has gone from protecting the throne (in the abstract) to defending the society to which she belongs.

Figure 14.1 As W'Kabi, Daniel Kaluuya Makes Black Panther's Collective Protagonist Visible. Screenshot taken by author.

W'Kabi makes the transition from supporting a king who will revenge the death of his parents to understanding that peace is best for everyone.

The presence of a collective protagonist in *Black Panther* follows the Third Cinema precedent in *Daughters of the Dust* (Julie Dash, 1991). Set in 1902, Dash's film explores the emotions underlying a momentous day for the Peazants, a multigenerational family that has lived on the Sea Islands along the southern Atlantic coast of the United States in relative isolation since the end of the Civil War. The extended family gathers to share a meal before some members move to the mainland. Yellow Mary (Barbara O.), the prodigal daughter, has come home for the occasion. Viola (Cheryl Lynn Bruce), a devout Christian, and Haagar (Kaycee Moore), who wants her children to grow up on the mainland, are the ones pushing for change. The matriarch Nana Peazant (Cora Lee Day) is reconciled to their move. Yet she worries that in their new lives, her relatives will lose their connection to the wisdom that has aided them on the islands. Exploring diverging ideas about the significance of the traditions that have sustained them, *Daughters of the Dust* also anticipates the debates that *Black Panther* negotiates.

In Dash's film, dialogue reveals characters' differing views about family and tradition. Yet its multiple registers of performance (voiceover, public declamations, and naturalistic passages) show the overriding need for formally enslaved people to cherish one another. Loving and supporting each other becomes key to the emotional journey Eula (Alva Rogers) and her husband Eli (Adisa Anderson) make as they work through the anguish that accompanies her pregnancy, because they do not know if the father is Eli or a White man who raped her. Sound–image relationships make time fluid, and the film's "progressive unfolding of events in time is less important to the narrative than a sense of time in which the past and future co-exist and impact the present."[75] *Black Panther* presents a comparable vision of time. Its depiction of "Wakanda is at once urban and rural, futuristic and traditional, technological and mystical."[76]

In both films, the actors' embodiment of their characters remakes popular memory. In *Daughters of the Dust*, even the tone of the actors' voices conveys the characters' "tremulous, sacred awareness that the course of their lives and the family name is now, more than ever, in their hands."[77] The "mise-en-scène of Grandma Nana, Haagar, Yellow Mary, and Eula in the center of the frame makes their space theirs, and their possession of the space makes them bigger than life."[78] For film scholar Manthia Diawara, the actors "become so associated with Ibo Landing that it becomes difficult to imagine [it] without the faces of these Black women. Analogically speaking, it is like imagining America in Western films without the faces of John Wayne, Kirk Douglas, and Gary Cooper."[79]

Modeled on *Daughters of the Dust*'s magnificent imagery of Black women joined together through shared history, *Black Panther*'s essentially all Black cast makes the characters' collective experiences visible and makes the aspirations of Diasporic people part of American popular culture. The actors' backgrounds reflect "the incredible breadth of the African diaspora," with players from the United States, Mexico, and the United Kingdom tracing their heritages to Zimbabwe, Kenya, Uganda, Guyana, and Tobago.[80] Casting underlines the story's investment in honoring familial (and group) connections. Esteemed South African actor John Kani portrays T'Chaka, while his son Atandwa Kani plays young T'Chaka. Forest Whitaker is Zuri, and his son Denzel Whitaker portrays Zuri as the young man who spies on N'Jobu.

Like other aspects of the film, the cast and their characters contribute to *Black Panther*'s social significance. As Faramelli notes, having "black people for the first time depicted in a major movie as kings, queens, inventors, and diplomats, rather than slaves, thugs, dealers and thieves, has given the movie a real-world political engagement not seen in other superhero films."[81] Writer and civil rights activist Shaun King places *Black Panther* alongside cultural moments like "Rosa Parks refusing to give up her seat on the bus in Montgomery" and Dr. King's 'I Have a Dream Speech.'"[82] The film is akin to moments like the "birth of hip hop, Michael Jackson's 'Thriller' becoming the best-selling album of all-time, [the] election of Barack Obama as our first Black President, [and] Colin Kaepernick taking a knee to protest police brutality and injustice in America."[83] King's sense of *Black Panther*'s cultural status recalls Diawara's view that *Daughters of the Dust*'s imagery is as significant as the iconography of Hollywood Westerns. Their observations point to both films' interventions in societies in which many of the "major battles have moved into the cultural front."[84]

Like *Daughters of the Dust*, the narrative in *Black Panther* rests on the interactions of Black characters who belong to a community. T'Challa and Killmonger/N'Jadaka are central figures, but the actions of other characters are also important. For example, while M'Baku's initial action disrupts T'Challa's uncontested coronation, his subsequent ones sustain the community. He resists the opportunity to enjoy the strength provided by the heart-shaped herb offered to him, and he eventually sets aside old grievances to support Wakandans seeking to avoid global war. The decisions that Okoye makes on the battlefield are also crucial; making the transition from her traditional duty to serve whoever is Wakanda's king to aligning herself with the peaceful pan-African contingent, she "has an arc that replays [the film's] central ideological conflict in microcosm."[85]

Nakia, Princess Shuri (Letitia Wright), and Queen Ramonda are important; they bring "T'Challa back from near death" and make "him strong because he listens to them."[86] Actions by Nakia, Shuri, and Okoye provide evidence that "the women of Wakanda drive the narrative."[87] For some, Nakia is the "moral and political heart of the film," because she first introduces the idea of ending Wakanda's "isolationist policies" and eventually persuades "T'Challa

Figure 14.2 Nakia (Lupita Nyong'o) Argues for One of Several Possible Paths for Wakanda. Screenshot taken by author.

to work toward the liberation of all oppressed peoples."[88] Existing alongside positions expressed by other characters, the argument Nakia makes early on, that "Wakanda is strong enough to help others and protect ourselves at the same time," ultimately shapes the next step in Wakanda's history (see figure 14.2.).

Black Panther's exploration of if, or how, Wakanda should engage with the outside world is not decided by a clash between two isolated individuals. It is a multigenerational process, involving T'Chaka, N'Jobu, their families, the people of Wakanda, and finally a re-imagined relationship between the First and Third Worlds. Its visualization of Black people implicitly united under the red, black, and green pan-African flag makes it relevant to the contemporary milieu, particularly for audiences seeking change. The film's mainstream status does not negate its Third Cinema politics. As Gabriel explains, "From Julio García Espinosa in Cuba to Ousmane Sembene of Senegal, from Miguel Litton of Chile to Haile Gerima of Ethiopia, the most persistent call has been [that] the future of cinema depends on popular culture and popular memory."[89] Using popular material, *Black Panther* reshapes popular memory by framing Black experiences and capabilities as key components of global history.

NOTES

1. See Nama 2011, Parham 2018, and S. Henderson 2018. As part of the MCU, Coogler's film builds on the initial success of *Spider Man* (Sam Raimi, 2002) and the films dominating the market since the release of *Iron Man* (Jon Favreau, 2008). Film and media productions featuring Black superheroes include *Abar* (Frank Packard,

1977), *The Meteor Man* (Robert Townsend, 1993), *Spawn* (Mark A. Z. Dippé, 1997), *Steel* (Kenneth Johnson, 1997), the trilogy starting with *Blade* (Stephen Norrington, 1998), *Luke Cage* (Cheo Hodari Coker, Netflix, 2016–2018), and *Black Lightning* (Salim Akil, CW, 2017–present).

2. See Nama 2011, Faithful 2018, and Riesman 2018. Stan Lee and Jack Kirby created the Black Panther character in 1966. In the mid-1970s, Don McGregor and artist Billy Graham shaped the comics. From 1996 to 2003, Christopher Priest complicated the superhero in part by framing him as a king. In the late 2000s, Reginald Hudlin and Jonathan Maberry contributed important female characters. In the 2010s, David Liss and Jonathan Hickman continued the narrative. In 2016, Ta-Nehesi Coates and Brian Stelfreeze updated the comic to have an "Afrofuturistic design" (Girish 2018, 32). Subsequent contributors include Roxane Gay, Alitha Martinez, and Afwa Richardson.

3. Renée T. White, "I Dream a World: *Black Panther* and the Re-Making of Blackness," *New Political Science* 40, no. 2 (2018): 422. See Nama 2011, Johnson 2018, Allen 2018, and Mattimore 2018. Mark Dery coined the term "Afrofuturism" in "Black to the Future: Interviews with Samuel R. Delany, Greg Tate, and Tricia Rose," published in *Flame Wars: The Discourse of Cyberculture* (1994). Like Delany, Octavia Butler, N. K. Jemison, and Nnedi Okorafor are important Afro-Futurist authors. As *A Pure Solar World: Sun Ra and the Birth of Afrofuturism* (2016) by Paul Youngquist shows, the musician is a key figure in Afro-Futurism. Details in *Black Panther* recall *Space is the Place* (John Coney, 1974), a film starring and co-authored by Sun Ra. His character's spaceship lands in Oakland, and he speaks with young people at a youth center. To recruit African Americans to settle the planet he has discovered, he sets up an "Outer Space Employment Agency."

4. Anthony R. Guneratne, "Introduction: Rethinking Third Cinema," in *Rethinking Third Cinema*, eds. Anthony R. Guneratne and Wimal Dissanayake (New York: Routledge, 2003), 3.

5. Julio García Espinosa, "For an Imperfect Cinema," in *New Latin American Cinema: Volume One: Theory, Practices, and Transcontinental Articulations*, ed. Michael T. Martin (Detroit: Wayne State University Press, 1997), 82, 81–82.

6. Ibid., 81.

7. Ibid.

8. Karen Good Marable, "Watch the Throne," *Essence*, March 2018, 81.

9. Espinosa, "For an Imperfect Cinema," 80.

10. Ella Shohat and Robert Stam, *Unthinking Eurocentrism: Multiculturalism and the Media* (New York: Routledge, 2014), 292.

11. Ibid., 25.

12. Ibid.

13. Ibid.

14. Ibid., 26, italics in original.

15. Guneratne, "Introduction: Rethinking Third Cinema," 10, italics in original.

16. Espinosa, "For an Imperfect Cinema," 80.

17. Renée T. White, "I Dream a World," 423.

18. Manohla Dargis, "'Black Panther' Shakes Up the Marvel Universe," *New York Times*, February 6, 2018, https://www.nytimes.com/2018/02/06/movies/black-panther-review-movie.html.

19. Devika Girish, "Out of this World," *Film Comment*, March-April 2018, https://www.filmcomment.com/article/black-panther-science-fiction/.

20. Tabassum "Ruhi" Khan, "Viewing *Black Panther* through a Postcolonial Feminist Lens," *Women and Language* 42, no. 1 (Spring 2019): 101.

21. Ibid.

22. Ibid.

23. Makeba Lavan, "To Whom Does Wakanda Belong?" *Africology: The Journal of Pan African Studies* 11, no. 9 (August 2018): 23.

24. Ibid., 24.

25. Khan, "Viewing *Black Panther* through a Postcolonial Feminist Lens," 100.

26. George Faithful, "Dark of the World, Shine on Us: The Redemption of Blackness in Ryan Coogler's *Black Panther*," *Religions* 9, no. 10 (October 2018): 10, https://www.mdpi.com/2077-1444/9/10/304.

27. Lavan, "To Whom Does Wakanda Belong?" 23.

28. Delice Williams, "Three Theses about *Black Panther*," *Africology: The Journal of Pan African Studies* 11, no. 9 (August 2018): 28.

29. Julian C. Chambliss, "*Black Panther*: The Evolution of the Idea," *Science Fiction Film and Television* 12, no. 3 (2019): 377, https://muse.jhu.edu/article/736771/pdf.

30. Ibid.

31. See Chambliss, "*Black Panther*: The Evolution of the Idea," 2019; Girish, "Out of this World," 2018.

32. Vann R. Newkirk II, "The Provocation and Power of *Black Panther*," *The Atlantic*, February 14, 2018, https://www.theatlantic.com/entertainment/archive/2018/02/the-provocation-and-power-of-black-panther/553226/.

33. Ibid.

34. Chambliss, "*Black Panther*: The Evolution of the Idea," 374.

35. Anthony Faramelli, "Liberation On and Off Screen: *Black Panther* and Liberation Theory," *Film Comment* 43, no. 2 (September 2019), https://quod.lib.umich.edu/f/fc/13761232.0043.202/--liberation-on-and-off-screen-black-panther-and-black?rgn=main;view=fulltext.

36. Ibid.

37. Ibid.

38. Derek Charles Catsam, "If You're (Concerned About) White You're Alt-Right: Racialized Conservative Responses to *Black Panther*," *Africology: The Journal of Pan African Studies* 11, no. 9 (August 2018): 53; see 54.

39. Ibid, 55.

40. Ibid, 56.

41. Ibid, 55.

42. Teshome H. Gabriel, "Third Cinema as Guardian of Popular Memory: Towards a Third Aesthetics," in *Questions of Third Cinema*, eds. Jim Pines and Paul Willemen (London: British Film Institute, 1989), 58.

43. Ibid.
44. Espinosa, "For an Imperfect Cinema," 81.
45. Jason Parham, "*Black Panther* is All a Superhero Movie Can Be, and More," *Wired*, February 18, 2018, https://www.wired.com/story/black-panther-review/.
46. Ibid.
47. Christopher Orr, "*Black Panther* Is More Than a Superhero Movie," *The Atlantic*, February 16, 2018, https://www.theatlantic.com/entertainment/archive/2018/02/black-panther-review/553508/; see White, "I Dream a World," 426.
48. David Edelstein, "*Black Panther* is Unusually Gripping and Grounded for a Superhero Film," *Vulture*, February 16, 2018, https://www.vulture.com/2018/02/black-panther-review.html#:~:text=Black%20Panther%2C%20starring%20Chadwick%20Boseman,accounts%20as%20Africa's%20poorest%20country.
49. Jim Pines, "Preface," in *Questions of Third Cinema*, eds. Jim Pines and Paul Willemen (London: British Film Institute, 1989), ix.
50. Gabriel, "Third Cinema as Guardian of Popular Memory," 55.
51. Ibid.
52. Teshome Gabriel, "Thoughts on Nomadic Aesthetics and the Black Independent Cinema: Traces of a Journey," in *Blackframes: Critical Perspectives on Black Independent Cinema*, eds. Mbye B. Cham and Claire Andrade-Watkins (Cambridge, MA: The Massachusetts Institute of Technology Press, 1988), 72.
53. Jorge Sanjinés, "Problems of Form and Content in Revolutionary Cinema," in *New Latin American Cinema: Volume One: Theory, Practices, and Transcontinental Articulations*, ed. Michael T. Martin (Detroit: Wayne State University Press, 1997), 66.
54. Ibid., italics in original.
55. Espinosa, "For an Imperfect Cinema," 76.
56. Ibid.
57. Ibid., 80; see Allen 2018, Johnson 2018, Parham 2018, White 2018, and Faramelli 2019.
58. Newkirk, "The Provocation and Power of *Black Panther*"; Adilifu Nama, *Super Black: America Pop Culture and Black Superheroes* (Austin: University of Texas Press, 2011), 4.
59. Marable, "Watch the Throne," 77.
60. Josh Horwitz, "'Black Panther' Dramatically Changed the Make-Up of the Superhero Movie Audience This Weekend," *Quartz*, February 19, 2018, https://qz.com/1210475/black-panther-dramatically-changed-the-make-up-of-movie-audiences-this-weekend/.
61. Ibid.
62. Marable, "Watch the Throne," 81.
63. Marsha R. Robinson and Caryn Neuman, "Introduction: On Coogler and Cole's *Black Panther* Film (2018): Global Perspectives, Reflections and Contexts for Educators," *Africology: The Journal of Pan African Studies* 11, no. 9 (August 2018): 1.
64. Ibid.
65. Shohat and Stam, *Unthinking Eurocentrism*, 26, italics in original.

66. Manthia Diawara, "Black American Cinema: The New Realism," in *Black American Cinema*, ed. Manthia Diawara (New York: Routledge, 1993), 11.

67. Clyde Taylor, "Preface: Once Upon a Time in the West . . . L.A. Rebellion," in *L.A. Rebellion: Creating a New Black Cinema*, eds. Allyson Nadia Field, Jan-Christopher Horak, and Jacqueline Najuma Stewart (Berkeley: University of California Press, 2015), xxii.

68. Ibid, italics in original.

69. Robert Stam, "Introduction: Alternative Aesthetics," in *Film and Theory*, eds. Robert Stam and Toby Miller (Malden, MA: Blackwell, 2000), 263.

70. Tre Johnson, "*Black Panther* is a Gorgeous, Groundbreaking Celebration of Black Culture," *Vox*, February 23, 2018, https://www.vox.com/culture/2018/2/23/17028826/black-panther-wakanda-culture-marvel.

71. Samantha N. Sheppard, "Bruising Moments: Affect and the L.A. Rebellion," in *L.A. Rebellion: Creating a New Black Cinema*, eds. Allyson Nadia Field, Jan-Christopher Horak, and Jacqueline Najuma Stewart (Berkeley: University of California Press, 2015), 229.

72. Williams, "Three Theses about *Black Panther*," 28.

73. Taylor, "Preface: Once Upon a Time in the West," xx, italics in original.

74. Sanjinés, "Problems of Form and Content in Revolutionary Cinema," 65.

75. Gladstone L. Yearwood, *Black Film as a Signifying Practice: Narration and the African American Aesthetic Tradition* (Trenton, NJ: Africa World Press, 2000), 225.

76. Dargis, "'Black Panther' Shakes Up the Marvel Universe"; see White (2018, 424); Girish (2018, 30, 32).

77. Richard Brody, "The Return of Julie Dash's Historic 'Daughters of the Dust,'" *The New Yorker*, November 18, 2016, https://www.newyorker.com/culture/richard-brody/the-return-of-julie-dashs-historic-daughters-of-the-dust.

78. Diawara, "Black American Cinema: The New Realism," 18.

79. Ibid., 18–19.

80. Newkirk, "The Provocation and the Power of *Black Panther*."

81. Faramelli, "Liberation On and Off Screen."

82. Shaun King, "*Black Panther* is One of the Most Important Cultural Moments in American History," *Medium*, February 20, 2018, https://medium.com/@ShaunKing/black-panther-is-one-of-the-most-important-moments-in-american-history-1fc9166a0972.

83. Ibid.

84. Gabriel, "Third Cinema as Guardian of Popular Memory," 55.

85. Odie Henderson, "*Black Panther*," *Roger Ebert.com*, February 15, 2018, https://www.rogerebert.com/reviews/black-panther-2018.

86. Robinson and Neuman, "Introduction: On Coogler and Cole's *Black Panther* Film (2018)," 6.

87. Girish, "Out of this World," 32.

88. Marlene Allen, "If You Can See It, You Can Be It: *Black Panther*'s Black Magic Woman," *Africology: The Journal of Pan African Studies* 11, no. 9 (August 2018): 21; Faramelli, "Liberation On and Off Screen."

89. Gabriel, "Third Cinema as Guardian of Popular Memory," 56.

WORKS CITED

Allen, Marlene D. "If You Can See It, You Can Be It: *Black Panther*'s Black Magic Woman." *Africology: The Journal of Pan African Studies* 11, no. 9 (August 2018): 20–22.

Brody, Richard. "The Return of Julie Dash's Historic 'Daughters of the Dust.'" *The New Yorker*, November 18, 2016. https://www.newyorker.com/culture/richard-brody/the-return-of-julie-dashs-historic-daughters-of-the-dust.

Catsam, Derek Charles. "If You're (Concerned About) White You're Alt-Right: Racialized Conservative Responses to *Black Panther*." *Africology: The Journal of Pan African Studies* 11, no. 9 (August 2018): 53–60.

Chambliss, Julian C. "*Black Panther*: The Evolution of the Idea." *Science Fiction Film and Television* 12, no. 3 (2019): 373–380.

Dargis, Manohla. "'Black Panther' Shakes Up the Marvel Universe." *The New York Times*, February 6, 2018. https://www.nytimes.com/2018/02/06/movies/black-panther-review-movie.html.

Diawara, Manthia. "Black American Cinema: The New Realism." In *Black American Cinema*, edited by Manthia Diawara, 3–25. New York: Routledge, 1993.

Edelstein, David. 2018. "*Black Panther* is Unusually Gripping and Grounded for a Superhero Film." *Vulture*, February 16, 2018. https://www.vulture.com/2018/02/black-panther-review.html#:~:text=Black%20Panther%2C%20starring%20Chadwick%20Boseman,accounts%20as%20Africa's%20poorest%20country.

Espinosa, Julio García. "For an Imperfect Cinema." In *New Latin American Cinema: Volume One: Theory, Practices, and Transcontinental Articulations*, edited by Michael T. Martin, 71–82. Detroit: Wayne State University Press, 1997.

Faramelli, Anthony. "Liberation On and Off Screen: *Black Panther* and Liberation Theory." *Film Comment* 43, no. 2 (September 2019).

Faithful, George. "Dark of the World, Shine on Us: The Redemption of Blackness in Ryan Coogler's *Black Panther*." *Religions* (October 2018): 1–15.

Gabriel, Teshome H. "Thoughts on Nomadic Aesthetics and the Black Independent Cinema: Traces of a Journey." In *Blackframes: Critical Perspectives on Black Independent Cinema*, edited by Mbye B. Cham and Claire Andrade-Watkins, 62–79. Cambridge, MA: The Massachusetts Institute of Technology Press, 1988.

Gabriel, Teshome H. "Third Cinema as Guardian of Popular Memory: Towards a Third Aesthetics." In *Questions of Third Cinema*, edited by Jim Pines and Paul Willemen, 53–64. London: British Film Institute, 1989.

Girish, Devika. "Out of this World." *Film Comment*, March-April 2018, 28–33. https://www.filmcomment.com/article/black-panther-science-fiction/.

Guneratne, Anthony R. "Introduction: Rethinking Third Cinema." In *Rethinking Third Cinema*, edited by Anthony R. Guneratne and Wimal Dissanayake, 1–28. New York: Routledge, 2003.

Henderson, Odie. "*Black Panther*." *Roger Ebert.com*, February 15, 2018. https://www.rogerebert.com/reviews/black-panther-2018.

Henderson, Shirley. "Hear them Roar: *Black Panther*'s Superwomen are the Very Definition of Power and Strength." *Ebony*, February 2018, 80–83.

Horwitz, Josh. "'Black Panther' Dramatically Changed the Make-Up of the Superhero Movie Audience This Weekend." *Quartz*, February 19, 2018. https://qz.com/1210475/black-panther-dramatically-changed-the-make-up-of-movie-audiences-this-weekend/.

Johnson, Tre. "*Black Panther* is a Gorgeous, Groundbreaking Celebration of Black Culture." *Vox*, February 23, 2018. https://www.vox.com/culture/2018/2/23/17028826/black-panther-wakanda-culture-marvel.

Khan, Tabassum "Ruhi." "Viewing *Black Panther* through a Postcolonial Feminist Lens." *Women and Language* 42, no. 1 (Spring 2019): 97–104.

King, Shaun. "*Black Panther* is One of the Most Important Cultural Moments in American History." *Medium*, February 20, 2018. https://medium.com/@ShaunKing/black-panther-is-one-of-the-most-important-moments-in-american-history-1fc9166a0972.

Lavan, Makeba. "To Whom Does Wakanda Belong?" *Africology: The Journal of Pan African Studies* 11, no. 9 (August 2018): 23–26.

Marable, Karen Good. "Watch the Throne." *Essence*, March 2018, 74–81.

Mattimore, Ryan. "The Real History Behind the Black Panther: Interview with Adilifu Nama." *History*, August 26, 2018. https://www.history.com/news/the-real-history-behind-the-black-panther.

Nama, Adilifu. *Super Black: American Pop Culture and Black Superheroes*. Austin: University of Texas Press, 2011.

Newkirk, Vann R II. "The Provocation and Power of *Black Panther*." *The Atlantic*, February 14, 2018. https://www.theatlantic.com/entertainment/archive/2018/02/the-provocation-and-power-of-black-panther/553226/.

Orr, Christopher. "*Black Panther* Is More Than a Superhero Movie." *The Atlantic*, February 16, 2018. https://www.theatlantic.com/entertainment/archive/2018/02/black-panther-review/553508/.

Parham, Jason. "*Black Panther* is All a Superhero Movie Can Be, and More." *Wired*, February 18, 2018. https://www.wired.com/story/black-panther-review/.

Pines, Jim. "Preface." In *Questions of Third Cinema*, edited by Jim Pines and Paul Willemen, vii–x. London: British Film Institute, 1989.

Riesman, Abraham. "The Man Who Made the Black Panther Cool." *New York* (January 22–February 4, 2018): 70–73.

Robinson, Marsha R., and Caryn Neumann. "Introduction: On Coogler and Cole's *Black Panther* Film (2018): Global Perspectives, Reflections and Contexts for Educators." *Africology: The Journal of Pan African Studies* 11, no. 9 (August 2018): 1–12.

Sanjinés, Jorge. "Problems of Form and Content in Revolutionary Cinema." In *New Latin American Cinema: Volume One: Theory, Practices, and Transcontinental Articulations*, edited by Michael T. Martin, 62–70. Detroit: Wayne State University Press, 1997.

Sheppard, Samantha N. "Bruising Moments: Affect and the L.A. Rebellion." In *L.A. Rebellion: Creating a New Black Cinema*, edited by Allyson Nadia Field, Jan-Christopher Horak, and Jacqueline Najuma Stewart, 225–250. Berkeley: University of California Press, 2015.

Shohat, Ella and Robert Stam. *Unthinking Eurocentrism: Multiculturalism and the Media*. New York: Routledge, 2014.
Stam, Robert. "Introduction: Alternative Aesthetics." In *Film and Theory*, edited by Robert Stam and Toby Miller, 257–264. Malden, MA: Blackwell, 2000.
Taylor, Clyde. "Preface: Once Upon a Time in the West ... L.A. Rebellion." In *L.A. Rebellion: Creating a New Black Cinema*, edited by Allyson Nadia Field, Jan-Christopher Horak, and Jacqueline Najuma Stewart, ix–xxiv. Berkeley: University of California Press, 2015.
White, Renée T. "I Dream a World: *Black Panther* and the Re-Making of Blackness." *New Political Science* 40, no. 2 (2018): 421–427.
Williams, Délice. "Three Theses about *Black Panther*." *Africology: The Journal of Pan African Studies* 11, no. 9 (August 2018): 27–30.
Yearwood, Gladstone L. *Black Film as a Signifying Practice: Cinema, Narration and the African American Aesthetic Tradition*. Trenton, NJ: Africa World Press, 2000.

FILMS AND TELEVISION

Abar, the First Black Superman. Directed by Frank Packard. United States: Mirror Releasing, 1977.
Black Lightning. Created by Salim Akil. United States: CW, 2017–present.
Black Panther. Directed by Ryan Coogler. United States: Walt Disney Studios Motion Pictures, 2018.
Blade. Directed by Stephen Norrington. United States: New Line Cinema, 1998.
Blade II. Directed by Guillermo del Toro. United States: New Line Cinema, 2002.
Blade: Trinity. Directed by David S. Goyer. United States: New Line Cinema, 2004.
Bush Mama. Directed by Haile Gerima. United States, 1979.
Coming to America. Directed by John Landis. United States: Paramount Pictures, 1988.
Daughters of the Dust. Directed by Julie Dash. United States: Kino International, 1991.
Iron Man. Directed by Jon Favreau. United States: Paramount Pictures, 2008.
Killer of Sheep. Directed by Charles Burnett. United States: Milestone Films, 1978.
Luke Cage. Created by Cheo Hodari Coker. United States: Netflix, 2016–2018.
The Meteor Man. Directed by Robert Townsend. United States: Metro-Goldwyn-Mayer, 1993.
Space is the Place. Directed by John Coney. United States: Rhapsody Films, 1974.
Spawn. Directed by Mark A. Z. Dippé. United States: New Line Cinema, 1997.
Spider Man. Directed by Sam Raimi. United States: Sony Pictures Releasing, 2002.
Steel. Directed by Kenneth Johnson. United States: Warner Bros., 1997.

Chapter 15

The Depiction of Homeschooling, Black Identity, and Political Thought in the Film *Black Panther*

Khadijah Z. Ali-Coleman

The Marvel Comics film *Black Panther*, directed by Ryan Coogler, is one of the country's highest grossing films of all time.[1] It offers viewers an action-packed Afro-futurist vision of a world where Black super-powered people exist. The movie emphasizes the differences between the protagonist character, T'Challa (Chadwick Boseman) and the antagonist character, Killmonger (Michael B. Jordan). The differences range from the way they treat women to how they serve as king. What the two cousins have in common, however, is that both of their fathers (who are biological brothers) take on the responsibility of home educating them as youth.

This depiction of homeschooling in *Black Panther* is a literal re-imagining of both blackness and education as it counters the national statistic that indicates that homeschooling is more often led by a student's mother and that Black families are less likely to homeschool when compared to White families.[2] However, by presenting homeschooling as the educational practice of both fathers, the audience is able to examine the ways both parents instilled in each son certain values. The film depicts the ways that homeschooling can be empowering. However, the film also illustrates the ways homeschooling is also used as a tool for Western indoctrination, often inherent in the learning experiences of colonized people throughout the world. My conclusion includes sentiments on how a meta-analysis of the film's themes suggest a conflation of African diasporic culture and imperialist ideology that often permeates our educational practice, whether we homeschool or engage in traditional school practice. Ultimately, I assert that the film's depiction of Killmonger offers a dystopian perspective of an African diasporic identity formed through homeschooling and cultural modeling despite overall visuals in the film that reflect a different story. I will use the storylines of both characters as impetus to discuss the role homeschool education plays in formulating identity using bell hooks' theory of education as liberatory practice. Overall, Mark Dery's concept of Afrofuturism[3] will undergird the analysis.

HOMESCHOOLING THROUGH STORYTELLING

As Black viewers, we were mesmerized by the breadth of images in this world of *Black Panther* that re-imagines blackness in ways we rarely have seen before within a popular mainstream series. I stood in line with my family when the movie debuted in 2018 in movie theaters across the globe, as did thousands of other Black Americans, anticipating a movie-watching experience that, although a work of fiction, represented some aspect of my cultural identity as a Black American woman.

In the movie, the superhero Black Panther hails from the country of Wakanda, ruling it by day as the African king, T'Challa. Wakanda is an African country where the most powerful element in the world, vibranium, exists, and Wakandans mask their vibranium supply and their country's technological advances from the rest of the world. The villain, Erik Killmonger, has other plans for the vibranium, polarizing audiences with his overtly violent behavior and sentiments that imply an interest in unifying Black people around the globe in an armed struggle.

While T'Challa's ideas stem from his father's teachings, revolving around keeping Wakanda focused solely on the well-being of its inhabitants, Killmonger's lessons from his father spark another direction. Killmonger hopes to implement a plan where oppressed Black people around the world are armed with the wealth and weaponry of Wakanda for a unified uprising against global supremacy. To call the interactions that we see between Killmonger and his father "homeschooling" is appropriate. Homeschool is PK-12 instruction that a student's parent(s) curates. The parents are either the lead instructors or they craft a curriculum taught by others who teach subject areas the parent may not have expertise in. It is also assumed that T'Challa had such a relationship as well with his father when a child. The film intimates that both fathers were the main teacher for the most part in the lives of both sons until the death of both fathers.

It is important to note that there are numerous methods that parents employ when homeschooling. In the movie, both fathers employ strategies of storytelling and oral traditions to impart knowledge to their sons. This method is commonly used in real-life by Black homeschooling families. In my 2020 study where I interviewed African American teens who were homeschooled and dual-enrolled in community college, some of them shared how they learned lessons from their parents through conversations and stories their parents shared with them directly or that they overheard when their parents spoke with each other. These lessons, in turn, offered information that they later felt helped prepare them to navigate college successfully.[4]

Black families in the United States choose to homeschool for a variety of reasons. A profile written by one journalist[5] illustrated through interviews with American families that Black families choose to homeschool because of the opportunity to infuse instruction with value-based content such as character-training. She also found that parents took children out of school to homeschool when there were environmental issues in the schools—from drugs to discipline issues of other children—and low expectations from teachers and administrators. I am a homeschooling parent who has been homeschooling my daughter off and on for twelve years. I have chosen to homeschool because homeschooling has afforded me the opportunity to emphasize course content through an Afrocentric lens. Seeing the movie *Black Panther* was a homeschooling field trip and an opportunity for me to watch a movie with my daughter that centered Black people and featured a rarity, a Black superhero. While I anticipated other elements of my cultural experience to be depicted on screen, because the title character is Black, I didn't expect to see homeschooling depicted and found it refreshing to see it included within a few scenes.

In the film *Black Panther*, we see evidence of Killmonger's homeschooling experience from the opening narrative. Later, there is a scene where Killmonger talks with his father in a cinematic flashback after opening the cabinet in the apartment where his father, N'Jobu (Sterling K. Brown), kept his journal about his Wakandan legacy and the artifacts that symbolize his cultural heritage. During the first narrative, Killmonger's father, N'Jobu, is telling young Killmonger the story of the powerful element vibranium and the history of his family line and the other tribes that make up the country's citizenry. Ending the narrative, the little boy asks, "And, we still hide, Baba?" While depicting the tradition of oral storytelling that is attributed to numerous African cultures throughout the diaspora, the story being told is one depicting ancestral practices of deification and tribalism fused with contemporary and futuristic visions of technology, flora, fauna, and design.

Although the audience is not aware immediately that the little boy being told the story of Wakanda is Killmonger, we later learn his true identity. The delay is necessary for our assumptions to drive our perception of what is good and what is evil (I address this framing later in this chapter). While we become more sympathetic to Killmonger as we become aware of who he was as a child and what his traumatizing experiences were leading up to his villainy, we are ultimately encouraged to root for his demise. Nevertheless, as we become aware that Killmonger's father has taught him all that he believes about the world, we understand the impact his homeschooling has had on his perception of the world.

The movie gives shape to Killmonger's story by making N'Jobu, his father, dimensional before he is killed by his own brother, the rightful king of Wakanda. We learn that N'Jobu lives as a Black American in the United States, hiding his true identity as an African prince. Killmonger's mother is absent from the storyline, but we can infer that she was Black and American born. With this backstory, Killmonger is navigating various Black identities, including those represented by class, ethnicity, and politics. We learn that he has grown up in an apartment in the inner city in California, living with his father as his custodial guardian. It is important to mention that the American city they are in is Oakland, California, the birthplace of the real-life political group, the Black Panther Party. During the tumultuous lifespan of the Black Panther Party from the late 1960s to the early 1980s, many of their action items included liberating Black people globally.[6] These ideas definitely seem to have played a hand in shaping and developing both the fictional character Killmonger and his father N'Jobu in this film. For example, N'Jobu speaks a passage to T'Chaka that is similar to a quote from Black Panther Party leader, the late Huey P. Newton. N'Jobu says, "Communities flooded with drugs and weapons. They are overly policed and incarcerated. All over the planet our people suffer because they don't have the tools to fight back. With vibranium weapons, they can overthrow every country and Wakanda can rule them all, the right way."[7] The quote by Newton found in a documentary featuring an interview of him in jail, said, "If the police were to withdraw from the community and the black community control its own police institution as well as all the other institutions within our community—we feel that law and order would exist."[8]

HOMESCHOOL AS LIBERATORY PRACTICE

Writer and theorist bell hooks, in her book *Teaching to Transgress*,[9] crafts a critical theory of education as liberatory practice that is applied in this analysis. One assertion of her theory is that education is always political and "we cannot enter the struggle as objects in order later to become subjects."[10] When using this theory to deconstruct the key elements of T'Challa and Killmonger's worldviews formed through teachings by their respective fathers, the themes of liberation and identity are inherent in both. N'Jobu and eventually his son Killmonger illustrate hook's position that education is always political. First N'Jobu, then Killmonger rejects the ideology of their Wakandan countrymen that maintains that their resources must stay hidden and that they must only serve the needs of the Wakandan people and not

Black people globally. Killmonger's central motivation is political, born from his father's lessons: he chooses to use his country's resources to arm Black people around the world.

In real life, many Black Americans who choose to homeschool their children are making a political choice. Regardless of socioeconomic class, they are often planning to use homeschooling as a tool to push back against mainstream ideologies of education. They are pushing back against systems that fail to educate Black children in ways that center their life experiences and the historical contribution of their ancestors.[11] The impact on student outcomes largely revolves around identity, too. Education researcher Jasmine Williams[12] studied African American males who were homeschooled prior to enrolling in a historically Black college or university (HBCU), by looking at their perceptions when transitioning from a homeschooling experience to an HBCU. While seeking to understand if a particular Afrocentric educational pedagogy exists among African American homeschooling families, she found that the students in her study were more likely to report that homeschooling had allowed opportunity for self-exploration and growth in an Afrocentric identity. Like Killmonger, African American males who were homeschooled reported being acutely aware of their place in the world through the homeschool education they received, feeling empowered to advocate for themselves when facing the world at-large, in general, and within their college classrooms, specifically.

The themes of freedom and identity are core in N'Boju's teachings to his son. Writer bell hooks said that education is liberatory when it becomes "that historical moment when one begins to think critically about the self and identity in relation to one's political circumstances."[13] Killmonger not only grows up believing that his place is on a throne, but he also believes that he is a savior for all Black people around the world and Wakandans specifically. Killmonger's actions up until this point in the film demonstrate a belief system where he believes his efforts are righteous and he is acting as a liberator. When he first arrives at Wakanda with the head of the White villain he murdered in a bag, he brags to the Wakandan people within earshot of T'Challa, "I'm standing in your house. Serving justice to a man who stole your vibranium and murdered your people. Justice your King couldn't deliver."[14]

The character T'Challa encounters a different experience. The teachings of his father serve an interest to maintain sovereignty at the expense of others. His African father—as most European kings are depicted in historical record, literature, and film—prepares his son for rulership that protects the self-interest of the nation first and foremost. The political aspect of education can be further deconstructed when examining how education shapes oppressive ideology that can disenfranchise others even when those teaching believe they are serving a higher good. Writer bell hooks' explains: "By reinforcing the idea that there is a split between theory and practice or by creating such a split, both groups deny the power of liberatory education for critical consciousness, thereby perpetuating conditions that reinforce our collective exploitation and repression."[15]

T'Challa's narrative provides space to analyze this split between theory and practice that hooks describes, resting on the resulting shift in his personal values and his choices toward the end of the film. While both characters differ along the lines of theory and practice, both received lessons from their fathers that were presented in an Afrocentric centering of the life experiences, achievements, historical turning points, and cultural significance of people of African descent. Black children who have been homeschooled report that this Afrocentric style of teaching effectively prepares them when navigating the world by building their self-identity and helping them understand who they are as people of African descent.[16]

BLACK IDENTITY AND POLITICAL THOUGHT

Despite the Afrocentric teaching style that both N'Jobu and T'Chaka utilize, their messages diverge along the lines of whose interests should be best served. The sons, T'Challa and Killmonger rage against each other throughout the movie in disagreement over these views. T'Challa and Killmonger's feuding depicts the nuance regarding the diverse manifestations of Black identity and agency in the world-at-large.

T'Challa, as depicted in the film, was not taught by his father to have a specific responsibility to Black people all over the world. Instead, he was raised as an isolationist, to be responsible for his countrymen and to take great care with his country's partnership with the United States and global government. In a scene where T'Challa is reunited with the spirit of his late father, T'Chaka, this sentiment of the father is expressed when T'Challa asks him why he didn't bring Killmonger home to Wakanda after he killed N'Jobu. T'Chaka tells T'Challa, "He . . . he was the truth I chose to omit . . . I chose my people. I chose Wakanda."[17] T'Challa "chooses Wakanda" in the epilogue of the movie when he does a series of things. First, he introduces Wakandan technology to the United Nations, then opens a recreational learning center in the neighborhood where his cousin and uncle lived and appoints his sister, a scientist, to head these activities that involve engaging with Black youth in America.

At first glance, these actions seem progressive and aligned with a vision to share the gifts of Wakanda with Black people outside of its borders, specifically those living in the United States who are disenfranchised, living as Killmonger did as an inner-city youth. But, upon closer inspection, it appears that T'Challa has chosen to offer STEM education to the youth of the Black inner city while offering vibranium to the powers that be, maintaining the status quo that already exists in the world. Fundamentally absent from his actions is the fact that he never addresses Killmonger's philosophy on why Wakanda has a responsibility to Black people around the globe.

It is easy to attribute Killmonger and T'Challa's ideologies in the film to historical Black figures who affirmed disparate solutions for Black people to exist in a world dominated by institutional racism. In fact, my daughter and I discussed at length after the movie whether we were pro-Killmonger or pro-T'Challa, trying to determine which character was best aligned with our own personal viewpoints. Killmonger's perspective in the *Black Panther* film is largely pan-African, a concept described in the 1975 article "The black diaspora in Pan-African perspective."[18]

This perspective centers the notion that all Black people of the world hail from Africa and are part of a subsequent community despite forced migration, enslavement, and other reasons that have led to people of African descent to leave the continent. Throughout the movie, Killmonger reiterates these messages consistently despite his misogynistic tendencies and indiscriminately violent behavior leading to the death or assault of several characters, including some from Wakanda.[19] An interesting finding in the historical trajectory of the Black Panther character finds that some of Killmonger's more overtly pan-Afrikan beliefs and Black liberation motifs were original to the title character in the comic before the film was made but quite a time after the character was created. Historian Marsha R. Robinson and cultural theorist Caryn Neumann explain that the character T'Challa was written in the Marvel comic later to mirror Black revolutionary political ideologies from the 1960s.[20] The eventual film, however, attributes more of the revolutionary perspectives to Killmonger in the film. Cultural studies professor Tim Posada writes about the way writer Reginald Hudlin shaped the character T'Challa from 2005 to 2009 when he penned the character's life in comics:

> Rather than avoid politics, as Marvel has done in the past, Hudlin places Black Panther in the midst of what was once a controversy, Afrofuturism and Power 629 this time elevating African Americanness on its own home turf. Even the cover of issue #34, by penciler Salvador Larroca and colorist Paco Roca, supports this. Storm, Black Panther's bride at the time, dons an afro, a leather skirt, boots, a military-style black sweater, and a sidearm. She's joined by two black militants, and the panther logo is redesigned to resemble Black Panther Party propaganda posters.[21]

While both perspectives are framed in Black political thought, the educational pedagogy is important to note. Hooks' theory of education as liberatory practice recognizes that "blackness is complex and multifaceted and that black people can be interpolated into reactionary and antidemocratic politics."[22]

But, T'Challa's interest in maintaining Western interests despite his rulership of a resource-rich African country is aligned with the theme of many Marvel comic stories that center whiteness and American jingoism. Marvel characters ranging from American-born Captain America and Iron Man harbor no greater patriotism than African-born character Storm or even Thor who is other-wordly. Each of these heroes display tremendous loyalty to this theme. Centering a protective stance over the technology and culture of his home country Wakanda, T'Challa epitomizes this positioning, decidedly loyal to the alliance his country has with the United States, evidenced by his close relationship with the White character, Everett Ross (Martin Freeman), a government official. Ending this point, T'Challa does not initially have a viewpoint that includes African Americans as cultural kin, instead possessing a loyalty to the dominant Western imperialism and global authority of White supremacy. This position is presented to T'Challa early and reinforced by his father's dominance in his identity-building process through homeschooling.

LIBERATION AS THE ENDGAME, OR IS IT?

In step with reality, the movie presents a scenario where outside of a cultivated Afrocentric environment, when a Black person enters the world after schooling—whether traditionally schooled or home-educated—they are expected to adopt a Eurocentric perspective. It is not far-fetched to believe that this film depiction of a world leader aligned with status quo politics. Black people must always be prepared to encounter and survive within a world where all spheres of dominant culture reflect a White perspective.[23] However, the film's narrative contradicts the audience's perception of the film as a culturally unifying pop culture artifact. There are two messages that both main characters received through their father's homeschooling practice. When actualizing these lessons, the question still remains as to who is being best served.

Can one consider T'Chaka's homeschooled messages to his son being effective when T'Challa inadvertently weaponizes Wakandan policy to not only stay out of national affairs, but further disenfranchise Black people globally through isolationist policies? In *Teaching to Transgress*, hooks' theory of education as liberatory practice confronts this idea that separateness is safe. She writes that "biases that uphold and maintain White supremacy, imperialism, sexism and racism have distorted education so that it is no longer about the practice of freedom."[24]

While Killmonger touted a pan-Afrikan sensibility, he revered the idea of imperialism, wishing to replace White imperialism with Black imperialism. This contrasts with T'Challa's choice to maintain Wakanda's role as a neutral participant, neither a disrupter nor a nation actively complicit in the maintenance of global dominance. It can be assumed then that for both Killmonger and T'Challa, liberation is not the final objective, assimilation is.

CONCLUSION

The message of assimilation and the adoption of imperialist ideology jolted me out of the romantic perception I initially had of the movie and its cast of beautiful Black faces and its depiction of African diasporic imagery from dress, movement, and vernacular. As a Black American scholar who is also a playwright, performance artist, and homeschooling mother, the permeating message of imperialistic virtue forced me to assess my own personal beliefs and assertions that often conflate cultural reverence with markers of culture that don't necessarily incorporate ideologies that reject a colonizing mentality. Let's be clear. I enjoyed *Black Panther* and believe it is a necessary addition to our archive of Afro-futurist art as it attempts to present a future that includes Black people within dominant society. But, our analysis of cultural representation needs to include analysis of the ideologies presented, careful to examine if our cultural images are being used to promote imperialist rhetoric. As hooks asserts, "critical interrogation is not the same as dismissal."[25] We should be able to hold close cultural works that have problematic elements and discuss them honestly to continuously reconcile our intentions with our outputs.

A theory of education as liberatory practice can be used to analyze the way that education is depicted and/or implemented, as has been done in this chapter. What this analysis has led me to understand is that a theory of education as liberatory practice can be used as a meta-communication tool, deconstructing the way the messages in art communicate ideologies and impact learning taking place as we engage in art and any programming that helps construct our general outlook. Therefore, I am proposing something broad in scope—namely, how to use the film as an educational tool beyond the film's take on the impact of homeschooling.

Meta-communication is the way we communicate about how we are communicating. Paulo Freire in his seminal work *Pedagogy of the Oppressed* asserts that "in order to communicate effectively, educator and politician must understand the structural conditions in which the thought and language of the people are dialectically framed."[26] As we re-imagine blackness, we can begin to determine how attached our view of ourselves is shaped by the intruding notions of imperialism despite the outer appearance of cultural uniqueness and authenticity. This practice actualizes the theory of education as liberatory practice where, whether children are homeschooled or enrolled in traditional schooling options, outcomes are always clear and reconciled with intent.

NOTES

1. Amanda Daily, "Why Hollywood Isn't As Liberal as We Think and Why It Matters" (Senior Thesis, Claremont McKenna College, 2019), https://scholarship.claremont.edu/cmc_theses/2230/.

2. Brian Ray, "Academic Achievement and Demographic traits of Homeschool Students: A Nationwide Study," *Academic Leadership: The Online Journal* 8, no. 1 (2010): 7.

3. Bennett I. Capers, "Afrofuturism, Critical Race Theory, and Policing in the Year 2044," *New York University Law Review* 94, no. 1 (April 2019).

4. This was part of my 2020 dissertation study. See Khadijah Zakia Ali-Coleman, "Dual Enrolled African American Homeschooled Students' Perceptions of Preparedness for Community College" (PhD diss., Morgan State University, 2020).

5. Nedra Rhone, "Homegrown Lessons / More African-American Families Turn to Homeschooling," *Newsday*, October 12, 2003. https://search-proquest-com.proxy-ms.researchport.umd.edu/docview/279789475?accountid=12557.

6. Nik Heynen, "Bending the Bars of Empire from Every Ghetto for Survival: The Black Panther Party's Radical Antihunger Politics of Social Reproduction and Scale," *Annals of the Association of American Geographers* 99, no. 2 (2009): 406–422.

7. *Black Panther*, directed by Ryan Coogler (Walt Disney Studios Motion Pictures, 2018).

8. *Huey P. Newton: Prelude to a Revolution*, directed by John Evans (Amazon Prime, 1998), www.amazon.com/Huey-P-Newton-Prelude-Revolution/dp/B079LV8CWY.

9. bell hooks, *Teaching to Transgress: Education as the Practice of Freedom* (New York: Routledge, 1994).

10. hooks, *Teaching to Transgress*, 46.

11. Cheryl Fields-Smith, and Monica Wells Kisura, "Resisting the Status Quo: The Narratives of Black Homeschoolers in Metro-Atlanta and Metro-DC," *Peabody Journal of Education* 88, no. 3 (2013): 265–283.

12. Jasmine D. Williams, "Homeschoolers: Experiences of African American Male Students A Phenomenological Study," *Urban Education Research & Policy Annuals* 4, no. 1 (2016): 110–121.

13. hooks, *Teaching to Transgress*, 47.

14. *Black Panther*, Coogler, 2018.
15. hooks, *Teaching to Transgress*, 67.
16. Ali-Coleman, "Dual Enrolled African American Homeschooled Students' Perceptions of Preparedness for Community College."
17. *Black Panther*, Coogler, 2018.
18. St Clair Drake, "The black diaspora in Pan-African perspective," *The Black Scholar* 7, no. 1 (1975): 2–13.
19. In the film *Black Panther*, Killmonger shoots and kills his girlfriend, strangles an elderly woman, and brutally fights members of T'Challa's family and all-female royal army.
20. Marsha R. Robinson and Caryn Neumann, "Introduction: On Coogler and Cole's *Black Panther* Film (2018): Global Perspectives, Reflections and Contexts for Educators," *Africology: The Journal of Pan African Studies (Online)* 11, no. 9 (2018): 1–12.
21. Tim Posada, "Afrofuturism, Power, and Marvel Comics's *Black Panther*," *The Journal of Popular Culture* 52, no. 3 (2019): 625–644.
22. hooks, *Teaching to Transgress*, 67.
23. In this qualitative study on the transition experiences of Black homeschooled students in the United States, the researcher found that when Black homeschooled children enrolled in predominantly white institutions, they described their course curricula as typically emphasizing a Eurocentric perspective that they were unfamiliar with. Read more in Taj'ullah X. Sky Lark, *From Homeschool to College: Exploring Transition Experiences of Homeschooled African American Students at Predominantly White Institutions* (Hampton University, 2014).
24. hooks, *Teaching to Transgress*, 29.
25. hooks, *Teaching to Transgress*, 46.
26. Paulo Freire, *Pedagogy of the Oppressed* (revised) (New York: Continuum, 1996), 96.

WORKS CITED

Ali-Coleman, Khadijah Zakia. "Dual Enrolled African American Homeschooled Students' Perceptions of Preparedness for Community College." PhD diss., Morgan State University, 2020.

Capers, I. Bennett. "Afrofuturism, Critical Race Theory, and Policing in the Year 2044." *New York University Law Review* 94, no. 1 (April 2019).

Daily, Amanda. "Why Hollywood Isn't As Liberal As We Think and Why It Matters." Senior Thesis, Claremont McKenna College, 2019.

Drake, St Clair. "The black diaspora in Pan-African perspective." *The Black Scholar* 7, no. 1 (1975): 2–13.

Fields-Smith, Cheryl, and Monica Wells Kisura. "Resisting the Status Quo: The Narratives of Black Homeschoolers in Metro-Atlanta and Metro-DC." *Peabody Journal of Education* 88, no. 3 (2013): 265–283.

Freire, Paulo. *Pedagogy of the Oppressed* (revised). New York: Continuum, 1996.

Heynen, Nik. "Bending the Bars of Empire from Every Ghetto for Survival: The Black Panther Party's Radical Antihunger Politics of Social Reproduction and Scale." *Annals of the Association of American Geographers* 99, no. 2 (2009): 406–422.

hooks, bell. *Teaching to Transgress: Education as the Practice of Freedom.* New York: Routledge, 1994.

Marech, Rona. "Home Schooling Draws More Blacks." *BaltimoreSun.com*, January 23, 2006, https://www.baltimoresun.com/news/bs-xpm-2006-01-23-0601230045-story.html.

Mokoena, Dikeledi A. "*Black Panther* and the Problem of the Black Radical." *Journal of Pan African Studies* 11, no. 9 (2018): 13–19.

Rhone, Nedra. "Homegrown Lessons / More African-American Families Turn to Homeschooling." *Newsday*, October 12, 2003. https://search-proquest-com.proxy-ms.researchport.umd.edu/docview/279789475?accountid=12557.

Ray, Brian. "Academic Achievement and Demographic Traits of Homeschool Students: A Nationwide Study." *Academic Leadership: The Online Journal* 8, no. 1 (2010): 7.

Robinson, Marsha R., and Caryn Neumann. "Introduction: On Coogler and Cole's Black Panther Film (2018): Global Perspectives, Reflections and Contexts for Educators." *The Journal of Pan African Studies (Online)* 11, no. 9 (2018): 1–12.

Sky Lark, Taj'ullah X. *From Homeschool to College: Exploring Transition Experiences of Homeschooled African American Students at Predominantly White Institutions.* Hampton University, 2014.

Williams, Jasmine D. "Homeschoolers: Experiences of African American Male Students A Phenomenological Study." *Urban Education Research & Policy Annuals* 4, no. 1 (2016): 110–121.

FILMS

Black Panther. Directed by Ryan Coogler. United States: Walt Disney Studios Motion Pictures, 2018.

Chapter 16

Two Paths to the Future

Radical Cosmopolitanism and Counter-Colonial Dignity in Black Panther

Neal Curtis

The superhero genre has been infamously resistant to diversity. While strides have been taken in the comics to incrementally improve representations of race, ethnicity, gender, and sexuality, the dominance of the White man as hero has remained evident in the genre's transition to box office dominance. With the exceptions of *Steel* (1997) directed by Kenneth Johnson, *Blade* (1998) directed by Stephen Norrington and *Catwoman* (2004) directed by Jean-Christophe Pitof, superhero films have largely been an exercise in hegemonic whiteness. As such they retain many of the colonial assumptions of White normality and superiority where their sense for the cosmopolitan rarely extends beyond the jet-setting and globe-trotting of billionaires or covert paramilitary elites. The significance of Ryan Coogler's *Black Panther* (2018) is notable, therefore, because it is a significant challenge to all of these prejudices. As a film with a Black director, a Black creative team and predominantly Black cast it was a significant step forward in a White dominated industry. As a film, however, it directly and forcefully engages with both the parochial and colonial attitudes that still organizes Hollywood's worldview, offering a vision of an Afro-infused political future based on radical cosmopolitanism and the dignity of counter-colonial struggle (see also chapter by Renee White in this volume).

These two political trajectories were actually set up in the earlier film that first introduced Wakanda and T'Challa (Chadwick Boseman) to the Marvel Cinematic Universe. In *Captain America: Civil War* (Anthony and Joe Russo, 2016), we see how T'Challa's father T'Chaka (John Kani) has already begun the process of engaging with the wider world when we learn that an explosion resulting from superhero activity killed eleven Wakandans on an outreach mission in Lagos, Nigeria. As a consequence, the world calls for control of superhero activity and establishes the Sokovia Accords. During the signing of the Accords at the UN building in Vienna, a terrorist bomb, supposedly planted by Captain America's long-time friend Bucky Barnes (Sebastian Stan), explodes and kills T'Chaka. This makes T'Challa next in line for the Wakandan throne and sets him on a mission to execute Bucky for his crime: a vengeful path that anticipates the anti-imperial rage of his antagonist, Erik Killmonger (Michael B. Jordan), in *Black Panther*, and undoes T'Chaka's earlier efforts to open Wakanda to the world.

In this chapter, I will argue that the two political trajectories of *Black Panther*, namely its post-national cosmopolitanism and the vengeful counter-colonial violence, are based on a critique and reformation of the traditional theory of sovereignty that defines the modern nation state. This is a theory that founds national sovereign power in threats to the security of its borders and the naming of the enemy. In the first instance, the film follows T'Challa's continuing journey from a king motivated by the punishment of Wakanda's enemies to becoming a champion of international engagement and ethical universalism, while Killmonger is shown to move from being an avatar for the covert U.S. war machine to the agent of counter-colonial dignity. While these two journeys and their outcomes are distinct, they are nevertheless closely connected. In many respects, their origins emanate from the exceptional power of the sovereign to suspend the law in a state of emergency. More specifically, as the legal philosopher and Third Reich jurist Carl Schmitt argued, this is the sovereign's capacity to decide on the exception and declare when the law no longer applies.[1] As I will argue shortly, it is the politics of exception that informs the actions of the younger T'Chaka in the opening scene of *Black Panther* and sets both narratives in motion.

After working through the key elements of Schmitt's theory of sovereignty and how it manifests in the early part of the film, the chapter analyses the two political visions of radical cosmopolitanism and counter-colonial dignity that are developed as alternatives to it. This also requires some consideration of the film's progressive gender politics—especially as understood from the perspective of Africana womanism[2]—as Nakia (Lupita Nyong'o, Shuri (Letitia Wright), Okoye (Danai Gurira), and Ramonda (Angela Bassett) are as important as the film's antagonist, Killmonger, to T'Challa's transformation. The chapter then proposes that while the radical cosmopolitanism of T'Challa seems to win out in the end, the film operates through a form of negative dialectics[3] in which the radical dissent of Killmonger is preserved in rather than negated by T'Challa's cosmopolitan turn. The chapter concludes by showing how this tension in *Black Panther* between the particular and the universal, the local and the global, is in keeping with what sociologist Julian Go calls "postcolonial cosmopolitanism."[4]

CARL SCHMITT AND THE SOVEREIGN DECISION

In *Political Theology,* Carl Schmitt defined the sovereign as "he who decides on the exception"[5] or the entity charged with deciding whether "a normal [legal/juridical] situation exists."[6] In other words, the essential feature of sovereignty is the capacity to suspend the law in response to a state of emergency understood as either civil unrest or an external threat. Responding to Schmitt, Italian philosopher, Giorgio Agamben argued the exceptional status of the sovereign renders any idea of the legal and the extra-legal problematic. What he calls the "anomic" element of sovereignty, namely the capacity to suspend the *nomos* (the Greek word for law), means sovereignty is the point where the law and its absence, the legal and the extra-legal "coincide."[7]

This exceptional politics is central to *Black Panther*, where the entire story is premised on a related phenomenon that Agamben calls the sovereign ban, a condition in which those elements the sovereign deems criminal, dangerous, or hostile are placed outside the law and exposed to violence. For Agamben, the spatial model for this is the camp where inmates are stripped of their personhood, and hence their protection under the law. When the film opens in Oakland—a location is chosen because it was the birthplace of the Black Panther Party[8]—we are introduced to N'Jobu (Sterling K. Brown), the younger brother of King T'Chaka who is visiting him. N'Jobu is living in Oakland as a Wakandan War Dog, an undercover agent supposed to feed intelligence about the outside world back to Wakanda. We learn, however, that N'Jobu has effectively gone rogue and is responsible for stealing some of Wakanda's precious metal vibranium, a crime he committed so that oppressed people around the world might have "the tools to fight back." It becomes clear that as a Black man living in America, he has become politicized by the racist legacy of colonialism and slavery he sees every day on the streets of Oakland.

In this scene, it is also revealed that his friend and accomplice "James" (Denzel Whitaker) is actually a Wakandan spy named Zuri (Forest Whitaker), sent to watch N'Jobu; he has reported N'Jobu's actions to T'Chaka. On discovering what he regards as a betrayal, N'Jobu attempts to kill Zuri, but T'Chaka steps in and kills N'Jobu instead. In this act, the law that would ordinarily protect N'Jobu is suspended and his actions that supposedly threaten the security of Wakanda justify his killing. Importantly, however, although we don't know this at the time, N'Jobu has had a son, Eric (the grown role is played by Michael B. Jordan), with an American woman and T'Chaka returns to Wakanda, thereby abandoning the boy. This abandonment of Eric as a child (Seth Carr), where he is left unprotected to face whatever violence Oakland might direct at a young Black man, thus becomes the premise for the entire film, because it is the return of Eric that drives the narrative and its themes of colonialism, slavery, and revolutionary politics.

When we first meet the adult Killmonger, he represents the "blowback" of colonialism when he raids a British Natural History museum to take back African artifacts stolen during the age of empire. Specifically, he has come to secure a piece of vibranium the museum doesn't even know it has. Here, he reverses the crucial colonial hierarchy that depicts the colonized as unenlightened and lacking knowledge. The ignorance of the White expert becomes an important early marker of the film's politics. This is also the first we see of Killmonger as a revolutionary subject. Prior to this, we learn he had been a soldier in covert U.S. operations aimed at counter-terrorism and regime change. The logic of this part of his backstory is unclear but was no doubt included to reference the contemporary forms of neo-colonialism that underlie the war on terror and American exceptionalism. It is what the British historian and cultural critic Paul Gilroy called the "new armoured cosmopolitanism" of U.S. president George W. Bush and British Prime Minister Tony Blair, a supposedly humanitarian interventionism still committed to the old imperial fantasy of "spreading civilization by force."[9]

From this aspect of Killmonger's biography, we also learn he has been so committed to this cause and so ruthless in his purpose that he has scarred his body with hundreds of cuts, each one the mark of someone he has killed while on active duty as part of the elitist SEALs for the U.S. government. Here, his scarification operates with all the ambivalence that critical theorist Homi Bhabha attributed to colonial mimicry. For Bhabha, colonialism always works by demanding mimicry of the colonizer by the colonized. However, it is a mimicry that is also supposed to reproduce the difference of colonial authority. In copying the language, manners, and style of the colonizer, the colonized show themselves to be "almost the same, but not quite."[10] Mimicry therefore carries with it an important ambivalence that reinforces colonial power, but this means it can also shift from mimicry to menace. In other words, identification through mimicry can also become "a sign of the inappropriate [. . .] that poses an imminent threat" to what is considered normal.[11] Coogler clearly knows to what extent the colonial gaze remains prevalent and that the scarification that keeps a corporeal record of U.S. neo-imperial adventures would be viewed as savage. According to Bhabha's view of mimicry, this identification is thus a *"double* vision" where the intensity of the identification with the neo-colonial project also "disrupts its authority."[12] The scars are testimony to Killmonger's commitment as U.S. soldier dedicated to U.S. covert operations, but they also represent the naked violence of those operations, stripped of the discursive, ideological balm that would normally accompany them.

This feature of Killmonger's skin is revealed when he returns to Wakanda and challenges T'Challa for the right to the throne during ritual combat. In this scene, he defeats T'Challa and supposedly kills him by throwing him off Warrior Falls, just as he did when they first met in the comic in 1973.[13] Having thus assumed the title of Wakandan king and then having partaken in the magical ritual through which a potent herb bestows on him the powers of the Black Panther, Killmonger proceeds to undermine the political and cultural institutions of Wakanda to ensure no one will be able to challenge him in the future. His stated desire is to use the resources of Wakanda to fight a heavily weaponized war against the ongoing exploitation of people around the world. At this point, although his cause remains just, Killmonger has now shifted from the role of anti-hero to full blown, tyrannical super-villain. In the process, the radical Black politics he represents are recast from legitimate and perhaps necessary to illegitimate and dangerous. However, I believe Coogler retained an important aspect of radical Black politics in Killmonger's character, but before I return to that I would like to say something about the politics that appears victorious at the end of the film.

RADICAL COSMOPOLITANISM

In the third act of the film, we discover that T'Challa did not die at Warrior Falls but was rescued by the Jabari Women. Having been de-powered for the ritual fight with Killmonger, his powers are given back to him by Nakia who managed to save one of the sacred plants before Killmonger had them all destroyed. The damage wrought in the ensuing and climactic battle between T'Challa and Killmonger makes T'Challa realize that Wakanda can no longer hide and must, once he re-secures his rightful place as king, engage with the outside world in order to improve people's lives. On first view, I took aversion to this ending. It seemed as if the film's radicalism was hopelessly lost and we were left with a very ideological vision of neoliberal governmentality where the success of public works relied on the benevolence and charity of billionaires. On reflection, this turned out not to be the case and T'Challa carries with him his own radicalism in the form of a commitment to a cosmopolitan humanism that has a long and significant heritage in Black politics, especially in the writings of figures like civil rights activist W. E. B. Du Bois and the psychiatrist and political philosopher Frantz Fanon.

As was noted earlier, however, the roots of T'Challa's cosmopolitan turn had already been sown by his father in the earlier film, *Captain America: Civil War*. It is no accident, then, that the first time we see T'Challa in that film, and therefore in the Marvel Cinematic Universe, is at the UN building in Vienna as if presaging his turn to openness and engagement, and his return to that very same building in the first of *Black Panther's* post-credit scenes. However, perhaps the most significant precursor to this new political engagement also took place in the earlier *Captain America* film when T'Challa, having discovered Bucky was framed, grants him refuge and asylum, and Shuri helps him recover from the wounds he has received. The importance of this granting of refuge is noted in *Black Panther* when T'Challa decides to take an injured Agent Everett Ross (Martin Freeman) back to Wakanda and Shuri points out he has brought "another broken White boy for us to fix." Her care of Bucky is then returned to in the second of the two *Black Panther* post-credit scenes.

At the beginning of *Black Panther*, this future path of openness and engagement is already being advocated for by Nakia who we see rescuing trafficked women in the Sambisa Forest in Nigeria. Having being called home for the ceremony to confirm T'Challa as king, he asks her to stay but she tells him "I've found my calling out there," going on to argue that Wakanda needs to "share what we have." So, while T'Challa becomes sovereign of a territory, the borders of which he is determined to protect, Nakia already represents the border crossings and "translocal solidarity" that are essential to the practice of cosmopolitan politics.[14] Shuri's care for the refugee and Nakia's defense of vulnerable foreigners are therefore Wakanda's future, even if the reluctant new king hasn't quite understood this yet. It is also worth noting—given this film is saturated with different aspects of Black politics—that this early scene where Nakia expresses her independence, by telling T'Challa she has no wish to be queen, and the ritual at Warrior Falls where she speaks for her tribe and concedes the throne to him, both need to be understood in terms of Africana womanism rather than Western feminism.[15]

In an excellent article on the topic, Zimbabwean feminist scholar Rosemary Chikafa-Chipiro (2019) explains that Africana womanism privileges race over both class and gender and speaks to "the wholeness of black peoples."[16] It therefore "champions negotiation and harmonious relations between black men and women."[17] In other words, "the women's centrality in the politics of Wakanda places more precedence on the commitment to the wholeness of Wakanda peoples and the state's sovereignty than to the women's individual subjectivities. Therefore, the women's roles privilege the communal over the individual" in order "to enable the realization of sustainable futures."[18] This sense of negotiation, however, does not in any way undermine the importance of the women to the film's politics. As Chikafa-Chipiro notes, the arrival of the Dora Milajes in the opening scene "heralds the centrality of Black womanhood in the power dynamics of Wakanda."[19] Indeed, the leader of the Dora Milajes, General Okoye, also epitomizes a second important aspect of Africana womanism that Hudson-Weems calls "nommo," or "women's sense of agency as self-namers and self-definers."[20] We see this explicitly when

Okoye decides to remain loyal to the Wakandan crown even after it is taken by Killmonger, which also means she is perfectly placed to rename T'Challa king when he returns; but it is the nommo of Nakia's self-definition that T'Challa ultimately follows.

As I have already noted, this path is the one that leads to T'Challa's embrace of the radical cosmopolitanism that has a long tradition in Black politics. For Paul Gilroy, the writings of W. E. B. Du Bois have always centered around a commitment to "world citizenship and world history."[21] Likewise, American studies scholar Günter Lenz, writing about Du Bois's lifelong relationship with German culture and intellectual life, has noted how his signature concept of "double consciousness" is primarily "a dynamic, bi-(or multi-)cultural mode of inquiry of African American experience, culture, thinking, and discourse."[22] In the same work, Lenz goes on to quote African American literature scholar Bernard Bell who argued "'African American double consciousness thus signifies a biracial, bicultural state of being in the world, an existential site of socialized cultural ambivalence and emancipatory possibilities of personal and social transformation'";[23] and philosopher Nahum Chandler who argues that Du Bois "never ceased to affirm this heterogeneity as *also* a good, a resource, in general," as well as a discourse on "impurity" that "opens a powerful critical reflection upon its own historical production."[24]

Consequently, Lenz concludes that Du Bois's "African American exploratory discourses are modes of a *radical cosmopolitanism*" in the sense of "an open, trans- (and post) national, diasporic discourse that acknowledges and negotiates intercultural multiplicity, heterogeneous interests and positions, and hybrid publics."[25] In his later writings, Du Bois developed the related concept of the "fourth dimension" whereby he proposed a new vision of global democracy and citizenship that countered both U.S. imperialism and racial division with a "social plan to place the politically marginalized and colonized 'colored world' at the centre of global democracy."[26] This was in turn motivated by "the expressive cultural tradition of African American calls for sanctuary."[27] This was something that T'Challa had, of course, earlier afforded Bucky.

Although Frantz Fanon is perhaps best known for his evocation of national consciousness as part of any counter-colonial struggle he, too, aimed toward a radical cosmopolitanism. In fact, according to Julian Go, the experience of colonialism lent itself to a politics that transcended parochial identities. For Go, "colonialism was generative of cosmopolitanism as colonialism's own victims ably seized upon the contradictions and envisioned their transcendence."[28] In other words, the exclusions of colonialism became "a condition for a new different type of cosmopolitanism."[29] Fanon can therefore be shown to have called for "decolonization in order to transcend the [. . .] contradictions of colonialism and realize a new humanism."[30] On this matter, it is no coincidence that the first page of Fanon's *Black Skin, White Masks* and the last page of *The Wretched of the Earth* are devoted to the human (humanism and then humanity respectively). As Go also notes, Fanon's conception of humanity "does not exclude the colonizer" because it is understood that colonialism has also corrupted them.[31] This is not to excuse the guilt of European colonizers because Fanon is clear about how they have failed. At the end of *The Wretched of the Earth,* he pointedly notes: "All the elements of a solution to the great problems of humanity have, at different times, existed in European thought. But Europeans have not carried out in practice the mission which fell to them," namely "bringing the problem of mankind to an infinitely higher plane."[32]

In Go's reading of Fanon, decolonization is not therefore a romantic return to an idyll but a radical transformation and "nationalism is merely a basis for its own supersession."[33] At the end of *Black Panther,* we consequently arrive at something akin to what Gilroy calls "geo-piety," which he defines as an attitude "that operates on an earthly scale and is not oriented by fundamental concern for the sovereign territory of national states."[34] Such a piety is exemplified in T'Challa's speech to the UN in the first of *Black Panther*'s post-credit scenes. Having already returned to the site of Eric's abandonment and transformed that site of sovereign exception into the headquarters of Wakanda's new cosmopolitan program of social and scientific outreach, he addresses the world:

> Wakanda will no longer watch from the shadows. We cannot. We must not. We will work to be an example of how we as brothers and sisters on this Earth should treat each other. Now, more than ever, the illusions of division threaten our very existence. We all know the truth: more connects us than separates us. But in times of crisis the wise build bridges, while the foolish build barriers. We must find a way to look after one another as if we were one single tribe.

However, to fully understand the significance of this speech, and therefore the true complexity of the film's politics, it is necessary to articulate why the film does not simply arrive at a liberal view of cosmopolitanism, but instead articulates Go's "postcolonial cosmopolitanism." To do that we need to return to and recover an aspect of Killmonger's politics that we have not yet properly explored.

SOVEREIGNTY, THE EXCEPTION, AND RADICAL DISSENT

While it can be argued that the defeat and death of Killmonger signals the delegitimation of his militant form of political activism, the film is in fact far more complex in its treatment of the counter-colonial violence that Killmonger advocates. Indeed, if the film is so clear-cut in its message, why did it encourage so many viewers to claim "Killmonger was right"? To understand this requires a closer examination of what happens to Killmonger after he defeats T'Challa at Warrior Falls, in particular, when he goes through the ritual that is supposed to give him the powers of the Black Panther. When we saw T'Challa partake of the sacred rite in the early part of the film, the ingestion of the magical herb took him to the Wakandan spiritual plane where he met his deceased father who tells him it is time for him to be king. The setting is especially "African" in its flora and fauna and is bathed in purple light, a color that manifests in T'Challa's Black Panther suit to indicate the presence of the spiritual realm whenever he assumes his superhero persona. By contrast, when Killmonger partakes of the sacred rite, he does not go to Wakanda but returns to Oakland, the same place where he had been left behind as a child, where he too meets his deceased father in the very apartment where Killmonger grew up and his father was killed.

This is important because it is the spirit of his father's dissent—and his political radicalization on the streets of Oakland—that Killmonger carries with him when he receives his superpowers. This is made explicit in the film because when Killmonger suits up he does not in fact manifest as the Black Panther but as a quite different beast, the White leopard known as Preyy. This animal first appears in the comics at the very moment we are introduced to Killmonger—previously known as N'Jadaka and the name of Killmonger's father in the film—who is shown violently assaulting T'Challa.[35] When we first see the two in battle, Killmonger's animal familiar is drawn standing behind and above him on a rock, but its position within the frame also makes it look like Preyy is standing on Killmonger's back.

To understand this, we need to know what caused N'Jadaka's transformation into Killmonger. In the comics, after first meeting the Fantastic Four,[36] T'Challa made several visits to the United States to work with them and the Avengers. While he was away and Wakanda was unprotected, colonizers captured and enslaved N'Jadaka and shipped him off to America. When he escaped, he returned to Wakanda and violently seized power in an effort to prevent any further incursions in Wakandan territory. When T'Challa himself returned, he found a country vastly different from the one he left, a country now under Killmonger's tyrannical rule. A year before, Marvel had also briefly renamed *Black Panther* as *Black Leopard*, feeling they needed to distance him from the increasingly visible Black Panther Party. In light of this, the use of a White leopard as Killmonger's totem animal is no coincidence. Where the *Black Panther* (Black leopard) represents autonomy and freedom, the White leopard represents the burden of colonialism that N'Jadaka carries and caused him to take such a destructive course of action. The animal stands as a clear warning about colonialism's damaging effects.

Returning to the film, Killmonger's manifestation as Preyy is clearly indicated both in the color of his suit, which is Black and gold, and the spotted pattern that is especially visible on his mask. So, when Killmonger seizes the power of Wakanda with the express desire to decolonize the world or liberate the "two billion people all over the world who look like us, whose lives are much harder," this choice of costume and characterization by Coogler is not accidental. From this, it is possible to see why people continued to take a liberatory reading of the character and let slide his seemingly tyrannical desire for the sun "to never set on the Wakandan empire." Killmonger literally carries the history and pain of colonial exploitation back to an indifferent Wakanda with the intention of using its wealth, resources, and technical advances for global political liberation.

That this turns violent is in keeping with Frantz Fanon's analysis of the struggle for decolonization which is "quite simply the replacing of a certain 'species' of men by another 'species' of men"[37] and the "native who decides to put the programme into practice, and to become its moving force, is ready for violence at all times."[38] The colonial world, Fanon goes on to note, is therefore "a Manichean world"[39] in which "the violence of the colonial regime and the counter-violence of the native balance each other and respond in an extraordinary reciprocal homogeneity. [. . .] The development of violence among the colonized people will be proportionate to the violence exercised by the threatened colonial regime."[40] Because this world is also a Schmittian world of friend and enemy, these echoes of Fanon lead back to the topic of sovereignty and the politics of the exception, and in a brilliant reading of both Agamben and Fanon by legal studies scholar Susan Dianne Brophy we can see how Killmonger might still be regarded as heroic and remain a champion of radical Black politics despite his autocratic adoption of violence.

In her essay entitled "Lawless Sovereignty," Brophy argues that the study of Fanon and colonialism more broadly suggests "another form of sovereignty can be appealed to as a means of challenging the state of exception" and the force of law that underpins it.[41] Brophy correctly points out that the colonial relation is the essence of exceptional politics where the colonizer is the source and embodiment of value and the colonized is "valueless [and] animalistic," and thereby reduced to bare life. In this condition, the law withdraws its protection, and the colonized are subject to extreme forms of violence and cruel treatment, epitomized in the slave trade. Here, the site of the sovereign ban also becomes the slave ship, the plantation, the auction, the hanging tree, and any place where the slave owner desires to enact his sovereign power.

In fact, in keeping with Agamben's analysis, it is this setting *outside* the bounds of legal protection that is *integral* to the sovereign power of the slave-owner. Here we have the intimate relationship between the legal and the extra-legal, the inside and the outside refigured in terms of colonial practice.

In other words, this *externalizing* of the colonized as animal or subhuman is a *constituent* element of colonial sovereign power and the *law* that the sovereign declares. However, remembering that the law is always infused with forms of violence that are turned against enemies, foreigners, outsiders, criminals, and animals from whom the sovereign withdraws the protection of the law, *and* that this setting outside of the law is intrinsic to the nature of sovereignty itself, the other form of sovereignty Brophy is seeking can only be found in a specific form of *lawlessness*. To reiterate, if the essence or inner truth of the law's legitimacy as well as its execution appears in setting certain entities outside the law, the "universalizable justice claim" that might found this alternative sovereignty can only be found beyond this topology of the mutually constituting inside/outside that defines the force and authority of law.

To find this lawlessness, Brophy needs to identify something genuinely external to sovereignty defined in terms of the politics of exception. In other words, she needs to locate a *remainder* that sovereign power can never grasp. Here, she turns to the dissent of the colonized, specifically the dissention that doesn't presume "a prior consent."[42] No matter what the colonized might consent to post-colonization in an attempt to secure or maintain a life, sovereign power is unable to take control of the fact the colonized never consented to the colonization in the first place. For Brophy, this originary dissent "is representative of a standpoint that is *always and already* external to the juridico-political order of the sovereign."[43] Understood in colonial terms, it is also a standpoint and a lawlessness that is "necessarily always already *universalized*" as a fundamental condition of all particular, local colonial experiences.[44] It is a "shared externality."[45] Consequently, this dissent and any action related to it "emerges from, reflects, and supports lawlessness in that it originates from outside the state of exception and necessarily *negates* the juridical power of a given state." Ultimately, it is a "constituting power that does not require law to supplement its force."[46]

In my reading of the very deliberate decision to have Killmonger manifest as Preyy when he undergoes the sacred ritual, and to have him visit the place from where he learned about the ongoing violence, discrimination, and exploitation of the postcolonial struggle, means he is always an avatar for radical Black politics. In particular, he is the manifestation of this originary dissent that gives access to the universalized justice claim at the root of a genuinely alternative politics. In effect, Killmonger represents the call to liberate every particular place that is still subject to this universal violence—represented in the film to some extent by government Agent Ross.

As I noted earlier, although Ross is confoundingly cast as the liberal, White ally, his presence is also a reminder of the global, neo-imperial role of militarized capital that continues to subject people to colonial violence in the name of regime change and Western conceptions of freedom. Colonialism remains a global, weaponized, trillion-dollar industry. As such, Killmonger's counter-violence needs to match it in scale and ferocity. He needs to produce his own "shock and awe." This also plays out at a time when the police violence and the extra-judicial killings of Black people that gave birth to the *Black Lives Matter* movement reminds us that the Manichean vision set out by Killmonger remains relevant. White supremacy has been under review and its culture has been subject to reform for the last 150 years, but decolonization it seems has not been achieved, far from it. In light of this, no matter how wrong Killmonger is shown to be, he remains the embodiment of the "never-having-consented dissent" that resists colonialism and its legacy in the post-colony.

ERIK KILLMONGER'S DEATH SCENE AND ITS POLITICS

Killmonger's death scene is therefore of the utmost importance because while T'Challa appears victorious, and his explicitly and clearly articulated shift toward cosmopolitan politics is shown to be the best political path to peace *and* justice, Killmonger does not concede that he was wrong nor does the film delegitimize his sense of continuing injustice. This is made explicit in the last words that Coogler writes for Killmonger. Fatally wounded in his final confrontation with Black Panther, T'Challa takes him out of the darkness in which they fought and into the softening light of the setting sun that signifies the end of this cycle of violence and anticipates a new day. As Killmonger collapses to his knees, T'Challa says: "Maybe we can still heal you," to which Killmonger replies "Why? So you can just lock me up? Nah. Just bury me in the ocean with my ancestors that jumped from the ships, 'cause they knew death was better than bondage." As he dies, then, Killmonger refuses to be the criminal whose action defines and legitimizes sovereign power. He refuses to offer his consent and retains his position of radical dissent and lawlessness where Brophy locates real justice.

This means the film offers a resolution of sorts, but it is not a synthesis of the two positions nor is it the positive overcoming of one (counter-colonial violence) by the other (cosmopolitanism). In fact, the brilliance of the film stems from the fact that it takes "a turn towards nonidentity" that Adorno argued is "the hinge of negative dialectics."[47] Understood in this way, T'Challa's turn to cosmopolitanism cannot be read as a positive result in which the challenge of Killmonger has been negated or subsumed because Killmonger's dissent continues to haunt T'Challa's future actions. This also applies to the justice assumed in Killmonger's counter-colonial struggle. Here, T'Challa's turn to universalism reminds us that Killmonger's politics is meaningless if it doesn't—as Fanon said it must—transcend itself and address the shared humanity it implies. Therefore, the sovereign dignity rooted in the never-having-consented of the colonized speaks to a fundamental recognition of human rights and the need for those rights to be equitably and substantively distributed.

Despite Fanon's advocacy for counter-colonial violence, he also knew that such politics must work to surpass itself and that the new situation that such violence was intended to bring about must not repeat the injustice it sought to free itself from. In *A Dying Colonialism* he writes, "The new relations are not the result of one barbarism replacing another barbarism, of one crushing of man replacing another crushing of man";[48] but this doesn't mean T'Challa's politics legitimates the dominant form of liberal cosmopolitanism. Speaking about what cosmopolitanism can learn from colonial and anti-racist struggles, Paul Gilroy argued that cosmopolitan solidarity "derives [. . .] from an instructive and humble confrontation with the bloody consequences of awesome imperial power."[49] This is precisely what Killmonger forces T'Challa to do. The fact that Killmonger's call against global injustice continues to haunt T'Challa also means that his cosmopolitan turn "is never a matter of forgetting what it took so long to remember,"[50] but a reminder that "the vigilance that is necessary to indict imperial modernity must be extended into the field of the future."[51] This idea that universal claims remain unrealized due to the persistence of universal injustice, especially as these inequities continue to manifest around "race" and ethnicity, is what I understand by Go's assessment of "postcolonial cosmopolitanism," and this is the complex but incredibly rich politics of *Black Panther*.

NOTES

1. Carl Schmitt, *Political Theology: Four Chapters on the Concept of Sovereignty* (Chicago: Chicago University Press, 1985), 5.

2. Clenora Hudson-Weems, "Africana Womanism: The Flip Side of a Coin," *Western Journal of Black Studies* 25, no. 3 (2001).

3. Theodor Adorno, *Negative Dialectics* (New York: Continuum, 1973).

4. Julian Go, "Fanon's Postcolonial Cosmopolitanism," *European Journal of Social Theory* 16, no. 2 (2013).

5. Schmitt, *Political Theology*, 5.

6. Schmitt, *Political Theology*, 13.

7. Giorgio Agamben, *Homo Sacer: Sovereign Power and Bare Life* (Stanford: Stanford University Press, 1998), 71.

8. The Black Panther Party was a radical civil rights and political liberation movement. According to Michael X. Delli Carpini, its philosophy and practice was "a mix of social contract theory as found in the U.S. Declaration of Independence,

individual rights as outlined in the U.S. Constitution, Marxist anti-capitalism, the national liberation theories of Frantz Fanon [. . .], the self-determination espoused by the black power movement, and the more generalized cultural and political radicalism of the New Left." Michael X. Delli Carpini, "Black Panther Party: 1966-1982," in *The Encyclopedia of Third Parties in America*, ed. I. Ness and J. Ciment (Armonke, NY: Sharpe Reference, 2000), 191. In addition, the Black Panther Party also viewed Black neighbourhoods and communities as colonies still ruled by a White police. Consequently, the film's direct reference to the birthplace of the Party against the backdrop of the Black Lives Matter movement that was continuing to protest against police violence and White supremacy meant the story had immediate political and cultural relevance.

9. Paul Gilroy, *Postcolonial Melancholia* (New York: Columbia University Press, 2005), 63, 62.

10. Homi Bhabha, *The Location of Culture* (London: Routledge, 1998), 86.

11. Bhabha, *Location*, 86.

12. Bhabha, *Location*, 88.

13. Don McGregor and Rich Buckler, *Jungle Action* 2, no. 6 (New York: Marvel Publications, 1973).

14. Gilroy, *Postcolonial Melancholia*, 76.

15. Hudson-Weems, "Africana Womanism."

16. Rosemary Chikafa-Chipiro, "The Future of the Past: Imag(in)ing Black Womanhood, Africana Womanism and Afrofuturism in *Black Panther*," *Image & Text*, no. 33 (2019): 2.

17. Chikafa-Chipiro, "Future of the Past," 6.

18. Chikafa-Chipiro, "Future of the Past," 7, 8.

19. Chikafa-Chipiro, "Future of the Past," 5.

20. Chikafa-Chipiro, "Future of the Past," 12.

21. Tommie Shelby and Paul Gilroy, "Cosmopolitanism, Blackness and Utopia," *Transition*, no. 98 (2008): 117.

22. Lenz, Günter, "Radical Cosmopolitanism: W. E. B. Du Bois, Germany, and African American Pragmatist Visions for Twenty-First Century Europe," *Journal of Transnational American Studies* 4, no. 2 (2012): 68.

23. Lenz, "Radical Cosmopolitanism," 68.

24. Lenz, "Radical Cosmopolitanism," 68.

25. Lenz, "Radical Cosmopolitanism," 88. Lenz also notes how Du Bois's radical cosmopolitanism speaks to "philosopher Anthony Kwame Appiah's reflections on the project of an open, dialogic, contested, 'rooted,' and 'partial' (in the double sense of the word) version of a cosmopolitanism that continually negotiates a kind of universalism with the recognition of local cultural differences, both Western and African (Ghana), as a 'shared search for truth and justice' that is permeated by the narrative logic of an inter/crosscultural imagination." (90) Lenz' quotes are found in Kwame Anthony Appiah's *Ethics of Identity* (New Jersey: Princeton University Press, 2005), 256.

26. Nicole Waligora-Davis, "W. E. B. Du Bois and the Fourth Dimension," *The New Centennial Review* 6, no. 3 (2011): 19.

27. Waligora-Davis, "Fourth Dimension," 24.
28. Go, "Fanon's Postcolonial Cosmopolitanism," 211.
29. Ibid.
30. Go, "Fanon's Postcolonial Cosmopolitanism," 213.
31. Go, "Fanon's Postcolonial Cosmopolitanism," 215.
32. Frantz Fanon, *The Wretched of the Earth* (London: Penguin, 1967), 253.
33. Go, "Fanon's Postcolonial Cosmopolitanism," 218. This is a point Fanon makes very clear in the essay "On National Culture" in *The Wretched of the Earth*. He writes: "The consciousness of self is not the closing of a door to communication. Philosophic thought teaches us, on the contrary, that it is its guarantee. National consciousness, which is not nationalism, is the only thing that will give us an international dimension." Fanon, *Wretched*, 199.
34. Gilroy, *Postcolonial Melancholia*, 72.
35. McGregor and Buckler, *Jungle Action* 2, no. 6.
36. Stan Lee and Jack Kirby, *The Fantastic Four* 1, no. 52 (New York: Marvel Publications, 1966).
37. Fanon, *Wretched*, 27.
38. Fanon, *Wretched*, 29.
39. Fanon, *Wretched*, 31.
40. Fanon, *Wretched*, 69.
41. Susan Dianne Brophy, "Lawless Sovereignty: Challenging the State of Exception," *Social & Legal Studies* 18, no. 2 (2009): 200. Brophy also tends to write 'force-of-law' to indicate that the force of law always entails the suspension of law under the logic of the exception.
42. Brophy, "Lawless Sovereignty," 208.
43. Brophy, "Lawless Sovereignty," 209.
44. Ibid.
45. Brophy, "Lawless Sovereignty," 211. In the original French, Fanon speaks of "positions globales," *Les damnés de la terre* (Paris: La Découverte/Poche, 2002), 52.
46. Brophy, "Lawless Sovereignty," 212.
47. Adorno, *Negative Dialectics*, 12.
48. Frantz Fanon, *A Dying Colonialism* (New York: Grove Press, 1965), 32.
49. Gilroy, *Postcolonial Melancholia*, 80.
50. Chikafa-Chipiro, "Future of the Past," 13.
51. Chikafa-Chipiro, "Future of the Past," 13.

WORKS CITED

Adorno, Theodor. *Negative Dialectics*. New York: Continuum, 1973.

Agamben, Giorgio. *Homo Sacer: Sovereign Power and Bare Life*. Stanford: Stanford University Press, 1998.

Bhabha, Homi. *The Location of Culture*. London: Routledge, 1998.

Brophy, Susan Dianne. "Lawless Sovereignty: Challenging the State of Exception." *Social & Legal Studies* 18, no. 2 (2009): 199–220.

Carpini, Michael X. Delli. "Black Panther Party: 1966-1982." In *The Encyclopedia of Third Parties in America*, edited by I. Ness & J. Ciment, 190–197. Armonke, NY: Sharpe Reference, 2000.
Chikafa-Chipiro, Rosemary. "The Future of the Past: Imag(in)ing Black Womanhood, Africana Womanism and Afrofuturism in *Black Panther*." *Image & Text*, no. 33 (2019): 1–20.
Fanon, Frantz. *A Dying Colonialism*. New York: Grove Press, 1965.
Fanon, Frantz. *The Wretched of the Earth*. London: Penguin, 1967.
Fanon, Frantz. *Les damnés de la terre*. Paris: La Découverte/Poche, 2002.
Gilroy, Paul. *Postcolonial Melancholia*. New York: Columbia University Press, 2005.
Hudson-Weems, Clenora. "Africana Womanism: The Flip Side of a Coin." *Western Journal of Black Studies* 25, no. 3 (2001): 137–145.
Go, Julian. "Fanon's Postcolonial Cosmopolitanism." *European Journal of Social Theory* 16, no. 2 (2013): 208–225.
Lenz, Günter. "Radical Cosmopolitanism: W. E. B. Du Bois, Germany, and African American Pragmatist Visions for Twenty-First Century Europe." *Journal of Transnational American Studies* 4, no. 2 (2012): 65–96.
Lee, Stan, and Jack Kirby. *The Fantastic Four #52*. New York: Marvel Publications, 1966.
McGregor, Don, and Rich Buckler. *Jungle Action* 2 no. 6. New York: Marvel Publications, 1973.
Schmitt, Carl. *Political Theology: Four Chapters on the Concept of Sovereignty*. Chicago: University of Chicago Press, 1985.
Shelby, Tommie, and Paul Gilroy. "Cosmopolitanism, Blackness, and Utopia." *Transition*, no. 98 (2008): 116–135.
Waligora-Davis, Nicole. "W. E. B. Du Bois and the Fourth Dimension." *The New Centennial Review* 6, no. 3 (2011): 57–90.

FILMS

Black Panther. Directed by Ryan Coogler. United States: Walt Disney Studios Motion Pictures, 2018.
Blade. Directed by Stephen Norrington. United States: New Line Cinema, 1998.
Captain America: Civil War. Directed by Anthony and Joe Russo. United States, Walt Disney Studios Motion Pictures, 2016.
Catwoman. Directed by Jean-Christophe Pitof. United States: Warner Bros., 2004.
Steel. Directed by Kenneth Johnson. United States: Warner Bros., 1997.

Chapter 17

My Bloodright

A Critical Analysis of Black Panther's *Erik Killmonger, Colonialism, and Hybrid Identity*

Gabriel A. Cruz

In 1966, the *Black Panther* of Wakanda made his debut in the pages of Marvel comics. Since then, Prince T'Challa has embarked on countless adventures and become a cultural icon. In the process, he has become proof that the Black imaginary belongs in the American canon of superheroes that are otherwise overwhelmingly White. Through the incorporation of themes, such as anticolonial critique and the politics of Afrofuturism, the Black Panther has carved a unique space for discourses related to race and society within the world of comics.[1] The character's longevity, popularity, and profitability eventually translated into the live-action film *Black Panther* (directed by Ryan Coogler), released in February of 2018, which made well over $1 billion dollars in the international box office.[2] The film is significant for many reasons beyond its ability to generate revenue, such as its commentary on issues like immigration, gender politics, and philosophical questions related to power and responsibility. In this chapter, I will discuss two such prominent and socially pertinent issues addressed within the text of *Black Panther*: colonialism and racial hybridity.

I contend that this text contains narrative logics regarding the need for reconciliation between colonial powers and the systems of inequality that they create through the exploitation of colonized communities. The creation of systems of inequality that are germane to colonial projects operate based on the direct exploitation of people and resources and generally continue even after the dissolution of the formal colonial project, leaving a postcolonial legacy of inequality and oppression.[3] In this chapter, I interrogate how this blockbuster film conceptualizes and narratively positions racialized hybridity, specifically within the character of Erik "Killmonger" Stevens/Prince N'Jadaka. Toward this end, I pose guiding research questions and apply narrative and visual rhetorical criticism, informed by critical race theory and postcolonialism to answer those questions. Next, I discuss the kingdom of Wakanda as a colonial power and the narrative logic of Killmonger acting as a symbol of hybridity that forces the kingdom to reconcile with its exploitative practices. I conclude this chapter by discussing the societal implications of my findings both in terms of the audience and the Marvel Cinematic Universe.

HYBRIDITY AND NARRATIVES

Understanding how the film constructs hybridity relative to power requires examining how hybridity is related to colonialism and how hybridity has been used within cinematic narratives. In this context, hybridity refers to the occupation of a racialized Third Space, a place in-between two racial/ethnic/national origins reflected in one's parentage that results in a lived experience along a supposed borderline.[4] This status of belonging to both-and-neither, existing in a liminal space that inherently disrupts and blurs otherwise clearly delineated categories of identity forces those that adhere to these demarcations of difference to reconcile the conceptualized categories and their significance with the reality of the body and personhood of one that violates these categories. In short, hybrids complicate socio-cultural narratives of hierarchies, value, and power.[5] As such, the hybrid poses a challenge to the system of power that helped to create it; a problem that must be resolved. In the worst-case scenarios, this can involve the expansion of oppressive laws and policies to include the oppression of those that have disrupted these boundaries. When systems of power are confronted with deviations from established norms that are meant to maintain hierarchical order, those systems recontextualize those boundaries so as to adapt and maintain the inequality.[6]

Wherever colonialism has occurred, hybridity has inevitably followed. Colonial endeavors by Britain, France, and Spain in the Americas has resulted in the creation of mixed communities and ethnically mixed offspring who have the genetic and cultural ancestries of both the colonized and the oppressed. Two particularly salient examples of hybrid populations created by colonial endeavors are the Mexican Mestiza/os and the Chicana/os of the Southwestern United States. Both groups trace their roots to the indigenous peoples of the Americas, and both groups are the result of forced migration at the hands of, and interpersonal mixing with, the colonial governments of Britain, France, Spain, and later the United States.[7] By the end of the nineteenth century, the colonial governments from Western Europe had been ousted from the Americas and the colonial projects as they had been originally conceived were dissolved. However, the governments that replaced the continental powers maintained colonial practices that kept the Mestizos and Chicanos socially and politically disenfranchised in a postcolonial system of oppression.[8] Postcolonialism can be understood as the influence of colonial projects beyond the direct subjugation of land and peoples by imperial forces;[9] and indeed colonialist legacies echo through postcolonial society through the cultural, political, economic, and racialized norms of these formerly colonized territories. Just as the laws from a colonial project may carry over into the new postcolonial government, so too does the status and significance of the hybrid. It is because the hybrid represents a challenge to the socio-political hierarchies of the postcolonial government that they are regulated officially through codified law or unofficially through cultural hegemony.

One particularly powerful way in which marginalized racial groups, such as those that occupy spaces of hybridity, Blackness, and Latinidad in the context of the United States, have been regulated is through mass-mediated narratives that are typically controlled by members of the dominant culture. Critical Race Theory holds that race is a concept that is socially constructed, and that within the United States non-White racialized identities are constructed in such a way that devalues them with legal, economic, social, and political implications.[10] Research has shown that mass media narratives often facilitate this devaluation of non-White racialized identities.[11] Narratives represented within the news often perpetuate stereotypes that characterize non-Whites as being criminals,[12] abusing public assistance programs,[13] and generally being unimportant.[14] Furthermore, creative works such as music or fictional narratives also often perpetuate stereotypes that non-White racial identities exist for the purpose of elevating White characters,[15] and are defined by intense violence,[16] sexual deviance,[17] and cultural savagery.[18] These narratives that are propagated through popular culture shape public perceptions of minority groups,[19] and thus influence the lived experiences of those that have non-White racial identities.

Those that occupy the racialized Third Space of hybridity have not been immune to the malignance of dehumanizing mass-mediated narratives. Those who desecrate the socially sacred ethnic categories by transcending them have historically been oppressed through the narrative logics related to hybridity. A prime example of this is the figure that was once termed the mulatto, those who are born of African and European ancestry in the United States. This figure has historically been represented as a tragic character in popular narratives; a pitiable miscreant for whom the audience may sympathize, because were it not for their unfortunate African lineage, they could be someone of significance.[20] This trope has existed in various forms and has evolved from heavy-handed arguments against integration to critiques of social norms regarding the treatment of disparate communities.[21] A few examples of characters of differing ethnic backgrounds who struggled whether externally or internally as a result of their bi-racial ancestry include Injun Joe from Mark Twain's *The Adventures of Tom Sawyer*, *Star Trek*'s Spock, and DC's Aquaman (both in comic narratives and his recent film adaptation).

This chapter is concerned with another such modern iteration of the hybrid identity, Erik "Killmonger" Stevens, also known as Prince N'Jadaka. In particular, I focus on the iteration depicted within the 2018 film *Black Panther* as opposed to the original comic book character that served as the basis for the film adaptation. Moving forward, I will be referring to this character as Killmonger for the sake of consistency. In the narrative of the film *Black Panther,* the character of Killmonger is the product of an inter-ethnic relationship between Prince N'Jobu (Sterling K. Brown) of Wakanda and an unnamed African American woman from Oakland, CA. While there are very few details about Killmonger's mother in the film, her absence plays a significant role in Killmonger's character arc as it is apparent that he is an orphan once his father is killed by King T'Chaka of Wakanda. In the movie commentary included in the Blu-ray edition of the film, director Ryan Coogler articulates the plight of Killmonger's mother, "The idea was when you see those guys talking over the paperwork in the beginning of the film, they're talking about a way to break her out of jail," Coogler explains. "The idea was they never got her out, and she passed away in prison, so Killmonger didn't come up with a mom either."[22]

This commentary from Coogler in addition to what is indicated in the film reinforces the tragic narrative of Killmonger's origins while also affirming his status as a hybrid. The villain is the result of a coupling between his American mother, who is represented as being held in a U.S. prison, and his Wakandan father. Due to Killmonger's dual ancestry of Wakanda and the United States, and in particular because of his internalized ethnic Wakandan identity and his upbringing in the United States, he occupies the Third Space. His hybrid identity is also reflected in the details of his aesthetic construction. Specifically, his use of African American Vernacular English representing his American cultural upbringing, and his War Dog tattoo that indicates his ancestry and also serves as a type of passport into Wakanda. Later in this chapter, I address Killmonger's hybrid identity and the implications within the narrative rhetoric of the text.

NARRATIVE + VISUAL CRITIQUE

This chapter is centered around answering three guiding questions related to narrative logics within *Black Panther*.[23] (1) How does the film conceptualize hybridity and the Third Space? (2) What narrative logics are present within the text regarding colonialism? (3) What narrative rhetorical assertions are made regarding reconciling postcolonial systems of inequality toward the ultimate goal of social justice?

In order to answer these questions, I have engaged in a close reading of the text and applied both Narrative and Visual Rhetorical critique informed by literature related to critical race theory, hybridity, and postcolonialism. Narrative critique involves the examination of stories and evaluating them in terms of their fidelity with the experiences of the audience, internal coherence, and the rhetorical values presented within the story.[24] In particular, this study focuses on the rhetorical values embedded in the narrative as well as the logics presented in the form of endorsed vs. villainized perspectives, behaviors, and ideologies. In doing so, I position the film *Black Panther*[25] as a persuasive text that attempts to appeal to audiences through certain messages related to race and power. Complementary to this analysis of the narrative, I also utilize visual rhetorical critique in order to further reveal the values and messages conveyed through the text as a visual medium.[26] Visual rhetoric holds that images are laden with persuasive ideological messages by virtue of their production by humans. Therefore, it is appropriate to apply visual rhetorical critique to this film as the purpose of this project is to uncover and engage with the persuasive messages present in the text related to matters of race and power. In the application of both methods, I have elected to prioritize the narrative logics within the text and use the visual elements of the film in service of supporting those logics. I engaged in another close reading of the text to examine the ways in which the narrative and visual elements within the film conveyed persuasive assertions related to hybridity, colonialism, and reconciling postcolonial oppression. They can be organized into three overarching categories that address each respective research question. The first category considers Wakanda as a colonial power, the second category addresses Killmonger's hybridity, and the third category discusses the narrative rhetorical logics regarding postcolonial inequality that are present within the text.

WAKANDA AS A COLONIAL POWER

To begin, it is important that we appropriately position Wakanda as a colonial power. In the film, Wakanda operates as an ostensibly isolationist country and maintains a guise of being a Third-World nation whose economy is primarily rooted in agricultural production. This external representation of being an impoverished nation is meant to deceive other nations and obscure the truth: that Wakanda is the most technologically advanced and wealthy country in the world. Wakanda's advancement as a society is perhaps best illustrated through the bewilderment of CIA Agent Everett Ross (Martin Freeman) when he awakes to discover that he has been healed by Wakandan medicine and marvels at the technological advancements of a nation he once understood to be impoverished. In addition, T'Challa's sister Shuri (Letitia Wright) is in charge of the vibranium labs and technological advancements. Yet, Wakanda's status as a secret international superpower state is not enough to categorize the nation as a colonial power. There are three elements of Wakanda that characterize the nation as an imperial power that engages in colonial projects: its national creation myth, the War Dog network, and the practice of its rulers in creating revisionist history.

In the beginning of the film, Prince N'Jobu regales the young Killmonger with a voice-over story about the origins of the first Black Panther and how he united the Border Tribe, River Tribe, Merchant Tribe, and Mining Tribe into a unified country while the Jabari Tribe refused the union and instead settled into the mountains of Wakanda. This narrative told by Prince N'Jobu serves as a national myth that emphasizes the unity of the tribes while glossing over important details that were likely present in the actual history of the founding of Wakanda. Details such as whether there was resistance from any of the four tribes, how the peace was actually brokered, whether there was insurrection at any time, or if there was any inequality in the original unification are missing. Indeed, quite a bit of detail is absent from this priming narrative. At the very least, one might expect N'Jobu to explain how the tribes became their modern iterations. Why was one tribe relegated to mining while another became the warrior tribe that defends Wakanda's borders? The mining of vibranium presumably falls under the purview of the Mining Tribe, does this give them a position of honor or are they instead a caste of exploited laborers? These details are conspicuously missing from the myth. This national myth reduces the dimensionality of the actual history of Wakanda, and instead offers a narrative that is devoid of details that might suggest a shameful past or less than utopic present, all for the purpose of creating a homogenous national identity for Wakandans. This type of myth is valuable for a colonial power that promotes an isolationist, and thus us-vs-them, national identity. Additionally, in the reference guide comic book *Marvel Atlas #1*,[27] Wakanda is described as having eighteen tribes, all of which have a seat in the nation's parliament. However for the film, the parliament was replaced with the notably less democratic royal council wherein elders from each of the five tribes advise the crown. This conceptualization of the Wakandan government reflects a more imperial imagining of Wakanda and reinforces the colonial aspect of the country.

This is consistent with modern iterations of colonial narratives about the creation of the United States such as the colonization of the Americas and alleged spreading of civilization to the First Nations.[28] Absent from such narratives about the founding of the United States or even modern narratives about the treatment of colonized populations are the historical details, the consequences of which have been felt if not explicitly heard. In this sort of myth-making, narratives about events, such as the genocide of Native Americans[29] or the brutal exploitation of immigrants for labor,[30] are omitted because they disrupt stories that are meant to instill national pride. In this way, Wakanda is culturally represented to the audience as a technological utopia of Afrofuturism devoid of any human rights violations that likely characterized its past.

The network of international Wakandan spies, referred to as the War Dogs, are the colonial project that Wakanda actively utilizes to exercise international influence for national interests. Typically, when one conceptualizes a colonial project, one thinks of the forceful occupation of territories and the direct subjugation of indigenous people. Within the context of the film, I position the War Dogs as a colonial project, because the ultimate function of the spy network is to extract resources, in the form of information, from nation-states without their knowledge or consent for the purpose of advancing the interests of the Wakanda leadership. The methods of doing so include covert operations, such as undercover reconnaissance and the use of lethal force, when necessary. Wakanda does not need to extract material resources from other countries, rather it harvests international information as that is the one resource that it needs that it cannot produce within its own borders.

The War Dogs were represented within the film in three distinct instances. The first involved Prince N'Jobu's post in the United States. While the actual goal of his official mission in the United States was unclear, it was apparent that it likely involved the surveillance of the United States's treatment of African-Americans and other minority groups within that country. During his conversation with King T'Chaka, Prince N'Jobu details all the ways in which the African American community has been oppressed, and he pleads unsuccessfully with the king to allow him to aid these communities. The second representation of the War Dogs is Nakia's (Lupita Nyong'o) mission to liberate women that are being trafficked by soldiers in Africa. This depiction of women being transported by armed guards that are clearly represented as villains appears to be a visual reference to the now infamous 2014 kidnapping of 276 school girls by the terrorist group Boko Haram in Nigeria.[31] Nakia's mission was to infiltrate the organization as one of the victims in order to presumably dismantle the entire human trafficking operation; however, the mission was cut short by the interference of Prince T'Challa (Chadwick Boseman) due to his need for her presence at his coronation ceremony. The mission ends with T'Challa and Nakia fighting and defeating the human traffickers, which suggests the permissibility of violence in this endeavor. It is also very likely that the mission would have resulted in Nakia using lethal force to dismantle the trafficking ring anyway, had the mission been allowed to continue and reach its intended conclusion. The third depiction is perhaps the strongest evidence that the War Dogs are a colonial project used to serve the interests of Wakanda. During Killmonger's brief reign as the King of Wakanda, he orders the arming of oppressed descendants of the African Diaspora for the purpose of overthrowing the global North, developed countries whose wealth was built through colonial projects and who were largely responsible for the historic enslavement of Africans. In order to do so, he uses the War Dogs network to arm these communities in places like New York City, London, and Hong Kong. The speed with which this plan was initiated suggests that (1) the War Dogs posed no significant resistance to Killmonger's vision of an overthrown global North, possibly due to a willingness to enact violence even on behalf of a newly crowned king of ostensibly foreign origin, and (2) previously established connections to oppressed communities in these different countries, likely for the purpose of gathering intelligence and perhaps even for instigating insurrection in those nations not unlike Killmonger's plan.

In addition to the use of national myths and the War Dogs colonial project, Wakanda can also be positioned as a colonial power by understanding its use of revisionist history. Similar to the national myth that likely depicts a mono-dimensional view of the country's history, the royalty of Wakanda, particularly King T'Chaka (John Kani) and to a lesser extent King T'Challa, attempt to rewrite Wakanda's recent past by denying the existence and legitimacy of Killmonger as the son of Prince N'Jobu and one who has a rightful claim to the throne of Wakanda. The news that Killmonger was the son of his uncle came as a shock to T'Challa, and when he had an opportunity to speak to his father in the Ancestral Plane, T'Challa confronted him. This moment of conflict is symbolic of T'Challa working to acknowledge and confront the broader colonial sins of Wakanda, while also setting the young king on his way to envisioning a different future. When T'Challa asked T'Chaka why he had left Killmonger in the United States as a boy, the deceased king answered that "he was the truth I chose to omit"[32] for the sake of Wakanda. This sentiment, that the truth of Killmonger's bi-ethnic heritage should be kept from others for the sake of Wakanda, was shared by T'Challa when Killmonger first confronted him in the throne room. During the interaction, T'Challa quietly acknowledges the truth of Killmonger's status as a member of the royal family but refuses to openly acknowledge it until it becomes clear that the only way to rid Wakanda of Killmonger is to fight him in ritual combat. T'Chaka and T'Challa's decision to ignore the legitimacy of Killmonger as Prince N'Jadaka represents a desire to revise Wakanda's history in a manner that is beneficial for the status quo and maintains the nobility associated with the kings as individuals and as symbols of the nation's morality. The truth of Killmonger's existence would inspire critique against the crown and invite potential challenges, especially since Killmonger's existence was tied to Prince N'Jobu's attack on Wakanda and his eventual plan to free Killmonger's mother from prison. Such a scandal would have instilled distrust of the royal family of Wakanda in the Wakandan public. In this way, it is clear that King T'Chaka's initial decision to revise history and obscure the existence of Killmonger was not only an attempt to keep his family from the shame of Prince N'Jobu's actions but to also prevent any potential threats to his rule. In the next subsection, I will discuss Killmonger's positionality as a hybrid who acts as a symbol of grievances against colonial power.

KILLMONGER AND HYBRIDITY

Drawing from Stuart Hall's concept of the Black aesthetic, which contends that characters that occupy the space of Blackness are textured with elements of Black culture in ways that are ideological,[33] I argue that Killmonger's Black hybrid aesthetic is also ideologically constructed. Within the film, Killmonger's hybrid identity is ideologically constructed in three distinct ways: through the composition of the character in terms of visual elements and his narrative arc; his hatred for his ancestry; and his desire to overthrow colonial oppression by inverting the global North/South dynamic.

Killmonger's hybridity is first established within the narrative when we learn that his parentage is both Wakandan and African American. At first, one might feel compelled to consider Killmonger's racial identity as monodimensionally Black. However, this would be a superficial assessment of the character as it ignores the cultural boundaries between Wakandan and African-American societies and their intersectional influences on Killmonger's life. Killmonger not only has a dual national identity granted through his birth in the United States and royal lineage, along with the Wakandan War Dog lip tattoo, he also has dual cultural identities. Killmonger may "pass" as traditionally African American in the context of the United States but his cultural identity is a defining component of his character in much the same way that ethnic identities have been an important part of immigrant groups that have come to the United States. This cultural identity is also reinforced visually and narratively in the text. One example of this is the War Dog tattoo that Killmonger possesses, a luminescent script tattooed on the inside of his lip that resembles his father's War Dog tattoo and clearly denotes his own status as being associated with the War Dogs. It is most likely that this tattoo came from his father and was created to denote Killmonger's claim to Wakandan society. In this way, Killmonger is visually marked as being Wakandan in addition to his cultural roots and lived experience in the African American community in the United States. His hybridity is also signified by his Wakandan name and his ability to speak Xhosa. In the text, Killmonger speaks both languages fluently, a code-switching tactic that helps him to cross the cultural boundaries that separate his ancestral roots. Killmonger also utilizes his Wakandan name, N'Jadaka, when confronting T'Challa for the throne of Wakanda. This scene in the film represents Killmonger's attempt at stepping out from his position in the Third Space and into the space of his father's cultural identity by virtue of claiming his right to challenge T'Challa for the throne.

These elements of the character position Killmonger as a hybrid, and I contend that he displays qualities consistent with the Mulatto trope. This is particularly evident when considering that the Mulatto is a tragic figure[34] whose disposition is rooted in their bi-racial origin. In this instance, rather than being defined by depression stemming from an African American heritage, as is typically the case with the Mulatto trope, Killmonger possesses a rage and hatred for Wakanda for two reasons. The first is that King T'Chaka murdered Killmonger's father and left him to die unceremoniously on the floor of his apartment. The second reason for Killmonger's rage is Wakanda's long-standing practice of refusing to intervene on a global level and help empower the oppressed. Killmonger's hate defines the character in much the same way that the Mulatto trope is defined by the tragedy that the character experiences.

The character's desire for revenge combined with his elite U.S. military training as part of the Army S.E.A.L.S. team and impressive record for lethal efficiency as a sniper allowed him to make his way into the Wakandan throne room, defeat T'Challa in ritual combat, and gain control of Wakanda's military might. Once Killmonger ascended to the throne of Wakanda, he became an imminent threat to the global North. Killmonger's positionality as a hybrid character and his defiance of colonial oppression is visually signified by his adornment of the Igbo Mgbedike, a mask associated with the Igbo tribe. Killmonger reclaims the mask when he visits the British Museum in London to retrieve a vibranium weapon from the exhibit with the help of the villain Ulysses Klaue (Andy Serkins), a criminal Caucasian arms dealer who has been an enemy of the Wakandans for decades.

The Igbo tribe earned a reputation for resisting the Trans-Atlantic Slave Trade, even to the point of suicide as illustrated in the folklore story of the

Igbo Landing.[35] According to the story, a group of Igbo Africans who were sold into slavery in Savannah, GA, violently overthrew their captors and committed mass suicide once free. The contention of the story is that the Igbo would rather die than live a life of slavery,[36] a strategy that is echoed in Killmonger's final battle with T'Challa. His defiance of colonial rule is a salient part of the character of Killmonger which in this context is rooted in his disgust in the oppression that stems from colonial/postcolonial power and influence. Visually, the image of Killmonger dressing and speaking in a way consistent with modern depictions of African American identity and then wearing an Igbo mask into combat as he initially rescued Klaue from captivity reinforced his corporeal symbolism of not just being hybrid but a militant hybrid with a strong connection to the African continent. Ultimately, Killmonger assassinates Klaue as a form of trophy kill and strongman to endear himself to T'Challa's allies as a superior warrior.

NARRATIVE LOGIC ABOUT RESOLVING POSTCOLONIAL INEQUALITY

Broadly, the narrative arc of the film centers around the conflict between Killmonger, the symbol of postcolonial inequality and hybridity, and King T'Challa, who encapsulates royalty and colonialist expansion through the covert interventionist program referred to as the War Dogs. Killmonger's origin and positionality as a traumatized occupant of the hybrid Third Space serves as symbol for the postcolonial effects that characterize former colonial projects such as the United States, Canada, and Mexico. In this way, the systemic socio-political violence and inequality, such as extreme-policing, economic discrimination, and political disenfranchisement, that often oppresses minority communities[37] who were incorporated into colonial projects in subordinate or subaltern positions become represented in the character of Killmonger. Following this interpretation of the text, the narrative arc of Killmonger ultimately seizing the throne of Wakanda and attempting to instigate international revolution and armed struggle against articulated colonial powers serves as a case for the need to reconcile the postcolonial legacies that haunt modern nations. In essence, the narrative logic here is that the trauma endured by racial minority groups persists and serves as a platform for the critique of society, and the voices that critique this power must be considered legitimate or else risk the deterioration of social fabric and collateral damage that would inevitably follow.

While Killmonger's methods of critiquing colonial power are clearly problematic by virtue of propagating violence, especially violence against civilian targets, his anger against the nation of Wakanda and its contribution to the dichotomy of the global North and South are justified. His justification is supported by not just his own personal trauma at the hands of the Wakanda royal family but for the reasons that he articulates in the film, wherein he asserts that Wakanda has a responsibility as a singularly advanced and powerful nation to aid in the liberation of those whose origins trace back to the African Diaspora and the Trans-Atlantic Slave Trade. At first, Killmonger convinces the fellow tribal leaders as well as General Okoye that he will use vibranium weapons to militarize the rest of the world for armed struggle. The Dora Milaje Amazonian warriors are loyal but then turn against the new king to embrace T'Challa's ideology of peaceful conflict resolution.

Ultimately, after a series of impressive fight scenes, King T'Challa recognizes the legitimacy of Killmonger's critiques against Wakanda both personally and systemically. I contend that the narrative logic within the text is that the morally correct approach to dealing with critical voices rooted in systems of oppression is to legitimize their grievances and recognize the validity of recommendations for working to end the postcolonial legacies of oppression. In the film, this perspective is represented in King T'Challa's ultimate decision to reveal the truth of Wakanda's power and wealth to the international community in the epilogue of *Black Panther* at the United Nations. Additionally, T'Challa creates an international outreach program based in Oakland, CA, in the childhood home of Killmonger (specifically the apartment complex where Prince N'Jobu was murdered). This is especially significant because of Oakland's above-average poverty rate and higher than average African American population.[38] These efforts suggest that the narrative arc endorses the logic that colonial forces and postcolonial legacies must be actively counteracted and that it is the burden of those in power to listen to marginalized voices and work toward equitable solutions for reconciling historical grievances particularly those that still shape the dynamics of modern society. Furthermore, the conclusion of the film suggests that T'Challa recognizes the struggles Killmonger endured and that the best way to help is to engage in direct educational outreach instead of relying on the federal government which has been largely responsible for the oppression of African-Americans as described by Prince N'Jobu in the beginning of the film. This outreach comes in the form of the initiative that is to be led by Shuri, and the decision for her to lead this program is evidence of a more boots-on-the ground approach from the royal family as opposed to having an intermediary run of the operation. The location and choice of leadership also suggests that this is a personal investment in the African American community rather than merely spreading the socio-political influence of Wakanda in the United States.

CONCLUSION

This film puts forth a few different logics about the validity of grievances rooted in colonial oppression and postcolonial systems of inequality and how those grievances should be addressed. Killmonger's racialized hybrid identity positions the character as an existential critique of Wakanda's colonial endeavors through the War Dogs program. Additionally, his actions in the film embody the argument that the nations of the global North have a responsibility to use their power and capital to reconcile with their colonial histories, that is, the descendants of the African Diaspora and the Trans-Atlantic Slave Trade. The rhetorical assertion made by the narrative endorses Killmonger's claims of the responsibility of the global North in the empowerment of the marginalized. The text simultaneously condemns acts of violence in service of this goal and instead endorses a more moderate and sustainable approach: outreach and socio-economic and political empowerment rather than violent extremism. However, it should be noted that the sustainability of this solution for reconciling historical grievances is predicated on the maintenance of systems of power that have historically and continue to benefit from the wealth generated by postcolonial legacies. Unfortunately, following this mode of reasoning, it is unlikely that such systems of power are likely to significantly suffer as these dominant power structures adapt to the shifting landscape that they are helping to create.

This is important to consider as the text also carries an underlying implication regarding the maintenance of colonial projects even in the face of systemic reform. Wakanda maintains, to the best of the audiences' knowledge, the War Dogs program which served as the initial impetus for this colonial critique and the creation of Killmonger as a resident of the Third Space. The implicit rhetorical assertion here is that even governing powers that enact anticolonial policies can still be trusted to maintain dominance through the preservation of colonial projects. In essence, governing powers may embrace change but only in as much as it does not threaten their dominance. As such, some postcolonial legacies of inequality will likely continue to be perpetuated.

My final contention is that the film functions as a pedagogical text relative to this understanding about the maintenance of power. In one sense, the narrative asserts that power that is inherently oppressive, as in the case of a monarchy that is founded on the exclusion of antiassimilationist perspectives (Jabari Tribe) and the maintenance of a rigid class system (the various Wakandan tribes), can ultimately be wielded for positive outcomes. However, following this logic to its natural conclusion would inevitably lead us to a stark understanding: an oppressive system of power and governance that is not radically reformed will continue to produce more violent extremists like Killmonger.

NOTES

1. Adilifu Nama, *Super Black: American Pop Culture and Black Superheroes* (Austin: University of Texas Press, 2011).

2. Mark Hughes, "'Black Panther' Stalks $1.3 Billion at the Worldwide Box Office," *Forbes*, April 2, 2018, https://www.forbes.com/sites/markhughes/2018/04/02/black-panther-stalks-1-3-billion-at-the-worldwide-box-office/#96f63f2ef966.

3. Ania Loomba, *Colonialism/Postcolonialism: The New Critical Idiom*, 2nd ed. (New York: Routledge, 2005).

4. Sayyed Rahim Moosavinia and Sayyede Maryam Hosseini, "Liminality, Hybridity, and 'Third Space': Bessie Head's a Question of Power," *Neohelicon* 45 (2018).

5. Gloria Anzaldua, *Borderlands/La Frontera: The New Mestiza*, 2nd ed. (San Francisco: Aunt Lute Books, 2007).

6. Michelle Alexander, *The New Jim Crow: Mass Incarceration in the Age of Colorblindness* (New York: The New Press, 2010).

7. Anzaldua, *Borderlands/La Frontera*.

8. Anzaldua, *Borderlands/La Frontera*.

9. Fetson Kalua, "Homi Bhaba's Third Space and African Identity," *Journal of African Cultural Studies* 21, no. 1 (2009).

10. Lisa A. Flores, "Critical Race Theory," in *Encyclopedia of Communication Theory*, ed. Stephen W. Littlejohn and Karen A. Foss (Thousand Oaks: Sage, 2009).

11. Dana Mastro, Elizabeth Behm-Morawitz, and Michelle Ortiz, "The Cultivation of Social Perceptions of Latinos: A Mental Models Approach," *Media Psychology* 9, no. 2 (2007).

12. Michael G. Lacy and Kathleen C. Haspel, "Apocalypse: The Media's Framing of Black Looters, Shooters, and Brutes in Hurricane Katrina's Aftermath," in *Critical Rhetorics of Race*, ed. Michael G. Lacy and Kent A. Ono (New York: New York University Press, 2011).

13. Gracie Lawson-Borders, "Tilted Images: Media Coverage and the Use of Critical Race Theory to Examine Social Equity Disparities for Blacks and Other People of Color," *Social Work in Public Health* 34, no. 1 (2019).

14. Laura C. Prividera and John W. Howard, "Masculinity, Whiteness, and the Warrior Hero: Perpetuating the Strategic Rhetoric of U.S. Nationalism and the Marginalization of Women," *Women and Language* 29, no. 2 (2006).

15. Matthew W. Hughey, "Cinethetic Racism: White Redemption and Black Stereotypes in "Magical Negro" Films," *Social Problems* 56, no. 3 (2009).

16. Matthew Oware, "Brotherly Love: Homosociality and Black Masculinity in Gangsta Rap Music," *Journal of African American Studies* 15 (2011).

17. David C. Oh and Doreen V. Kutufam, "The Orientalized 'Other' and Corrosive Femininity: Threats to White Masculinity in *300*," *Journal of Communication Inquiry* 38, no. 2 (2014).

18. Richard C. King, "Alter/native Heroes: Native Americans, Comic Books, and the Struggle for Self-Definition," *Cultural Studies/Critical Methodologies* 9, no. 2 (2009).

19. Mastro, Behm-Morawitz, and Ortiz, "The Cultivation of Social Perceptions of Latinos."

20. Donald Bogle, *Toms, Coons, Mulattoes, Mammies, and Bucks: An Interpretive History of Blacks in American Films, Updated and Expanded*, 5th ed. (New York: Bloomsbury Academic, 2016).

21. Bogle, *Toms, Coons, Mulattoes, Mammies, and Bucks*.

22. Ryan Parker, "'Black Panther': Ryan Coogler Reveals What Happened to Killmonger's Mother," *The Hollywood Reporter*, May 4, 2018, https://www.hollywoodreporter.com/heat-vision/black-panther-what-happened-killmongers-mother-1108754.

23. *Black Panther*, directed by Ryan Coogler (United States: Walt Disney Studios Motion Pictures, 2018).

24. Walter Fisher, "The Narrative Paradigm: An Elaboration," *Communication Monographs* 52 (1985).

25. *Black Panther*, directed by Ryan Coogler.

26. Trischa Goodnow, "Empowerment Through Shifting Agents: The Rhetoric of the Clothesline Project," in *Handbook of Visual Communication: Theory, Methods, and Media*, eds. Ken Smith, Sandra Moriarty, Gretchen Barbatsis, and Keith Kenney (New York: Routledge, 2011).

27. Michael Hoskin, *Marvel Atlas #1* (New York: Marvel Comics, 2007).

28. Michael Ray FitzGerald, "The Indianized White Man and the Anglicized Indian: Imperial and Anti-Imperial Discourse in NBC's Daniel Boone, 1964-1970," *Journal of American Culture* 37, no. 3 (2014).

29. Gregory W. Rutecki, "Forced Sterilization of Native Americas: Later Twentieth Century Physician Cooperation with National Eugenics Policies?," *Ethics & Medicine* 27, no. 1 (2011).

30. J. Justin Castro, "Mexican Braceros and Arkansas Cotton: Agricultural Labor and Civil Rights in the Post-World War II South," *Arkansas Historical Quarterly* 75, no. 1 (2016).

31. Amanda Holpuch, "Stolen Daughters: What Happened After #BringBackOurGirls?," *The Guardian*, last modified October 22nd, 2018, https://www.theguardian.com/tv-and-radio/2018/oct/22/bring-back-our-girls-documentary-stolen-daughters-kidnapped-boko-haram.

32. *Black Panther*, directed by Ryan Coogler.

33. Angela M. Nelson, "Studying Black Comic Strips: Popular Art and Discourses of Race," in *Black Comics: Politics of Race and Representation*, eds. Sheena C. Howard and Ronald L. Jackson II (London: Bloomsbury Academic, 2013).

34. Bogle, *Toms, Coons, Mulattoes, Mammies, and Bucks: An Interpretive History of Blacks in American Films, Updated and Expanded*.

35. Terri L. Snyder, "Suicide, Slavery, and Memory in North America," *Journal of American History* 97, no. 1 (2010).
36. Snyder, "Suicide, Slavery, and Memory in North America."
37. Alexander, *The New Jim Crow*.
38. "Quick Facts: Oakland City, California," *United States Census Bureau*, accessed December 14, 2019, https://www.census.gov/quickfacts/oaklandcitycalifornia.

WORKS CITED

Alexander, Michelle. *The New Jim Crow: Mass Incarceration in the Age of Colorblindness*. New York: The New Press, 2010.

Anzaldua, Gloria. *Borderlands/La Frontera: The New Mestiza*. 3rd ed. San Francisco: Aunt Lute Books, 2007.

Bogle, Donald. *Toms, Coons, Mulattoes, Mammies, and Bucks: An Interpretive History of Blacks in American Films, Updated and Expanded*. 5th ed. New York: Bloomsbury Academic, 2016.

Castro, J. Justin. "Mexican Braceros and Arkansas Cotton: Agricultural Labor and Civil Rights in the Post-World War II South." *Arkansas Historical Quarterly* 75, no. 1 (2016): 27–46.

Goodnow, Trischa. "Empowerment Through Shifting Agents: The Rhetoric of the Clothesline Project." In *Handbook of Visual Communication: Theory, Methods, and Media,* edited by Ken Smith, Sandra Moriarty, Gretchen Barbatsis, and Keith Kenney. New York: Routledge, 2011.

Fisher, Walter. "The Narrative Paradigm: An Elaboration." *Communication Monographs* 52 (1985): 347–367.

FitzGerald, Michael Ray. "The Indianized White Man and the Anglicized Indian: Imperial and Anti-Imperial Discourse in NBC's Daniel Boone, 1964-1970." *Journal of American Culture* 37, no. 3 (2014): 281–289.

Flores, Lisa A. "Critical Race Theory." In *Encyclopedia of Communication Theory*, edited by Stephen W. Littlejohn and Karen A. Foss. Thousand Oaks: Sage, 2009.

Holpuch, Amanda, "Stolen Daughters: What Happened After #BringBackOurGirls?" *The Guardian*. Last modified October 22, 2018. https://www.theguardian.com/tv-and-radio/2018/oct/22/bring-back-our-girls-documentary-stolen-daughters-kidnapped-boko-haram.

Hoskin, Michael. *Marvel Atlas #1*. New York: Marvel Comics, 2007.

Hughes, Mark. "'Black Panther' Stalks $1.3 Billion at the Worldwide Box Office." *Forbes*, April 2, 2018. https://www.forbes.com/sites/markhughes/2018/04/02/black-panther-stalks-1-3-billion-at-the-worldwide-box-office/#96f63f2ef966.

Hughey, Matthew W. "Cinethetic Racism: White Redemption and Black Stereotypes in "Magical Negro" Films." *Social Problems* 56, no. 3 (2009): 543–577.

Kalua, Fetson. "Homi Bhaba's Third Space and African Identity." *Journal of African Cultural Studies* 21, no. 1 (2009): 23–32.

King, Richard C. "Alter/native Heroes: Native Americans, Comic Books, and the Struggle for Self-Definition." *Cultural Studies/Critical Methodologies* 9, no. 2 (2009): 214–223.

Lacy, Michael G., and Kathleen C. Haspel. "Apocalypse: The Media's Framing of Black Looters, Shooters, and Brutes in Hurricane Katrina's Aftermath." In *Critical Rhetorics of Race*, edited by Michael G. Lacy and Kent A. Ono. New York: New York University Press, 2011.

Lawson-Borders, Gracie. "Tilted Images: Media Coverage and the Use of Critical Race Theory to Examine Social Equity Disparities for Blacks and Other People of Color." *Social Work in Public Health* 34, no. 1 (2019): 28–38.

Loomba, Ania. *Colonialism/Postcolonialism: The New Critical Idiom.* 2nd ed. New York: Routledge, 2005.

Mastro, Dana, Elizabeth Behm-Morawitz, and Michelle Ortiz. "The Cultivation of Social Perceptions of Latinos: A Mental Models Approach." *Media Psychology* 9, no. 2 (2007): 347–365.

Moosavinia, Sayyed Rahim, and Sayyede Maryam Hosseini. "Liminality, Hybridity, and 'Third Space': Bessie Head's a Question of Power." *Neohelicon* 45 (2018): 333–349.

Nama, Adilifu. *Super Black: American Pop Culture and Black Superheroes.* Austin: University of Texas Press, 2011.

Nelson, Angela M. "Studying Black Comic Strips: Popular Art and Discourses of Race." In *Black Comics: Politics of Race and Representation*, edited by Sheena C. Howard and Ronald L. Jackson II. London: Bloomsbury Academic, 2013.

Oh, David C., and Kutufam, Doreen V. "The Orientalized 'Other' and Corrosive Femininity: Threats to White Masculinity in 300." *Journal of Communication Inquiry* 38, no. 2 (2014): 149–165.

Oware, Matthew. "Brotherly Love: Homosociality and Black Masculinity in Gangsta Rap Music." *Journal of African American Studies* 15 (2011): 22–39.

Parker, Ryan. "'Black Panther': Ryan Coogler Reveals What Happened to Killmonger's Mother." *The Hollywood Reporter.* Last modified May 4, 2018. https://www.hollywoodreporter.com/heat-vision/black-panther-what-happened-killmongers-mother-1108754.

Prividera, Laura. C, and John W. Howard. "Masculinity, Whiteness, and the Warrior Hero: Perpetuating the Strategic Rhetoric of U.S. Nationalism and the Marginalization of Women." *Women and Language* 29, no. 2 (2006): 29–37.

Rutecki, Gregory W. "Forced Sterilization of Native Americas: Later Twentieth Century Physician Cooperation with National Eugenics Policies?" *Ethics & Medicine* 27, no. 1 (2011): 33–42.

Snyder, Terri L. "Suicide, Slavery, and Memory in North America." *Journal of American History* 97, no. 1 (2010): 39–62.

"Quick Facts: Oakland City, California." *United States Census Bureau.* Accessed December 14, 2019. https://www.census.gov/quickfacts/oaklandcitycalifornia.

FILMS

Black Panther. Directed Ryan Coogler. United States: Walt Disney Studios Motion Pictures, 2018.

Chapter 18

The Other Worlds of *Black Panther*'s Purple Heart-Shaped Herb

Paul Karolczyk

INTRODUCTION

The fictional ritual of the purple heart-shaped herb in Marvel's Afrofuturist superhero film *Black Panther* (Ryan Coogler, 2018) examines the cultural importance of psychotropic plant use in African traditional religion and healing, and probes into the present-day implications of the indigenous traditional knowledge that it embodies. Psychotropic plant use in Africa likely evolved from origins among early human foragers exploring the flora of Pleistocene ecosystems. Although studying these enduring practices can expand our knowledge of psychotropic plant influences on human consciousness, religious cosmology, and psychospiritual healing, Western researchers long assumed that Africa's plant traditions had little to teach them.[1] However, the heart-shaped herb's timely cinema debut coincides with a rekindled ethnobotanical interest in psychotropic plant use in Africa, specifically with hallucinogenic species, that is shining new light on this neglected and misunderstood feature of indigenous culture that belongs to humanity's cultural ecological heritage.[2]

The herb's sacramental portrayal in the film reconsiders the ancient pan-cultural practice of psychotropic plant use in sacred rites and spiritual healing. As the film suggests, Africa's indigenous plant traditions may hold solutions to some of Earth's current major anthropogenic dilemmas. Viewed in this way, the heart-shaped herb not only challenges persistent racist stereotypes of African traditional religion, but it also gives visibility to a Black perspective that is missing from prevalent discourses, including in literature and film, that express the West's fascination with hallucinogenic plants. Consequently, *Black Panther* stands out in American popular cinema as a film that gives sacred and medicinal psychotropic plant use a cultural presence that rarely appears in comparison to the widely visible imagery of socially approved secular recreational drug and alcohol use. This ethnobotanical essay considers *Black Panther's* heart-shaped herb as an invitation to the humanist study of African indigenous psychotropic plant uses to capture some of their meaning in traditional and contemporary world culture.

IF THEY ONLY KNEW

A branch of cultural anthropology, ethnobotany seeks to build knowledge about past and present plant uses in their traditional contexts. Plants first gained cultural importance when early humans discovered geographically diverse flora that helped meet their physical, social, and psychological needs. Through the ages, plants have shaped the evolution of language, foodways, medicine, tools, agriculture, art, religion, architecture, and many other cultural dimensions. Ethnobotanists' interests include plant physiology, ecological functions, biogeography, and evolution of uses.[3] The ethnobotany of psychotropic plants examines the relationship between plants, culture, and cognition, showing that plants have far more importance than just providing food, fiber, and medicine.[4] Fieldwork indicates that psychotropic plant use in indigenous religious rites may shape basic symbolic structures of human consciousness, influencing language, ideas, beliefs, and perceptions about the natural and spiritual worlds. Indeed, a major focus of the ethnobotany of psychotropic mind-altering plants is to learn about their cultural meanings and their psychocultural effects.[5] Examples include studying the presence of sacred hallucinogenic plant motifs in the pre-colonial sculpture of Central and South America and the sacramentalization of cannabis in several religious traditions around the world.[6]

YOU MAY SAY I'M A FORCE OF NATURE

Most psychotropic plants alter human consciousness through active nitrogen-containing, water-soluble compounds called alkaloids that affect brain chemistry.[7] Well-known plant alkaloids include caffeine, nicotine, cocaine, and morphine. Popular hallucinogenic varieties include mescaline in the peyote cactus and psilocybin in several types of "magic" mushrooms. However, not all psychotropic plants produce their effects through alkaloids. For instance, the psychoactive power of cannabis comes from tetrahydrocannabinol (THC), a fat-soluble cannabinoid compound.[8] Mental effects range from mild to intense changes in sensory perception, mood, and cognition, while physical effects span from slight changes in pupil dilation and heart rate to nausea and vomiting.[9] Methods of consuming psychotropic plants vary with religious, medicinal, and recreational uses and may take place through absorption, ingestion, inhalation, or injection. As psychoactive chemicals can concentrate in different parts of plants, users may consume seeds, stems, roots, bark, leaves, flowers, resin, or fruit. Users may consume a plant in natural or cured forms or after processing it into a snuff, tincture, poultice, or crystal extract.[10] Dosages depend on potency, availability, desired effects, user experience, risk of harm, and other factors.

Black Panther's purple heart-shaped herb blends African American sci-fi comic book imagination with aspects of real plants, ecology, and culture. The herb appears to be a palm-sized vascular plant with a gently glowing purple heart-shaped body (see figure 18.1). In Africa, the color purple variably symbolizes royalty, wealth, wisdom, and healing, all of which are themes in the film. The color purple also functions to market and brand the movie, and plays a role in costume design as one can trace with the character of the high priest Zuri (Forest Whitaker) as discussed later in the text. In Wakanda, the plant's purple neon glow may be an effect of exposure to vibranium, the nation's prized metal, but it also demonstrates bioluminescence, a naturally occurring chemical process that produces self-generated light in organisms to support their reproduction. Bioluminescence mostly occurs in aquatic animals, fungi, and bacteria, but rarely in terrestrial plants.[11] The herb grows nested in a solitary, trumpet-shaped purple flower where the reproductive organs, the pistil and stamens, typically form. Short root-like structures anchor the herb to the flower's interior base instead of penetrating the ground. As fictional characteristics, these relationships obfuscate whether the herb replaced the flower's reproductive organs, if it contains them, or if it survives

Figure 18.1 *Black Panther's* Heart-Shaped Herb. Screenshot taken by author.

epiphytically. The flower also lacks a sepal and stem, as its roots grow directly from its base into loose soil. It thrives alongside a ground-creeping plant with small, delicate, simple dark green leaves. The closeness of the herb, flower, and ground-creeping plant reflects ecological symbiosis, a natural strategy of interactive co-dependence.

The heart-shaped herb's introduction in *Black Panther's* animated opening scene of Wakanda's origin story gives few clues about its native habitat. The scene does show, however, an iconic globe that situates Wakanda in present-day Rwanda near the Western Rift Valley, one of Africa's most biodiverse regions.[12] While it is reasonable to assume that the herb evolved in the wild, the movie shows it only as a cultivated plant growing inside of a large religious rock temple dedicated to the panther goddess Bast. The structure's flickering torch-lit interior suggests that the herb is genetically adapted to dimness that would kill most normal plants. The temple's internal gardens are large enough to contain three adult gardeners, who are also priests. Clothed in colorful traditional garments, the gardeners use simple hand tools to tend the low growing plants. Their kneeling posture while working may also symbolize reverence for the goddess.

SPACE IS THE PLACE

The rock temple in *Black Panther* is not mere backdrop but a sacred spatial symbol of Wakanda's religious cosmology, especially as it is the physical ceremonial space of the ritual of the heart-shaped herb, in addition to being the herb's cultivation site. As a religious landscape feature, the temple represents a transcendental portal between the material world of earthly ephemeral existence and the interminable spiritual plane of deities and ancestors. Although fictional, the temple nevertheless highlights the prominence of religious spaces in Africa, such as the pyramids, obelisks, and sun temples of ancient Kemet and Kush, the Ethiopian Orthodox stone churches of Lalibela, and the Songhai Empire's mud-and-wood tombs in Timbuktu. However, these eminent places contrast in size, function, influence, and visibility with smaller ones, such as shrines in homes and other locally known built and natural spaces. Having many possible functions, temples and shrines can greatly differ from each other in their religious purposes and additional abilities to fill socio-emotional needs, mark territory, display cultural identity, and preserve sacred traditions.[13]

Cultural anthropologist Wim Van Binsbergen's highly cited fieldwork in Zambia classifies shrines according to material layout and attributes, associated ideology, cult organization, and nature of the associated group.[14] These analytical foci can be useful to postulate the deeper meaning of the film's temple as it incorporates aspects of real African sacred spaces. Glimpses of the temple's exterior layout appear briefly in a daytime shot that shows it on a foggy peak surrounded by lushly forested hills, and in a night shot where it stands covered in darkness cut with shards of torchlight. The temple appears as a complex of three upright, semi-oval rock structures that resemble smooth carved granite rather than ragged geological outcrops. The presence of rock in temples and shrines symbolizes the sacred everlasting relationship between humans and nature.[15] Rock's durability also makes it desirable for memorializing historic sites, shielding worshippers and sacred objects from physical and spiritual enemies, and giving visible permanence to tradition. The temple's natural setting and upward structures may also symbolize African traditional animist beliefs in animal deities and spirits occupying the sky, mountains, forests, rivers, and other natural features and phenomena.[16]

Several extended film scenes show the temple's symbol-laden interior as a large, dusky, cavernous space. Torches and small fires splatter dim amber light on timeworn stone walls enveloped in wet green moss, heavy ropes of vine, and thickly knotted roots. Large carved columns rise and fade into an infinite shadow ceiling. The temple's inner sanctum holds its primary architectural feature: the ritual chamber of the heart-shaped herb. The chamber's annulus-shaped slab floor encircles a pit of red sand that ritual participants use to cover subjects in symbolic burials to denote sacrifice. A large fifteen-step slab staircase ascends in a counterclockwise spiral around the floor's circumference to a platform overlooking the pit. A ring of columns marks the chamber's perimeter. Wide, elevated slab walkways and platforms converge at the chamber and divide the temple's floor space into equal quadrants. Stone slab borders halve the quadrants and form narrow walkways that also meet at the chamber. One-half of each main quadrant contains a dark shallow pool of water where a smooth, gleaming larger-than-life Black Panther statue stands. The other half holds a raised-bed garden where the heart-shaped herb grows. Several large waist-high rocks in the gardens provide spiritual protection. The gardens' presence in the temple sanctifies the human–nature relationship and gives religious significance to the herb's cultivation.[17]

WHERE PATHWAYS MEET

Clues about the temple's religious cosmology emerge in sacred circular and spiral motifs that permeate Wakanda's cultural landscape. These repeating features resemble the sacred geometry of the Kongo cosmogram or *Tendwa Nzá Kongo*, a religious ideogram from central Africa's Bantu-speaking Kongo culture that crossed the Atlantic with the slave trade (see figure 18.2).[18] The

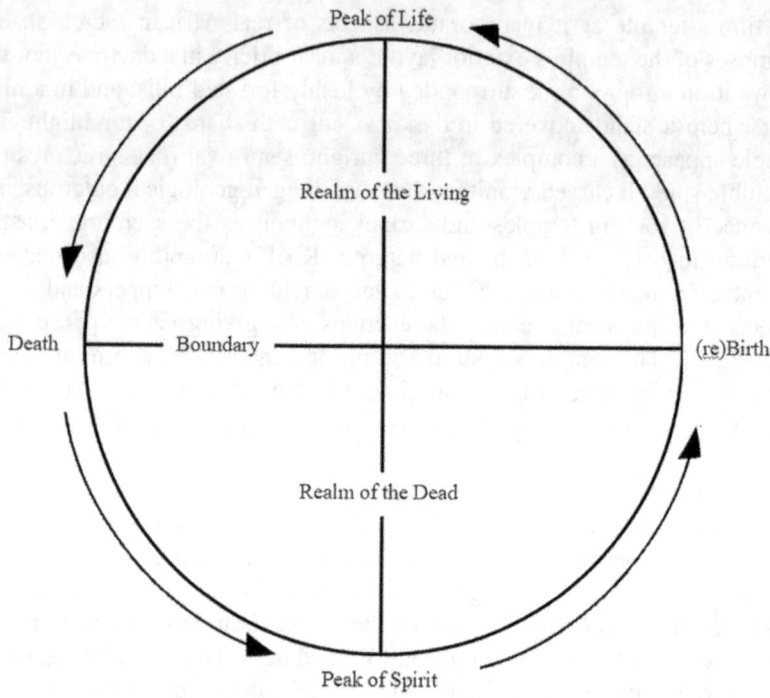

Figure 18.2 Kongo Cosmogram. Screenshot taken by author.

cosmogram offers a suitable interpretive framework that may help elucidate the ritual of the heart-shaped herb's underpinning religious cosmology. The Kongo cosmogram often appears as a cross within a circle, though it can also be a diamond or spiral. Counterclockwise movement around the cosmogram represents the spiritual journey through life and death, mirroring the sun's arc in the sky above the Kongo culture region's location in the southern hemisphere. The symbolic movement also appears clearly in a spinning 360° counterclockwise panning shot of scientist Princess Shuri's (Letitia Wright) lab in the scene where she is treating the wounded American secret agent.

The cosmogram's main cruciform feature, the *Yowa* cross, consists of two equilateral intersecting lines that divide it into quarters, a pattern reflected in the walkways that split the temple's floor into quadrants.[19] The cross' horizontal line signifies a boundary between the worlds of the living and the dead. Kongo religious traditions describe this boundary as an ocean or other waterbody, which may explain the presence of the temple's pools.[20] The boundary's east and west points correspond with sunrise and sunset, implying birth and death. The cross' vertical line denotes the transcendent relationship between the living and the dead. The line's north and south points indicate peak moments in a person's earthly and spiritual existence. The cross' intersection marks the crossroads or meeting place between the realms of life and death as does the convergence of the walkways around the temple's burial pit.

The film's animated story of Wakanda's origin indicates that visionary experiences predated the discovery of the heart-shaped herb. Indeed, the Black Panther's warrior-shaman ancestor saw the panther goddess Bast in a vision before she led him to find the herb.[21] Perhaps, the ancestor, as a hunter-gather, prayed to the animal goddess to use her divine maternal powers of fertility and protection to help him find food, enable healing, and overcome other adversities. Although the story spotlights the ancestor's shamanic vision as a crucial link to the Black Panther's genesis, the ritual of the heart-shaped herb does not follow a shaman's leadership but the direction of the temple's priests instead. In reality, shamans and priests can both officiate at rituals, but only shamans ingest hallucinogenic plants to accompany ritual subjects into visionary planes.[22] The film's priests lead the ritual and assist the king along his journey, but they never appear to ingest the herb, a plant reserved only for the monarch who himself inherits the shamanic role from the ancient ancestor. With Zuri heading it, the temple's hierarchical priesthood features a mixed gender and intergenerational composition that demonstrates the African traditional social values of umoja (unity) and ujima (collective work and responsibility). Despite placing a man at the top of Wakanda's religious leadership, the film challenges notions of patriarchy in religious cosmology by having a goddess instead of a god as the Black Panther religion's chief deity.

DOOR OF THE COSMOS

T'Challa (Chadwick Boseman) and Killmonger's (Michael B. Jordan) ritual experiences are the film's foremost scenes to highlight the heart-shaped herb's sacred and healing aspects. This section explores both of their rituals by applying from cultural anthropology, Arnold van Gennep's model of rites of passage, and Victor Turner's related concept of liminality, and also from behavioral psychology, the concepts of set and setting.[23] Van Gennep's model views all rites of passage as having a tripartite structure consisting of separation, liminality, and aggregation.[24] A ritual subject's passage through this sequence signifies their transition or initiation from a previous state, condition, or identity to a new, different one. Separation happens when the subject temporarily leaves their usual socio-cultural milieu upon entering the ritual. Liminality takes place when the subject enters the indeterminate position between their past and future states.[25] Aggregation concludes the ritual when the subject rejoins their community with their new identity and status.

A ritual's sequences, symbolism, and socio-physical environment merge with a subject's mental state during the ritual. Ingesting a hallucinogenic plant can take a ritual subject through a kaleidoscope of emotions, perceptions, and physiological responses.[26] The concepts of set and setting have helped to explain such responses since clinical psychologists first applied them in psychedelic drug research in the 1960s.[27] Set represents the subject's personality structure, including their attitude, mood, emotions, inhibitions, expectations, and motivations, and their cultural views about what constitutes reality at the time of the ritual. Setting refers to the subject's socio-physical environment, including the ritual site's location and material conditions, and the presence of other participants, including their functional roles and relationships to the subject.

T'Challa is already moving between full separation and partial liminality when his heart-shaped herb ritual begins. His separation occurred earlier when he left his family to engage in ritual combat in the perilous waters of Warrior Falls.[28] T'Challa's liminal phase becomes evident when symbols of social transition appear that change his identity and status into that of an ordinary vulnerable man. This occurs when T'Challa relinquishes his Black Panther powers to become equal with his challenger. His ritual's liminal phase continues in the temple's inner chamber where he replaces his symbolic adornments from combat for those of a shaman preparing for mystical flight. For his symbolic burial in the chamber pit, T'Challa wears only shorts and a bead and bone coronation necklace representing connection to the royal ancestors. He lies on the pit's red sand with his arms crossed over his torso to signify passage through the crossroads of life and death as symbolized in the Kongo cosmogram.

OUTSIDE THE TIME ZONE

T'Challa's ritual ingestion of the potent purple plant begins when a female priest picks a single herb from a flower in one of the temple's gardens. She puts the fresh herb into a small handheld mortar, mashes it with a pestle, and then pours the resulting purple poultice into a bowl. Wearing the ceremonial garments and face paint of a high priest, Zuri steps into the chamber pit holding the bowl in his hand to administer the sacramental drink to T'Challa (see figure 18.3).[29] When T'Challa gulps it down, Zuri pronounces, "allow the heart-shaped herb to restore the powers of the Black Panther and take you to the ancestral plane." A purple neon glow pulsates from T'Challa's body when his supernatural powers return. When Zuri sees the herb's psychoactive

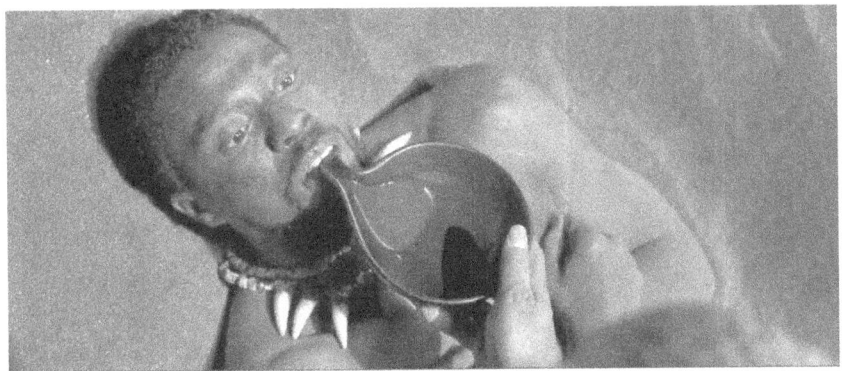

Figure 18.3 T'Chaka Drinking Herbal Poultice. Screenshot taken by author.

effects intensify, he invokes the king's father in the ancestral plane, saying, "T'Chaka we call on you, come here to your son." The scene then changes to show T'Challa's arrival in the ancestral plane.

It is hard to distinguish whether T'Challa's herb-induced vision is a complex hallucination or a dream, because although his eyes close during the burial, it is unclear if this means he has fallen asleep. The distinction is important, because as mental phenomena hallucinations typically occur during wakefulness and dreams during sleep.[30] Ethnobotanists have documented numerous plants that African traditional religions use to produce both effects. Perhaps the most studied is *Tabernanthe iboga*, a hallucinogenic perennial rainforest shrub having religious and medicinal uses in the Fang's Bwiti and Mbeiri cults in Gabon.[31] Researchers have also observed ritual uses of hallucinogenic plants in South Africa's Tsonga and Zambia's Ndembu cultures.[32] Ethnobotanists use the term "oneirogenic" to describe plants that produce or enhance dreams.[33] Southern Bantu diviners in South Africa use several types of such plants, including *Rubia, Silene, Hippobromus, Chamaecrista*, and *Dianthus* species. *Black Panther's* fictional herb resembles *Datura metel (fastuosa)*, a purple flowering plant that the Tsonga of Mozambique use as an oneirogen and hallucinogen in fertility rituals (see figure 18.4).[34] Often describing such species as "Plants of the Gods," "Flesh of the Gods," and "Food of the Gods," ethnobotanists have considered their hallucinatory effects as potentially forming the ancient experiential basis of religion itself. Indeed, humans have long interpreted such hallucinations as evidence of deities, ancestors, and distinct spiritual universes.[35]

Indigenous traditional religions often interpret plant-induced hallucinations as "visions" and "journeys" as depicted in *Black Panther*.[36] The purple heart-shaped herb's ability to transport T'Challa and Killmonger from Wakanda's ordinary here and now to mental states of shifting spatial, temporal, and

Figure 18.4 *Datura metel (fastuosa)*. Uploaded to Wikimedia Commons by photographer, user Llez.

emotional experiences of the past, present, and otherworldly makes the plant itself a symbol of transition and liminality. T'Challa's vision opens with a childhood memory of seeing himself as a young boy interacting affectionately with his father, King T'Chaka (John Kani), in the temple's inner chamber. T'Challa's vision then flashes forward to his early adulthood when he witnessed and failed to stop his father's death. The herb's power to make this traumatic memory resurface in T'Challa's consciousness alludes to the traditional medicinal use of hallucinogenic plants as psychospiritual healing agents—a practice now gaining increased attention in the West, although indigenous cultures may view trauma as a spiritual rather than psychological problem.

Back in the ritual chamber, Zuri looks down at T'Challa in the pit and responds in a Xhosa word meaning, "praise the ancestors." The priest's assistants, including young children, cover T'Challa with shovelfuls of the pit's red sand in a symbolic burial denoting the king's crossing over to the world of the dead. T'Challa's vision then shows him awakening in a serene, hazy, purple-hued savannah dreamscape. He emerges cross-armed from the ground wearing a traditional long dashiki made of embroidered white fabric that symbolizes ancestral connection. Before him stands a large acacia tree, a versatile African plant symbol, with several black panthers perched on its thick branches. As the king steps toward the tree, one of the large cats jumps down and transforms into T'Chaka, who is wearing black and white kente cloth. T'Challa hugs his father and kneels in front of him with a remorseful look on his face. T'Chaka replies by sternly commanding his son to stand up and behave like a king. The two engage in quiet discussion, but T'Challa's vision abruptly ends when T'Chaka quells his son's doubts about leading Wakanda without his physical paternal presence. An astonished T'Challa suddenly rises in the burial pit, gasping for air, in awe of what he had just experienced. Zuri urges the king to breath, calming him. An astonished T'Challa smiles and tells Zuri, "He was there. He was there, my father." T'Challa's return from the ancestral plane to normal consciousness ends the ritual's liminal sequence. The ritual's aggregate phase occurs when T'Challa reenters society with his new status, authority, and confidence as the Black Panther and Wakanda's king, fortified by the ancestral guidance received during his vision.

THEY CAN'T ACCEPT ME

The film uses Killmonger's ritual to show a contrasting turbulent kind of experience that hallucinogenic plant use is also capable of producing. Although Killmonger and T'Challa's rituals both took place in the same temple, vast differences in their social settings may have shaped their divergent experiences. Killmonger's hostility toward Wakanda's traditions, including the ritual of the heart-shaped herb, invited resistance toward him from the priests. By murdering Zuri, Killmonger disrupted the temple's social organization, forcing the slain elder leader's female assistant (Sope Aluko) to replace him. Anguished and unwilling to take Zuri's place, she submits to his killer's demands with great reluctance. This observation is crucial because forcefully changing a ritual's traditional symbols and social organization may violate deep religious beliefs, distressing participants and directing resentment toward transgressors.

Killmonger's ignorance of Wakanda's sacred traditions prevents him from seeing that his ritual lacks several symbols of liminality that appeared in

T'Challa's ritual. He does not wear the coronation necklace that T'Challa wore to symbolize continuity with the royal ancestors. Despite resembling a form of African traditional skin art, the permanent row-patterned scars on Killmonger's body display violent power-laden symbolism that may conflict with Wakandan cultural requirements for ritual subjects to strip their bodies of status symbols. Another notably missing feature in Killmonger's ritual is the presence of children that was evident in T'Challa's ritual. Cultural insiders may interpret the absence of traditional symbols or their replacement with incongruous ones as insurmountable obstacles to the ritual subject's spiritual passage. The priests' abhorrence toward Killmonger and his ritual's incomplete assemblage of traditional symbols indicate an unwelcoming social setting that lacks the hope, optimism, and acceptance that characterized T'Challa's ritual.

In terms of set, Killmonger and T'Challa's disparate personal histories and cultural backgrounds conditioned them to respond differently to the heart-shaped herb's mind-altering power. Killmonger's upbringing in Oakland, California, far from his father's African homeland, filled him with knowledge, attitudes, motivations, and expectations that his rival cousin from Wakanda did not have. Conversely, T'Challa, steeped in Wakanda's traditions, understood the herb's cultural significance, and long expected to one day experience its legendary visions as a requirement of royal succession and attainment of the Black Panther's supernatural powers. While Killmonger knows of the herb's ability to give the Black Panther his powers, he lacks the cultural preparation needed to navigate its psychospiritual effects. Although Killmonger's vision begins as T'Challa's did with a traumatic memory of his own father's murder, the similarities quickly end. Killmonger never makes it to the mystical savannah that welcomed T'Challa's arrival. Instead, his vision becomes a chain of nightmarish images from his childhood apartment that show him as a boy (Seth Carr) tormented by the specter of his father's death and his desperation for answers about his own identity.

The desolation of Killmonger's vision breaks only for a slight moment when he discovers his father's secret notebook that reveals his connections to Wakanda. His hopeful excitement crashes when his father, N'Jobu (Sterling K. Brown), appears behind him in the apartment. The startled boy responds indifferently to N'Jobu's tender greetings, averting the possibility of a warm embrace as observed in T'Challa and T'Chaka's reunion. Rather, father and son discuss questions of social exclusion, violence, and death. Killmonger's vision amplifies the self-doubt, anger, and loneliness that he feels from his abandonment by his royal family. He finds himself trapped in liminality, stuck in an endless time cycle that shifts back and forth between childhood and adulthood, boy and man. When Killmonger cannot find solace, he wakes from his vision in confused rage. Blaming the heart-shaped herb for his disturbing experience, he commands the female priest to burn the herb gardens, threatening her when she protests. Without having gained the royal ancestors' blessings, Killmonger's belligerent short-lived rule ends when T'Challa, restored to health by the heart-shaped herb's physical healing power, returns to defeat him.

CONCLUSION: YOU THOUGHT YOU COULD BUILD A WORLD WITHOUT US

An ethnobotanical approach shows that the purple heart-shaped herb in *Black Panther* is cinematized comic book fiction inspired by the real-world significance of African indigenous traditional psychotropic plant uses that belong to humanity's heritage of religion, ritual, medicine, and cultural ecological adaptation. The herb's sacramental use in the film's royal initiation rituals and healing practices specifically underscores the importance of psychotropic plants in African traditional social, political, and religious rites and spiritual healing. Unlike their secular meanings in Western recreational drug contexts, psychotropic plants in traditional cultures are keys that open doors to other worlds where spirits, deities, and ancestors dwell. Such views demonstrate a relationship between nature, plants, and human consciousness that Westerners may better understand through a cultural relativist lens. The religious use of psychotropic plants lays at the core of indigenous consciousness and cultural identity in a way that is comparable to the sacramental use of grape wine for members of Judeo-Christian religions. Furthermore, such plants symbolize historical cultural ecological connections between indigenous peoples and the places and environments where they cultivate and use their plants. The purple heart-shaped herb's relationship to Wakanda's people and their consciousness mirrors what Tabernanthe iboga means to Gabon's Fang, peyote to Mexico's Huichol, and ayahuasca to the Peruvian Amazon's Urarina.

From an Afrofuturist standpoint, the heart-shaped herb's ritual use prompts us to question the place of African indigenous traditional knowledge (ITK) in our untethered, materialistically driven high-tech world. It would be wrong to assume that such knowledge is antithetical to modern technological progress. The film's portrayal of the herb's visionary and medicinal power represents African ITK as a guiding force that fosters ethical development and use of high technology for the elimination of human suffering and the advancement of environmental sustainability. In this view, the herb's symbolism embodies empowerment, healing, and environmental stewardship that can together counterbalance hyper-technological culture with a desire for a better future on a healthy planet. The herb's significance in the film symbolizes cultural reverence for nature and promotes a social consciousness that shuns ideas, beliefs, and attitudes that fuel the inequity, violence, and economic expansion that are destroying Earth's cultural and natural richness.

An opposite destructive expression of social consciousness gains visibility in the climactic burning of the herb garden, initiated by Killmonger, a scene that is perhaps the film's most cinematic moment. It is the equivalent of anarchy, since Killmonger thinks he can do without Wakanda's traditional plant-based magic, defying the power of the ancestors. His decision to set the garden ablaze contradicts his character's image as a revolutionary enemy of White power. The arson actually seems more likely to symbolize White power's genocidal history of erasing indigenous culture, identity, consciousness, and environmental knowledge. This history lives on today as environmental racism and other forms of oppression against Black, Indigenous, and People of Color.

The burning of the garden also raises questions about the ongoing drug debate, namely the relationship between drug criminalization and the freedom to use psychotropic plants for personal psychological, spiritual, and medicinal purposes. As anthropological evidence shows, such uses have an ancient legacy in many cultures, so what interests do policymakers really have in criminalizing them? Criminalization supporters have viewed illegal psychotropic plants as a scourge, while their opponents have underscored the importance of education, research, and legalization. The spreading decriminalization and legalization of cannabis, and to a still much smaller degree, psilocybin, is showing a recent gradual shift in social attitudes toward these plants. This demonstrates that a cultural change is happening because wider segments of society are discovering psychotropic plants to have beneficial personal and social value. If the plants could speak, what would they say to us? Perhaps they have been speaking to us all along; we just have not learned how to listen.

NOTES

1. Peter Mitchell and Andrew Hudson, "Psychoactive Plants and Southern African Hunter-Gatherers: A Review of the Evidence," *Southern African Humanities* 16 (2004): 40; J. F. Sobiecki, "A Review of Plants Used in Divination in Southern Africa and their Psychoactive Effects," *Southern African Humanities* 20 (2008): 1–2; Richard Evans Schultes and Albert Hoffman, *Plants of the Gods: Their Sacred, Healing and Hallucinogenic Powers* (Rochester: Healing Arts Press, 1992), 26, 27–30.

2. J.F. Sobiecki, "A Preliminary Inventory of Plants Used for Psychoactive Purposes in Southern African Healing Traditions," *Transactions of the Royal Society of South Africa* 57, no. 1&2 (2002): 1–24.

3. Judith A. Carney, "African Traditional Plant Knowledge in the Circum-Caribbean Region," *Journal of Ethnobiology* 23 no. 2 (2003): 167–185; Schultes and Hoffman, *Plants of the Gods*, 26–30.

4. Peter T. Furst, "Introduction" in *Flesh of the Gods: The Ritual Use of Hallucinogens*, ed. Peter T. Furst (New York: Praeger Publishers, 1972), xi–xv; Peter T. Furst, *Hallucinogens and Culture* (San Francisco: Chandler & Sharp Publishers, Inc., 1976), 10; Weston LaBarre, *Culture in Context* (Durham: Duke University Press, 1980), 62–84; Terrence McKenna, *Food of the Gods: The Search for the Original Tree of Knowledge* (New York: Bantam Books, 1992), 15; Schultes and Hoffman, *Plants of the Gods*, 9, 65, 184–185.

5. Schultes and Hoffman, *Plants of the Gods*, 184–185; LaBarre, *Culture in Context: The Selected Writings of Weston LaBarre*, 40–41.

6. William A. Emboden, Jr., "Ritual Use of Cannabis Sativa L.: A Historical-Ethnographic Survey," in *Flesh of the Gods: The Ritual Use of Hallucinogens*, ed. Peter T. Furst (New York: Praeger Publishers, 1972), 214–236; LaBarre, *Culture in Context*, 93–107; Schultes and Hoffman, *Plants of the Gods*, 87, 92–101, 145, 148–149, 154.

7. Ralph Metzner, "Hallucinogenic Drugs and Plants in Psychotherapy and Shamanism," *Journal of Psychoactive Drugs* 30, no. 4 (1998): 5; Schultes and Hoffman, *Plants of the Gods*, 172–175.

8. Schultes and Hoffman, *Plants of the Gods*, 99.

9. Theodore X. Barber, *LSD, Marihuana, Yoga and Hypnosis* (Chicago: Aldine Publishing Company, 1970), 9, 20; Schultes and Hoffman, *Plants of the Gods*, 10–14, 176–177.

10. Schultes and Hoffman, *Plants of the Gods*, 26–27.

11. Steven H. D. Haddock and James F. Case, "The Bioluminescence Web Page," *The Bioluminescence Web Page*, University of California at Santa Barbara, updated 2011, accessed December 1, 2019, https://biolum.eemb.ucsb.edu/.

12. A later scene confirms this location when it shows Killmonger finding a map with geographical coordinates in his father's notebook.

13. Allan Dawson, "Introduction," in *Shrines in Africa: History, Politics and Society*, ed. Allan Dawson (Calgary: University of Calgary Press, 2009), vii–xii; Judith Sterner and Nicholas David, "Pots, Stones, and Potsherds in Shrines," in *Africa: History, Politics and Society*, ed. Allan Dawson (Calgary: University of Calgary Press, 2009), 5–9; Wim M. J. van Binsbergen, *Religious Change in Zambia: Exploratory Studies* (New York: Routledge, 2009), 103.

14. Binsbergen, *Religious Change in Zambia*, 103.

15. Timothy Insoll, "Shrine Franchising and the Neolithic in the British Isles: Some Observations based upon the Tallensi, Northern Ghana," *Cambridge Archaeological Journal* 16 (2006): 227–236.

16. Sterner and David, "Pots, Stones, and Potsherds in Shrines," 11–13.

17. The movie does not explain why the herb's cultivation takes place in the temple.

18. Robert Farris Thompson, *Flash of the Spirit: African & Afro-American Art & Philosophy* (New York: Vintage Books, 1984), xv–xvi.

19. Thompson, *Flash of the Spirit*, 109–110.

20. Robert Farris Thompson, "Bighearted Power: Kongo Presence in the Landscape and Art of Black America," in *Keep Your Head to the Sky: Interpreting African American Home Ground*, eds. Grey Gundaker and Tynes Cowan (Charlottesville: University Press of Virginia, 1998), 41.

21. The movie certainly adopts Bast from the ancient Kemetic (Egyptian) cat goddess of the same name who served as protector of the pharaohs and the sun god, Ra.

22. While Bast led the first Black Panther's ancestor to discover the heart-shaped herb in a vision, the movie does not explain what caused his vision in the first place; Victor Turner, "Religious Specialists," in *International Encyclopedia of the Social Sciences*, ed. David L. Sills, vol. 13 (New York: Macmillan Company and The Free Press, 1972), 439.

23. Furst, *Hallucinogens and Culture*, 15; Metzner, "Hallucinogenic Drugs and Plants," 4–8; Schultes and Hoffman, *Plants of the Gods*, 177–181.

24. Arnold van Gennep, *The Rites of Passage*, trans. Monika B. Vizedom and Gabrielle L. Caffee (Chicago: The University of Chicago Press, 1960), 11.

25. Victor Turner, *The Ritual Process: Structure and Anti-Structure* (New Brunswick: Aldone Transaction, 2008), 95.

26. LaBarre, *Culture in Context*, 56.

27. Barber, *LSD, Marihuana, Yoga and Hypnosis*, 14–19; Timothy Leary, Ralph Metzner, and Richard Alpert, *The Psychedelic Experience* (Secaucus: The Citadel Press, 1964), 11.

28. The movie does not explain how the prince got his Black Panther powers before he became the king.

29. This drinkable form of ingestion contrasts with the movie's opening scene which shows the warrior-shaman picking and eating a single herb that gives him his Black Panther powers and made him Wakanda's first king.

30. LaBarre, *Culture in Context*, 39–41.

31. James W. Fernandez, "Tabernanthe iboga: Narcotic Ecstasis and the Work of the Ancestors," in *Flesh of the Gods: The Ritual Use of Hallucinogens*, ed. Peter T. Furst (New York: Praeger Publishers, 1972), 237–260; Harrison G. Pope Jr., "Tabernanthe iboga: An African Plant of Social Importance," *Economic Botany* 23, no. 2 (1969): 174–184.

32. Sobiecki, "A Review of Plants Used in Divination in Southern Africa and their Psychoactive Effects," 338–339.

33. Sobiecki, "A Review of Plants Used in Divination in Southern Africa and their Psychoactive Effects," 338.

34. Thomas F. Johnston, "Communication with the Fertility God via Hallucinogens in Tsongaland," *Religion* 4, no. 2 (1974): 87–88.

35. LaBarre, *Culture in Context*, 50, 62; Weston LaBarre, "Hallucinogens and the Shamanic Origins of Religion," in *Flesh of the Gods: The Ritual Use of Hallucinogens*, ed. Peter T. Furst (New York: Praeger Publishers, 1972), 261; McKenna, *Food of the Gods*, 24; Schultes and Hoffman, *Plants of the Gods*, 61.

36. Fernandez, "Tabernanthe iboga," 237, Johnston, "Communication with the Fertility God," 88; Pope Jr. 180, Schultes and Hoffman, *Plants of the Gods*, 112–113;

Sobiecki "A Review of Plants Used in Divination in Southern Africa and their Psychoactive Effects," 335–338; Jean-Francois Sobiecki, "Psychoactive *Ubulawu* Spiritual Medicines in the Initiation Process of Southern Bantu Diviners," *Journal of Psychoactive Drugs* 44, no. 3 (2012): 217, 219.

WORKS CITED

Barber, Theodore X. *LSD, Marihuana, Yoga and Hypnosis.* Chicago: Aldine Publishing Company, 1970.
Binsbergen, Wim M.J. van, *Religious Change in Zambia: Exploratory Studies.* New York: Routledge, 2009.
Carney, Judith A. "African Traditional Plant Knowledge in the Circum-Caribbean Region." *Journal of Ethnobiology* 23, no. 2 (Fall/Winter 2003): 167–185.
Dawson, Allan. "Introduction." In *Shrines in Africa: History, Politics and Society*, edited by Allan Dawson, vii–xvii. Calgary: University of Calgary Press, 2009.
Edmonds, Ennis Barrington. *Rastafari: From Outcasts to Culture Bearers.* New York: Oxford University Press, 2003.
Fernandez, James W. "Tabernanthe iboga: Narcotic Ecstasis and the Work of the Ancestors." In *Flesh of the Gods: The Ritual Use of Hallucinogens*, edited by Peter T. Furst, 237–260. New York: Praeger Publishers, 1972.
Furst, Peter T. "Introduction." In *Flesh of the Gods: The Ritual Use of Hallucinogens*, edited by Peter T. Furst, vii–xvi. New York: Praeger Publishers, 1972.
Furst, Peter T. *Hallucinogens and Culture.* San Francisco: Chandler & Sharp Publishers, Inc., 1976.
Gennep, Arnold van. *The Rites of Passage.* Translated by Monika B. Vizedom and Gabrielle L. Caffee. Chicago: The University of Chicago Press, 1960.
Haddock, Steven H. D. and James F. Case. "The Bioluminescence Web Page." *The Bioluminescence Web Page.* University of California at Santa Barbara, updated 2011. Accessed December 1, 2019. https://biolum.eemb.ucsb.edu/.
Insoll, Timothy. "Shrine Franchising and the Neolithic in the British Isles: Some Observations based upon the Tallensi, Northern Ghana." *Cambridge Archaeological Journal* 16, no. 2 (2006): 223–238.
Johnston, Thomas F. "Communication with the Fertility God via Hallucinogens in Tsongaland." *Religion* 4, no. 2 (1974): 85–95.
LaBarre, Weston. "Hallucinogens and the Shamanic Origins of Religion." In *Flesh of the Gods: The Ritual Use of Hallucinogens*, edited by Peter T. Furst, 271–278. New York: Praeger Publishers, 1972.
LaBarre, Weston. *Culture in Context: Selected Writings of Weston LaBarre.* Durham: Duke University Press, 1980.
Leary, Timothy, Ralph Metzner and Richard Alpert. *The Psychedelic Experience: A Manual Based on the Tibetan Book of the Dead.* Secaucus: The Citadel Press, 1964.
McKenna, Terrence. *Food of the Gods: The Search for the Original Tree of Knowledge.* New York: Bantam Books, 1992.

Metzner, Ralph. "Hallucinogenic Drugs and Plants in Psychotherapy and Shamanism." *Journal of Psychoactive Drugs* 30, no. 4 (1998): 1–10.

Mitchell, Peter, and Andrew Hudson. "Psychoactive Plants and Southern African Hunter-Gatherers: A Review of the Evidence." *Southern African Humanities* 16 (2004): 39–57.

Pope Jr., Harrison G. "Tabernanthe iboga: An African Plant of Social Importance." *Economic Botany* 23, no. 2 (1969): 174–184.

Schultes, Richard Evans, and Albert Hoffman. *Plants of the Gods: Their Sacred, Healing and Hallucinogenic Powers*. Rochester: Healing Arts Press, 1992.

Sobiecki, J.F. "A Preliminary Inventory of Plants Used for Psychoactive Purposes in Southern African Healing Traditions." *Transactions of the Royal Society of South Africa* 57, no. 1&2 (2002): 1–24.

Sobiecki, J. F. "A Review of Plants Used in Divination in Southern Africa and their Psychoactive Effects." *Southern African Humanities* 20 (2008): 333–351.

Sobiecki, Jean-Francois. "Psychoactive *Ubulawu* Spiritual Medicines in the Initiation Process of Southern Bantu Diviners." *Journal of Psychoactive Drugs* 44, no. 3 (2012): 216–223.

Sobiecki, Jean-Francois. "Psychoactive Plants: A Neglected Area of Ethnobotanical Research in Southern Africa (Review)." *Ethno Medicine* 8, no. 2 (2014): 165–172.

Sterner, Judith, and Nicholas David, "Pots, Stones, and Potsherds in Shrines." In *Africa: History, Politics and Society*, edited by Allan Dawson, 1–21. Calgary: University of Calgary Press, 2009.

Thompson, Robert Farris. *Flash of the Spirit: African & Afro-American Art & Philosophy*. New York: Vintage Books, 1984.

Thompson, Robert Farris. "Bighearted Power: Kongo Presence in the Landscape and Art of Black America." In *Keep Your Head to the Sky: Interpreting African American Home Ground*, edited by Grey Gundaker and Tynes Cowan. Charlottesville: University Press of Virginia, 1998.

Turner, Victor. "Religious Specialists." In *International Encyclopedia of the Social Sciences*, edited by David L. Sills, vol. 13. New York: Macmillan Company and The Free Press, 1972.

Turner, Victor. *The Ritual Process: Structure and Anti-Structure*. New Brunswick: Aldone Transaction, 2008.

FILM

Black Panther. Directed by Ryan Coogler. United States: Walt Disney Studios Motion Pictures, 2018.

Index

accents: in *Black Panther*, 188, 192–94. *See also* code-switching
action cinema: Black, 54–55, 68; Hong Kong, 53–54, 60, 68; martial arts, 58–60, 67
activism: Black, 224–25, 229–31, 233–37; digital, 90–91. *See also* Black organizations; Du Bois, W. E. B.; hashtag activism; Ruffin, Josephine St. Pierre; Trotter, William Monroe; Washington, Booker T.
adored ones, 154–55. *See also* The Dora Milaje
aesthetics: African, 187, 245, 247; Black, 323; Black action, 55–56, 68; Chinese, 57–58; Hong Kong action cinema, 53–54
Africa: economy of, 108; in Hollywood films, 107; labor division in, 204, 208–9; metalworking in, 250–52; psychotropic plant use in, 333, 341; religious spaces in, 336–37; scholarship on, 208, 249; women warriors in, 204, 207
African American: identity, 109, 187–88, 197–98, 207. *See also* double-consciousness; identity; Killmonger, Erik

African diaspora, 5, 23, 129, 220, 249, 273–74, 277, 289, 293
African indigenous traditional knowledge (ITK), 345
Afrofuturism, 4, 22–23, 129, 227, 279n3, 345–46; divine feminism of, 203–4; rewriting queerness in, 92–93; view on race, 129–30; of the Underground Railroad, 127–30, 139–40. *See also* Dery, Mark; race as technology
Agamben, Giorgio, 301, 308
Amadiume, Ifi, 209. *See also* gender roles
Aneka, 155; relationship with Ayo, 87, 93–94, 158–59, 161–62, 166n32, 206. *See also* Ayo, relationship with Aneka
Artificial Intelligence, 247–48. *See also* Griot
Auer, Peter, 189–90, 197
Augenbraum, Eric, 88. *See also* hashtag activism
authenticity, cinematic, 54, 59–60, 70n31; in *Black Panther* fighting, 60–61; in Hollywood films, 67
Avengers: Endgame (dir. Anthony and Joe Russo), 161, 164

Avengers: Infinity War (dir. Anthony and Joe Russo), 161, 164
Ayo, 155; in *Avengers: Civil War*, 159; relationship with Aneka, 87, 93–94, 158–59, 161–62, 206

Baer, Hester, 90–91. *See also* feminism, hashtag
Bassett, Angela, 79
Bast goddess, 250, 336, 339, 348n21
Berry, Halle, 80
Berube, Michael, 179. *See also* disability studies
Bhabha, Homi, 302. *See also* colonialism
Big Tech: challenging the ethics of, 259
Bingham, Dennis, 75, 82n10. *See also* genre, biopic
Birth of a Nation (dir. D.W. Griffith), 3, 6–7
Black actors: transition from biopic to superhero, 79–80, 82n15
Black Arts Movement, 23–24, 216
Black elite, 215–16, 230–32, 234–37
blackface, 34–35. *See also* paint down
BlacKkKlansman (dir. Spike Lee), 5–7, 9
Black Lives Matter movement, 7–8, 69n9, 89, 217; influence of, 228. *See also* activism; hashtag activism
Black manhood, 230, 232–33; in *Black Panther*, 234. *See also* masculinity, Black
Black organizations, 233, 237; League of Women for Community Service (LWCS), 224, 229; National Association for the Advancement of Colored People (NAACP), 229, 233, 237. *See also* activism; Black Panther Party
Black Panther (dir. Ryan Coogler): African-American perspective in, 109–10; American perspective of, 187–88, 196–97; ancestral plane in, 62–64, 307; box office success of, 1, 10, 103, 315; casting of, 277; fight style/stuntwork in, 43–47, 162–64; heart-shaped herb in, 183–84, 335–36, 342, 345; impact on Black community, 4–5, 28, 78, 171, 184, 228, 272–73, 288; as a progressive text, 268–71; queerness in, 183–84; religion in, 336–37, 339; ritual combat in, 59–61; as Third Cinema, 269–73, 275–78
Black Panther Party, 111–12, 177, 237, 290, 301, 307, 311n8; references/imagery in *Black Panther*, 109–10, 177, 222. *See also* activism, Black organizations
Black Panther/T'Challa (character): creation of, 2, 110–11; evolution of, 22, 110–12, 114, 154, 279n2, 293. *See also* Kirby, Jack; Lee, Stan; T'Challa/Black Panther (in *Black Panther* film)
Black Panther Volume Six (writ. Ta-Nehisi Coates), 93, 161–62; interpretation of the Dora Milaje, 158. *See also* Ta-Nehisi Coates
Black Panther Volume Three (writ. Christopher Priest), 153–58
Black Power Movement, 110–11, 311n8
The Black Stuntmen's Association (BSA), 37–39. *See also* The Coalition of Black Stuntmen and Women
Blankman (dir. Mike Binder), 22, 173
Blaxploitation films, 55–56
Bordwell, David, 59
Boseman, Chadwick, 1–2, 73–75, 82n7; audience response to, 78
Brophy, Susan Dianne, 308–9
Brown, Calvin, 37–38. *See also* The Black Stuntmen's Association
Brown, William Wells, 132
Bullock, Barbara, 189
Bush Mama (dir. Haile Gerima), 274
Bynum, Sadiqua, 44, 47

camera shots, 180: jumpcut, 176, 179; rotating shot, 175, 179
Cape Jr., Robert W., 174. *See also* disability studies
Capoeira Angola, 45. *See also* martial arts
Captain America: Civil War (dir. Anthony and Joe Russo), 107–8, 159, 163, 299–300, 303–4
Captain America: The Winter Soldier (dir. Anthony Russo & Joe Russo), 76
Carrington, Andrew, 92–93
Carter, Ruth E., 1, 9, 24, 129
Catsam, Derek Charles, 270–71
Central Intelligence Agency (CIA), 270: against Africa, 113; against the Black Panther Party, 113–14
Chambliss, Julian C., 270
Changling, Wang, 57–59
Charlottesville Unite the Right 2017 Rally, 7–9
Cheadle, Don, 80
Chikafa-Chipiro, Rosemary, 304. *See also* womanism, Africana
Civil Rights Movement, 111, 217, 225–26, 237
Cleaver, Kathleen, 112. *See also* Black Panther Party
The Coalition of Black Stuntmen and Women, 39–40. *See also* The Black Stuntmen's Association
code-switching, 188–89, 192–93, 195–99, 324
Cohen, Cathy, 176, 180, 182. *See also* deviance as resistance; queer theory
colonialism, 24, 305–10; colonial mimicry, 302; effects of, 315–16, 325–26. *See also* hybridity; postcolonialism
Coogler, Ryan, 1, 6–8, 22, 110, 190, 206, 318
cosmogram (*Tendwa Nzá Kongo*), 337–40
cosmopolitanism, 300, 302–4; postcolonial, 306, 311; radical, 305–6, 312n25

costume design: in *Black Panther*, 24, 129, 274, 308. *See also* Ruth E. Carter
COVID-19 pandemic, 46, 218
critical race theory, 317
critique: narrative, 319; visual rhetorical, 319
Crumpton, Taylor, 4

Daughters of the Dust (dir. Julie Dash), 275–77
decolonization, 55, 103, 305–6, 308, 310, 313n33
Dery, Mark, 4, 22, 129, 227
deviance as resistance, 176–77, 180. *See also* Cathy Cohen
Diawara, Manthia, 276–77
disability studies, 174–75, 179. *See also* Killmonger, Erik, as psychologically disabled; Klaue, as psychologically disabled; trope, supercrip
The Dora Milaje, 8; challenging Eurocentrism, 204, 207; portrayal in the comics, 153–58, 161–62, 205; portrayal in the MCU, 157, 159–64, 203, 304–5; portrayal in *World of Wakanda*, 158–59, 205–6; as warriors, 162–64. *See also* Aneka; Ayo; Midnight Angels; Nakia; Okoye; Queen Divine Justine
double consciousness, 187–88, 197–99, 207, 305; of T'Challa/Black Panther, 194–95
Douglass, Frederick, 131, 135, 137
drug addiction in the US, 217–18
Du Bois, W. E. B., 187, 198–99, 207, 220, 225, 235–36, 305
DuVernay, Ava, 1, 9, 17n1

education: Afrocentric lens, applied to, 291–92; as a liberatory practice, 290–91, 294–96. *See also* bell hooks
Ejiofor, Chiwetel, 80
English, African American (AAE), 190, 197–98

Epper, Jeannie, 38. *See also* Stuntwoman's Association of Motion Pictures
equanimity, cinematic: in Black action films, 70n34: in *Black Panther*, 62–66
erasure: Black, 23; Black lesbian, 94–95
Espinosa, Julio García, 267–69, 271–72. *See also* Third Cinema
ethnobotany, 334, 341, 345
Eurocentrism, 26, 205, 207, 294
Eusebio, Jonathan, 44
expressivity, cinematic: of Black action films, 55–56; in *Black Panther*, 62–63

fandom, 93–95; online, 90
Fanon, Frantz, 2, 24, 55, 188, 195, 198, 305–6, 308, 311, 313n33
Faramelli, Anthony, 270, 277
feminism: Black, 224–25, 229–31; divine, 203, 206, 210; hashtag, 90–91
fiction, speculative, 172, 219, 227
42 (dir. Brian Helgeland), 77
Foxx, Jamie, 80, 173
Freire, Paulo, 295–96
Fruitvale Station (dir. Ryan Coogler), 79, 110

Gabriel, Teshome, ix, 271–72
Gay, Roxane, 22, 158, 205. *See also World of Wakanda*
Gebru, Timnit, 259
gender: constructs, 232–33; hierarchy, 208–9; politics, 300, 304–5. *See also* womanism, Africana
gender roles: European, 208; precolonial African, 204, 207–10
genre, biopic, 73–75, 77–79; *Black Panther* as, 74; Marvel films as, 75–76
genre, superhero: films, 75–76, 82n10; lack of Black representation in, 2, 4, 21, 299

Gilroy, Paul, 302, 305–6, 311
Go, Julian, 300, 305–6, 311
Graham, Billy, 3, 279n2. *See also* Black Panther/T'Challa (character)
Graham, Danny, 45–46
Green Book (dir. Peter Farrelly), 9
The Green Mile (dir. Frank Darabont), 173
Griot, 247–48. *See also* Artificial Intelligence
Guerrero, Ed, 55–56
Gurira, Danai, 79, 94, 275

Hampton, Fred, 177. *See also* Black Panther Party
Hancock (dir. Peter Berg), 22, 80, 173
The Harlem Renaissance, 216
Harris, Joi "SJ," 42. *See also* stuntwork
Harvey, David, 105. *See also* neoliberalism
hashtag activism, 87–91, 114
heroism: Black, 74, 77, 81
Hippolyte, Maria, 46–47
Hobbs & Shaw (dir. David Leitch), 173
Hollywood: appealing to non-Western audiences, 67–68; blacklisting in, 38–40; (mis)representing Blackness, 21, 55–56, 68; whiteness of, 1, 9
homeschooling: in *Black Panther*, 287–92; in Black US families, 288–89, 291
hooks, bell, 290–92, 294–95
housing projects, 175. *See also* Shabazz, Rashad
Hudlin, Reginald, 21, 279n2, 293
hybridity, 316; hybrid populations, 316–17. *See also* colonialism, double consciousness

ideation, 57–58; martial, 54, 58–59, 65–68. *See also* authenticity; expressivity; equanimity; tranquility
identity, 89, 92–95, 190–93; Black, 4, 187–88, 204, 288–94, 323; language as, 190–92. *See also* African American; hybridity

identity, secret: in *Black Panther*, 194–95, 198; of superheroes, 194
Igbo tribe, 324–25
intersection: of Blackness and queerness, 92–95, 176, 182–83
isolationism: debate in *Black Panther*, 108–9, 117, 191, 196, 254–56, 271, 278, 292–93

Jabari tribe, 107, 248, 253–54, 257, 320
Jackson, Andrew, 138. *See also* slave narratives
Jackson, Samuel L., 80
Jasanoff, Sheila, 247, 254, 256–57
Jim Crow laws, 226, 230–32
Johnson, Julie Ann, 39–41. *See also* Stuntwoman's Association of Motion Pictures; stuntwork
Jordan, Michael B., 79, 110
Jungle Action Featuring the Black Panther (comic series), 3, 111, 114. *See also* Black Panther/T'Challa (character)

Keynesianism, 104–5
Khan, Tabassum "Ruhi," 269–70
Killer of Sheep (dir. Charles Burnett), 274
Killmonger, Erik (in *Black Panther*): as African American, 183, 198, 290, 318; character differences between comic and film, 109, 112–13; hybrid identity of, 318, 323, 325, 327; language of, 198; as Mulatto trope, 324; politics of, 8, 10, 27–28, 65, 288, 291, 293, 295, 302–3, 308–10, 346; as Preyy, 307–9; as psychologically disabled, 172, 174–81, 184; as queer, 182–84; as radicalized, 220, 235, 237–38; religious ritual of, 63–64, 343–45; scarification of, 61, 178, 302. *See also* N'Jadaka, Preyy
King, Jr. Martin Luther, 225, 237–39
Kirby, Jack, 2, 22, 110–11, 154, 187–88. *See also* Black Panther/T'Challa (character)

Klaue (in *Black Panther*), 26–27, 178, 191, 195, 222, 234, 247, 252, 324–25; as psychologically disabled, 181–82
Klein, Naomi, 105

language: in *Black Panther*, 189–91, 195–98, 199n14. *See also* Xhosa/isiXhosa
L.A. Rebellion film movement, ix–xi; films of, 273–74. *See also* Third Cinema
Lavan, Makeba, 269–70
Lee, Spike, 5–7, 22
Lee, Stan, 2–3, 22, 111, 154, 187–88. *See also* Black Panther/T'Challa (character)
Lenz, Günter, 305, 312n25. *See also* cosmopolitanism, radical
Leonhard, Gerd, 253, 256–59
#LetAyoHaveAGirlfriend, 87, 91–95, 98n44, 99nn47–8. *See also* erasure; hashtag activism; Twitter
Lindsey, John W., 133. *See also* slave narratives
linguistics: bilingual, 189, 191; monolingual, 189, 191–92. *See also* code-switching
Los Angeles uprisings, ix, 27. *See also* L.A. Rebellion film movement
Lynne, Monica, 156–57. *See also* The Dora Milaje; *Jungle Action Featuring the Black Panther*

Malcolm X, 108, 219, 238
Marshall (dir. Reginald Hudlin), 73–74
martial arts, 44–45, 162
masculinity: Black, 222, 232–37; in *Black Panther*, 233–34
M'Baku, 60–61, 221–22, 258, 278; as psychologically disabled, 181
McGregor, Don, 3, 279n2. *See also* Black Panther/T'Challa (character)
Micheaux, Oscar, 3
Midnight Angels, 155, 159, 163. *See also* Aneka; Ayo; *World of Wakanda*

mythmaking: of a colonial power, 321; of Wakanda, 25, 252, 320–21
mythology: of Prester John, 221; of superhero films, 75, 81

Nakia: language of, 191, 195; politics of, 116–17, 223, 254–56, 271, 278, 304; portrayal in MCU, 114, 160, 321–22; portrayal in the comics, 155–57, 205
Nama, Adilifu, 4, 272–73
narrative logic: of *Black Panther*, 325–26
narratives, mass media: against non-whites, 317–18. See also trope
Navar-Gill, Annemarie, 93, 95
Neal, Larry, 23
neoliberalism, 104–5; benefitting the one percent, 106; racism of, 106–7
Neumann, Caryn, 273, 293
Newkirk, Vann R., 270, 272
Newton, Huey P., 110, 222, 290. See also Black Panther Party
N'Jadaka: in the comics, 109–10, 307. See also Erik Killmonger, Preyy
N'Jobu, 27, 63–64, 104, 109–10, 220, 222, 321, 344; language of, 192–94; politics of, 176–77, 255, 290, 301
Nyong'o, Lupita, 79–80

Oakland, 109–11, 175–77, 183, 222, 246, 257–58, 290, 301, 326
Okoye: language of, 191, 196; portrayal in MCU, 87, 94, 160–64, 179–80, 203, 207, 238, 275, 304–5; portrayal in the comics, 155–56, 205
Oyiboke, Amen, 77

paint down, 34–37, 41, 47. See also blackface; stuntwork
Pan-Africanism, 112, 204, 206–7, 271, 293
patriarchy, 208–9; in *Black Panther*, 221, 270, 339
Peters, Micah, 3

Poitier, Sidney, 38, 55–56
politics: Black, 303–5; exceptional, 301, 308; respectability, 231, 235
postcolonialism, 317; confronting, 325–27. See also colonialism
Preyy, 307–8. See also Killmonger, Erik; N'Jadaka
Priest, Christopher, 153–58, 205. See also Black Panther/T'Challa (character); *Black Panther Volume Three*
psychotropic plants, 333–35, 341, 345–46

Queen Divine Justice, 155, 157–58
queer theory, 95, 182–83

race as technology, 130. See also Afrofuturism
Radio (dir. Michael Tollin), 173
Ray (dir. Taylor Hackford), 173
religious ritual, 339–40; in *Black Panther*, 62–63, 307, 309, 336–45. See also psychotropic plants
representation: Black, 22, 28, 55–56, 68, 73–74, 77–80, 184, 205, 228, 274, 299; Black disabled, 172–73, 184; Black queer, 88, 91–93; queer, 91, 94
revisionist history: of Wakanda, 322–23. See also Wakanda
Robinson, Marsha R., 273, 293
Roosevelt, Teddy, 233
Ross, Agent Everett, 25–26, 113, 181–82, 194, 196, 234, 270, 309–10, 320
Ruffin, Josephine St. Pierre, 215–16, 224, 229–32. See also activism; Black elite; Black organizations

Sanjinés, Jorge, 272, 275
Sankofa, 23, 29
#SayHerName, 89. See also hashtag activism; Twitter
Schalk, Sami, 171–72; bodyminds, theory of, 174; disability metaphor, concept of, 174–75; "Reevaluating the Supercrip," 172, 180–81, 185n3

Schmitt, Carl, 300–301
Science Fiction, 22, 103, 129, 136, 216–17, 227, 267
Scott, Suzanne, 90, 94
Screen Actors Guild (SAG), 33; founding of, 35–36; stuntwork diversity policy of, 39–42
Shabazz, Rashad, 175. *See also* housing projects
Shuri, 66, 247, 253, 255–56, 258, 304, 326
Silicon Valley, 246, 256, 258–59
slave narratives in America, runaway, 131–34; freedom as outer space, 137–39; use of technology, 134–37
Smith, Will, 80
social media: as resistance, 87–90. *See also* hashtag activism; social movements, online; Twitter
social movements, online, 87–88, 90. *See also* hashtag activism; social media; Twitter
sovereignty, theory, 300–301, 304; and colonialism, 308–11. *See also* Susan Dianne Brophy
Stanfill, Mel, 93, 95
Storming of the US Capitol (2020), 218, 229
Stuntmen's Association of Motion Pictures, 36–37, 39. *See also* stuntwork
Stuntwoman's Association of Motion Pictures (SWAMP), 37–38. *See also* Epper, Jeannie; Johnson, Julie Ann; stuntwork
stuntwork: Black, 37–38, 43–48; diversity policies of, 39–44; exclusion in, 34–37; female, 38–39. *See also* The Black Stuntmen's Association; paint down; Stuntmen's Association of Motion Pictures; Stuntwoman's Association of Motion Pictures; wig down
subtitles, 190, 196–97

Sweet Sweetback's Baadasssss Song (dir. Melvin Van Peebles), 56
symbolism, 335–37; in *Black Panther*, 26, 62–66, 109, 190–91, 195–97, 203, 316, 322–23, 325, 340, 342–46

T'Challa/Black Panther (in *Black Panther* film), 53, 65–66; fighting style, 45, 60–61; identity of, 194–95; language of, 191, 196; politics of, 8, 29, 62–63, 115–17, 223, 234–35, 238–39, 269–70, 291–95, 303, 306, 310–11, 322, 326; religious ritual of, 62, 340–44. *See also* Black Panther/T'Challa (character)
technological: conservatism, 248, 253; determinism, 254; progressivism, 248, 253–54, 256
technology: changes, 249–50; ethics of, 252–59; opting out of, 257; risk assessment of, 254, 256
Terrell, Mary Church, 229–30
Third Cinema, 23–24, 267–69, 271–73; collective protagonist in, 275–77; films, 274–76; humanity in, 273–75
Third Space, 317–18, 324. *See also* hybridity
Third world country, 25, 181, 197, 320
Third World filmmaking, 268–69
Thor: Ragnarok (dir. Taika Waititi), 76
tranquility, cinematic, 54, 57–59; in *Black Panther*, 64–68
trope: Bury Your Gays, 91; ebony saint, 55; good negro, 225; magical Negro, 22; noble Negro, 55; supercrip, 172–73, 180–81; tragic Mulatto, 317–18; white savior, 9, 22, 25, 270
Trotter, William Monroe, 216, 220, 235–36
Tubman, Harriet, 132–33
The Turner Diaries (writ. William Luther Pierce), 226
The Tuskegee Institute, 221. *See also* Washington, Booker T.

Twitter: Black, 89, 171; social movements on, 87–89. *See also* #BlackLivesMatter; hashtag activism; #SayHerName; social media

Underground Railroad: as Afrofuturistic, 127–30, 140; imagery in *Black Panther*, 127, 140; origins of, 130–31
The Underground Railroad (writ. Colson Whitehead), 128, 139
utopia: Black, 215–17, 226–27; white, 225–26
utopian texts, 219, 226–27

Van Peebles, Melvin, 55–56
vibranium, 23, 68, 104, 107, 118n9, 162–63, 219, 288, 302, 320, 335; archaeological perspective on, 246, 248, 250–54
visibility: Black queer, 92–95. *See also* erasure; representation

Wakanda, 2, 7–8, 23–26, 104; as a colonial power, 319–23, 327; etymology of, 187–88; foreign policy of, 109, 114–17; geography of, 108; government in, 107, 115; history of, 219–20; patriarchy in, 221, 270, 339; technology in, 245–47; tradition *vs.* modernity in, 221

Walters, Marvin, 39. *See also* The Black Stuntmen's Association; stuntwork
War Dogs: of Wakanda, 179, 321–22, 324, 327. *See also* Wakanda
Washington, Booker T., 220, 225, 234–37
The Way of the Dragon (dir. Bruce Lee), 53
Webb, William, 139. *See also* slave narratives
Whitaker, Forest, 79
White, Renée T., 267, 269
white superiority myth, 217, 219, 225–26
white supremacy, 6–8, 22, 27–28, 226, 228–29, 233, 249, 268, 294
wig down, 34, 36–37, 39. *See also* stuntwork
Wills, Henry, 40–41
W'Kabi, 180, 182, 222–23, 234, 271, 275
womanism, Africana, 304–5. *See also* gender politics
World of Wakanda (writ. Roxane Gay, Yona Harvey, Rembert Browne), 87, 158–59, 205–6

Xhosa/isiXhosa, 199n11; use in *Black Panther*, 190–91, 196, 198, 199nn14, 324. *See also* language

Yazsek, Lisa, 23

About the Contributors

Khadijah Z. Ali-Coleman is a multidisciplinary artist and independent scholar who studies the intersections of African American culture, history, and scholarship. She has engaged in recent research that focuses on African American dual-enrolled and homeschooled students and practitioner work focused on arts-integration and high-impact learning practices. As a playwright and cultural curator, she engages in comprehensive research to develop historical theater works and museum exhibits. She is a 2019 Fulbright-Hays scholar and the 2020 Scholar-in-Residence at Prince George's County African American Museum and Cultural Center where she served as a teaching artist before COVID-19 closed most public venues. She is founding director of the multidisciplinary arts company *Liberated Muse Arts Group which* she has led since 2008 and is cofounder of the education think tank Black Family Homeschool Educators and Scholars (BFHES). She is coeditor of the forthcoming book *Black Children in the United States: An examination of homeschooling in practice, theory and popular culture* (2021).

dann j. Broyld is an associate professor of African American History and Public History at Central Connecticut State University. He earned his PhD in nineteenth-century United States and African Diaspora history at Howard University. His work focuses on the American-Canadian borderlands and issues of Black identity, migration, and transnational relations, as well as oral history, material culture, and museum–community interaction. Broyld's most recent article is titled: "The Underground Railroad as Afrofuturism" and he is currently finishing a book on American runaways to Canada before the Civil War.

About the Contributors

Cynthia Baron is a professor in the Department of Theatre and Film and an affiliate faculty in the American Culture Studies doctoral program at Bowling Green State University. She is the author of *Denzel Washington* (2015) and *Modern Acting: The Lost Chapter of American Film and Theatre* (2016). She is the coauthor of *Reframing Screen Performance* (2008), *Appetites and Anxieties: Food, Film, and the Politics of Representation* (2014) and *Acting Indie: Aesthetics, Industry, and Performance* (2020). She is the BGSU Research Professor of Excellence for 2017–2020.

Dolita Cathcart, an associate professor of history at Wheaton College, was raised in the Bronx, New York, by two immigrant parents from Germany and Cuba who briefly stopped in the United States on their way back to Cuba. They stayed in the United States when their plans were interrupted by the Cuban Revolution. Cathcart attained her A.B. degree from Harvard-Radcliffe Colleges, a master's in American Civilization from the University of Massachusetts, Boston, and a doctoral degree in history from Boston College. Originally interested in practicing medicine, Dolita "discovered" her love of African American history while collaborating on *Freedom Bound: A History of America's Civil Rights Movement* with Robert Weisbrot of Colby College from 1982 to 1989. Cathcart coedited the volume *Crossing Borders, Making Homes: Stories of Resilient Women* with Dalia J. Llera and Eleanor Roffman. She has appeared in the Independent Lens, PBS, documentary "Birth of a Movement" and in National Geographic's documentary series, "Origins." Currently, Cathcart is working on *Collateral Damage*, a book on how racism, sexism, and classism negatively affect white America, white males, and American democracy.

K. Sean Chaplin graduated with his PhD in sociology from the Texas A&M University. He is in the department of sociology and criminology at John Carroll University. He studies race, culture, and sport.

Gabriel A. Cruz holds a PhD in media and communication studies from Bowling Green State University. His primary area of scholarship is race, comic book-related popular culture, and the rhetoric of White Nationalism. Cruz currently teaches at the University of North Carolina at Greensboro and has taught a variety of classes related to media studies, popular culture, propaganda, and superhero-based fiction. His work has appeared in the academic periodicals *Journal of Alternative and Community Media* and *Howard Journal of Communications,* and also in the book *Deadpool and Philosophy: My Common Sense is Tingling.*

Neal Curtis is associate professor in media and communication at the University of Auckland. His most recent books are *Idiotism: Capitalism and the Privatization of Life* (2013) and *Sovereignty and Superheroes* (2016).

About the Contributors

Zeinabu irene Davis is an independent filmmaker and full professor of communication at the University of California, San Diego. She is comfortable working in documentary, narrative, and experimental genres. Her work is passionately concerned with the depiction of women of African heritage. Her most recent feature documentary on the filmmakers of the LA Rebellion film movement, *Spirits of Rebellion: Black Cinema from Los Angeles* (2016), won seven awards, including the African Movie Academy Award for Best Diasporic Documentary and Best Feature Documentary & Audience Award from the BlackStar Film Festival. Her films are distributed by Cinema Guild, Women Make Movies, and Third World Newsreel. She frequently writes articles on Black cinema which have been published in *Cineaste* and *Shadow & Act*.

Mikal J. Gaines, PhD, is an assistant professor of English at Massachusetts College of Pharmacy and Health Sciences University in Boston, MA. He is the author of "Staying Woke in Sunken Place, or The Wages of Double Consciousness" featured in Jordan Peele's *Get Out Political Horror* (2020), "They Are Still Here: Possession and Dispossession in the 21st Century Haunted House Film" in *The Spaces and Places of Horror* (Vernon, 2020), and "Strange Enjoyments: The Marketing and Reception of Horror in the Civil Rights Era Black Press" in *Merchants of Menace: The Business of Horror Cinema* (2014). His research areas include African American Literature, Film, and Popular Culture, Horror and Gothic Studies, and Critical Theory.

Giselle Greenidge is an assistant professor in the Behavioral Sciences Division in the School of Health Science and Wellness at Northwest Missouri State University. She received her doctoral degree in sociology from the University of North Texas. She currently teaches general sociology, race and ethnic issues, social stratification, and research methods in the social science. Her research interests include race and ethnicity, culture, globalization, and visual ethnography.

Paul Karolczyk has a PhD in geography with an anthropology concentration from Louisiana State University and a MS in geography and BS in industrial technology from Central Connecticut State University. His PhD dissertation, *Subjugated Territory: The New Afrikan Independence Movement and the Space of Black Power* (2014), used ethnographic fieldwork, archival research, discourse analysis, and GIS to examine the radical geography of Black revolutionary nationalism in the United States. He lives in Washington State.

Clarence Lusane is a professor of international relations and former Chair of the Political Science Department at Howard University, and also emeritus professor at American University. He is an activist and scholar, and a well-respected expert in the areas of human rights, African American politics, global race relations, U.S. elections, and international relations. He has lectured and taught on these topics in over seventy countries including China, Colombia, Cuba, England, France, Germany, Haiti, Japan, the Netherlands, New Zealand, Panama, Russia, Rwanda, S. Korea, Switzerland, the United Kingdom, Ukraine, and Zimbabwe among others. He is a former Commissioner on the D.C. Commission on African American Affairs and the former Cochair of the Civil Society Committee for the U.S.–Brazil Joint Action Plan to Eliminate Racial Discrimination, a bi-lateral agreement involving the United States and Brazilian governments and civil society in both nations. He is the author of more than 100 scholarly articles and eight books on human rights, U.S. and Black politics, globalization, and European history. Dr. Lusane's latest book is *The Black History of the White House*. The book led to two presentations at the White House during the Obama presidency: the Millennium and Pipe Dream Blues: Racism and the War on Drugs among others. His next book, *$20 and Change: Harriet Tubman, Andrew Jackson, and the Struggle for a Radical Democracy* is scheduled for release in 2021.

Paul Moffett is an instructor of English at Memorial University of Newfoundland. He holds a PhD in English Literature from Memorial University and his primary research focus is on intersections of the sacred and the secular in late medieval Arthurian literature. He maintains an enthusiastic secondary research interest in popular culture, especially comics and television, as well as an interest in critical adaptation theory. He is currently working on a project on piety in Sir Thomas Malory's *Le Morte Darthur* and on a teaching project focused on monsters, from medieval werewolves to modern zombies.

Shayla Monroe is a doctoral candidate in anthropology at University of California, Santa Barbara (UCSB). She specializes in faunal analysis, the social zooarchaeology of Sudan and Egypt, the archaeology of ethnicity the ancient Nile Valley, and African pastoralism. Monroe earned her MA in Anthropology from UCSB in 2014. Since 2013, she has worked as an archaeologist at the 3rd Cataract of the Nile River in Sudan, first at the Egyptian colonial site at Tombos, and then at the Kerma hinterlands site, Abu Fatima, also in northern Sudan. Monroe began her career at Howard University, where she earned degrees in Anthropology and English (2012). She also spent two seasons (2010 and 2011) working at L'Hermitage plantation (also known as the Best Farm Slave Village) with the National Park Service in Frederick, Maryland.

Karen A. Ritzenhoff is a professor in communication as well as women, gender, and sexuality studies at Central Connecticut State University. In

2019, she coedited and published two books: *The Handmaid's Tale: Teaching Dystopia, Feminism, and Resistance across Disciplines and Borders* (with Janis L. Goldie) and *New Perspectives on the War Film* (with Clémentine Tholas and Janis L. Goldie). She recently completed another war related coedited volume on *Mediated Terrorism in the 21st Century* (2021), coedited with Elena Caoduro and Karen Randell.

Sarah E. S. Sinwell is an associate professor in the Department of Film and Media Arts at the University of Utah. She has published essays on Kickstarter, *Green Porno* and *Mysterious Skin* in *A Companion to American Indie Film*, *Women's Studies Quarterly* and *Asexualities: Feminist and Queer Perspectives*. Examining shifting modes of independent film distribution and exhibition on YouTube, Netflix and SundanceTV, Sinwell is an assistant professor in the Department of Film and Media Arts at the University of Utah. She has published essays on Kickstarter, *Green Porno*, and *Mysterious Skin* in *A Companion to American Indie Film*, *Women's Studies Quarterly*, and *Asexualities: Feminist and Queer Perspectives*. Examining shifting modes of independent film distribution and exhibition on YouTube, Hulu, Netflix, and SundanceTV, her recently published book *Indie Cinema Online* (Rutgers University Press, 2020) redefines independent cinema in an era of media convergence.

Lauren Steimer is associate professor of media arts and film and media studies at the University of South Carolina. Her book, *Experts in Action: Transnational Hong Kong-style Stunt Work and Performance* (2021), traces embodied histories of transnational exchange by identifying and defining unique forms of expert performance common to contemporary globalized action film and television genres.

Myron T. Strong graduated with his PhD in sociology from the University of North Texas. He is currently an Assistant Professor of Sociology at the Community College of Baltimore County in Baltimore, Maryland. His current research explores Afrofuturism, race, gender and other social factors in modern comics. He has published in academic journals, anthologies, and encyclopedias. Recently, he won the Barbara K Walters Community College Award from the Eastern Sociological Society for his article *The Emperor Has No Clothes: How Outsider Sociology Can Shift the Discipline in Sociological Forum*.

Joshua Truelove graduated with a BA in history from Central Connecticut State University and is enrolled at Boston College where he is working on a PhD in twentieth-century U.S. history. His work focuses on comedy and popular culture.

About the Contributors

Renée T. White is provost and professor of sociology at Wheaton College in Massachusetts. She is a scholar on race, gender, and social inequality. White has published in a wide variety of venues such as *The Black Scholar, New Political Science, Health Promotion Practice* and the *Council of Europe Higher Education* Series. She is author *of Putting Risk in Perspective: Black Teenage Lives in the Era of AIDS* (1999) and coeditor of three books: *HIV/AIDS: Global Frontiers in Prevention/Intervention* (2009), *Spoils of War: Women of Color, Cultures, & Revolutions* (1997), and *Frantz Fanon: A Critical Reader* (1996). Renée White currently serves on the editorial review board for the *Journal of Women and Gender in Higher Education*.

Wayne Wong is a lecturer at The Hong Kong Polytechnic University. His articles have been published in peer-reviewed journals including *Asian Cinema, Global Media and China, Journal of Contemporary Chinese Art, Martial Arts Studies* and edited volumes such as *The World of John Wick*. His research interests include comparative film theories and philosophies, Chinese and transnational cinemas, and martial arts studies and cultures. He is currently working on a book about the aesthetics of Hong Kong martial arts cinema titled *Action in Tranquillity: Sketching Martial Ideation in Kung Fu Cinema*.

Dominique Young is a fourth-year PhD student in English at the University of Maryland, College Park, and a 2018 SSRC Mellon Mays Predoctoral Research Fellow. She received her BA in English from CUNY Brooklyn College. Her research focuses on African American women's popular fiction, film, and music videos from the 1990s. This past semester, she taught a 200-level undergraduate course titled, "Late 20th Century African American Women's Popular Fiction and Culture." This course examined seminal twentieth-century African American women's popular fiction, and visual productions that center working-class Black women. Through this course and in her own research, Young is invested in exploring the popular form as, what Kara Keeling calls, a radical existing space, for representations of some of the most marginal African American women in the 1990s.

www.ingramcontent.com/pod-product-compliance
Lightning Source LLC
Chambersburg PA
CBHW061704300426
44115CB00014B/2560